# Men of Blood

This book examines far more thoroughly than ever before the treatment of serious violence by men against women in nineteenth-century England. During Victoria's reign the criminal law came to punish such violence more systematically and heavily, while propagating a new, more pacific ideal of manliness. Yet this apparently progressive legal development called forth strong resistance, not only from violent men themselves but from others who drew upon discourses of democracy, humanitarianism, and patriarchy to establish sympathy with "men of blood."

In exploring this development and the contest it generated, Professor Wiener, author of several important works in British history, analyzes the cultural logic underlying shifting practices in nineteenth-century courts and Whitehall and locates competing cultural discourses in the everyday life of criminal justice. The tensions and dilemmas highlighted by this book are more than simply "Victorian" ones; to an important degree they remain with us. Consequently this work speaks not only to historians and to students of gender but also to criminologists and legal theorists.

Martin J. Wiener is the Mary Gibbs Jones Professor of History at Rice University. His previous books include *Between Two Worlds: The Political Thought of Graham Wallas* (1971), *English Culture and the Decline of the Industrial Spirit* (1980), and *Reconstructing the Criminal* (1990).

# Men of Blood

## Violence, Manliness and Criminal Justice in Victorian England

Martin J. Wiener

*Rice University*

CAMBRIDGE
UNIVERSITY PRESS

PUBLISHED BY THE PRESS SYNDICATE OF THE UNIVERSITY OF CAMBRIDGE
The Pitt Building, Trumpington Street, Cambridge, United Kingdom

CAMBRIDGE UNIVERSITY PRESS
The Edinburgh Building, Cambridge CB2 2RU, UK
40 West 20th Street, New York, NY 10011-4211, USA
477 Williamstown Road, Port Melbourne, VIC 3207, Australia
Ruiz de Alarcón 13, 28014 Madrid, Spain
Dock House, The Waterfront, Cape Town 8001, South Africa

http://www.cambridge.org

First published 2004

Printed in the United States of America

*Typeface* Baskerville 10/12 pt.     *System* LATEX 2ε     [TB]

*A catalog record for this book is available from the British Library.*

*Library of Congress Cataloging in Publication Data*
Wiener, Martin J.
Men of blood : violence, manliness and criminal justice in Victorian England /
Martin J. Wiener.
p.   cm.
Includes bibliographical references and index.
ISBN 0-521-83198-9
1. Homicide – England – History – 19th century.   2. Violence in men – England – History –
19th century.   3. Women – Violence against – England – History – 19th century.   4. Wife
abuse – England – History – 19th century.   5. Sexism – England – History – 19th century.
6. Criminal justice, Administration of – England – History – 19th  century.   I. Title
HV6535.G42E64   2003
364.15′23′094209034 – dc21          2003048566

ISBN 0 521 83198 9 hardback

*for Rebecca and Vivian*

# Contents

vii

# Figures and Tables

# Preface

This book is located in the imprecise but vital realm in society where cultural representations and public actions meet; more exactly, the space in the life of the criminal law where discourse and dispositions come together. In exploring this space, I hope to bring cultural and criminal justice history closer together, and to demonstrate how much each can contribute to the other. In recent years historians have begun to appreciate how intertwined representations and actions are, how discourse is not just talk but structures action, is a mode of action; how, conversely, action always happens within some discursive frame. Yet it is one thing to appreciate this in principle, quite another to carry it through in practice, without privileging one or the other. How well I succeed in this challenging task will be for readers to judge.

In a previous work I attempted a cultural history of criminal policy in Victorian and Edwardian Britain, describing patterns of thought surrounding and helping to shape the central government's construction and treatment of criminal offenders. In one sense, this book extends that enterprise, moving from the general to the more particular – from crime in general to homicide (and rape) in particular – and from national policymaking to the disposition of particular cases; in locale, from Parliament, the Home Office, and the organs of the national "intelligentsia" to the assize courtrooms of England, and to the popular reporting and discussing of what went on there, in newspapers, periodicals, pamphlets, and broadsides, as well as, again, the rooms of the Home Office. The present work is chiefly based on two "archives": one of them public – newspaper and other published accounts of killings and the legal proceedings that followed them – and one private – discussions between Home Secretaries, their civil servants, and judges, together with appeals from condemned prisoners and others for mercy. The first archive was immediately and widely known to contemporaries, the second confidential and closed, presumably forever. The hundred-year, then seventy-five-, and finally fifty-year rule has opened this second archive. Taken together, both with their own specific agendas and biases, they afford a fuller view than has previously been possible of what was thought and what was done about men committing major violence in Victorian England.

In this sphere, as others, what was thought and what was done were, as already suggested, not neatly separable, and they are not treated separately here. The law was at the same time both precise and compelling, and open (even by judges devoted to precedent) to interpretation, especially in questions of "crimes against the person," and most especially when strong feelings were roused, as was almost always the case when charges of homicide and rape were raised.

One aim of this work is simply to better understand the meaning and treatment of serious violence by men, especially against women, in Victorian England. Another, more general, is to more closely connect cultural and criminal justice history. Yet a third aim is to contribute to the understanding of the roles played by gender in criminal justice history and by criminal justice in gender history. Even as scholarly work has begun to link the two fields, it has suffered from a marked imbalance: nearly all of it has been focused on the treatment and experiences of women; the other half of the population has only just begun to be examined as a gender. Scholarly work on the relations of men, as men, to the criminal justice system is much needed, particularly for the nineteenth century, which formed a watershed not only in criminal justice but in gender constructions and relations, and the two watersheds were in fact, as I will argue, closely connected. "Masculine criminality" was undergoing significant reconstruction in this era.

As such an observation suggests, this work has a thesis. Simply put, it is that men's violence, particularly against women, became in this period a matter of greater import than ever before, evoking strong but complex and often conflicting sentiments and legal actions and that in the end, for all the complexity, contradiction, and conflict that went on around it, such violence was viewed with ever-greater disapproval and treated with ever-greater severity. The story told here is one of both contestation and change, and both facets have their place. Yet, ultimately, it is argued, the most important thing about the story is the change that took place, in the way such violence was understood and, inseparable from this, in the way in which it was dealt with by the organs of the law.

To highlight change in this realm, in particular change in the direction of diminished tolerance of men's violence against women, is to risk being accused of glossing over the continuing mistreatment of women in this era. This would be a serious misreading. This book does not seek to evaluate the Victorians by the standards of the early twenty-first century. It attempts to understand them, not to judge them, and to understand them more in relation to their predecessors than to their successors. How did they differ, in both their contradictions and their changes, from the generations that went before them? What kind of legacy did they leave the twentieth century?

Within the field of criminal justice history, this book is unusual in that rather than examining one county or one judicial circuit over a more limited period of time, it ambitiously (or foolhardily) takes the entire nation, over nearly a century, for its subject. In so doing, of course, it must sacrifice some degree of thoroughness and "definitiveness." At the same time, it does not attempt, even superficially, to cover all aspects of male violence and the law, but confines itself to the crimes of homicide and rape. Nor does it examine all levels of the system, but confines itself to the highest courts of original jurisdiction, the assizes, where such serious charges were tried. It draws, as noted, upon both published and unpublished sources, some of which have never been made use of before. It is both quantitative and qualitative, making general statements based on wide and in one area virtually complete data while closely reading texts from both archives to elucidate the contours and complexities of what might be called "discourses of male violence." It is built upon a unique database of detailed information on several thousand Victorian criminal cases, including virtually every case of spouse murder that went to trial, a large sample of spouse manslaughter, and other homicide and rape cases from this period and for some years earlier and later.[1] Of course, cases officially noted and dealt with did not include all cases of "actual" homicide and certainly not of "actual" rape, as we (or even Victorians) would define them.[2] Contemporaries were well aware of this: as the *Times* noted in 1876, "the absolute numbers of murders tells us nothing. It only says how many murderers have been brought to justice."[3] Therefore, quantification can only take us part of the way. Much of this work is "qualitative," closely examining discourses and dispositions that defined and interpreted men's violence. The sources for such examination are vast, very much more extensive than for earlier periods, and far beyond the ability of any one person, or group of persons, to fully read. The Victorian era saw an explosive growth in both the public and private archives – newspapers grew in number and multiplied their circulation, and after an 1836 Act allowing time after murder convictions for consideration of appeals the relevant Home Office files greatly expanded. Selectivity and discrimination are inevitable, as in most

---

[1] This is as far as I know a larger and more complete database than has ever been compiled on these crimes in this era. It was compiled primarily from reports in the *Times*, supplemented by those in other newspapers. From the early 1840s onwards the *Times* covered almost every assize, reporting virtually every murder trial. In general, its court reporters were, unusually at the time, barristers; thus its accounts are likely to be, at least on legal issues, reasonably accurate. [Alfred Chichele Plowden, *Grain or Chaff? The Autobiography of a Police Magistrate* (London, 1903), p. 109.] One way to check the completeness of its coverage is against the listing from 1858 on in the Annual Judicial Statistics of the names of all persons found guilty of murder; I have confirmed that every one of these was also reported in the *Times*. By "spouse" I have taken all cases where the two parties were living together for an extended period of time, "common-law" marriage being not at all unusual, especially among the poor.
[2] On the limitations of official criminal statistics, see Allison Morris, *Women, Crime and Criminal Justice* (London and New York, 1987), and Monica Walker, ed., *Interpreting Crime Statistics* (Oxford, 1995); for the nineteenth century, see Clive Emsley, *Crime and Society in England, 1750–1900* (London; second edition, 1996).
[3] *Times*, 6 January 1876, p. 4.

scholarship that attempts to address significant issues. Certainly the patterns uncovered here, both of change and of conflict, are not the only ones that can be found in this material, nor are they immune from challenge. They are, however, patterns that have for the most part not hitherto been noted, or much examined. They need to be.

# Acknowledgments

Over the decade of its composition, parts of this argument were tried out in many venues: American Society for Legal History; Australian Victorian Studies Association; Australian Modern British History Association; Balliol College, Oxford; British Criminology Association; Third Carleton Conference on the History of the Family; Catholic University of America; First European Social Science History Conference, Amsterdam; European University Institute, Florence; George Washington University; Georgetown University Law Center; Hebrew University of Jerusalem; Institute for Crime and Policing at the Open University; International Conference on the History of Violence, Liverpool; Keele University; Leeds Centre for Victorian Studies; Maison des Sciences de l'Homme, Paris; North American Conference on British Studies; Princeton University; University College, Northampton; Victorian Studies Association of Western Canada; Victorians Institute; and the Western Conference on British Studies. I am greatly in the debt of those who hosted me, listened to my thoughts-in-process, and most of all to those whose responses led me to revise them to the point where I can send them into the world on their own. In particular I greatly profited from the advice, assistance, and criticism of John Archer, Roger Chadwick, Carolyn Conley, Joel Eigen, Clive Emsley, Vic Gatrell, Jim Hammerton, Tom Haskell, Martin Hewitt, Peter King, Helena Michie, Randy McGowen, David Philips, George Robb, Gail Savage, Greg Smith and Michael Willrich. I wish also to thank Carolyn Conley, Barry Godfrey and Stephen Farrall, Peter King, Louis Knafla, Greg Smith, Howard Taylor, and John Carter Wood for allowing me access to as-yet unpublished work.

For support at a critical time, and encouragement that what I was doing was indeed social science history, I am deeply grateful to Erik Monkkonen, James Q. Wilson and Harmon Hosch, the open-minded director of the National Science Foundation's Law and Social Sciences Division. I am also most appreciative of the faith the Woodrow Wilson International Center for Scholars and its former director, Charles Blitzer, placed in my capacity to say something worthwhile about such an "eccentric" subject.

A number of my students over the years have rendered invaluable assistance: Jim Good, Susan Hanssen, Bill Jahnel, Melissa Kean, Krisztina Robert, Kim Szatkowski, Elaine Thompson, Martin Wauck, Katie Wells and Tammy Whitlock. I would have been at sea without the computing knowledge of Katy McKinin and Carolynne White and the editing skills of Catherine Howard. I am greatly indebted to the staff of the Fondren Library at Rice, most of all those in the Interlibrary Loan office, who dealt with my numerous requests with friendly efficiency. Two Deans of Humanities – Judith Brown and Gale Stokes – steadily supported my work, as did my departmental chairs, Tom Haskell and Jack Zammito. In the members of my department I have always found collegiality and comfort. I am also in the debt of former Rice President George Rupp, for giving strong backing when it was most needed to research in the humanities.

Some of the material in chapter 4 has appeared in the *Journal of British Studies* vol. 40, no. 2; in chapter 6 in *Social History* vol. 24, no. 2; in chapter 7 in *Law and History Review*, vol. 17, no. 3.

My wife, Meredith Skura, has given me steadfast advice, support, and understanding, and our daughters, to whom this work is dedicated, have ensured that in my absorption with dreadful family crimes in the nineteenth century I did not forget the happier world of family love and warmth.

# Introduction

Whatever else may be included in the education of the people, the very first essential of it is to unbrutalise them; and to this end, all kinds of personal brutality should be seen and felt to be things which the law is determined to put down.

. . . . J.S. Mill and Harriet Taylor, 1853[1]

### The Problem of Male Violence

In the modern world, one of the most fundamental obstacles to social order and peace has been the nature of males. A mass of scientific study has established that from birth, males on average tend to be more aggressive, restless and risk-taking than females, and in general less amenable to socialization. History as well as anthropology bears out the implications of the scientific studies, for it would appear that all settled societies, past and present, have been faced with the twin tasks of putting to use and reining in these male propensities.[2]

This book addresses one such propensity: with greater physical strength combined with greater aggressiveness, men are and have always been far more seriously violent than women. Perpetrators of homicide, excepting the special case of infanticide, have in almost all times and places been largely male, often overwhelmingly so. It is in fact a cliche of criminology that violent criminals are far more likely to be male than female.[3] The problematic nature

[1] *Remarks on Mr. Fitzroy's Bill for the More Effectual Prevention of Assaults on Women and Children* (London, 1853) [published anonymously].

[2] For a stimulating survey of this question, James Q. Wilson, "On gender," *The Public Interest* no. 112 (Summer 1993), 3–26.

[3] As David Levinson summarized the findings of many studies in 1994, "in all places at all times in human history men have been far more likely to murder than have women, and men have been far more likely to kill other men than women have been likely to kill other women." Levinson, *Aggression and Conflict: A Cross-Cultural Encyclopedia* (New York, 1994), p. 4. Also see David Levinson, *Family Violence in Cross-Cultural Perspective* (New York, 1989). Recent statistics for the United Kingdom are analyzed in *Gender and the Criminal Justice System* (London: Home Office, 1992).

of this male propensity has if anything grown in modern times, with the emergence of a way of life very different from that in which male inclinations to violence developed. As evolutionary psychologists and anthropologists have argued, this is a trait that has lost much of its former functionality, but because of its long gestation, it is not one that is easy to banish.[4]

Thus, it is safe to say that homicide, whether the victims are female or male, is and as far as we can ascertain always has been highly gendered behavior and ought to be looked upon from that angle more than it has been. The obverse of this claim is that how homicide is treated by society, both today and in other times and places, can reveal much about notions of masculinity and their changes, just as the excavation and elucidation of such notions help in turn to make sense of homicide's treatment. Even though of course killing is highly unusual behavior, fortunately peripheral to everyday life, "what is *socially* peripheral," the cultural historians Peter Stallybrass and Allan White have reminded us, is "frequently *symbolically* central."[5] This book argues that this was certainly true of nineteenth-century homicide, especially homicides adjudged to be intentional. Putting such claims into practice, this book attempts to demonstrate how intertwined criminal justice, gender and the wider culture were in one particular place and period – Britain in the Victorian age.

In recent decades, education, legislation and the media have all been invoked and employed to discourage male violence. Yet social intervention to reshape this sort of male behavior has not been a phenomenon of only the past generation. It has a history, a neglected one, reaching back at least several centuries, and was especially prominent in nineteenth-century England, a society undergoing the most rapid transformation experienced since the invention of agriculture. The age of Victorianism, despite some of the staid associations that still cling to the term, was anything but static.

### Victorian England and Homicide

Over this era, several broad changes took place in the recorded incidence and treatment of homicide. Most significant for this work's concern, public,

This appears to be true for the past as well as the present, for example Hertfordshire in Shakespeare's time: Carol Z. Wiener, "Sex Roles and Crime in Late Elizabethan Hertfordshire," *Journal of Social History* (1975), 38–60, and Peter Lawson, "Patriarchy, Crime and the Courts: The Criminality of Women in Late Tudor and Early Stuart England," in *Criminal Justice in the Old World and the New*, ed. Greg T. Smith, Alyson N. May and Simon Devereaux (Toronto: Centre of Criminology, University of Toronto, 1998).

[4] The best single work on our subject from this perspective remains Martin Daly and Margo Wilson, *Homicide* (Hawthorne, N.Y., 1988). For a recent study of gender and evolutionary psychology, see David P. Barash and Judith Eve Lipton, *Gender Gap: The Biology of Male-Female Differences* (New York, 2002).

[5] Peter Stallybrass and Allan White, *The Politics and Poetics of Transgression* (Ithaca, N.Y., 1986), p. 5.

normally male-on-male, killing apparently was declining markedly, while "private," domestic or other intimate killing was failing to show clear evidence of diminution. Along with these trends went a trend in treatment by the criminal justice system towards greater punishment for major crimes against the person and easing punishment for crimes against property, and within the treatment of crimes against the person a shift in severity of punishment from public to private violence, most especially murder. What might such shifts mean? Several things. For one, as has been much discussed by historians of crime, the nineteenth- and early twentieth-century decline in recorded violence was part of a long-term social tendency for life-threatening violence to diminish, at least in public, under both the pressures of authority against such "disorderliness" and the gradual rise in material standards of living and social standards of self-discipline and "civility."[6] The Victorian era greatly developed its inheritance from previous eras, racheting up the pressures of authority and, along with improving material conditions, raising the social standards of self-discipline. By its later years these efforts were being rewarded by a sustained rise in most indices of "civility." This move against interpersonal violence meshed with a second trend to shape the treatment of male violence, particularly that directed against women.

This second trend was a "reconstruction of gender," begun in the eighteenth century but only coming to fruition in the nineteenth. Women were increasingly seen as both more moral and more vulnerable than hitherto, while men were being described as more dangerous, more than ever in need of external disciplines and, most of all, of *self*-discipline. This re-imagining of gender played a crucial if as yet unappreciated role in criminal justice history, just as developments in the latter were contributing to the former. From this re-imagining, as it joined with the increasing intolerance of violence, came a tendency to see women as urgently needing protection from bad men, which brought acts of violence against women, more often than not taking place in the home, out from the shadows.

During the sixty-four-year reign of a woman, the treatment of women in Britain and in the burgeoning empire became a touchstone of civilization and national pride. As a young queen came to the throne in 1837, and after her marriage and the start of childbearing, there was much talk of her reign as a

---

[6]The *locus classicus* for theoretical discussions of this is Norbert Elias, *The Civilizing Process* [orig. pub. Zurich, 1939; Eng. trans. 1978 & 1983] (rev. ed., Oxford, 2000). The broad process of "pacification" has been examined by many historians: in particular see Lawrence Stone, "Homicide and Violence," in *The Past and the Present Revisited* (London, 1987); James A. Sharpe, "The History of Violence in England: Some Observations," *Past & Present* 108 (August 1985), 206–215; Jean-Claude Chesnais, "The history of violence: Homicide and suicide through the ages," *International Social Science Journal* 44.2 (May 1992), 217–234. The most authoritative study of this long-term trend and discussion of its possible causes is Manuel Eisner, "Modernization, Self-Control and Lethal Violence: The Long-Term Dynamics of European Homicide Rates in Theoretical Perspective," *British Journal of Criminology* 41 (2001), 618–638.

new age in which "family" values would spread their influence. One writer in praising the Queen after her marriage typically depicted a "beautiful chain," not the traditional one of hierarchy from Sovereign down to subject, but one of common family life: "which should be fastened at one end to the cottage, at the other end to the palace, and be electric with the happiness that is carried into both."[7] Indeed, when seeking a symbol of the nation's humanity and morality, the use of the female national symbol, "Britannia," was given a new life. After Victoria's accession several new coins were minted carrying the image of Victoria as Britannia, and the new bronze penny of 1860 had Victoria on one side and an older version of Britannia on the other. Elsewhere, Britannia appeared more often in magazine cartoons as "the apotheosis of values central to the dominant elites, Justice, Liberty and The Empire," and by the end of the century had become a matriarch conflated with Victoria herself. Britannia became, in Peter Bailey's phrase, "the Angel of the House, made the Matron at large and On Guard."[8] One way it was felt in which the new era distinguished itself from what went before was in the heightened moral influence of women and attention to their protection (at home and around the world) from a variety of evils, not least among them the violence of men.[9]

Of course, as many scholars have pointed out, this kind of protection often amounted to little more than rhetoric, and even when it did make a real difference in ordinary lives, it conferred its benefit at a price: abroad, by

[7]Quoted in John Plunkett, "Queen Victoria: the Monarchy and the Media 1837–1876" (Ph.D. thesis, University of London 2000), in turn quoted in Regenia Gagnier, "Locating the Victorians," *Journal of Victorian Culture* 6, no. 1 (Spring 2001), 118.
[8]For further information, see Roy Matthews and Peter Mellini, "John Bull's Family Arises," *History Today* (May 1987), 20, and "From Britannia to Maggie," *History Today* (September 1988), 18.
[9]One of the chief rationales of empire was its protection of women in other societies against their own menfolk; the abolition of suttee in India being only the most famous of many examples cited throughout the century. From another angle, the uncovering of female suffering itself helped justify empire: as Cannon Schmitt has argued about "Gothic" themes in Victorian writing, "women are [repeatedly] figures whose victimization calls forth Englishness from (implicitly male) spectators. This configuration, whereby women must suffer to produce or confirm Englishness [in men], is intensified and generalized as the century progresses, reaching something of an apogee during the Indian Rebellion." *Alien Nation: Nineteenth Century Gothic Fictions and English Nationality* (Philadelphia, 1997), p. 161.
The Victorian era also saw revived interest in the legendary national hero, King Arthur, which focused particularly upon Arthur's efforts to transform a warrior society based upon bloodthirsty conquest into a realm based upon a gentler, less combative code of conduct. Indeed, as Stephanie Barczewski has observed, "nineteenth century authors often utilized the legend to explore definitions of a new kind of masculinity capable of functioning in an increasingly domestic sphere" – while at the same time anxious that such a "new man" might be an emasculated one. [*Myth and National Identity in Nineteenth Century Britain* (London and New York, 2000), p. 169.]

justifying the domination of other peoples, and at home, by similarly justifying male paternalism – widening gender distinctions and making the home almost the only proper place for women, while men ran politics, business and much of the rest of public life. This is not to mention that it also produced new pressures on women to shape themselves behaviorally to fit the ideal of "true womanhood" worthy of such care and protection. Yet for all this it will not do to simply dismiss the ideal of protecting women as nothing but a hypocritical instrument of a new kind of white male domination. As scholars of class have shown, "Victorian values" did not simply tighten social controls; they also challenged and reconfigured existing relationships of power. It is past time for gender historians to heed what historians of class have painfully learned – while not ceasing to show how ideas and ideals can be employed to support existing distributions of power, at the same time to appreciate the multiple effects of values and sentiments, and how they sometimes create the conditions for real change in social relations.

In nineteenth-century Britain the seemingly endless (and well-studied) discussions of true womanhood were paralleled by a similar (if less studied) preoccupation with true manhood. Ill-defined terms like "manly" and "unmanly" appear everywhere in Victorian discourse, hinting at a continual gnawing on this indigestible bone.[10] If women were having their "nature" delimited, so too in some significant ways were men.[11] The concern of respectable persons to protect women more effectively easily allied with the other concern already in evidence – to reduce violence and "civilize" men in general (especially, though not exclusively, working-class men) in all their social relations. In the eighteenth century manliness' close association with bearing arms or fighting upon insult had already loosened; the gentry for the most part ceased carrying weapons and became more reluctant to get into duels or other affrays. Gentlemen dramatically yielded their once-prominent place in the rolls of violent offenders, while at the same time even plebeian men were resorting less often to lethal violence.[12] In the nineteenth century

[10] See J.A. Mangan and James Walvin, eds., *Manliness and Morality: Middle-Class Masculinity in Britain and America, 1800–1940* (Manchester, 1987); Michael Roper and John Tosh, eds., *Manful Assertions: Masculinities in Britain since 1800* (London, 1991); Stefan Collini, "Manly Fellows: Fawcett, Stephen, and the Liberal Temper," in *Public Moralists: Political Thought and Intellectual Life in Britain 1850–1930* (Oxford, 1991), pp. 170–196; John Tosh, *A Man's Place: Masculinity and the Middle-Class Home in Victorian England* (New Haven, 1999).

[11] On nineteenth-century restriction of male "nature," see the brilliantly suggestive remarks of Alain Corbin, "The 'Sex in Mourning'," in his *Time, Desire and Horror: Towards a History of the Senses* (Cambridge, Mass., 1995): "the range of masculine gestures shrank ... tears went out of fashion. The photographic pose emphasized the calm, gravity and dignity of men. ... We need to listen carefully; we then perceive the depth of male suffering. ... The unhappiness of women flowed from the misery of men."

[12] See Robert Shoemaker, "Male Honour and the Decline of Public Violence in Eighteenth-Century London," *Social History* 26 (2001), 190–208.

this decline continued, and efforts to reduce it further both broadened and became more specifically gendered. More kinds of violence came to fall within the circle of condemnation and punishment, including, more than ever before, those directed against women. While men's prerogatives in relation to women expanded in certain directions, they narrowed in others. In particular in nineteenth-century England, even as much traditional tolerance continued towards violence against women, especially wives, such violence was increasingly investigated, censured and punished by more active – or intrusive – agents of criminal justice. In this way, the protection of women came to pose the question of the "reconstruction" of men, and the criminal justice system became a site of intense cultural contestation over the proper roles of and relations between the sexes.

Indeed, not only was male violence coming more and more to be denounced as a relic of benighted ages and a practice of barbaric peoples, but more generally, the elevation of the family values ever more associated with women's natures (such as religiosity, nurturing, sensitivity to the feelings of others and of course sexual self-denial) fed a questioning (even in the face of a surge of imperial enthusiasm in the late decades of the century) of the values of bravery, self-assertion, physical dominance and others traditionally associated with masculinity. The ideal of the "man of honor" was giving way to that of the "man of dignity," which required in place of a determination to avenge slights whatever the danger involved the qualities of reasonableness, forethought, prudence and command over oneself.[13] The newer expectation for men, to manifest peaceableness and self-restraint in more and more areas of life, well established among gentlemen by the end of the eighteenth century, was extended in the following century in two directions: from gentlemen to all men, and from public, male-on-male violence to "private" violence against subordinates, dependents and the entire female gender. Both extensions met strong resistance, from customary notions of masculinity among much of the populace in which violence had an essential place, from similarly customary notions of social hierarchy, and from related notions of gender relations, in which women's weapon of the tongue was met by men's weapon of the fist. Nonetheless, by the end of the nineteenth century newer standards of manliness had made great headway. In these movements and contestations, the Victorian era was witness to a powerful "second stage" in the centuries-long reconstruction and, to a degree, "domestication" of male ideals and, to a lesser but nonetheless significant extent, of male behavior – one that has not as yet received its due.[14]

---

[13]See John Tosh, "The Old Adam and the New Man: Emerging Themes in the History of English Masculinities, 1750–1850," in *English Masculinities 1660–1800*, ed. T. Hitchcock and M. Cohen (London, 1999), pp. 217–238.

[14]This is not of course to argue that Victorian criminal justice victimized men or favored women. The actual circumstances of women and men in the dock often

At the same time however "Victorianism" itself was conflicted, and had no simple approach to the "problem of men." This was particularly so in regard to the mistreatment of "bad" women, for heightened expectations of female virtue and domesticity, when unmet, could mitigate the otherwise-heightened offensiveness of male violence against members of the opposite sex. In addition, the idealization of the family home made intrusion into it by the state or other social actors even more questionable. Thus, efforts to "civilize" men often encountered cross-currents generated not simply by a persistence of older values but by parallel changes in expectations of women and of domestic life, making their advance a good deal less than straightforward.

This effort to change men's behavior, along with its accompanying conflicts and contradictions, was played out in the working of the criminal justice system.[15] Legal institutions are of course also cultural institutions. In the everyday implementation of the law can often be seen put into practice the generalizations of preachers and moralists as well as of ordinary people. As the law has a cultural dimension, cultural history also has a legal dimension. The cloth of cultural history is woven from diverse fabrics, some of these legal – discourse in the courtroom, among lawyers and officials, and in the press as well as in essays and conduct books, fiction and art. A crime, a trial, a reprieve effort, and public and private accounts of them are all potentially revealing cultural texts. We shall attempt to see what they can suggest of notions of violence and conceptions of manliness, and how these were put into practice in the century of the "pax Victoriana."

This book deals only with one area of the law – the criminal – and within that area only one statistically minor part – the treatment of major crimes of violence, chiefly homicide (predominantly that which had female victims) and also rape. Homicide embraces only a very small proportion of crimes of violence, and even rape only a part of sexual offenses. Moreover, recorded offenses, even of homicide, by no means represented all such acts, and certainly the number of rape prosecutions in the nineteenth century only hinted at the total amount of sexual violence against women. Yet very little can be said with any confidence about unrecorded violence, beyond the claim that

---

differed sufficiently to justify differential treatment. The actual behavior of men may possibly have merited even more punishment, and that of women less, than was actually handed out, then and now, as Susan Edwards, among others, has argued. [*Sex and Gender in the Legal Process* (London, 1996), pp. 371–372.] However, this study is not concerned with rights and wrongs, but with historical developments and their explanation.

[15] As James Sharpe has noted, "historians are only just beginning to study how masculinity was socially and culturally constructed in early modern England, yet it would seem that male criminality would offer a relatively well-documented way into this problem." [*Crime in Early Modern England* (rev. ed. 1999), p. 159.] This is true of more recent periods also, as this book hopes to demonstrate.

it existed and was ubiquitous. The gap between actual and recorded lesser violence was particularly great, and even when such violence was recorded, the records are usually not very forthcoming. Extreme crimes like homicide or rape can reveal more, for they arouse much more official and public interest and generate far more material of various kinds than do lesser offenses. Their legal prosecution produces a disposition, of course – a man goes free, goes to prison, or is hanged, to cite the most common outcomes – but such prosecutions do more: they engage a wide range of persons in reflection, discussion and pronouncement, often with life-or-death consequences, on deep moral questions. How does one define violence, how does one identify circumstances that justify, excuse or mitigate such violence, and what should one expect of persons placed in various provoking situations, or of those whose responsibility for their actions, for one reason or another, may be in question? The principles of the law, of course, offer some guidance for such questions, but they do not operate in a world of their own; principles, rules and procedures always arise and are applied within specific social and cultural contexts. How in relation to these major crimes of violence did the criminal law evolve, how was it applied, and what did it mean for widely-held understandings of masculinity? To these questions this book seeks to supply some answers.

# 1

# Violence and Law, Gender and Law

In nineteenth-century England, the problem of violence, the meanings of gender, and the workings of law were all assuming more prominent places in culture and consciousness. As they did, the three converged on one issue in particular – that of more effectively controlling male violence, particularly in order to better protect women. Of course, such a morally and politically stigmatized concept as "violence" is not simply descriptive of an objective set of actions but, particularly at its margins, subject to multiple, changing and often competing definitions. In some definitions, violence has not needed to be physical (it might, for example, be verbal, in the form of threats or insults, or the "mental cruelty" as cited in divorce law); in others, the infliction of physical pain and even injury has not necessarily been violence (in medical procedures or in the punishment of children, until very recently). New forms of "violence" are continually discovered, while behavior considered "violent" may in time cease to be so labeled.

Even today, in a climate of opinion more hostile to the use of physical coercion perhaps than any previous era, views still differ on when (legal) force becomes (illegal) violence. The banning in ever more jurisdictions of physical punishment of children, the establishment of the crime of marital rape and the controversies in legal cases concerning consensual sexual violence illustrate the difficulty even in one period of finding universal agreement on the definition or boundaries of violence.[1] In past times the concept of violence, however tangible and self-evident it may have seemed, was at least as mutable, constructed and contested. As William Ian Miller has observed, "the word violence is a depository for a large number of utterly incommensurable

---

[1] On the last, the case of *R.v. Brown* 1993, in which the House of Lords found consensual homosexual sado-masochistic acts to be unlawful violence, is instructive. See Leslie J. Moran, "Violence and the Law: The Case of Sado-Masochism," *Social and Legal Studies* 4 (1995), 225–251; Carol Smart, *Law, Crime and Sexuality: Essays in Feminism* (London and Thousand Oaks, Calif., 1995), pp. 115–120. Also highly relevant is the 1991 legal recognition of marital rape as a crime: see Keith Soothill, "Marital rape in the news," *Journal of Forensic Psychiatry* 5 (1994), 539–549.

activities, each with its own sociology and psychology."[2] The study of social context and social expectations is thus an integral part of any history of violence.

Violence, however precisely defined, is certainly a powerful and meaningful subject, today and in the past. Claims involving it carry a special weight and an inherent connection with morality. As its etymology (linked with "violate") suggests, violence is not only the force its perpetrator uses, or the physical injury he inflicts, but also the act's aim and effect – a "violation." To cite Miller once more: violence "is distinguished from more generalized force because it is always seen as breaking boundaries rather than making them."[3]

Nonetheless, the constituents of violence are not so "incommensurable" or its distinction from "mere" force not so clear as scholars like Miller suggest. The use of physical force or threat of force is not just another means of social communication. It is an especially dangerous means, and thus always of great import to societies and states, most of all to modern societies, for whose members personal safety and social peaceableness has come to be one of the most basic expectations. Much of the rise of this expectation, and the associated stigmatization of most violence, can be followed in the nineteenth century, in Britain as much or more than anywhere.

While the content and definition of violence is not stable, the subject is a universal and trans-historical one. The employment of force itself is ubiquitous, while the notion of violence is to be found wherever and whenever one looks.[4] Wherever communities are formed and maintained, there "violence" is discovered, defined and dealt with in some way. Rules and values governing the use of force, however varying, seem to follow from the rootedness (strongly argued by evolutionary psychologists) of inclinations to the use of force in human (and predominantly male) nature. Universal yet mutable; resting on nature, yet a creature of culture – violence in history is a rich subject not only for measurement but even more for interrogation. Interrogation to understand the notion of violence itself, and to elucidate its relations with other social concepts grounded in nature, like gender, and with social institutions, like the law.

There is a specific and generally agreed-upon historical trend in which this current study must be located, and that is the centuries-long decline, in England and most of the West, in the incidence of the kinds of force broadly

---

[2]William Ian Miller, *Bloodtaking and Peacemaking: Feud, Law and Society in Saga Iceland* (Chicago, 1990), p. 77. See also Robert Muchemblad, "Anthropologie de la Violence dans la France Moderne [15th –18th s.]," *Revue de syntheses* (1987), 21–55.
[3]Miller, ibid., p. 60.
[4]See David Riches, ed., *The Anthropology of Violence* (New York, 1986); Levinson, *Aggression and Conflict* (New York, 1994); Dorothy Counts, Judith K. Brown and Jacquelyn C. Campbell, eds., *Sanctions and Sanctuary: Cultural Perspectives on the Beatings of Wives* (Boulder, Colo., 1992).

acknowledged, then as now, as violence.[5] Officially recorded homicides (the only kind of violence for which at least some usable figures survive for a long period) fell in England from something like 20 per 100,000 annually in medieval times to about one per 100,000 at the opening of the twentieth century, and this trend was similar, if most often not as pronounced, in other parts of Western and Central Europe.[6] Although many causes can be found for this decline, such as the growth of commercial–industrial society, of popular education and of the standard of living, one prominent and more direct source was a deliberate "civilizing offensive" waged by emerging and strengthening states and other institutions of social order like churches and schools against behavior now perceived as "barbaric," of which serious interpersonal violence was perhaps the most central mode.

Such a "civilizing offensive" was certainly at work in British history. Over several centuries, much unwanted infliction of physical (and sometimes mental) suffering was increasingly stigmatized, and exceptions to such stigmatization – the chastisement of children and other dependents, or social inferiors – were ever more reduced. The Victorian era formed a landmark in this long offensive. From one angle, Victorian England's heightened condemnation of interpersonal violence was but one chapter in a story of state-driven "pacification" of life going back at least to the sixteenth century, and broader than merely English.[7] Yet the Victorian chapter made fundamental contributions

[5]This trend, of course, applies only to violence *within* societies, and in particular to that between private groups or individuals. During the same centuries the amount of violence wreaked on those *outside* Western societies rose very greatly.

[6]James A. Sharpe, "Crime in England: Long-Term Trends and the Problem of Modernization" [p. 22], and Pieter Spierenburg, "Long-Term Trends in Homicide: Theoretical Reflections and Dutch Evidence, Fifteenth to Twentieth Centuries" [pp. 64–66], in *The Civilization of Crime: Violence in Town and Country since the Middle Ages*, ed. Eric A. Johnson and Eric H. Monkkonen (Urbana, Ill., 1996); V.A.C. Gatrell, "The Decline of Theft and Violence in Victorian and Edwardian England," in *Crime and the Law: the Social History of Crime in Western Europe since 1500*, ed. V.A.C., Gatrell, Bruce Lenman and Geoffrey Parker (London, 1980), p. 287.

[7]The leading explanatory model for this longterm "pacification" is that of Norbert Elias, *The Civilizing Process* [orig. pub. 1939] (London, 1978 & 1983; rev. ed. 2000); a sympathetic but knowledgeable evaluation of the model and its uses by historians is provided in Pieter Spierenburg, "Elias and the History of Crime and Criminal Justice: A Brief Evaluation," *International Association for the History of Crime and Criminal Justice Bulletin* no. 20 (Spring 1995), 17–30. In England, both the level of interpersonal violence and the tolerance of both state and public towards it diminished over the seventeenth and eighteenth centuries. In a 1996 paper ("Crimes Against Persons in Elizabethan Kent"), Louis Knafla found that a thorough examination of all levels of criminal courts in the last years of the sixteenth century uncovered at least twice as many crimes against the person as previously thought, and underlined the leniency of their punishment, as compared to that meted out to even trifling crimes against property. On the decline in recorded offenses against the person thereafter, see James Sharpe, *Crime in Early Modern England, 1550–1750* (London and New York, 1999), John Beattie, *Crime and the Courts in England 1660–1800* (Princeton, 1986) and James

to this story. Two crucial things were added in these years to the "civilizing project" in Britain: First, just when one might have expected a relaxation of the drive, apparently begun in the Tudor era, to suppress interpersonal violence, instead the Victorian era saw a major intensification, as crimes of violence came to be taken more seriously by the state than ever before.[8] It may at first puzzle us that, while (as we now know) the recorded homicide rate had fallen to its lowest level in English history, and lesser violence had very probably also diminished, both officials and members of the writing and reading public exhibited greater fear and outrage in the face of interpersonal violence than ever before. Typically for its time, the liberal *Law Magazine,* in drawing the line of criminal law reform at mid-century at the death penalty, justified its retention by what it called "the immense increase which has notoriously taken place in the whole catalogue of personal injuries, from common assaults up to attempts to shoot, stab, and poison."[9]

The puzzle becomes less baffling if we remember, for one thing, that contemporaries had only very minimally reliable data on the incidence of crime, violent and otherwise, and thus continued to feel threatened by an apparently rising tide of violent crime well into the second half of the century. Even more important, they were living in a time of unprecedentedly rapid change, in which industrialization, urbanization, population growth, and vastly increased mobility and anonymity appeared to many in the comfortable classes to threaten to overwhelm the degree of "civilization" that had been gradually attained, and plunge society into disorder and insecurity. It was only in part a fear of dispossession: if anything, as an ever-more productive economy spread material goods, it cheapened them, causing fears of crimes against property to at least become less ferocious. Yet economic growth seemed to most to do nothing for the security of the person (indeed perhaps diminishing it by, for example, making it more affordable for more people to drink themselves into belligerent intoxication). A new "modern" form of barbarism seemed possible (particularly as violence had diminished in the previous century more drastically among "gentlemen" and the middling sort than among the laboring classes, thus widening class differences in this realm).[10]

Cockburn, "Patterns of Violence in English Society: Homicide in Kent 1560–1985," *Past and Present,* no. 130 (February 1991), 70–106.

[8] James Sharpe and Roger Dickinson, in their preliminary report to the Economic and Social Research Council, "Violence in Early Modern England, Research Findings, Initial Results" (2000), p. 3, noted their strong impression that "fatal criminal violence was, in the early modern period [1600–1800], punished with surprising leniency by the courts."

[9] *Law Magazine* 44 (August–November 1850), 122.

[10] The gentry, formerly over-represented, virtually vanished from homicide prosecutions between 1700 and 1800, while middling men became rarer there. See Robert Shoemaker, "Male Honour," *Social History* 26 (2001), 190–208. Many assault

At the same time, the new economic, social and political order taking shape made personal self-discipline, orderliness and non-violence both more valuable and more necessary than ever before. Self-discipline, proverbially the way to better oneself morally and materially, meant restraining anger as well as lust, a gospel now preached more widely than ever before, in both religious and secular venues, to every member of society. Pushed by fears of a new barbarism especially in the growing numbers of working people congregated in towns and cities, and pulled by visions of never-before-attained levels of personal and social security, dignity and betterment, authorities and middle-class publicists went to work to narrow further the boundaries of tolerable interpersonal violence. And as the gospel of self-management spread, impulsive and violent behavior became all the more threatening, by its actual growing rarity, at least in the circles frequented by self-improving persons, and by the increasing contrast it made with the self-improving way of life.

Diminishing acceptance of interpersonal violence was perhaps heralded by an emerging unease about violence against animals, most visibly practiced by the lower-class men who handled and employed them. In 1822, a year in which penalties for manslaughter were sharply increased, cruelty to animals was first criminalized, by means of Richard Martin's bill against cruel practices to cattle. Two years later the Society for the Prevention of Cruelty to Animals was established, and in 1835, while prosecution and punishment of violent offences was being legislatively advanced, a sweeping act prohibited cockfighting and bull-baiting, and extended the protection of Martin's Act to domestic pets.[11]

Not that the new intolerance was of violence everywhere, even among humans: the intensified drive against interpersonal violence within the country went along with the development and employment of ever-larger and more destructive military forces, as British power spread worldwide. In very few years during the century were British forces not engaged in some war or another. Ironically, this imperial expansion could assist internal pacification, as many of the young men most prone to violence joined the military or became settlers overseas, in either case finding large opportunities to unleash their aggressive impulses against non-Europeans. From this angle, the increasing disapproval of violence within Britain provided a discourse readily put to use in attacking empire, while at the same time in its effects complementing and even supporting empire. However in conflict they were on one level, in both internal pacification and external aggression can be seen the lineaments

prosecutions formerly brought by middling men against each other seem to have migrated to the civil courts where they appeared as actions for damages. See Greg T. Smith, "Masculinity, Honour and Non-Lethal Violence at the King's Bench, 1760–1820," unpublished essay.

[11] See Harriet Ritvo, *The Animal Estate: The English and Other Creatures in the Victorian Age* (Cambridge, Mass., 1987), pp. 126–128.

of the increasing state monopolization of violence that has characterized modern history. The discourse of pacification, moreover, came to be drawn upon to provide the central moral justification of the British role overseas: as Britain came to rule over ever-growing numbers of less-developed peoples, they saw themselves as bringing law and order to those who possessed little of them. However, for this mission Britons themselves – soldiers and sailors as well as administrators – needed to be models of law-abiding, orderly virtues, and thus, even if abroad, they too eventually became targets of the civilizing offensive.[12]

In this repression of violence, law – primarily its criminal side – took a leading role. The law was a complex entity, shaped by many players. Legislators, politicians, civil servants, newspaper editors and reporters, amateur and professional magistrates, judges, jurors, lawyers and others all played parts in this broad movement. Offenses were redefined and penalties were increased, either statutorily, through judicial review of cases, or by judges presiding over particular cases. Judges delivered their views publicly in trial summations and privately to Home Secretaries and civil servants, who themselves contributed through their decisions in appeals. Lawyers argued both the law and the facts, and jurors rendered their verdicts, with newspapers and others commenting. The many players involved, and the complexity of law's imbrication with social institutions and relations, local as well as national, meant that it could never be (at least not in England) a single instrument of social policy. Rather, it mixed policies, interests, sentiments and values from this great range of social actors, with often unpredictable results.

Thus, while powerfully influenced by the priorities of the governing class, law was not simply its instrument. Neither, for that matter, could it have a single aim, effect, or even logic. In the comparatively open English system, even the criminal law's application was invoked by many persons, for various reasons, and its operation involved the collaboration of different persons and groups, who did not necessarily agree in general values or in specific instances. Further, in the daily operation of the criminal law at least, case law was as important as statute law, and case law rarely spoke with one voice. In the nineteenth century it was made by twelve and then fifteen High Court

---

[12]This issue came into the open at moments of crisis, such as in the debates over the handling of the Ceylon uprising of 1848 or the Jamaica disturbances of 1866. Many on both sides of those arguments accepted the need for Englishmen in the empire to serve as models for subject peoples; in part, their difference was over how they saw the rule of law in non-English societies to be best safeguarded – by decisive, if brutal, action or by self-restraint and avoidance of unnecessary violence. [See R.W. Kostal, "A Jurisprudence of Power: Martial Law and the Ceylon Controversy of 1848–51," *Journal of Imperial and Commonwealth History* 28 (2000), 1–34; Bernard Semmel, *The Governor Eyre Controversy* (London, 1962); Catherine Hall, "Competing Masculinities: Thomas Carlyle, J.S. Mill and the case of Governor Eyre," in Hall, *White, Male, and Middle Class* (New York, 1992), 255–295.]

judges over the course of very many particular prosecutions, each with its own peculiar set of circumstances. Sentences varied enormously, because of both the extensive personal discretion given judges, and the great diversity of circumstances between one case – even of the same offense – and the next. Juries also, while excluding women and all persons without property, varied a good deal in social circumstances and opinion from one to another.[13]

However diverse and flexible, the law's tasks were being expanded.[14] Even civil law was increasingly involved in dealing with questions of bodily harm and violence. Nineteenth-century tort law (the law governing liability for harms that do not fall under either criminal or contract law) exhibited diminishing acceptance of preventable personal injury. In previous centuries civil law had shared with criminal law what would seem to modern sensibilities to be a striking lack of concern about personal injury and even death as compared to damage to property interests. Although in principle any "trespass" – unauthorized contact with the person or property of another – was actionable, in practice such suits seem to have overwhelmingly dealt with property damage and only occasionally personal injury (and then disproportionately among the upper classes). In addition, the law made little allowance for indirect injury, however serious or even fatal. Moreover, grounds for civil action were removed by death; the heirs or dependents of a person killed by another had no right of civil redress.[15]

This situation, like the parallel one in criminal law, changed in the nineteenth century, as imputations of responsibility expanded and tort litigation grew.[16] Just as a fear of a "crime wave" exercised many early Victorians, so too did parallel fears of an "accident wave" (and not only in the new industries), producing state intervention in the form of a wide variety of safety

[13]On the complexity and variability of the criminal law in practice in that century, see Clive Emsley, *Crime and Society in England, 1750–1900* (London, 1996) and Carolyn Conley, *The Unwritten Law: Criminal Justice in Victorian Kent* (Oxford and New York, 1991); much of what Peter King has magisterially established for later eighteenth- and early nineteenth-century criminal justice continued in good measure to apply: see P. King, *Crime, Justice and Discretion: Law and Social Relations in England 1740–1820* (Oxford, 2000).

[14]As the Commissioners of Bankruptcy and Insolvency in 1840 declared, the law was "the most powerful of all teachers in showing men their social duties, and in compelling their performance."

[15]See P.W.J. Bartrip and S.B. Burman, *The Wounded Soldiers of Industry: Industrial Compensation Policy 1833–1897* (Oxford, 1983); Elisabeth Cawthorn, "New Life for the Deodand: Coroners' Inquests and Occupational Deaths in England, 1830–46," *American Journal of Legal History* 33 (1989), 137–147.

[16]In this, the way was led by Americans: see Peter Karsten, *Head Versus Heart: Judge-Made Law in Nineteenth-Century America* (Chapel Hill, N.C., 1997). America also led in the related development of medical malpractice litigation. See Kenneth Allen De Ville, *Medical Malpractice in Nineteenth-Century America: Origins and Legacy* (New York, 1990); De Ville discusses English case law precedents for American litigation on pp. 159–161.

legislation as well as more indirect use of the state through growing litigation and expanding imputations of legal responsibility.[17] These two sets of fears were not unrelated.

In recent years, the view that the "negligence" principle that developed in the nineteenth century chiefly served the purpose of restricting wider pre-existing notions of "absolute liability" for harms has been sharply revised.[18] Notions of absolute liability have turned out upon closer examination to have been confined to certain very limited areas of social interaction. Non-liability seems to much better describe the legal character of most pre-Victorian instances of harm.[19] As they were doing in regard to criminal liability, nineteenth-century legislators, judges and juries – despite oft-expressed concerns about opening "floodgates" to litigation – nonetheless were indeed extending civil liability.[20]

In 1846 the Fatal Accidents Act gave dependents for the first time a claim in certain cases of accidental death. Although limiting amendments were added by mining and railway interests, the act opened a new field of litigation. Even in cases of non-fatal injuries, more remote forms of liability were being successfully claimed, and at the highest levels of law. In an 1841 case in which a child had been injured by a cart that he had unlawfully entered and that had been set in motion by one of his fellows, Chief Justice Denman affirmed the judgment of Middlesex magistrates that the owner of the cart was liable for damages, for leaving it unattended where children were playing.[21] Despite nineteenth-century judicial reverence for "privity of contract" (the principle that a contract creates a legal relationship only between the parties directly involved in making it)[22] third parties began in the 1830s to win damage suits. In 1837 a man whose hand had been shattered by a defective gun bought by his father won a £400 judgment against the seller, though his only relation

---

[17]Whereas the "crime wave" has long been debunked by historians, a simplistic functionalism still tends to prevail in regard to the "accident wave," which may have been less pronounced than contemporaries believed, influenced as they were by expanded social investigation, by coroners, government inspectors and newspapers.

[18]Such a view is argued in F.H. Lawson, *Negligence in the Civil Law* (Oxford, 1950); the most influential statement of it is in Morton Horwitz, *The Transformation of American Law 1780–1860* (Cambridge, Mass., 1977).

[19]See Robert L. Rabin, "The Historical Development of the Fault Principle: A Reinterpretation," *Georgia Law Review* 15 (1981), 925–961, and Gary T. Schwartz, "Tort Law and the Economy in Nineteenth Century America: A Reinterpretation," *Yale Law Journal* 90 (1981), 1717–1775.

[20]See J.L. Barton, "Liability for Things in the Nineteenth Century," in *Law and Social Change in British History*, ed. J.A. Guy and H.G. Beale (London, 1984).

[21]*Lynch v. Nurdin* (1841) 1 Q.B. 29. The original case was heard at Middlesex Quarter Sessions in 1839.

[22]See P.S. Atiyah, *The Rise and Fall of Freedom of Contract* (Oxford, 1979).

to the defendant was as a third party to a contract entered into by the defendant.[23] In 1858 another and even more removed third party triumphed – a passenger injured on a ferry whose crew had been hired for the day by the ferry operator successfully sued not the ferry operator but the man from whom he had leased the crew. Mr. Justice Erle, soon to become Chief Justice, upheld the jury's verdict of culpable negligence despite the fact that the plaintiff had nothing to do with the contract governing the employment of the crew.[24]

In like fashion, the liability of employers for harms to their employees expanded. The new and ingenious restrictive legal doctrines of common employment and assumption of risk, which have received much attention from critical historians, served only to limit, not to halt, this expansion.[25] The famous 1837 case of *Priestley v. Fowler*,[26] later taken as the first enunciation of the doctrine of common employment, used to limit employers' liability, was nonetheless also the first time in the long history of the common law, as D.J.P. Read pointed out, that the master had been informed "that he was under an enforceable duty to provide for the safety of his servant."[27] The early Victorian period saw the appearance of many new legal duties of care, enforceable civilly and sometimes criminally, in a growing effort to diminish the toll of avoidable injury and death. Such developments were very much in tune with the parallel increased determination to reduce the level of interpersonal violence.

While civil law was increasingly involved in rethinking responsibility for physical harm, the chief arena for this was of course criminal law. In this era criminal prosecutions grew enormously. The number of recorded crimes in England and Wales rose almost sevenfold between 1805 (the earliest date for which there are national statistics) and 1842.[28] This leap was seen by contemporaries as recording a proportionate increase in actual criminal activity, but a large part of it, as V.A.C. Gatrell has argued, must be ascribed to much more thorough, expensive and efficient machinery for detecting crimes, apprehending suspects and trying, convicting and punishing them. The creation of such expensive social machinery betokened an intensification of interest, inside and outside government, in repressing crime and ensuring order in society.

---

[23] *Langridge v. Levy* (1837) 2 M.&W. 519.
[24] *Dalyell v. Tyrer* (1858) El. Bl.&El. 898.
[25] See Bartrip and Burman, *Wounded Soldiers of Industry*, op. cit.
[26] 3 M.&W. 1; M.&H. 305.
[27] D.J.P. Read, "The History and Development of the Tort of Negligence in the Nineteenth Century" (Ph.D. thesis, University of Kent, 1983), p. 110.
[28] V.A.C. Gatrell, "Crime, Authority, and the Policeman-State, 1750–1950," in *The Cambridge Social History of Britain, 1750–1950*, vol. 3, ed. F.M.L. Thompson (Cambridge, 1990), pp. 243–310.

Along with increased legal scrutiny of violence went similarly increased scrutiny of "unnatural death." Coroners were given more work to do and more funding and legal backing to get it done.[29] Inquests became more common and much more thorough, bespeaking a new determination to uncover the causes of unexpected death, violent and other, and so to diminish its incidence. An 1836 statute provided for the first time for the payment of the cost of postmortem and toxocological examinations, and for the payment of medical witnesses at coroners' inquests. In case payment was not sufficient, legal penalties were also for the first time set out for medical practitioners who failed to comply with coroners' requests to carry out such examinations or appear as such witnesses.[30] All these changes improved fact-finding about the causes of sudden death. General verdicts like "act of God" or "found dead," which leap out from the pages of coroners' reports of the early years of the century, gradually yielded to more specific ones.[31] A second act of the same year established the first nationwide registration of deaths and created a government department to track births and deaths.[32] The first statistical head of this department, William Farr, began immediately to crusade for greater vigilance and vigor in seeking the causes of deaths, natural *and* unnatural. After 1836, more professional and more thorough inquests (together with improvements in medical science) were increasing the likelihood of detecting unnatural and perhaps culpable deaths and providing evidence for more successful prosecutions.[33] With more active coroners establishing culpability in a greater number of deaths, criminal prosecution of dangerous behavior, whether driving vehicles in the streets, handling machinery and equipment at workplaces, or misusing firearms, rose. Indeed, coroners' inquests were themselves seen as an increasingly important part of the criminal justice system, a key player in the repression of violent acts, whose role by late in the century embraced behavior in the home. In the words of a 1900 *British Medical Journal* article (when concern about mistreatment of children had taken center stage from that about violence against

---

[29] See J.D.J. Havard, *The Detection of Secret Homicide* (London, 1960); Gary Greenwald and Maria W. Greenwald, "Medicolegal Progress in Inquests of Felonious Deaths: Westminster, 1761–1866," *Journal of Legal Medicine* 2 (1981), 193–264; Thomas R. Forbes, *Surgeons at the Bailey: English Forensic Medicine to 1878* (New Haven, Conn., 1985); Ian Burney, *Bodies of Evidence: Medicine, Public Inquiry, and the Politics of the English Inquest, 1830–1926* (Baltimore, 2000).

[30] Medical Witnesses Act 1836. After 1836 more cases were recognized as violent [Greenwald].

[31] Marybeth Emmerichs, "Getting Away With Murder? Homicides and the Coroners in Nineteenth-Century London," *Social Science History* 25 (2001), 93–100.

[32] Birth and Death Registration Act 1836.

[33] Havard and Greenwald both argue that numerous cases of homicide went undetected before the Victorian era, when detection improved.

adults), "the publicity of its proceedings acts as a strong deterrent to parents and others (a very numerous class) whose conduct borders on 'criminal neglect.' "[34]

Simultaneous with the revival and enhanced use and prestige of coroners, a second, better-known new administrative development did even more to increase official scrutiny of harm-causing behavior. Between 1829 and the late 1850s, professional police forces were established throughout the country.[35] Established initially chiefly out of fear for the safety of property in an era of social dislocation, these forces came to press down on disorderly and violent activity as well as thefts. They patrolled places of public gathering, preventing a great deal of violence from getting started or from getting out of hand, and made a surprisingly large number of arrests.[36] A recent scholar of the early police forces has remarked on "the sheer size of the police intervention," which marked a significant departure from previous practice.[37] Even private violence felt their impact: it is notable how often in domestic homicides and near-homicides a constable, once called by neighbors, was quickly on the scene taking offenders into custody. Such offenders rarely sought to escape, seeming to accept the inevitability of arrest.

As more efficient machinery for detecting and apprehending offenders was being constructed, the criminal law itself was being redrawn to extend and toughen the punishment of violence more broadly defined. For eighteenth-century English criminal law, personal injury was in principle and practice a secondary concern. While theft of property valued as low as a shilling was a felony, punishable at least in principle by hanging, assault, no matter how vicious, was not – unless the victim died. Even manslaughter – culpable but non-intentional killing – carried a maximum penalty of only a year's imprisonment, and even that punishment was very rarely applied. Indeed,

---

[34] Quoted in Burney, *Bodies of Evidence*, op. cit., p. 85.

[35] David Philips and Robert D. Storch, *Policing Provincial England, 1829–1856: The Politics of Reform* (Leicester, 1999).

[36] See Philips and Storch, ibid., p. 225, and Chris A. Williams, "Counting crimes or counting people: Some implications of mid-nineteenth century British police returns," *Crime, History and Societies* 4 (2000), 77–94.

[37] Williams, ibid., 86. In Sheffield 1844–62 arrests totaled twenty times the number of indictable offenses recorded; the great majority of arrests were for public order offenses like "drunk and disorderly," which no doubt nipped a great deal of violence in the bud. Arrests for common assault were also frequent, 96% of these of men. [Williams, ibid.] Sometimes they served a classic detective function: The *York Herald* in 1842 heaped praise upon an Inspector from the Metropolitan Police who solved the murder of a widow, tracing it to a former employee who sought money from her [appendix to John Carter, *A Sermon preached . . . the Sunday after the murder of Mrs. Jane Robinson, with an appendix, as to the proceedings of Mr. Inspector Pearce, in tracing out the murderer* (Whitby, 1842)].

most incidents of private violence in the eighteenth century seem not to have reached the courts, and even those that did were generally viewed as essentially private matters.[38]

There were signs of diminishing legal tolerance of interpersonal violence in the late eighteenth century,[39] with administration preceding the formal law. Few assault complaints in the first half of the eighteenth century ever went to trial (instead being "settled" between the parties before, or even in court).[40] From about 1780, such cases, at least for working-class offenders, began to move from being treated civilly to being treated criminally. The size of fines for assault tended to increase, while courts became increasingly willing to order some time in jail in cases of serious violence. In general, by 1820 the typical penalty for most assault convictions had altered from a nominal fine to the clearly harsher one of imprisonment.[41] Similarly, in manslaughter cases by the turn of the century the jury's finding that the victim's death came by way of accident did not necessarily, as earlier, lead to a discharge; in such cases, if offenders had shown recklessness or imprudence, they were increasingly likely to be sentenced to some jail time.[42]

Many forms of reckless disregard for the safety of others were being taken more seriously by the law. Traffic and occupational accidents resulting in a death appear to have become more likely to lead to prosecutions for

[38]John Beattie, "Violence and Society in Early Modern England," in *Perspectives in Criminal Law,* ed. A.N. Doob and E.L. Greenspan (Aurora, Ont., 1985), pp. 42–43, 49–50; also Beattie, *Crime and the Courts,* op. cit., pp. 75–76, 457–461; Clive Emsley, *Crime and Society,* op. cit., p. 141; Greg T. Smith, "The State and the Culture of Violence in London, 1760–1840," (Ph.D. thesis, University of Toronto 1999).

[39]*Popular* tolerance also seems to have begun to wane not long after official tolerance: examples of execution crowd execration of murderers cited in V.A.C. Gatrell, *The Hanging Tree: Execution and the English People, 1770–1868* (Oxford, 1994) all date from after 1820.

[40]Norma Landau, "Indictment for Fun and Profit: A Prosecutor's Reward at Eighteenth-Century Quarter Sessions," *Law and History Review* 17. 3 (Fall 1999), 507–536.

[41]Peter King, "Punishing Assault: The Transformation of Attitudes in the English Courts [1748–1821]," *Journal of Interdisciplinary History* 27 (1996–1997), 43–74.

[42]Beattie, *Crime and the Courts,* p. 609; Beattie, "Violence and Society," pp. 48–49; King, "Punishing Assault." Concern for personal security also seems a major motive behind the war on juvenile crime which began in the 1790s and accelerated after 1815. Just as the growing intolerance of violence was chiefly impacting upon men, this new effort against youthful delinquency was disproportionately directed against boys, whose prosecution rose faster than that of girls. Boys, who were far more likely than girls to combine theft with a degree of personal violence, were perceived as a threat in a way that girls were not. See Peter King and Joan Noel, "The Origins of 'The Problem of Juvenile Delinquency': The Growth of Juvenile Prosecutions in London in the Late Eighteenth and Early Nineteenth Centuries," *Criminal Justice History* 14 (1993); the inference concerning violence is mine.

manslaughter or occasionally even murder.[43] Moreover, the criminal law was reaching now into locales as well as types of offenses it had hitherto little touched. The courts were showing a newfound interest in prosecuting violence in and by the military, which like sea-borne offenses had hitherto been left alone, or to military or naval authorities. James Cockburn found soldiers first appearing in assize court in the county of Kent as accused killers in 1806, although that county's dockyards and ports had long been home to an unruly military population. He also uncovered a series of early nineteenth-century cases in Kent in which efforts were made for the first time to impose liability upon ships' masters who had killed men under their command.[44] The wartime expansion and increased visibility of the Navy and merchant marine made behavior on board a greater concern, and in 1799 Parliament expanded the jurisdiction of the criminal sessions of Admiralty Court to reach all offenses of whatever kind committed at sea. The growth of the empire demanded further expansion, and an 1817 act permitted naval officials to arrest and try British subjects for homicides committed outside British territory.[45] One of the provisions of the 1828 Offences Against the Person Act empowered magistrates in both England and Scotland to investigate suspected homicides of or by British subjects anywhere overseas, and gave judges throughout the empire authority to act on any such indictments.[46] Later this jurisdiction was further extended by a clause of the 1867 Merchant Shipping Act to any crime committed by any British subject on a foreign ship "to which he does not belong" (was not a member of its crew).[47] The reach of English law was continually widening, most of all in regard to acts of violence.

By legal categories, the nineteenth century's hardening approach to interpersonal violence is clear. Just as many property offenses were having their penalties reduced in the 1830s, maximum sentences for various kinds of assault were actually raised, both in law and in practice. By the opening of Victoria's reign the transition from "civil" to "criminal" treatment of assault was almost complete. Within the criminal courts that handled assaults – petty sessions and Quarter Sessions – the hitherto usual practices of dropping assault charges upon reconciliation or imposing a nominal fine upon some kind

---

[43] Unlike earlier: as John Beattie concluded [*Crime and the Courts* p. 86]: "For most of this period [1660–1800], men were rarely charged with a criminal offense when death occurred in accidents."

[44] Cockburn, "Homicide in Kent," op. cit.

[45] 57 Geo. III, c.53.

[46] 9 Geo. IV, c.31, s.12.

[47] This clause was inserted to enable magistrates in the empire and in English ports to deal with British seamen boarding foreign ships and there causing trouble. See Geoffrey Marston, "Crimes by British Passengers on Board Foreign Ships on the High Seas: The Historical Background to Section 686(1) of the Merchant Shipping Act 1894," *Cambridge Law Journal* 58 (1999), 171–196.

of compensation to the complainant were increasingly subject to criticism by magistrates and judges, and giving way more often to the imposition of some term of imprisonment.[48]

This process was gradual: in its 1814 edition, Burn's *Justice of the Peace*, the standard handbook for magistrates, instructed that in assault cases "the court frequently recommends the defendant to talk with the prosecutor, that is, to make him amends for the injury done him," and thereafter impose a small fine.[49] By the 1825 edition, the usual punishments inflicted (fine, imprisonment and the finding of sureties to keep the peace) were listed, and mention of private negotiation was confined to "cases where the offence more immediately affects the individual."[50] But this was a gradually shrinking category: more and more, interpersonal violence was seen as affecting the public as a whole.

While magisterial practices on assault were already changing, other changes in treatment of crimes against the person, chiefly affecting the higher courts of assize, were being made legislatively. The first piece of legislation to deal generally with violence, commonly known as Lord Ellenborough's Act, was passed in 1803. Ellenborough replaced a limited bill proposed by another Lord to repress an outbreak of face-slashing attacks in Ireland that numbered among its victims "respectable" members of the public with a broader one applying to England as well, and addressing a wider range of violent acts, indeed most that aimed at or resulted in "grievous bodily harm," a term left undefined. Ellenborough and his supporters seem to have been particularly determined to do away with armed robberies, hitherto dealt with essentially as crimes against property rather than against the person. Since they were already subject to the sentence of death, armed robberies did not need any augmentation of penalties, but now it appears the injury to persons, even if only from having a loaded pistol in their faces, was bulking larger in the Lords' outrage than even the loss of property. Ellenborough's bill provided an alternative way to capitally prosecute such offenses, as offenses against the person. It made attempts to kill, or even only to inflict grievous injury, if employing firearms or such potentially lethal instruments as swords or knives, punishable by death. The bill also removed the necessity of proving previous malice or intention in woundings. It passed fairly easily into law and soon came to be used more widely than simply against armed robberies;

---

[48] King, "Punishing Assault," op. cit.; Smith, "The State and the Culture of Violence," op. cit. Robert Shoemaker has noted the focus of complaint in defamation suits shifting in the course of the eighteenth century from words to "inappropriate physical conduct ... as if it was the pushing, beating, mobbing and spitting that was as much the source of complaint as the actual words used." ["The Decline of Public Insult in London 1660–1800," *Past and Present*, no. 169 (2000), 117].

[49] Burn, *Justice of the Peace*, 22nd ed. (1814), 3: 185.

[50] Burn, *Justice of the Peace*, 25th ed. (1825), 3: 231.

gradually, a wide range of violent acts were brought under its aegis, including serious violence between men and women.[51] The passage of this act in retrospect seems a milestone in criminal justice, even if the actual disposition of cases shifted only slowly thereafter.[52] Henceforth, more violent offenses were charged at assizes, where they received more severe punishments.[53]

When the French wars ended, anxieties about violence in Britain also rose further, and not only about political violence. By 1826 criminal law enforcement had become a salient political issue; that year Home Secretary Robert Peel (also working to establish the first professional police force on English soil) saw an Act through Parliament to encourage the prosecution of the more serious forms of assault by extending to them the provision of expenses to witnesses as well as prosecutors which already obtained in capital prosecutions.[54] Two years later, the laws on violence were consolidated and much further hardened by the Offences Against the Person Act of 1828 (9 Geo. IV c. 31), which was, in the judgment of its most recent student, "the first truly comprehensive piece of legislation designed to address interpersonal violence in British society."[55] Known as Lord Landsdowne's Act (for the Home Secretary at the moment it was introduced) it was actually in large part the result of efforts by Robert Peel during his tenure at that post. It was a part of Peel's broader program to improve the effectiveness of law enforcement, and (unlike Lord Ellenborough's Act) it was immediately made use of in the courts. This measure eliminated the earlier act's requirement of the use of offensive weapons – henceforth, even simpler assaults could, if considered sufficiently threatening, be prosecuted capitally. It also expanded the scope of that act by explicitly describing various behaviors that could be

[51] For example, in 1811 at the Surrey assizes Thomas Livermore was convicted under this act for attempting to murder his wife (he had cut her throat, but she survived) [*Times*, 1 April 1811, p. 3]. The following year Ann Sheldon was similarly charged with administering poison to her husband, but was acquitted [*Times*, 14 August 1812, p. 3].

[52] Looking back from the height of the Victorian era, James Fitzjames Stephen observed that "the very grossest and worst class of offences against the person were, till 1803, treated with the capricious lenity which was as characteristic of the common law as its equally capricious severity." *History of English Criminal Law* (London, 1883) 3: 116.

[53] Charges of attempted murder, already generally handled at assizes, gradually rose thereafter. For example, there were twenty convictions at the Old Bailey for attempted murder (apart from cases of attacking constables or other agents of the state) in the almost half-century from 1756 through 1803, but thirty-five in the almost quarter-century from 1804 through 1827, almost twice as many in half the time. [Throughout, however, acquittals on this charge continued to well outnumber convictions.] [Humphry Woolrych, *History and Results of the Present Capital Punishments in England* (London, 1832), pp. 128–132.]

[54] The Criminal Justice Act 1826, 7 Geo. IV, c.64.

[55] Greg T. Smith, "The State and the Culture of Violence" op. cit., p. 108.

capitally prosecuted. This act also shifted a very large body of lesser cases from quarter sessions to petty sessions, encouraging the prosecution of more non-capital violent offences.[56] At assizes, indictments and convictions for attempted murder significantly increased after its passage.[57]

Both of these changes – broadening the definition of violent offenses and facilitating their prosecution and conviction – were carried further in the next important measure, the 1837 Offences Against the Person Act (1 Vict. c.85). Enacted together with another better-known law eliminating the death penalty for most property offenses,[58] it *extended* the death penalty, at least in principle, to *more* cases of serious violence. In particular, it revised the 1828 Act to make an attempt to murder by "any other means whatsoever" liable to the same capital penalty as the use of a knife or other sharp instrument.[59] It also made it clear that failed attempts to kill where no bodily injury had been produced were still felonies, liable to punishment of up to transportation for life.

This extension of the meaning of wounding was taken in the courts to apply also when no intent to kill could be proved. In 1843, Chief Baron Abinger, citing this statute, held in a trial of a man who, when kicking another man, caused severe injury, that an instrument of some sort was no longer necessary to establish the serious charge of "wounding" (rather than the mere misdemeanor of "assault"): all that was necessary was to prove that some wound had been inflicted in the course of an assault.[60] The 1837 act

[56]After the 1828 act, cases in Middlesex Quarter Sessions were on average more serious, yet despite the diversion of the less serious ones their number did not fall, suggesting either (or both) an increase in such offenses or an increased propensity to prosecute [Smith, ibid.]

[57]At least at the Old Bailey, where the rate of convictions more than doubled in the less than five years from 1828 through Sept. 1832, from a yearly average of about 1 1/2 to one of about 3 1/2; in 1833 alone there were five convictions [Woolrych, op. cit., 131–132]. The *Times* reported only ten prosecutions (and eight convictions) for all forms of attempts to murder in the quarter-century from 1803 to 1828, but it only took another five years to report another eleven prosecutions (and nine convictions). Even though in this period the *Times* reported criminal trials only very erratically, the increase is suggestive.

[58]1 Vict. c.91.

[59]Lord John Russell, introducing the bill: *Parliamentary Debates*, S.3, 37 (1837): 723. 1 Vict. c.85, s.3.

[60]As often happened, however, the jury refused to follow his direction and found only assault [*R.v. Duffill* (1843): 1 Cox C.C. 49; *Lincolnshire Chronicle*, 21 July 1843, p. 1]. Even for judges some wound remained necessary to make the offense a felony, as Baron Rolfe reminded a Lancashire grand jury in 1845. Citing the case before them of "a man charged with having assaulted, kicked, and beaten a woman with intent to do grievous bodily injury. I must point out that . . . to kick a person, if it does not cause a wound, is no felony. Without a wound there is no felony in such cases, except in some attempts to strangle. . . . I can easily see how gentlemen are desirous,

also allowed a prisoner to be charged for common assault at the same time as a more serious count, which diminished the likelihood of acquittal.[61] If a jury was unwilling to convict of a more serious offense, it would often be ready to convict of the lesser, the penalty for which the act increased to as much as three years' imprisonment.[62]

Fatal violence as well was receiving fresh legislative attention. Manslaughter was a charge virtually confined before the nineteenth century to quarter or even merely petty sessions.[63] Its status as a clergyable offense lasted through most of the eighteenth century, and those convicted were usually simply burned in the hand and discharged. Even when felons began to be punished by imprisonment later in the century, its use for those found guilty of manslaughter remained highly exceptional; more common in that case was to also impose modest fines.[64] All this changed in the nineteenth century, when more kinds of killing came to be prosecuted as manslaughter, punishment for this offense increased, and it came to be tried exclusively at assizes.[65] To uphold this charge, unlike that of murder, intent to kill did not

---

in what I conceive to be the present imperfect state of the law, and in bad assaults to bind over parties for feloniously wounding, but really it is a violation of the law." Rolfe concluded by hoping for yet another tightening of the law on crimes against the person [*Liverpool Mercury*, 15 August 1845, p. 10].

[61] Burn, *Justice of the Peace*, 29th ed. (1845), ed. Thomas Chitty, p. 285. Several years later the trying of manslaughter in any court below the assizes was formally prohibited (5 and 6 Vict. c.38, s.1).

[62] Though this maximum was rarely applied, it did provide a potential weapon in the judicial armory, and a strong public statement on the seriousness with which some behavior that might only be convictable of common assault was now being viewed.

[63] For Surrey between 1660 and 1800, Beattie could find (in assize but also surviving quarter sessions records) 309 murder indictments, but only 6 for manslaughter [*Crime and the Courts*, op. cit., p. 83]. Sarah Anne Barbour-Mercer ["Prosecution and Process: Crime and the Criminal Law in Late Seventeenth Century Yorkshire" (Ph.D. Thesis, University of York, 1988)] similarly noted for that county from 1650 to 1700 the rarity of manslaughter charges in either assize or surviving quarter sessions records: she found 393 murder charges, but only 12 of manslaughter (and three murder charges downgraded by the grand jury to manslaughter). These examinations, however, while complete for assizes are much less so for quarter sessions, and there would appear to have been a good deal more manslaughter indictments brought there than these would indicate. Sharpe and Dickinson's ESRC project on violence in early modern England has uncovered many. For example, in Chester 1600–1800 coroners' inquests returned 307 findings of murder and 295 of manslaughter ["Initial Results" (2001), op. cit., p. 1.]

[64] John Beattie, *Crime and the Courts*, op. cit., pp. 89–96.

[65] By 1850, in England and Wales as a whole, there were 192 persons committed for trial at assizes on the charge of manslaughter, compared with 52 on a murder charge. [*Judicial Statistics for England and Wales for the Year 1850*]; certainly some of the rise in manslaughter charges reflected a down-charging of killings that would formerly have been charged as murder (perhaps in acknowledgment that a jury was likely to find

need to be shown; mere lack of regard for the lives of others was sufficient. Such indifference to life was coming to appear more dangerous and more heinous than ever before. As the Victorian jurist James Fitzjames Stephen later pronounced, "the danger to the public consists in the wilful infliction of deadly violence, and is not affected by the intention with which it is inflicted." Nor was it just a question of public safety: the moral guilt was not obviously less: "Is there anything," he rhetorically asked, "to choose morally between the man who violently stabs another in the chest with the definite intention of killing him, and the man who stabs another in the chest with no definite intention at all as to his victim's life or death, but with a feeling of indifference whether he lives or dies?" Indeed, he went on to suggest that "cases may be put in which reckless indifference to the fate of a person intentionally subjected to deadly injury is, if possible, morally worse than an actual intent to kill."[66]

As imprisonment became typical rather than exceptional for those convicted of manslaughter, one year no longer seemed an appropriate maximum. In 1822 the penalty ceiling for the offense was raised from one to three years' imprisonment,[67] and in the Offences Against the Person Act of 1828 raised again, all the way to transportation for life. After the latter act such stiff sentences did indeed begin to be handed down, and the 1837 Act specifically re-enacted this liability.[68] Now appearing only at the highest level, the assizes, such cases began to receive not only more severe punishment but also more publicity, thus heightening the potential for "instructive" impact upon the populace.

Finally, although murder had of course long been recognized as the most morally heinous and socially dangerous of offenses and been capitally punished, its treatment also was undergoing changes. On the one hand, growing discomfort with the death penalty and increasingly cautious charging practices were contributing to a decline in the number of murder charges per capita; without a good likelihood of conviction, magistrates began to hesitate to issue an indictment for murder, preferring to charge manslaughter.

only manslaughter anyway), but much was due to the charging in cases that might previously have been charged less seriously, or even escaped criminal charges, such as deaths produced by reckless driving, occupational negligence, or public-house or domestic quarrels.

[66] Stephen, *History*, op. cit., 3: 92.
[67] 3 Geo. IV c.38.
[68] Transportation sentences were being given by the following year: see *R.v. Manion* 1829 (manslaughter of a wife) and *R.v. Davis* 1829 (a prize-fight). Most manslaughter trials, however, though substantially increasing in number, ended in acquittal, and most convictions produced sentences lighter than transportation. For example, in the session year 1844–45, seventeen manslaughter trials at the Old Bailey (substantially more than most previous years) yielded only five convictions, just one of which received a sentence of transportation.

On the other hand, as they came in the course of the 1830s to be virtually the only remaining proceedings that could lead to hangings, murder trials increasingly occupied a category all their own, and as newspaper coverage expanded and town populations rose, they became much more publicly visible and culturally freighted.[69] The year of Victoria's accession, 1837, was the first in which execution was in practice reserved for murderers and, in rare cases, attempted murderers. The gap between murder, with its punishment of death, and all other offenses now widened to the chasm it remained until the abolition of the death penalty in the second half of the twentieth century.

Thus, as in so much else, the 1830s was a decade of major transition in criminal justice. The ending of the "bloody code" was accompanied by intensified social surveillance and regulation of public order and also a heightening of the penalties for violent behavior. By mid-century, fears for the safety of property were to ease, and "criminal anxieties" were to shift in the direction of crimes against the person. One chapter in English criminal justice history was closing and another was opening. As crimes against property evoked less fear, crimes against the person were evoking more. Correspondingly, the prosecution and punishment of the former eased. Alongside this easing went hardening treatment of the latter.[70] The everyday proceedings of justice, case by case, level by level, gradually turned a rising hostility to interpersonal violence into specific action. The rise in prosecution and punishment of assaults that began in the late eighteenth century continued through most of the nineteenth. Attempted murder charges increased in number. Manslaughter prosecutions increased in number and moved into assize courts. Finally, the crime of murder came in the early Victorian years to stand out in the public mind as never before, the only crime for which persons were executed. As such, it came to occupy a special place of its own in the world of criminal justice. Compared with all other criminals, accused murderers made a much greater impression on the public mind and were dealt with by coroners and inquest juries, grand jurors, and trial juries and judges with especial solemnity and severity. In such ways the priorities of criminal law gradually were rearranged. As the Conservative editor of the *Law Times* declared in an authoritative 1877 treatise, "the foremost object of all legislation is security

---

[69] This status as the only offense punished in practice capitally was essentially attained by 1837, by which time the capital penalty had been removed from property offenses and hanging for rape and for sodomy had fallen into disuse (the last rapist was hanged in 1836, and the offense was formally decapitalized in 1841 [4&5 Vict. c.56]). The only hangings thereafter other than for murder were three men, in 1841, 1855, and 1861, for attempted murder. In 1861 liability to the death penalty was removed from all offenses but murder and high treason (24&25 Vict. c.100).

[70] By the 1890s, larceny sentences at assizes (unless for repeaters) were much lighter than earlier (usually one to six months), even though only more serious cases were being dealt with there, petty cases being now handled summarily. On the other hand, treatment of crimes against the person largely resisted the trend to leniency.

for *the person*. The security of property is second in importance to this."[71] The *Law Times* would not have made such a declaration a half-century earlier.

Moving from legal categories to social ones, the same change in view of violence is evident. In the first half of the century certain kinds of "provoked" attacks – killings in defense of honor or reputation – were losing their traditional excusable character. Dueling, much less common than a century earlier but refusing to disappear, had long been technically criminal, but little punished. Now it began for the first time to be seriously prosecuted. In 1838 a successful prosecution for murder placed the institution in the dock of public opinion, leading within a few years to a revision of the military code providing severe penalties for the practice. At the same time more common "set fights," the ordinary man's duels, were also receiving more official condemnation. Even fights involving less premeditation were drawing more serious treatment. Drunkenness, which undermined the ability to control oneself, was becoming less likely to mitigate one's responsibility for violent or disorderly behavior. In a variety of ways, judges and juries were coming to expect men to exercise a greater degree of control over themselves than ever before.

Yet this movement was neither applied across the board of forcible behavior, nor were its sentiments shared by all. In a variety of ways, it was resisted and its force deflected. Distinctions were made between more and less excusable acts of violence. Older attitudes approving of male aggressiveness continued, even among the middling classes and the governing elite. Alternative notions of manliness – such as the widespread tradition of the "fair fight" – persisted and ensured that some killings would be treated more gently than others. And as always class made a large difference: the war on violence was felt by many workingmen and their spokesmen to bear down chiefly on them, and the old theme of "one law for the rich man, and one for the poor man" was re-sounded in this arena, all the more loudly as workingmen advanced towards inclusion in the political nation. There was much to justify their sense of a class war, for not only was violence more a part of working-class life, that life, at least below the skilled labor "aristocracy," was often characterized by organs of respectability as fundamentally primitive, a match for any practices found among indigenous peoples of the empire. Such a tarring of whole classes was intensely resented, as were related

---

[71] Edward W. Cox, *The Principles of Punishment, as Applied in the Administration of the Criminal Law, by Judges and Magistrates* (London, 1877), p. 93 [italics in original]. As he explained: "It is even more necessary to repress by punishment crimes of violence [than crimes against property] because they are more noxious to the community by the terror and distrust they occasion, by their dangerous tendency to incite irregularly constructed minds to imitation and the dissolution of society itself that would result from any extensive following of the example." [p. 77] Cox was also an active barrister and then magistrate, and knew the criminal justice system intimately as a practitioner as well as an observer.

characterizations of entire districts like Liverpool docklands or Lancashire mining areas as barely civilized. Even drink, so strongly condemned by "civilizing" reformers, was seen by many as a part of English tradition and as an Englishman's (though not an Englishwoman's) right, and thus the extent of personal responsibility for crimes committed under the influence could be, and was, heatedly disputed. One face of the war on violence was certainly a class war, and it was often vigorously resisted in these same terms.

Yet class, and the differences in perceptions of violence and outright contestations over its perpetrators' culpability and punishment it encouraged, was not the only social framework through which the war on violence was waged. A second, arguably even more important, was that of an ongoing "reconstruction of manliness." The nineteenth-century criminal justice process simultaneously applied its universalistic language as an instrument of "social control" in two ways – against members of the working classes and against men (and thus, of course, particularly – though never exclusively – against working-class men). However, the criminal law and its administration was always more than a simple instrument of control: it was throughout a structured public arena (and also private seminar, when after murder convictions cases went to the Home Office) in which general and difficult questions of responsibility were argued, and decisions were arrived at with immediate practical (sometimes life-or-death) consequences for potentially any member of society. These public and private discussions themselves depended on how a variety of cultural notions were constructed – respectability, Englishness, manliness and womanliness high among them. Both faces of criminal justice, of control-and-resistance and of general moral debate, were real and fundamental; each shaped the context for the other; both stories need to be told, together.

### Gender, Violence and Law

As the first half of the nineteenth century saw a heightening concern about personal security and a consequent intensified fear of interpersonal violence, it also saw another, perhaps even more profound, development: a sea change in constructions of femininity and masculinity, or as contemporaries would have said, "womanliness" and "manliness." This change had many facets, but at its core was a newly-sharpened image of women as more moral, spiritual and religious – if weak and fragile – and men as stronger, more energetic and more "rational." While needing the protection of the stronger sex, and refraining from the necessary but inevitably conflictual worlds of business and politics, woman was, in the characteristic phrase of Charles Kingsley, "the natural and therefore divine guide, purifier, inspirer of the man."[72] This

---

[72] Quoted in Walter Houghton, *The Victorian Frame of Mind 1830–1870* (New Haven, 1957), p. 251n.

emotionally powerful allocation of qualities by gender, most identified with the Evangelical movement so important in shaping Victorian Britain, was widely absorbed far beyond the middle class alone in the early years of the century, transforming among other things the nature of British Christianity. As Callum Brown has argued, after many centuries in which not only the Church of England but religiosity itself had been a predominantly male enterprise, around 1800 piety became noticeably feminized, and women "pietized." As women's spirituality came to be privileged, men's was increasingly seen as problematic. Nineteenth-century religious literature (which grew explosively) portrayed women almost always as exemplars of goodness and even holiness, while even exemplary men's stories emphasized their great struggle to overcome the snares of their male nature.[73] It now came to be assumed, by Radicals as much as by Conservatives (part of the master Victorian narrative, one might say) that men were in need of women to elevate them and save their souls, as domestic and intimate "angels."[74] However, if this was so then a new and fundamental spiritual and moral task faced the nation: not simply the reform of social or political institutions, but the "reform" of men themselves. And, until that ambitious aim could be accomplished, the nation was presented with the immediate task of protecting women from mistreatment by unreformed men.

Independently of the Evangelical movement, the new culture of sensibility that emerged in the eighteenth century in the ruling classes similarly rendered customary constructions of manhood problematic by elevating the value of the more "delicate" feelings hitherto left for the most part to women and by criticizing most expressions of male aggressiveness, particularly towards women. "Rakes" became, as G.J. Barker-Benfield has put it, "the most egregious representatives of a male culture now being defined by its incompatibility with a new sense of public 'decency,' that is, order in the streets and the nonbrutalization of women."[75] This cultural shift, like Evangelicalism, was brought to a head by the impact of the French Revolution, which moved order and virtue to the fore of anxious "state of the nation" discussions. A "moral panic" that accompanied the political panic

---

[73]Callum G. Brown, *The Death of Christian Britain* (London and New York, 2001), pp. 59, 88–114.

[74]Alex Tyrrell has shown that in his most radical period of the late 1830s and 1840s, Samuel Smiles propagated, along with calls for middle- and working-class cooperation to extend the franchise and obtain social reforms, a "vision of a world that would be reformed – not through the masculine agency of politics, but through the feminine agency of motherhood." "Samuel Smiles and the Woman Question in Early Victorian Britain," *Journal of British Studies* 39 (2000), 185–216.

[75]G.J. Barker-Benfield, *The Culture of Sensibility: Sex and Society in Eighteenth-Century Britain* (Chicago, 1992), p. 49.

of these years focused fresh attention on the state of the family and caused upper-class adultery, as brought into public view by a rising number of criminal conversation and divorce trials, to become more of a "social problem" than ever before. These trials, and the public discourse surrounding them, "used political events," as Katherine Binhammer has argued, "to consolidate and promote the domestic ideal of women."[76] But they did more: they similarly consolidated and promoted a "domesticated" ideal of men, for the central conflict of these dramas was rarely focused on the wife; instead, it typically highlighted the conflict between two men over one's wife, in which contrasting male behavior was of the greatest concern. Such dramas stimulated discussion of what proper manliness consisted of, and in general encouraged the heaping of abuse upon their usual "villain," the "other man," the "seducer" of a susceptible woman and the "destroyer" of a home.

Encouraged by these several converging cultural streams, the treatment of women, even before the accession of a woman to the throne, was being cited as a measure of civilization, and the law-abiding, self-disciplined, marriage- and woman-respecting Englishman (and Scotsman) was emerging as a cultural ideal and, increasingly, archetype. By the opening of the nineteenth century, this archetype had a new mirror image, that of the impulsive and fractious "native" overseas, who also generally mistreated his womenfolk. Evangelicals and Utilitarians shared in propagating this image to the home public. William Wilberforce described to the House of Commons in 1813 "the evils of Hindostan" as "family, fireside evils," paying particular attention to the ill-treatment of women as evidenced by polygamy and suttee, among other practices, contrasting this with the equality and respect to which women were entitled "in all Christian countries."[77] A few years later, James Mill in his influential *History of British India* generalized far beyond Hindustan: "among rude people," he observed, "the women are generally degraded, among civilized people they are exalted."[78] For decades thereafter, such statements were endlessly repeated.[79] One

---

[76]Katherine Binhammer, "The Sex Panic of the 1790s," *Journal of the History of Sexuality* 6 (1996), 409–434. See also the earlier characterization of the 1790s as a time of particular "moral panic" in Lawrence Stone, *The Road to Divorce: England 1530–1987* (Oxford and New York, 1990).

[77]William Wilberforce, "Substance of the speech of William Wilberforce, Esq., on the clause of the East India Bill for promoting the religious instruction and moral improvement of the natives of the British dominions in India, on the 22nd of June and the 1st and 12th of July, 1813," *Pamphleteer* (London), vol. 3, no. 5 (March 1814), p. 70.

[78]*History of British India* (London, 1818), vol. 1, p. 383.

[79]See for example Clare Midgley, *British Feminism in the Age of Empire* (London and Boston, 2003).

influential missionary wrote in 1843 of just-freed Jamaican slaves brought from Africa that, "like the inhabitants of all uncivilised nations . . . the men treated the women as inferior in the scale of being to themselves, exercising over those who composed their respective harems a kind of petty sovereignty."[80] The "protection of women" became an important justification of empire.[81]

The woman-mistreating native had a parallel in the "British barbarian" at home, now no longer the disappearing "rake" but, far more frighteningly, those degraded men in the lower reaches of society whom neither Christianity nor the broader influences of civilization had yet reformed.[82] In regarding them also, the treatment of women became a touchstone. Such a trope flourished particularly in the second half of the century. A gang rape by Lancashire pitmen of a tramp woman they found lying drunk in a ditch in 1874, who died of her injuries, provoked the *Daily Telegraph* to compare such people unfavorably with the African savages recently described by Dr. Livingstone and declare that "the most brutal, the most cowardly, the most pitiless, the most barbarous deeds done in the world, are being perpetrated by the lower classes of the English people." The *Times* complained in 1872 that a succession of killings "has presented a picture of drunken brutality such as might be more fitly expected in some savage island in the far Pacific, where the natives had just tasted for the first time the terrible poison of drink."[83]

If at home as abroad, the protection of women became a powerful justification for the exercise of power and the disciplining of populations, in both locales it was a good deal more. This insistence was too strong to simply be

---

[80] James Mursell Phillippo, cited in Catherine Hall, *Civilising Subjects: Metropole and Colony in the English Imagination 1830–1867* (Chicago, 2002), p. 187. The position of women came to serve as a marker by which to rank peoples. Lord Arthur Gordon, praising to William Gladstone in 1876 the Fijians he was governing, observed that "two things have struck me especially as showing that they are a good way from barbarism, the high position of women, and their respect for agricultural labour." [Paul Knaplund, ed., "Gladstone-Gordon Correspondence," *Transactions of the American Philosophical Society* 51.4 (1961), 67.]

[81] And of even "imperial feminism" as well. For the use of the image of the "downtrodden woman" of colonized societies to advance the emancipation of women in Britain and their power abroad see Antoinette Burton, *Burdens of History: British Feminists, Indian Women, and Imperial Culture, 1865–1915* (Chapel Hill, N.C., 1994).

[82] See for example Tim Barringer, "Images of Otherness and the Visual Production of Difference: Race and Labour in Illustrated Texts, 1850–1865," in *The Victorians and Race*, ed. Shearer West (Aldershot, 1996), pp. 34–52.

[83] *Daily Telegraph*, 17 December 1874, quoted in Richard Altick, *Victorian Studies in Scarlet*, p. 295; *Times*, 21 December 1872, p. 9.

FIGURE 1. "Victorian Era: Justice" (*Punch*, Jan. 30, 1901). One of a series illustrating the chief characteristics of the age. Here Britannia wields the sword to protect non-European women from their own men.

used to justify other purposes; it in turn used those other purposes, and in doing so helped reshape both the empire and Britain itself. As scholars of domestic and imperial reform have demonstrated, it was an aim continually appealed to by persons and groups pushing a wide range of changes – reforms or deformations, as they might variously be seen – many having lasting effects. If protecting women became a justification for exercising power over other peoples, in the process the justification became a force in itself. What E.P. Thompson observed about the eighteenth century "rule of law" applies here; an authority so justified, to maintain itself, had to actually frequently take actions that did indeed, for all the cultural misunderstanding behind them, work to protect subject women from many harms. Moreover, rhetoric in itself can be a powerful force; in this case, it empowered critics, British and indigenous, of existing forms of masculine authority, sometimes to the vexation of British governors.[84]

At home, any general stigmatization of violence was inevitably going to impact not only on the working classes more than their social superiors, but on men much more than women, since men have always been the chief perpetrators of violence. At its core, therefore, if a general intensification of sanctions against violence was already necessarily "classed," it was also necessarily gendered, all the more as the leading form of female lethal violence – the murder of newborns – was being treated ever more leniently. But with the "protection of women" assuming a place at the heart of "civilization" and "Englishness" (the two taken to be almost the same thing), it is not surprising that the war on violence began to assume a more explicitly gendered cast, as the evocative figure of the female victim advanced to center stage.[85] Yet it was not only the sharp distinction between masculinity and femininity, so associated with Victorianism, that made this figure so prominent, but other equally important developments, even those usually portrayed as reactions against Victorian gender ideology. The growing recognition of women's political rights in the second half of the century reinforced Victorian gender ideology in this sphere by making more prominent women's right to bodily security, against both beatings and coerced sex. The two cultural revolutions

---

[84]Jean and John Comaroff (hardly apologists for imperialism) have noted how the "egalitarian rhetoric" of British missionaries in southern Africa attracted and mobilized women: "Some early [female] converts," they observed, "said explicitly that Christianity would reverse [their] disabilities, that it 'raised them to an equality with their husbands.'" *Of Revelation and Revolution: Christianity, Colonialism and Consciousness in South Africa*, vol. 1 (Chicago, 1991), p. 240.

[85]The same development has been noted taking place at this time, or even earlier, in America: see Scott Martin, "Violence, Gender and Intemperance in Early National Connecticut," *Journal of Social History* 34. 2 (Winter 2000), 309–325, which examines an 1815 wife murder trial and finds a transformation of the victim "from drunken scold to brutalized victim," illustrating "in microcosm what would occur later in the antebellum temperance movement and beyond."

regarding women which were proceeding through the Victorian era – what we might call the "paternalist" or "gender protectionist" (sometimes called "new model patriarchy")[86] and the feminist – often pictured as contesting with each other, more often worked together in this sphere, *both* of them causing male violation of female bodily integrity to be more stigmatized and more punished. The well-known movements in the 1870s and 1880s to repeal the Contagious Diseases Acts and to raise the age of consent exhibited how these two cultural revolutions (their heirs today in opposite camps) could reinforce each other in that era. In such ways the imperative to "protect the gentler sex" contributed to women's emancipation, and together with a just-emerging feminism provided the ideological scaffolding for the nineteenth century war on male violence.

Thus, for all that the nineteenth-century intensification of the war on interpersonal violence needs to be brought out, that era's second contribution to the long civilizing offensive was at least as important. The focus of the offensive gradually moved from violence between men – and at times between women – (particularly in public) to violence committed by men against women and other dependents (more often in private). At first, even as the courts stepped up prosecution and punishment of violence from the 1770s they continued to deal almost exclusively with the chiefly public violence that took place between men, and to a lesser extent among women also. Prosecutions for domestic violence were rare. For practical purposes, the notion of "criminal assault" did not yet embrace, other than on special occasions, violence by husbands against wives. Only after the Napoleonic Wars were expressions of outrage at violence against women, of any class, noticeable in the courts, and only thereafter were increased efforts made to discover, punish and reduce it. In this shift of focus, the long era of rising pressure against interpersonal violence merged with changing gender ideologies. As women came to appear ever more moral and spiritual but at the same time that much more vulnerable than men, increasing offense was taken at their physical mistreatment, by men as well as by women themselves.

As more crimes against the person were defined and prosecuted, and as conviction and the severity of punishment, in crimes against property as well as against the person, came increasingly to depend upon the degree of violence, or threat to personal security, involved, the ranks of those criminally prosecuted and, even more, of those punished for crimes against the person began to become even more male than formerly. This development was very likely accentuated by the increasing outrage at offenses against women's persons from the 1840s. And if the movement towards a virtual male monopolization of the roles of serious offenders was encouraged by the changing pattern of concerns, it in turn made the image of females as victims of

[86] In, among other works, Ian Duncan, *Modern Romance and Transformations of the Novel: The Gothic, Scott, Dickens* (Cambridge, 1992).

violence and the complementary image of men as natural perpetrators of it all the more compelling.

Although the general increase in criminal prosecution of the first half of the century leveled off in the 1840s and later in the century went into reverse, this was much more true for female than for male defendants.[87] An emerging disenchantment with the use of imprisonment focused first on its use for women.[88] At the same time, while a growing number of deviant women were coming to be seen as mentally ill, and diverted to asylums and reformatory institutions, this psychiatrizing tendency was slower to affect deviant males.[89] In consequence, the male proportion of those prosecuted at the Old Bailey (London's chief criminal court for serious offences) rose from about 3/4 in the 1830s to well over 90% by the end of the century.[90] On a national level, men formed an increasing proportion of those proceeded against by indictment (the more serious form of criminal proceeding), rising from 73%

[87]See V.A.C. Gatrell, "Decline of Theft and Violence," op. cit. Even as the total number of persons apprehended for indictable offences (those more serious offences which had not been turned over to summary jurisdiction) fell between 1857 and 1890 almost by half (from 32,031 to 17,678) the female proportion of this declining total fell from 27 to 19%. The female proportion of those committed for trial fell even more, and of those convicted and imprisoned still more yet [Lucia Zedner, *Women, Crime, and Custody in Victorian England* (Oxford, 1991), pp. 316–323].

[88]See Martin Wiener, *Reconstructing the Criminal: Culture, Law and Policy in England 1830–1914* (Cambridge, 1990), pp. 309–310. Already by the early Victorian years punitive language was softening: whereas in 1825 the Evangelical Elizabeth Fry argued that women prisoners should be "humiliated" by cutting off their hair, in 1842 she had changed her mind: "the poor [female] prisoner," she now wrote, "should be humbled by her faults [but] she should not always carry about in the view of others the crime she has committed, it hardens and makes them worse than before." [Kay Daniels, *Convict Women* (St. Leonard's, NSW: 1998), p. 115.]

[89]See Roger Smith, *Trial by Medicine: Insanity and Responsibility in Victorian Trials* (Edinburgh, 1981); Zedner, op. cit.

[90]Malcolm M. Feeley and Deborah M. Little found this to have risen from an eighteenth-century average of about 2/3, and barely more than half early in the eighteenth century. ["The Vanishing Female: The Decline of Women in the Criminal Process, 1687–1912," *Law and Society Review* 25 (1991), 722.] However, Peter King, in an as-yet unpublished essay, has reanalyzed and questioned Feeley and Little's findings for the eighteenth and early nineteenth centuries, concluding that there was little change in gender proportions before mid-century; however, the pronounced shift during the second half of the nineteenth century, found also by Philippe Chassaigne for the Old Bailey and by Lucia Zedner more generally, has not been challenged. [Zedner, op. cit.; Philippe Chassaigne, "La Meurtre à Londres à l'Epoque Victorienne: Structures Sociales et Comportements Criminels, 1857–1900" (Thèse de Doctorat, University of Paris, 1991).] According to Chassaigne, the proportion of women among those tried at the Old Bailey, which was devoting a growing part of its caseload to serious crimes against the person, decreased by about 62% between 1860 and 1911 (from 21 to 8%).

of the total in 1857 to 81% by 1890.[91] Moreover, throughout the century male defendants remained somewhat more likely to be convicted and to receive longer sentences, and thus formed an even higher proportion of those undergoing criminal punishment. By 1900, more than 85% of inmates of local prisons (for short sentences) and about 96% of convict (longer sentence) prisoners were male.[92] Apart from property offenses, the same pattern still held: in prosecuted "crimes against the person" taken alone, the proportion of female defendants fell. And in the most serious criminal charge of all, murder of a non-infant, women were ever less often defendants. Even women's killing of their infants, more often offering evidence of intention than most killings, drew through the period a steadily smaller proportion of murder convictions, and after 1843 never an execution, while male killing of women was drawing a growing proportion of murder convictions.

As with the repression of violence, so also in the reconstruction of notions of manhood that went along with it, the law took a leading role. Even marriage law was affected, both by diminishing tolerance for violence and for male mistreatment of women. It was of course, unlike most law, directly connected to changing expectations of how men ought to act with women, and new influences can be seen in the expanding concept of "cruelty" in marriage litigation. The first sign of this was Lord Stowell's 1790 ruling in *Evans v. Evans* that "apprehension" of violence, though it had to be "reasonable," could take the place of actual violence as grounds for divorce. The impact of this concession was limited not only by judicial conservatism but by the very small amount of divorce litigation carried out under the extremely restrictive procedures in effect until the creation of the Divorce Court in 1857. Once established, however, that Court dramatically widened the stream of litigation and accelerated the development of case law: within the next few years the threshold of "reasonableness" for such apprehensions was lowered by a series of rulings. At the same time, the threshold of provocation for marital violence was raised, and a much greater degree of wifely misbehavior came to be necessary to make husbandly violence excusable.[93]

---

[91] Zedner, op. cit., p. 36.

[92] Annual reports of the Prison Commissioners; Annual judicial statistics.

[93] A.J. Hammerton, *Cruelty and Companionship: Conflict in Nineteenth-Century Married Life* (London, 1992), pp. 120–129. For example, in the 1860 case of *Pearman v. Pearman* (not mentioned by Hammerton) Justice Cresswell ruled that a wife's drunken violence did not excuse a husband's beating her. "Although," he allowed, "a husband might restrain his wife from using personal violence to him when she lost control through drink, yet there was no law which allowed a man to beat a drunken wife, and if he lost his temper and did beat her he was no doubt guilty of cruelty" [*Times*, 30 January 1860, p. 9]. This ruling did not directly help the wife, because while she sought a separation because of her husband's cruelty, he sought a divorce on grounds of her adultery, which was also proven. Yet even here Cresswell stressed that if [the court] "had reason to believe that the misconduct of the wife had been occasioned by the

Before the nineteenth century criminal courts saw comparatively few prosecutions for violence against women within the home. Sexual violence received even less attention: not only did the law make rape extremely difficult to prove, resulting in a very high acquittal rate, but most complaints of rape or attempted rape were dismissed by JPs or grand juries without ever reaching trial. Indeed, in either area it is only in the 1820s that signs of change begin to appear.

Much of the toughening of the criminal law already noted was stimulated in part by a new concern about violence against women. The same 1828 Offences Against the Person Act that raised penalties for crimes of violence included important provisions increasing the chances of convicting for rape. In introducing, in the next toughening bill in 1837, the clause that made an actual breaking of the skin not necessary for conviction of either the felony of wounding or the capital felony of attempted murder, Home Secretary Lord John Russell cited as his prime example of the need for this revision a case of atrocious violence against a wife. In this 1834 case, a man had attacked his wife with a heated poker, beat her insensible, set her clothes on fire, and was only prevented from killing her by the interference of neighbors, yet because he had not inflicted an incised wound could only be punished for an aggravated assault.[94] Henceforth, such a man could be convicted of attempted murder.

In such ways, the nineteenth-century criminal courts – in spite of their all-male composition – focused more and more on men.[95] Of course it was working-class men, by and large, whose behavior was at issue, evaluated by upper-class magistrates and judges and middle-class juries. Without this class difference, it is unlikely that the courts could have become major instruments for the reshaping of "manliness." And yet, class-prejudiced as they no doubt were, they did in fact become instruments of a development with implications beyond class. In regard to behavior towards females, both criminal and often civil justice rhetoric and activity revealed heightened conflict, but also movement. From newspapers and magazines to fiction to politics to the administration of the law, violence against or even serious mistreatment of women was being regarded more gravely and argued about more intensely.

---

misconduct of the husband [through cruelty] it would exercise [its] discretion by refusing a decree" and instead granting the wife a separation. However, in the end the jury found it had not been so occasioned, and the husband received his divorce.
[94] *Parliamentary Debates*, S.3, 37 (1837), 723. [1 Vict. c.85, s.3.]
[95] Recently, in the first extensive examination of late Victorian petty sessions prosecutions for minor violence, Barry S. Godfrey and Stephen Farrell have concluded that, even after taking the specific circumstances and characteristics of offences into account, as compared with women, men suffered disproportionately harsh penalties. ["Explaining differential patterns of punishment for men and women convicted of violent offences in the late Victorian period," unpublished paper, 2003.]

Nor was the movement to restrict male violence confined to offenses against women. Gender concerns were present even in views of violence between men. We will turn first to examine related changes in, and contests over, the law's treatment of this sort of violence, chiefly when it turned lethal, before looking at greater length at how the criminal law came to treat the major forms of men's violence against women.

# 2

# When Men Killed Men

On a summer evening in 1838 Mr. Francis Eliot and Mr. Charles Mirfin, together with two "seconds" each and a doctor, met on Wimbledon Common. While attending the Epsom Races earlier that year, Eliot's carriage had upset Mirfin's, fracturing the latter's ribs in the fall, and an altercation that followed had led to Eliot striking a blow upon the already-injured Mirfin, and departing the scene. When, months later, Mirfin discovered the identity and address of his malefactor, he demanded satisfaction. Refusing Eliot's offer of a verbal apology, Mirfin insisted upon "satisfaction" of a duel with pistols. The first round ended with misses; a second, insisted upon by Mirfin, resulted in his death.

In past years, that would have usually led to a merely pro forma indictment. This time, however, the inquest jury quickly returned verdicts of willful murder against all surviving parties, and a magistrate preferred indictments under the Offences Against the Person Act passed just the previous year against all except Eliot (who the justice no doubt felt had had no choice, as the man was threatening to shoot him one way or the other). The case went to the Old Bailey, where it was received differently than its predecessors had been. Defense counsel, as one might expect, made much of the fact that, as one put it, "men of rank and station, legislators, and lawyers, had been engaged in dueling" for many years, going on to remind the jury of the remark of the renowned judge Lord Erskine as counsel in an 1803 dueling trial that "there were feelings which occasionally actuated parties – feelings of wounded honour, which, if they ceased to exist, the welfare of society and the prosperity of the country would cease with them." In that case Erskine had won an acquittal. However, this citation of Erskine was rebuffed by Justice Vaughan, who declared that the jury in the 1803 trial had clearly decided wrongly. Despite further perorations of several skilled counsel and many highly respectable character witnesses, Eliot's two seconds were convicted of murder (the jury even declaring that the doctor should also have been charged). The verdict was a novelty, the first murder conviction of a duelist or second at the Old Bailey since at least 1756, and as such made a deep public impression.[1] Gaveling down the surprised outcries from

[1]For the period 1756–1831, see Humphry Woolrych, *History and Results of the Present Capital Punishments in England* (London, 1832), pp. 115–120, 127–132. Thereafter, the

spectators, Vaughan declared his full approval of the verdict. Of course he then announced that they would not hang, but suffer imprisonment. Their sentence was eventually set at imprisonment for twelve months in the House of Correction at Guildford, the last month of which was to be solitary, a sentence which they indeed served (after an appeal was denied). It was a great humiliation for gentlemen (even gentlemen of trade, as the defendants were), and a very public demonstration that juries and judges had begun to view dueling deaths in a new way.[2]

The next year, this time in Somerset, another set combat, this one a fist-fight in a lower social milieu, also ended fatally after no fewer than one hundred rounds. In this case, even though the fight had been conducted fairly, a middle-class man, Charles Rudge, who had not taken part in the fight itself, but had held the money stakes was tried for manslaughter, convicted and sentenced to a year's imprisonment. When his supporters (including all the jurors) petitioned for mitigation, Justice Coleridge (in the first years of what was to be a long and highly influential judicial career) explained his verdict to the Whig Home Secretary, noting that "my rule is to punish manslaughter occasioned in prize fights, or fights for money previously arranged, with some severity." However, since the man's character appeared good and his "station" quite a respectable one, Coleridge was ready to bend: "Now that the benefit of the example has been had," he concluded, "I shall be very glad, if Lord Normanby should feel with me, that some remission may properly be made." The sentence was reduced to four months.[3]

It was a time of example-setting. Violent and life-threatening defenses of one's honor, or even mere tests of one's prowess, once routine public rituals, were no longer considered manly by either state authorities or a growingly "respectable" public. Changes in the law, as we have seen, were making more kinds of violence against the person liable to prosecution, and prosecution in higher courts, where more severe punishment was possible; and the amount of such prosecution rapidly rose in the first half of the century. The great, and growing, bulk of this prosecution was of men, most of whom were charged with violence against other men.[4]

---

*Old Bailey Sessions Papers* [contemporary reports on all trials there until 1834; hereafter cited as OBSP] show no murder conviction in a duel.

[2] *Times*, 22 September 1838, p. 6. See also *Times*, 27 August 1838, p. 7; *Annual Register* 80, Part 2 (1838), p. 142; G. T. Crook, ed., *The Complete Newgate Calendar*, vol. 5 (London, 1926), 290–293.

[3] HO18/6/1 [August 1839].

[4] The basic source for prosecutions is the *Annual Judicial Statistics*, published from 1805 and more systematically and reliably from 1856. Recorded crime and its disposition during the nineteenth century have been valuably examined in David Philips, *Crime and Authority in Victorian England: the Black Country 1835–1860* (London, 1977); V. A. C. Gatrell, "The Decline of Theft and Violence in Victorian and Edwardian England," in *Crime and the Law: The Social History of Crime in Western Europe since*

What was the meaning of these changes in the law and its administration? Besides enumerating legislative enactments and totaling court caseloads, we need to understand what these cases of violence receiving official cognizance were like, their social character as well as their legal status. Making up the legal categories of assault, manslaughter and murder were specific kinds of violence, arising out of particular social situations and stimulating much moral and social discourse and argument. The rest of this chapter, and most of this work, will examine more closely the types of violent encounter most significant for notions of manliness and the response they called forth in the legal process and in the public mind.

The most common form of male-on-male violence was a public fight. Such physical altercations were ubiquitous in the early nineteenth century, and in both dispute settlement and "sporting" forms had for long been entrenched in popular culture. As one magistrate observed in 1829, the "habit of fighting from boyhood" was deeply ingrained in most Englishmen.[5] On occasion such fights had a fatal outcome. The most common single cause of adult deaths that produced inquests in eighteenth century London were punches and kicks received in fights (many arranged, still more spontaneous).[6] The number of such deaths exceeded the number recorded: cases have been found in which the death of a combatant was laid by coroners' inquests to natural causes though evidence was recorded that contradicted that conclusion, and other similar cases are almost sure to exist.[7] Coroner's juries, with their relatively popular composition, would seem to have been fairly tolerant of such violence and reluctant to see someone brought formally to justice for an ostensibly consensual and fair fight, however lethal its outcome. At a higher social level, as many as fifteen per cent of the homicides that came before the Old Bailey in sample years between 1690 and 1780 were produced

---

*1500*, ed. V.A.C. Gatrell, Bruce Lenman and Geoffrey Parker (London, 1980), pp. 238–337; Carolyn A. Conley, *The Unwritten Law: Criminal Justice in Victorian Kent* (Oxford and New York, 1991); Philippe Chassaigne, "La Meurtre à Londres à l'Époque Victorienne: Structures Sociales et Comportements Criminels 1857–1900" (Thèse de Doctorat, University of paris, 1991); Clive Emsley, *Crime and Society in England, 1750–1900* (London, rev. ed. 1996).

[5] Barber Beaumont, Esq., Middlesex magistrate, letter to the *Morning Post* 18 September 1829, cited in John Carter Wood, " 'The Shadow of Our Refinement': Violence, Custom and the Civilizing Process in Nineteenth-Century England" (Ph.D. dissertation, University of Maryland, 2001) p. 185. Wood's dissertation is the most thorough exploration of the "culture of fighting" in the English working classes during the nineteenth century.

[6] Thomas R. Forbes, "Inquests into London and Middlesex Homicides, 1673–1782," *Yale Journal of Biology and Medicine* 50 (1977), 212.

[7] Forbes, "Crowner's Quest," *Transactions of the American Philosophical Society* 68 (1978), 39–40.

by duels; it appears likely also that many others never reached the higher courts.[8]

Yet, after the wars with France, with military virtues no longer so needed, and with the nation, formerly seeming so united, now threatened by social unrest, anxiety about internal disorder and violence in general mounted in the respectable classes. One legal response to such fears for the safety of both property and person was to create professional police forces to make apprehension and prosecution more sure and ultimately to deter and prevent criminal acts; another was for the courts to toughen their treatment of violent death. Treatment of property crime, when brought to court, was already proverbially tough, indeed more so than could be sustained under increasing public criticism. Violent deaths of adults were nearly always at the hands of men. Such tightening seemed all the more urgent, as at least the more formal of these practices were not diminishing on their own. Dueling's appeal in the early years of the century was even spreading beyond the aristocracy and gentry to socially ambitious middle-class gentlemen like Eliot and Mirfin. Prizefights also were growing in popularity, with George IV's enjoyment of them and with urbanization and improved transport bringing larger numbers together, in this case to witness debasing spectacles. In such a situation, they both came to seem public dangers to a degree they had not before. Although not political, the formalized public violence of duels or prizefights, and even the violence of less formal but more common pub- and street-fighting, appeared now a danger to law and order that could no longer be tolerated.

Gentlemen had long dueled, first with rapiers and then with pistols, while plebeians used their fists, or, not infrequently, whatever came to hand. Even when a participant died, unless there had been some gross unfairness, those indicted could expect quick acquittals.[9] As usually premeditated, and often carefully arranged events, duels more flagrantly violated the law, even as it stood in the eighteenth century. However, they were widely accepted as a ancient privilege – and obligation – of high rank. They had come under a rising tide of criticism during the latter years of that century, as feeling against both aristocratic codes that existed outside the law and against lethal violence came to the fore in official as well as "respectable" circles.[10] Such sentiments, however, failed to diminish their frequency. The gradual weakening of the legitimacy of the duel was for some years counterbalanced by a rise in the

[8]Robert Shoemaker, "Male Honour and the Decline of Public Violence in Eighteenth-Century London," *Social History* 26 (2001), 190–208.
[9]Ibid.
[10]See Donna T. Andrew, "The Code of Honour and its critics: The opposition to dueling in England, 1700–1850," *Social History* 5 (1980), 409–434.

numbers of middling men who took to the duel as a mark of higher status.[11] So duels remained frequent into the fourth decade of the nineteenth century. By the 1820s, however, the institutions of criminal law had become unfriendly to these practices, and within a few years, a sharp change in the attitudes and policies of persons in authority and leaders of opinion brought about a sudden collapse of the practice.

When one of the combatants in a duel died, the matter usually came to court. However, judges continued for the most part to avoid directly confronting duels; often, they would highlight any impulsive, "passionate" facets to allow the jury to be forgiving, as it almost always seemed to want to be.[12] Even in 1826, an army officer charged with manslaughter at the Admiralty Court for shooting to death the ship's surgeon on a voyage home from Madras received merely a fine of £10. The court heard from him and his witnesses that the victim was a good friend and that a drunken quarrel between them over a woman had led to a duel with pistols, with the fatal result.[13] But after the well-publicized conviction of the Eliot party in 1838, public and legal tolerance of dueling seems to have evaporated. No less a personage than the Earl of Cardigan was put on trial in 1841 before the House of Lords, even though no death had occurred, on charges of attempted murder (along with lesser offenses) resulting from a duel (like Eliot, he was indicted under the 1837 Act). Not surprisingly his fellow peers acquitted the Earl of all charges, but the impression on the public made by the avidly followed trial was great.[14] Regardless of the status of the participants, in an age of popular unrest duels had become widely regarded among the middle and upper classes as an intolerable threat to public order. After Lord Cardigan's celebrated acquittal the *Times,* warning of "the aptness of the lower orders to learn evil from their betters," declared that "we are firmly convinced that no more pernicious or anarchical principle than that of the defenders of dueling was ever broached by Chartism, or even Socialism itself."[15]

By this point, though some public tolerance persisted, judicial language had become clear and direct. After a duel between a Lieutenant and a Lieutenant-Colonel at Camden Town in 1843 resulted in the latter's death, four men, all officers, were charged with murder at the Old Bailey. Justice

---

[11] See Antony E. Simpson, "Dandelions on the Field of Honor: Dueling, the Middle Classes, and the Law in Nineteenth-Century England," *Criminal Justice History* 9 (1988), 99–155.

[12] Jeremy Horder, "The Duel and the English Law of Homicide," *Oxford Journal of Legal Studies* 12 (1992): judicial attitudes only became "unyieldingly hostile" in "the nineteenth century." See also Robert Baldick, *The Duel* (London and New York, 1965).

[13] *Annual Register for 1826,* Appendix, pp. 40–43.

[14] The Lords seized upon a tenuous technicality of a possible flaw in the indictment. *Times,* 17 February 1841, pp. 5–6; *Annual Register for 1841,* Appendix, pp. 242–278; G.T. Crook, *The Complete Newgate Calendar* (London, 1926), vol. 5, pp. 313–318.

[15] Quoted in Baldick, op. cit., p. 113.

Williams declared it the unanimous view of the judiciary that "when two persons go out to fight a deliberate duel and death ensues, all persons who are present, encouraging and promoting that duel, will be guilty of murder." He seems to have pushed the jury too hard by not allowing the jurymen to find manslaughter. Not surprisingly balking at finding murder, they acquitted all four.[16] Yet there was to be no turning back: the Whig as well as Radical press denounced the acquittal, and an Anti-Dueling Association with broad political support was now in existence to press for its suppression. The *Spectator* used the verdict to attack the entire practice, putting it on a par with "vulgar" killing. "The only argument," the politically moderate paper observed, "ever urged by the duelist to gloss his crime is based on the assertion that there is a sort of nobleness in periling his own life equally with that of his opponent." But it noted that this same self-recklessness was found just as much among lower-class "vulgar shedders of blood" as among gentlemen: "Recklessness of self-destruction is usually found to prevail in a similar ratio with recklessness for the destruction of others: and accordingly the high civilisation which begets a prevailing idea of the sacredness of life, manifests itself in lessening these twin evils arising from the activity of one morbid impulse."[17]

In the spring of 1844, after discussing the matter with a sympathetic Queen, Prime Minister Peel had the War Office issue a revised code for officers making clearly punishable, if necessary by a general court-martial, any encouragement of or participation in a duel. The following year, a fatal duel saw the survivor flee to France, and reports of duels thereafter virtually ceased.[18] The last fatal duel known of in England took place in 1852 and was fought, appropriately enough, between two Frenchmen.[19] As the practice continued

[16] *R.v. Cuddy:* Carrington & Kirwaun, *Reports of cases argued and ruled at nisi prius in the courts of Queen's bench, common pleas and exchequer ... (& crown cases ...) 1853–53* (London, 1845–55), 1: 210. The duel took place on 1 July 1843.

[17] *Spectator,* quoted in the *Morning Post,* 10 July 1843, p. 4. The Tory *Morning Post* criticized what it called the "excessive condemnation" of dueling by Radicals who ignored greater evils like child labor in factories, but even it was now careful to acknowledge that the practice was a crime. The Middlesex Coroner, the popular Radical Thomas Wakley, made his view clear by ordering one of the seconds held in custody, even after he had been granted bail, forcing his supporters to obtain a habeas corpus writ to free him [*Morning Post,* 8 July 1843, p. 6].

[18] Robert Baldick, *The Duel* (London and New York, 1965), pp. 108–114.

[19] With French seconds as well [*Annual Register for 1852,* Chronicle pp. 169–171]. The survivor of this duel was convicted of manslaughter and apparently received only a brief period of imprisonment. An indication of the changing climate of opinion was the outrage expressed by the *Annual Register* that he had not been found guilty of murder. As it turned out, within two years he went to the scaffold for shooting a man to death in a quarrel. [*R.v. Barthelmy: Times,* 11 December 1854, p. 9 & 22 December 1854, p. 9.]

THE "SATISFACTION" OF A "GENTLEMAN."

FIGURE 2. "The 'Satisfaction' of a 'Gentleman.'" *Punch*'s scornful view of the duel [vol. 4 (1843), p. 58].

into the twentieth century on the Continent, this contrast was to become for Englishmen a marker of the nation's exceptional respect for law.[20]

While duels came to an end, plebeian set fights continued through the century. They were of two kinds, one usually for money stakes and flourishing as an organized source of popular entertainment, the other to settle private quarrels, often echoing duels in involving the protection of impugned honor,

[20] Fearing the return, among sailors and such men, of the return of the duel in a new guise, Justice Willes declared in *R.v. Morelli* 1868 that "the mere existence of a belief in a man's mind that his own life was in danger would not justify him in killing an assailant. If it were otherwise, the result might be to encourage among a class of men for whom he had great respect – sailors, who, of whatever country, had very little control over their own passions when drunk – a practice which, happily, in this country had been exterminated among the higher classes – viz., the practice of dueling, and they would have men resorting to knives on a mere tiff of passion." [*Times*, 31 January 1868, p. 9]. The *Times* produced many denunciatory leaders after the occurrence of (mostly foreign) duels: see for example 2 March 1842, p. 5; 23 September 1842, p. 4; 20 July 1843, p. 4; 15 March 1844, p. 2; 2 June 1845, p. 7; 24 June 1845, p. 7; 20 July 1846, p. 4; 19–21 August 1847, p. 4; 24 May 1852, p. 5; 15 March 1856, p. 9; 20 May 1858, p. 8; 1 October 1861, p. 9; 9 October 1861, p. 7; 21 November 1862, p. 12; 7 September 1868, pp. 8–9; 22 November 1878, p. 3; 2 March 1895, p. 7; 8 June 1901, p. 11.

reputation or status. Prizefights shared with duels the criminal element of some prior deliberation but, on the other hand, a history of social acceptance and, even more, entertainment. Indeed, for many eighteenth-century writers and commentators, they were a fundamental part of English national character.[21] Even more than duels, however, they were difficult to reconcile with new Victorian sensitivities. As their most recent historian has observed, while a prizefight had rules ("one couldn't hit his opponent while he was down, and strikes below the belt were considered 'foul' "), by later standards "it was a brutal affair. Fights could last an hour or two, with as many as thirty or forty rounds or even more. Injuries were often severe and fatalities not entirely unusual. Fighters were cheered on by spectators of all classes, and the working classes adopted the ritual of the prizefight when they 'stepped outside' to settle a dispute or to decide who would buy the next round of beer."[22] Eighteenth-century arguments over prizefight rules had rarely concerned its brutality. "The need to avoid pain," one historian has noted, "did not have a high priority among [the sport's] promoters and followers."[23]

By the nineteenth century, if a prizefight protagonist died the survivors were likely to be to prosecuted for manslaughter. Sometimes the judicial censure could be quite direct; in 1803, the year of his Act against crimes of violence, Lord Ellenborough tried several prizefighters for fighting a duel and for riotous assembly, and in summing up denounced prizefighting as "infinitely mischievous in its immediate effect to the limbs and lives of the combatants themselves" as well as in its drawing of "industrious people away from the subject of their industry" and its promoting brawls among spectators.[24] Perhaps most notable was the pride of place he gave to the harm inflicted on the participants, something rarely before complained much of.

Yet as with duels, denunciations by influential persons had for years little lasting effect on the workings of the apparatus of law. Prizefights continued after Ellenborough, even growing in numbers and size of audiences. More often than not, they were passed over by the legal authorities or only half-heartedly prosecuted. Police and jurymen, and also many magistrates, continued to feel much sympathy with both the "sporting" aspect of prizefighting, and with "manly English [fist-]fighting" in general, as long as it

---

[21]Their most recent historian has cited the editor of the *Connoisseur* as early as 1754 arguing that "the sturdy English have been as much renowned for their boxing as for their beef; both of which are by no means suited to the watery stomachs and weak sinews of their enemies the French." See John C. Wood, " 'The Shadow of Our Refinement': Violence, Custom and the Civilizing Process in Nineteenth-Century England" (Ph.D. dissertation, University of Maryland, 2001).
[22]Ibid.
[23]Dennis Brailsford, *Bareknuckles: A Social History of Prizefighting* (Cambridge, 1988), p. 20.
[24]Ibid., p. 45, taking the quotation from an 1811 history.

stayed within certain bounds.[25] However, as audiences grew in the 1820s, denunciations not only from newspapers but from judges and magistrates also grew in number and vigor. As the reign of George IV, the last monarch to publicly enjoy prizefighting, was drawing to a close, courts, partly perhaps out of fear of things getting out of hand, were becoming emboldened to action: even a fists-only prizefight that remained within rules could result in prosecution, conviction, and imprisonment. In 1829, many people were shocked at the outcome of an Old Bailey trial of a fighter and both seconds of the deceased in a contest for both honor and money that ended in one fighter's death. All three were convicted; more shocking than that were the sentences: Justice Gaselee accepted that the fighter may have had some excuse, "as it might be supposed that he had received insult," and gave him twelve months in the House of Correction, but he declared that the seconds, who had kept the deceased fighting after he was gravely injured, "had no excuse whatever," and sentenced them to transportation for life.[26] A drastically severe judgment, too much so to be much followed thereafter, it nonetheless sent a message (as no doubt intended) to the metropolitan public that arranged public fights were henceforth to exist under a sharp legal sword. Indeed, as the result of another case, the next edition of Burn's *Justice of the Peace* added even "countenancing a prize-fight" to its list of activities liable to criminal prosecution![27]

Two similar cases in the fall of 1833 and spring of 1834, heard in London and at York, found both seconds and surviving fighters tried for fighters' deaths. The first fight had degenerated after several rounds into a brawl, and the brother of the "winning" fighter (who escaped) was convicted of manslaughter. In the second, it was felt that the fight should have been halted by the defendants well before its fatal end, and two of them were convicted. In these cases, however, the sentences were more typical (if nonetheless stiffer than in the previous century) – respectively two months and four months at

---

[25] For example, John Morris and three other men were acquitted at Exeter in 1825 after a doctor refused to state with confidence that a fighter's death soon after was the direct result of the prize fight in which he had been knocked out [*Times*, 1 August 1825, p. 3; *Star*, 2 August 1825]. Three years later at the Old Bailey James Morgan and three others were acquitted after evidence from witnesses that the deceased had sworn he would fight till he died [*Times*, 13 September 1828, p. 3].

[26] *R.v. Davis et. al.* (1829): *Times*, 11 September 1829, p. 3; *Morning Chronicle* 12 September 1829. It is not clear whether these sentences were reduced by the Home Office. Although they had been formally liable to prosecution along with principals since a leading case in 1789, criminal prosecution of seconds had been rare before being mentioned in the 1820 edition of Burn's *Justice*. Two years after that an assize judge warned that not only were seconds liable, but even an attendee could be charged with aiding and abetting manslaughter. [Brailsford, op. cit., p. 73].

[27] Burn, *Justice of the Peace* 25th ed. (1830), 1:220.

hard labor.[28] The rule was established throughout the country that, as it came to be stated in Burn by 1845, "all persons present, assisting by their presence, at a prizefight, are guilty of manslaughter, if one of the combatants be killed."[29] In 1838, the death of a leading prizefighter, "Brighton Bill," produced manslaughter convictions for four men, a formal complaint by the jury that local magistrates in Hertfordshire had done nothing to prevent the match although it had been widely publicized, and subsequently a circular from the Home Office urging local authorities to put down the practice.[30] From then on, one of the tasks of the new police forces became preventing prizefights, and manslaughter charges when a fight nonetheless took place and a fighter died became routine.[31]

The legal system, however, never spoke with a single voice on prizefights. In cases of deaths from prize or set fights Victorian judges usually pressed juries for a conviction but then awarded or recommended modest sentences of a few months or less; they were not interested in punishing offenders heavily but in establishing the principle that such killings would be branded as criminal, and treated as such.[32] Yet even in this they did not always get their way. Coroner's juries not infrequently returned verdicts of accidental death.[33] Magistrates sometimes let the surviving parties off with scoldings and warnings. When such cases did reach trial, juries (drawn from a somewhat higher class than coroner's juries, but not so high as to usually include professional or other gentlemen) tended to be more ambivalent about such cases than were judges, and could be effectively appealed to by defense counsel, now

[28]*R.v. Murphy: Times,* 30 November 1833, p. 3; *R.v. Wilkinson et. al: Times,* 3 April 1834, p. 3.

[29]Burn, *Justice of the Peace,* 29th ed. (1845), 3:806.

[30]*Annual Register for 1838,* Chronicle, pp. 40–41. The following year's act encouraging counties to establish police forces made it possible for the first time to routinely expect such prevention.

[31]See for example David Philips, *Crime and Authority in Victorian England: the Black Country 1835–1860* (London, 1977), p. 255. The year of the death of "Brighton Bill" also saw the promulgation of a set of new rules for prizefighting, to bring a greater order and acceptability to the sport by diminishing unpalatable violence and reducing the chances of death or crippling [Brailsford, op. cit., p. 97].

[32]See for example *R.v. Beddesford* 1842, *R.v. Partridge* 1849, *R.v. Smith and Yales* 1851, *R.v. Gregory* 1851.

[33]Many homicides of all kinds seem to have been "missed" by coroner's inquests; see John Archer, " 'The Violence We Have Lost'? Body Counts, Historians and Interpersonal Violence in England," *Memoria y Civilizacion* 2 (1999), 171–190; Mary Beth Emmerichs, "Getting Away With Murder? Homicides and the Coroners in Nineteenth-Century London," *Social Science History* 25 (2001), 93–100; Howard Taylor, " 'The unpleasant proceeding of taking the skull cap off in a private house': The investigative burden of potential murder cases in England and Wales from the mid-nineteenth century to the mid-twentieth century," (unpublished paper 2001).

ubiquitous. When William Gill was charged at Kingston assizes in 1851 with manslaughter in a prizefight, witnesses called by the prosecution were highly reluctant, refusing, among other things, to definitely identify the prisoner. Defense counsel Henry Hawkins (ironically, when later raised to the Bench to gain a reputation as " 'hanging Henry Hawkins") argued that "whatever might be the opinion in some quarters with regard to these exhibitions of prizefights, it should not be forgotten that at one period persons of the highest station had not scrupled to countenance them by their presence and support." The jury deadlocked; Baron Parke sent them back to deliberate for several more hours; but in the end they acquitted Gill.[34] Even later, acquittals in prizefight deaths appear to have been more likely than in manslaughter charges taken as a whole. For instance, thirteen of the thirty men charged at the Old Bailey for this in the twenty years 1856–75 were acquitted, and sentences for the convicted seventeen never exceeded six months.[35]

Rooted as they were in popular culture, prizefights held on for many years against the weight of official denunciation. Yet the combination of police interference and judicial action gradually took their toll and by the end of the mid-Victorian years prizefights in the old unregulated form were disappearing. Their most recent historian has noted that most leading prizefighters left for more hospitable America in the 1850s and '60s, and between 1868 and 1870, "the prize-ring gradually faded from the columns" of the leading sporting newspaper, *Bell's Life*. By 1870 prizefights had thoroughly lost the kind of social approval, or at the least tolerance, they had enjoyed earlier in the century. They continued, but now their practitioners by their actions automatically classified themselves as "brutish" men of the lower classes.[36] Even a judge being lenient on a manslaughter case resulting from a set fight that started as a quarrel made a point of condemning matches "got up for money" as "brutal and disgraceful."[37] A "civilized" form, with rules drawn up by the eighth Marquess of Queensberry to limit damage, was first set out in 1867 and a later 1877 version became the basis of the modern rules of professional boxing.[38]

While prizefighting came to be in part criminalized and in part tamed into a regulated and much less bloody sport, fist-fighting (not for money) between not grossly ill-matched protagonists was tolerated longer. Particularly among the working classes, ritualized fist-fighting had long been a part of everyday life, one not to be easily rooted out. Nor was there always the desire to root it

[34] *R.v. Gill: Times*, 28 March 1851, p. 7.
[35] R. Anderson, "Criminal Violence in London, 1856–1875" (Ph.D. thesis, University of Toronto, 1991) p. 466. A complete study of prizefighting prosecutions has yet to be done.
[36] Brailsford, op cit., pp. 139, 156.
[37] *R.v. Tubbs: Times*, 10 April 1875, p. 9 [Justice Brett].
[38] Brailsford, op. cit., p. 161.

out: among their "betters" such fighting (when it did not involve betting and money prizes) was often praised as both a national and a manly tradition. As Thomas Hughes declared in his best-selling 1857 novel *Tom Brown's School Days*, "Fighting with fists is the natural and English way for English boys to settle their quarrels," and urged middle-class youth to learn to box.[39] Though Hughes expected boys to grow out of settling quarrels with their fists when they became men, continuing appreciation of fist-fighting by men of all classes (however much the "respectable" themselves refrained from participating in such behavior) modified and limited the drive to "civilize" the lower classes. Instead of warring on all fighting, the drive was largely diverted into "civilizing" fighting by sharply distinguishing "good old English stand-up fist-fighting" from the use of underhanded methods like kicking a downed man, or, worst of all, using a weapon, usually a knife. Nonetheless, in the second half of the century ritualized fist-fights declined as an accepted public activity. This decline was encouraged by the institutions of the law, as police increasingly took a hand in preventing or breaking them up, and judges were increasingly likely to condemn such behavior. If they declined in social or legal acceptability, they certainly never vanished like duels. Much more than dueling, pub and street fighting were deeply-rooted in working-class culture, and even the use of knives may have been reduced but by no means done away with.[40] Yet such fights, certainly when they resulted in a death, now came to produce outrage and serious prosecution.

In fist-fights where a death ensued, homicide charges only gradually came to be brought.[41] Whereas in the eighteenth and early nineteenth centuries such deaths appear to have often been ruled accidental by inquest juries, in the course of the 1830s, as all deaths began to be treated more seriously and the work of coroners was expanding and better supported, deaths from "fair" fights became for the first time more likely to be sent on to the criminal courts.[42] Some judges were eager to establish the principle that causing death

[39] Thomas Hughes, *Tom Brown's School Days* [1857] (New York, 1986), p. 246.
[40] For the persistence of such fighting through the century, see Andrew Davies, "Youth Gangs, Masculinity and Violence in Late Victorian Manchester and Salford," *Journal of Social History* 32 (1998), 349–369.
[41] For a discussion of legal leniency towards "fair fights," see Carolyn Conley, "Violence: Fair Fights and Brutal Cowardice," *The Unwritten Law*, op. cit., ch. 2. Also see John Archer, "'Men Behaving Badly?' Masculinity and the Uses of Violence, 1850–1900," in *Everyday Violence in Britain, 1850–1960*, ed. Shani D'Cruze (London, 2000), pp. 41–54. The Middlesex Criminal Registers and Sessions Court Books for the 1830s and 1840s show that a large proportion of the assaults that were prosecuted took place in groups, thus violating the accepted understandings of a "fair fight." By the late years of the century, at least in Middlesex, group attacks made up a much smaller proportion of prosecuted assaults.
[42] See Gary and Maria Greenwald, "Medico-legal Progress in Inquests of Felonious Deaths: Westminster, 1761–1866," *Journal of Legal Medicine* 2 (1981), 193–264. There

even in consensual fights carried out according to agreed rules was felonious. In an 1830 Lancaster case in which the deceased had challenged the prisoner to fight, "the jury were consulting together when his Lordship [Justice Park] interrupted them, by saying there could be no question as to his guilt." He then began, without waiting for them, to sentence the prisoner, but himself was interrupted by the clerk, who pointed out the jury had not spoken. "Gentlemen," Park then said, "I am bound to tell you, unless you find him guilty you will violate your oaths." They then did as they were told, and Park sentenced the man to pay a fine of one shilling.[43] Clearly Park was interested in a conviction, not in punishment. Such judicial high-handedness rarely appeared thereafter, but the same judicial approach was frequently repeated. In one manslaughter case at York in 1841, Baron Rolfe declared the fight "a fair one," but still summed up for conviction: he took some pains to overrule the defense objection that death arising from a consensual fight, an "amicable contest," could not be manslaughter. After the guilty verdict, however, "in consideration solely of the long period of imprisonment they had already undergone," he, like Park a decade earlier, fined the defendant one shilling.[44] Again, it was the conviction and not punishment that was important to the judge. Often defendants would already have spent months in jail awaiting trial, so the prosecution itself could be said to involve substantial punishment. Moreover, it was becoming more usual to sentence participants or abettors of "fair fights" to some jail time, if rarely exceeding a few months. Still, this was enough to mark them and the practice as highly disreputable. Judges were more concerned to establish the principle that causing deaths in such a way was felonious than to try to award heavy punishments that would have outraged many people.

As long as deaths even in fair fights were officially recognized as manslaughters, some judges then might express sympathy with defendants. Typical in this was Justice Erle, who, a colleague later recalled, "detested the Prize Ring," and was "sure to get a conviction" for manslaughter from a prizefight.[45] Yet for an 1864 death in a fair stand-up fight between two youths, his sentence was a mere one day.[46] Even where strong cases of self-defense or of accident were made out, a judge might nonetheless push for a manslaughter verdict, only to award a token fine.[47] As Baron Bramwell observed in an 1862

were no manslaughter indictments at the Old Bailey for deaths resulting from set fights in any decadal year beginning with 1760 until 1830, nor for deaths resulting from spontaneous fights until 1840 [John Betts, CCCSP 1839–40, #392].

[43] *R.v. Case* (1830): *Times*, 15 March 1830, p. 6.
[44] *R.v. Dawson et. al.* (1841): *Times*, 17 March 1841, p. 6.
[45] *Reminiscences of Sir Henry Hawkins* (London, 1904), p. 136.
[46] *R.v. Andrews et. al.*, *Lloyds' Weekly*, 27 March 1864.
[47] *R.v. Bethell*, *Times*, 22 August 1850, p. 7. This case had both defenses. A pub quarrel had led to "settling the matter" outside, but credible evidence established that the prisoner had unsuccessfully tried to avoid fighting; moreover, the deceased in falling

trial of three men, "legally the prisoners were all guilty, and all who took part in the fight were guilty in the eyes of the law." However, here "death had been an accidental result not at all intended." The fight was a fair one, and he "rejoiced" to find that out of nearly ninety prisoners [at the assize session] "not one of them was charged with the atrocious practice of stabbing." He thus gave the men merely four days' imprisonment.[48]

Even a group brawl, less acceptable than a one-on-one fight, would some-times be treated indulgently if fairness had prevailed. In an 1873 Kent case, four soldiers stood in the dock after one of their opponents died; as usual, they were found guilty of manslaughter, but each was sentenced to only four days in jail. As Justice Brett noted, "although they had been guilty of an offence against the laws, they would return to their regiments without a stigma on their characters, as it had been a fair stand-up fight and the knife had not been used."[49]

Two years later, after a man died in a fair and formalized stand-up fist-fight, Justice Brett similarly awarded just one week's imprisonment, again underlining the distinction: "we who are sitting here to administer the law are [not] bound to note that when men quarrel it is any great sin if they would only fight fairly with their natural weapons – their hands." If this fight had been prolonged too far, that was "practically the fault of the deceased" who had displayed "a courage which he liked to see in an Englishman."[50] However Brett was aware that his view had become less acceptable, for he described his decision and opinion as "bold." Sure enough, his stance was immediately attacked by the *Times*. The paper agreed with him on the heinousness and alien character of knives: "it has been generally regarded with justice as a redeeming point in even the violence of Englishmen that they have maintained the spirit of fair play and have refrained from gratify-ing their revenge, as in some other countries, by the safe and therefore cow-ardly use of the knife or dagger." But the paper complained that the rules which restrained men to the use of so-called "natural weapons" still allowed violent death to be inflicted, and in public. Middle- and upper-class men had long since given up such behavior; it was time for men of the working classes to follow. The paper called Brett's sentence merely "nominal," one that would encourage the working classes to bypass the law. "It is one of the first conditions of civilised society, not to mention Christianity or morality," it insisted, "that men should abstain from fighting out their quarrels, and

had struck his head on a curbstone. After getting a manslaughter verdict, Baron Platt awarded a one-shilling fine.

[48] *R.v. Roots et. al.: Times*, 29 July 1862, p. 10.

[49] Cited by Conley, op. cit., p. 50. She noted that "in the 63 cases [heard in Kent from 1859 through 1880] in which persons died as a result of brawls, 86% of those convicted were sentenced to less than eighteen months." But "exception might be taken when weapons were used."

[50] *R.v. Tubbs: Times*, 10 April 1875, p. 9.

that they should be content to seek from the law the redress of any real injury they may suffer. The mass of people are not of so mild a temper that a laxer doctrine can be safely encouraged among them."[51]

Already in 1858, this point had been emphasized by Justice Byles. Trying a death resulting from a set fight conducted fairly, he took immediate issue with defense counsel and declared that "there could be no doubt but that *all fights* were unlawful, *and all persons present,* if death ensued, were guilty of manslaughter." This left little for the jury to decide, and it duly convicted. Byles then gave the surviving fighter a comparatively stiff sentence of six months imprisonment at hard labor.[52] Six years later, trying two men after a fight resulted in a death, Baron Channell stressed that although in a murder trial, defendants not actually having struck the fatal blow could not, unless party to a common design to kill, be found guilty, "it was otherwise in this respect as to manslaughter." Here a wider net could and should be cast: "if several were parties to an unlawful act of violence, as a beating, and death, though not intended, resulted from that unlawful act, they were all guilty." "This," he went on, "was constantly exemplified in cases of fighting. However fair the fight might be, and although only one person struck the fatal blow, yet *all* engaged were guilty of manslaughter." Channell acknowledged the prisoners' previous good character, but still (for a group fight could never be as "fair" as a one-on-one fight) dealt out to each a very severe sentence of five years' penal servitude.[53]

Yet wherever leader-writers and judges might lead, juries (especially attached to the notion of "fairness" in fighting) did not always follow. When a Stockton butcher was charged in 1876 with manslaughter for killing a man in a fight, even though the prisoner's own counsel "said he could not resist the charge" and Justice Mellor consequently directed the jury to find him guilty, they acquitted him. Apparently, the fact that the man killed had been the aggressor weighed heavily enough with the jury for them to acquit, on the grounds of provocation. The judge was "astonished" and observed that the verdict "was theirs, not his. They were masters of the situation, and had taken the law into their own hands after his counsel had very properly admitted he was guilty and his Lordship himself had told them he was so in point of law." However, he added, "the justice of the case was not materially affected, because the sentence he should have passed upon him would have been of the smallest description."[54] On the issue of deaths resulting from fair fights, the contest between judges and juries, even if some "respectable"

[51] Ibid.

[52] *R.v. Lidstone* (1858): *Times,* 11 December 1858, p. 9. Italics original.

[53] *R.v. Staples and Turner* (1864): *Times,* 17 December 1864, p. 11. In *R.v. Knock* (1877), another old defense was excluded by the ruling that fighting on a challenge could not be considered fighting in self-defense [14 Cox C.C. 1].

[54] *R.v. Walker: Times,* 7 March 1876, p. 11.

editorial-writers chafed, was more on the principle of criminality than on the degree of punishment. While at no time in the Victorian period were even all "respectable" Englishmen of one mind about what constituted criminal violence, they were not in practice all that far apart. "Fair fights" were natural, manly and English, but for all that too liable to get out of control; they needed to be firmly discouraged, and when someone died in one, it needed to be publicly marked as a felonious act.

While all fights were declared unlawful, some, it was generally agreed, were much worse than others. "Unfair" fights – as common, it would seem, as "fair" ones – were a different story.[55] If fights conducted according to well-understood rules and with no weapons but fists were more often than not viewed comparatively generously, at least in many courts, it was clear that any fight breaking these bounds would be increasingly proscribed. Even without the use of lethal weapons, harsh sentences could still follow. In 1830 John Booth and another man agreed to settle their pub quarrel outside; his opponent died, but not before he told the surgeon attending him that he bore no ill will towards the prisoner, for he was as much at fault; nonetheless, Booth received three months' hard labor. The sentence, Justice Jervis told the court, "would have been more lenient had not the prisoner brutally kicked the deceased when on the ground."[56] This attitude continued to shape outcomes in such cases. As the jurist Edward Cox was to observe, "a blow with the fist is often to be excused . . . [but] in no case is kicking to be forgiven."[57]

By 1831 the principle had been firmly established that it was not necessary to use a weapon of any sort to be liable to be convicted of manslaughter. In *R.v. Briggs* that year the Twelve Judges unanimously upheld such a conviction for a kicking death. "Whether," they pronounced, "the wound was from a blow with a stick or a kick from a shoe, the indictment was equally supported, and the conviction was therefore right." This decision was thereafter cited in similar cases, whether the wounding was fatal or not.[58] John William Greaves discovered this, when he killed a man who had "much aggravated" him in a weaponless but no-holds-barred "up and down" fight which included kicking

---

[55] As the prosecuting counsel in *Briggs* (1831) observed, deaths by kicking were "common." In the 1834 prizefight case of *Wilkinson et al.*, noted above, Baron Alderson observed that "though fighting with fists was unlawful, and when death was the consequence it was felony, he should make a marked distinction between this case and those which had come before him when dangerous weapons were used, and kicks as well as blows resorted to" [*Times*, 3 April 1834, p. 3].

[56] *Times*, 17 April 1830, p. 3.

[57] Edward W. Cox, *The Principles of Punishment* (London, 1877), pp. 87–88.

[58] 1 Moody CC 318 [*Crown Cases Reserved for Consideration and Decided by the Judges of England, From the Year 1824 to the Year 1837*, London, 1844]. Such a citation was made in *R.v. Duffill* 1843 [1 Cox C.C. 41]. [In 1837 the Offenses Against the Person Act similarly made kicking sufficient for conviction for attempted murder.]

and biting, in Lancashire in 1840. Greaves was convicted of manslaughter and, after Justice Coleridge denounced "the brutal and disgraceful mode of fighting adopted in this county," sentenced to eighteen months at hard labor.[59]

In addressing a Liverpool grand jury in 1845, Baron Rolfe condemned the "sort of brutal violence which is found rarely except in this district and other parts of this county" and observed that deaths in these fights might even reach the level of murder:

> Parties may act with brutal violence towards one another upon little provocation. They may quarrel, go out and fight, and the result may be death. Is that manslaughter or murder? It is a question often very difficult of solution. The only way to decide it is this, to say that in those cases where the violence has been of a character that to any man, rationally reasoning, it must be evident the result would be death, undoubtedly that is murder. It is commonly said the distinction is where a deadly weapon has been used. That is perhaps an illustration of the rule instead of the rule itself, for there may be brutal violence used without any deadly weapon, and in my opinion, that is as much murder, as if a dagger or pistol had been used.[60]

Of course, when a deadly weapon was employed harsher punishment often awaited, as the very use of such weapons, even if no fatality ensued, was not to be tolerated. In 1832 Daniel Lynch, who had responded to a fist in his face by pulling out a common bread and cheese knife he was in the habit of carrying about and stabbing his attacker to death, was found guilty at the Old Bailey only of manslaughter, but given two years' imprisonment (rather severe given the physical attack upon him, and the unthinking immediacy of his response). This ordinary case became a leading one, for in it Chief Justice Tenterden made a point of laying down the dictum that "it is not every slight provocation, even by a blow, which will, when the party receiving it strikes with a deadly weapon and death ensues, reduce the crime from murder to manslaughter."[61] The next year on the Oxford Circuit George Hayward was less fortunate. After being kicked out of a house, he ran home, got a kitchen knife and returned to fatally stab his kicker. After Justice Tindall reminded the jury that "the exercise of contrivance and design denoted rather the presence of judgment and reason, than of violent and ungovernable passion," he was found guilty of murder.[62] The year after this Joseph Heeley

---

[59] *Times* April 4, 1840, p. 6; *Liverpool Mercury*, 10 April 1840, p. 124.

[60] *Liverpool Mercury*, 15 August 1845, p. 10.

[61] *R.v. Lynch* (1832): 172 *ER* 995; see also *OBSP* 1831–32, #855, and *Times* 6 April 1832, p. 6. This ruling became well known among legal officials after being cited at length in Burn, *Justice*, 28th ed. (1837), 1: 322.

[62] Tried 2 August 1834: 172 ER 1188. This ruling also was cited in Burn from 1837 on [1: 323].

was hanged at York for another fatal stabbing; in this case the defendant was shown to have started the fight, which the deceased had tried to avoid. Heeley's judge decided (without any specific evidence) that he had intended all along to use his knife, so told the jury, and got the murder verdict.[63]

Even when no death ensued, the use of a knife brought out Justice Coleridge's most severe inclinations. In the 1839 Liverpool assize session at which he tried Greaves for an unfair but weaponless killing, Coleridge tried also seven stabbing cases, and "expressed himself in the strongest terms against that practice, which, he said, was more prevalent in this part of the country than in any other." He went on to announce that all the Judges were determined to put down such "a brutal and outrageous" mode of proceeding in quarrels; and that whenever a clear case was made out before him, he "invariably sentenced the prisoner to transportation for life."[64]

1839 was a busy year for prosecution of fighting deaths. That year, despite the facts of the defendant's being only fifteen and the deceased's being an older, larger and stronger man, Justice Williams declared in the murder trial of George Coker that he "could not sufficiently deprecate the un-English and unmanly practice of resorting to the use of a knife in sudden quarrel, and it was with deep regret he found that the offence of stabbing was on the increase in this country. It became the bounden duty, therefore, both of judges and magistrates to check so disgraceful a practice as far as the law could do so." When the jury, as in most such cases, convicted only of manslaughter, the judge imposed the maximum sentence of transportation for life. As a reporter noted, "the prisoner dropped senseless in the dock, on hearing the sentence."[65] Particularly from this time on, the use of knives was frequently to be described as not only unfair, but un-English (despite the ubiquity of knives, and the commonness of knife assaults in the past, and even the present). For example, in *R.v. Pumford*, a wounding case a few years later, the judge noted "the un-English practice of using the knife in cases of quarrels, as required to be put down by the strong arm of the law."[66]

Also in 1839, two Lancashire workman had gotten into a Saturday night pub fight that continued out in the street. It ended when one pulled a knife and stabbed his opponent, from which wound the man died. On trial for murder, the stabber's counsel argued that his client had been completely

---

[63] *R.v. Heeley: Times*, 6 April 1835, p. 4.

[64] *Liverpool Mercury*, April 10, 1840.

[65] *R.v. Coker* (1839): *Times*, 16 August 1839, p. 7.

[66] [1851] Cited in David Philips, *Crime and Authority in Victorian England: The Black Country 1835–1860* (London, 1977), p. 264.] However, Greg T. Smith has observed from his study of criminal records "how commonly men went about armed in the late eighteenth and early nineteenth centuries." ["The State and the Culture of Violence in London, 1760–1840," (Ph.D. Thesis, University of Toronto, 1999), p. 245.] And Philips has pointed out that whatever judges may have thought, Victorian workingmen carried knives for cutting tobacco, cheese or bread, whittling sticks, and other tasks, which were easily turned into weapons.

intoxicated and hadn't known what he was doing, and that, moreover, the earlier insults by the deceased provided sufficient provocation to reduce the crime to at the most manslaughter. The jury did find manslaughter but went on, quite unusually, to declare that manslaughter to be "aggravated," just short of murder, and the judge, Baron Parke, approvingly responded with the maximum sentence of transportation for life. In doing so, he explained that "so often had he to lament the careless manner in which human life was sacrificed in this county, that he had resolved in all such instances to pass a severe sentence with the hope of deterring others." This verdict and sentence, like Coleridge's, was also received with some surprise.[67] In 1841, after a similar killing, James Oldbrook was tried for murder before Baron Parke, and the defense counsel, relieved when the judge ruled that the particular offense did not reach murder (perhaps because Oldbrook had only used a clasp knife, commonly possessed), accepted a manslaughter verdict and expressed his hope that "this would be a lesson to the people not to accustom themselves to carry such deadly weapons about them, alien as they were from English feelings. . . ."[68]

The notion that using knives in fights was (or certainly ought to be) alien to Englishmen suffused attitudes to lower-class foreigners in England, notably the growing number of foreign sailors in English ports that accompanied the economic boom of the mid-Victorian decades. At Liverpool in 1853, Baron Alderson sentenced a Spanish seaman, Edmund Montero, to transportation for twenty years for fatally stabbing another sailor in a fight; "if he had not been a foreigner," Alderson told the court, "I should have transported him for life."[69] When another Spanish seaman, Bernardo Henriquez killed a fellow foreigner in Thameside London three years later, in a scuffle by stabbing him in the belly with "a very formidable knife," he was convicted of murder, but saved from the gallows by a mercy recommendation from the jury, "on account of his being a foreigner"; presumably he did not know any better.[70] The following year yet another Spanish sailor, Jose de Rosario, stabbed to death a Greek sailor. The victim, it was reported, had wanted to fight "in the English fashion" and Rosario had agreed, but then in the course of the fight pulled a knife. Charged with murder, but convicted only of manslaughter, he was given fifteen years' penal servitude – it was, after all,

[67] *Times*, 28 March 1839, p. 7. The following spring John Allen was convicted at Liverpool of wounding another man with intent to do grievous bodily harm and for this non-fatal attack was surprisingly transported for fifteen years. He had drunkenly started a quarrel with an inoffensive neighbor, stabbed him very seriously; and had had to be restrained from trying to stab him again. Lord Coleridge in announcing the sentence declared "the determination of the judges, if possible, to put [knife attacks] down." *Times*, 4 April 1840, p. 7 ; also see *Liverpool Mercury*, 10 April il 1840.
[68] *R.v. Oldbrook: Times*, 1 April 1841, p. 6.
[69] *Times*, 10 December 1853, p. 9; see also *Liverpool Mercury*, 9 December 1853, p. 3.
[70] *R.v. Henriquez* (1856): *Times*, 21 June 1856, p. 11.

again a quarrel between two foreigners.[71] Yet use of a less common weapon even by foreigners might eliminate this "alien allowance": when a Brazilian sailor killed a compatriot in a Liverpool pub fight in 1861 by pulling not the ubiquitous seamen's knife but a razor and with it cutting his opponent's throat, he was given penal servitude for life.[72]

On the whole, foreign killers (especially if their victims were also foreigners, or at least similarly lower-class Englishmen) tended not to be held, in view of their less civilized state, quite as responsible as Englishmen.[73] In 1868, the defense counsel for an Italian sailor, John Morelli, explicitly made the "foreigners don't know any better" argument. He warmly agreed that "the use of a knife was extremely reprehensible, but [he went on] it was to be borne in mind the prisoner was an Italian." Justice Willes "protested against the proposition that they were to make any distinction between men of different countries," and indeed complained of Italians carrying about knives, making "the streets of this metropolis . . . not so safe as they used to be," but after getting this off his chest he nonetheless sentenced Morelli, whose fight had been forced upon him, to only eighteen months' imprisonment.[74]

A more merciful stance towards the punishment of foreign sailors (at least when they only killed other foreigners), though perhaps surprising, made some sense from the official, if not the popular, point of view: the civilizing mission of the English criminal courts was aimed at Englishmen; foreign seamen, only temporarily in England, and effectively segregated in their close quarters by the docks, posed no significant threat to the continued moral progress of England. Americans, however, as "cousins," did not merit the same indulgence. John Moody, who fatally stabbed another American seaman while docked at Newcastle in 1859, was given the maximum sentence for manslaughter of penal servitude for life.[75]

By the 1860s, a number of developments had come together to further heighten the urgency of the criminal law's "civilizing" mission. The

---

[71] *R.v. Rosario: Central Criminal Court Sessions Papers* [hereafter CCCSP] no. 1058; *Times* 31 October 1857, p. 9.

[72] *R.v. Francisco: Liverpool Mercury*, 2 April 1861; *Times*, 4 April 1861, p. 11.

[73] Or perhaps lower-class foreigners' lives were not valued quite as highly as those of Englishmen.

[74] *R.v. Morelli: Times*, 31 January 1868, p. 9. Willes revealed a broader social fear in rejecting also another part of the defense, that Morelli had believed his life to be in jeopardy. "The mere existence," he declared, "of a belief in a man's mind that his own life was in danger would not justify him in killing an assailant. If it were otherwise, the result might be to encourage among a class of men for whom he had great respect – sailors, who, of whatever country, had very little control over their own passions when drunk – a practice which, happily, in this country had been exterminated among the higher classes – viz., the practice of dueling, and they would have men resorting to knives on a mere tiff of passion."

[75] *R.v. Moody* (1859): *Times*, 9 December 1859, p. 11.

population of poor Irishmen in England had rapidly grown in the aftermath of the Famine, the transportation of convicts overseas was ceasing, piling up convicted felons at home, and now working-men were advancing in political power, with large numbers in the towns gaining the franchise in 1867 and opening up the vista – or specter – of universal suffrage. Judges, as others, seemed in consequence newly determined to wipe out the remaining enclaves of "barbarism" in England before they infected increasingly popular public institutions. From the 1860s murder verdicts began to appear frequently in cases of knife slayings during impulsive fights, previously usually considered simple manslaughter, even if such convictions rarely led to the scaffold. Patrick Hirley in 1863, Henry Hughes in 1865, and George Nuttall in 1868, all were so convicted.[76] Such cases usually had some aggravating circumstance which judges were at pains to emphasize: for instance, Hughes' knife had no cutting edge but only a sharp point – it was useful only for stabbing, while Nuttall had many previous convictions.

However, when judges insisted that intent to kill could be inferred from such evidence as simply the use of a lethal weapon, they frequently found themselves in conflict with members of the public, and sometimes with juries. John Anderson, a Newcastle mason who in 1878 stabbed a man who struck him in anger for his refusing to shut a farm gate, was, after the man died from the wound, convicted of murder, even though the victim had struck first. Both judge and jury recommended mercy, which was granted (with the usual commutation of sentence to one of penal servitude for life).[77] Yet others, not only fellow working men but also gentry of the region, believed that Anderson's act did not constitute murder. Writing from the Carlton Club, a stronghold of Tory landed gentry, and citing the agreement of his friends, the Northumberland gentleman John Brewer called the offense a clear case of manslaughter: "Anderson had no intention of killing King prior to the physical assault made upon him."[78] Country gentlemen like Brewer once played a major role in criminal proceedings, and had exerted great influence over the operations of the royal mercy.[79] Yet by 1878 his opinion and those of his Carlton Club friends on this case made little impression on the Tory Home Secretary, Richard Cross. Without clearly making new law, in this area Victorian judges (with the approval of Home Secretaries)

---

[76] *R.v. Hirley: Return of Capital Convictions 1861–81*, Home Office; *R.v. Hughes* (1865): HO45/9363/34032; *R.v. Nuttall* (1868): HO144/13/34262.

[77] Typically, such prisoners were (with satisfactory behavior) released after twenty years.

[78] *R.v. Anderson:* HO144/31/78506; *Times*, 29 October 1878, p. 9.

[79] See Douglas Hay, "Property, Authority, and the Criminal Law," in *Albion's Fatal Tree: Crime and Society in Eighteenth-Century England*, ed. Douglas Hay et. al. (London, 1975), pp. 17–63.

were pushing the law's envelope by rendering premeditation unnecessary, in practice as well as principle, for a murder verdict.[80]

If a fatal stabbing in a fight appeared not entirely impulsive, the defendant might go all the way to the gallows. Edward Gough, one of fifteen men in County Durham to hang within the four years 1873–76, when the official war on "barbarism" crested, had gotten drunk, challenged an equally drunk man to fight, and as the man was pulling off his coat outside, preparing to fight, rushed at him and stabbed him in the groin, from which wound the man shortly died. The jury recommended to mercy because of the "great excitement" of the moment, and the Home Office received letters giving some exculpatory context, one from a clergyman explaining Gough's behavior as being provoked by "a long series of insults, threats and blows" previously. But Justice Honyman and the Home Office ignored both, and Gough hanged.[81]

Even when lethal weapons were not used, "unfair" fights were increasingly severely punished. Killing a man by kicking him while down, for instance, could now lead to the gallows. In particular, a moral panic over "kicking deaths" in areas of large Irish settlement and in mining areas flared up, reinforced by intensified anti-Irish prejudices. While many brawls continued to be thought of as fair fights, and remained usually lightly treated, "unfair" fights, even those without weapons, often involving groups of men and frequently carried out by such reputedly dangerous types as miners or Irish laborers, was felt to be a threat that was growing rather than diminishing.[82] When someone died in such an encounter, outraged juries, judges, and the Home Office now came down hard. Of four Irishmen in Durham who in 1872 dragged a man from his own door and kicked him to death before his wife's eyes, two were hanged, and two (an eighteen-year-old and a thoroughly drunk participant) were given life imprisonment – despite the absence of weapons and the likely lack of any intent to kill.[83] More than ethnic prejudice was at work here: even an Englishman who kicked to death an Irishman in an ethnically-motivated fight around the Durham pits in 1873 was found guilty of murder, if afterwards reprieved.[84] This kind of fights, as we have seen, had always been treated more seriously, but the difference (and the association with national identity) markedly increased in the second half

---

[80] The rule that intention could be imputed was not rejected until the Criminal Justice Act 1967 [A. Kiralfy, ed., *The Burden of Proof* (Abingdon, 1987)].

[81] *R.v. Gough* (1873): 15 December 1873, p. 10; HO45/9354/29470.

[82] In 1845 a death in a brawl between two groups of Irishmen led to an Old Bailey sentence of seven years' transportation, while the other four manslaughter sentences that year in that court were all under three months. *R.v. Carroll:* CCCSP 1844–45, #1742.

[83] *R.v. Slane et. al.* 1872: HO144/5/18516.

[84] *Times*, 16 July 1873, p. 12.

of the nineteenth century. Fights that ended in a death continued to take place, and if conducted "fairly" continued to receive lenient treatment, but not as lenient as in the past, and if "unfair" such fights were now liable to sharp judicial denunciation and serious criminal sanctions. The law was now more deeply involved than ever before with the conflicts among poor men, as well as among their betters – more protective of the weak, more punitive towards the violent, and more regulative in general of working-class practices that fell short of "respectability."

Beyond fights, the sanctions of the law were expanding to proscribe men's harm-doing in a wider range of situations than hitherto. In the first half of the century there were many more manslaughter indictments for recklessness on the roads or at work when it cost the lives of others.[85] Occupational deaths were overwhelmingly male, as were the objects of prosecution. "Running-down cases" were highly gendered in two ways: not only were almost all those charged men (as men constituted nearly all drivers), but charges seem to have been more likely to be brought if the victim were female (as with other categories of person deemed in special need of care: children and old and feeble men). Rapid urbanization and the growth of large-scale mechanized industry had increased dangers to life and limb for many both on city streets and at work, and thus also increased the desirability of foresight, care and self-management in the general population. Tort law was increasingly involved in cases where lack of sufficient care led to harm, but also now when death resulted, the criminal law was often called upon. By 1865 the Recorder of London could inform a grand jury that "there was no doubt that everybody who was driving a vehicle through the streets was bound to exercise ordinary caution, and that if he did not do so, and death in consequence ensued, he was guilty of manslaughter."[86] Although in practice the failure to exercise "ordinary caution" was difficult to prove beyond a reasonable doubt, an important legal principle had become established in the course of the first half of the century, one that set up new pressures for men to regulate themselves more closely.[87]

---

[85] Lindsay Farmer has noted a similar rise in nineteenth-century Scotland in charges of "culpable homicide", the equivalent in Scots law of manslaughter, for such negligent deaths. [*Criminal Law, Tradition and Legal Order: Crime and the Genius of Scots Law, 1747 to the Present* (Cambridge, 1997), p. 150; also p. 33, note 86]

[86] *Times*, 19 September 1865, p. 9.

[87] In the leading cases of *R.v. Swindall & Osborne* (1846) and *R.v. Longbottom* (1849), it was established that the contributory negligence of the deceased did not eliminate the criminal liability of the accused. In the first it was ruled that "It is no ground of defence [to a manslaughter charge] that the death was partly caused by the negligence of the deceased himself, or that he was either deaf or dumb at the time" [2 Cox C.C. 141]; in the second more generally that "there is a very wide distinction between a civil action for pecuniary compensation for death arising from alleged negligence and a proceeding by way of indictment for manslaughter.... There is no balance

The military, hitherto left for the most part to its own laws, came in this century more clearly under the authority of the common law courts. These courts displayed in the early years of the century a newfound interest in prosecuting violence by military men. As has been noted, soldiers, for example, appeared for the first time as accused killers in assize court in the county of Kent in 1806, although that county's dockyards and ports had long been home to an unruly military population. Another expansion of the legal war on violence can be seen in a trend to more consistently impose liability upon ships' masters who had killed men under their command.[88]

Indeed, in a variety of ways the crackdown on violence was more than simply "class control" – the use of force by men in authority was generally coming under greater legal scrutiny.[89] The authority of masters was broadest in the military, of course, and next to that, among merchant seamen. Here, isolated from outside scrutiny and from the usual supports to authority on land, brutal discipline was virtually the norm. Yet the Napoleonic Wars, demanding unprecedented and lengthy mobilization of the populace, brought discipline and mistreatment more prominently into public view. The trial and conviction for murder at Admiralty Court in 1802 of Joseph Wall, former Governor of the trading and military base of Goree, in West Africa, for having, twenty years earlier, ordered a soldier under his command to be given 800 lashes with a even fiercer whip than that in normal use, was a landmark, often cited thereafter, in establishing legal bounds for even military discipline. The Lord Chief Baron pointed out to the jury "the distinction between wholesome correction and excessive severity, whether with respect of parents to their children, masters to their servants, or officers to their men...." In pronouncing the death sentence, the Recorder of London declared that "It was fit that every body should be impressed with this great

of blame in charges of felony" [3 Cox C.C. 439]. Towards the end of the century prosecutions for such negligent homicide declined. Systems of traffic management and occupational safety regulations, and quite likely more careful public behavior, were reducing the number of such fatal accidents, while new conceptions of social risk and its management led to the creation of new and more easily proved statutory duties.

[88]James Cockburn, "Patterns of Violence in English Society: Homicide in Kent 1560–1985," *Past and Present* no. 130 (February 1991), 70–106, cites some cases; some significant cases from other counties are discussed below.

[89]One of the lesser-known provisions of the Poor Law Amendment Act of 1834 was to prohibit the use of corporal punishment in workhouses, which if not putting a stop to this practice at least placed it clearly outside the law. As William Shaen, head of the Society for the Protection of Women and Children, could argue in evidence to the Contagious Diseases Act Commission in 1871, offenses should be considered "doubly criminal" when committed by someone who "occupies a position involving special duties towards the injured person" such as "parent against child...master against servant, or by a medical man against a patient." [P.P. 1871 XIX.1, Q 19,548]

truth – that no man, however high his station, however great his power, would be at liberty to dispose of the life of a fellow creature. . . . It was a murder of the most deliberate and malignant kind."[90]

In 1809, another military officer, Capt. James Sutherland, was hanged for fatally stabbing a cabin boy, the chief witness being a black sailor.[91] Three years after that a naval lieutenant, was tried by court-martial and hanged at the ship's yardarm for similarly stabbing a sergeant, who had refused a command. In response to this, the commanding Admiral sent round a circular to every ship, warning officers "never to treat with cruelty or violence those over whom he is to command" and also sailors never "by disobedience or disrespect to rouse the passions of those whom it is his duty to obey and respect."[92] No doubt there were other such instances which went unpunished; still, the wide interest that these hangings excited helped instill a new standard of expectations for military officers.

During these wars and especially in their aftermath the chief judge of the High Court of Admiralty, Lord Stowell, solidified such new expectations into precedential rulings.[93] Building on the distinction already made in the eighteenth-century Admiralty Court between cases of moderate and immoderate correction of seamen (the latter was liable to payment of costs and damages), Stowell was more likely to consider a particular correction case "immoderate," tended to award higher damages, and appears to have increased the likelihood that suits for damages by seamen against officers would be won. In a number of cases he awarded quite large damages to seamen for assaults upon them by captains. Along with this, he also attempted to make the maritime punishment of sailors more subject to notions of due process. Even when punishment by the master of a vessel was within the law, Stowell insisted in 1824 that it must be applied with moderation and that on the seas as on land "in all cases which will admit of the delay proper for inquiry, due inquiry should precede the act of punishment; and, therefore, that the party charged should have the benefit of that rule of universal justice,

---

[90]"Trial of Governor Wall . . .", in *British Trials* [microform] (Alexandria, Va., 1990–2000).

[91]*Times* 24 June 1809, p. 3; "Trial and execution of John Sutherland, Captain of the transport The Friends, for the murder of Richard Wilson, his cabin boy, on the 5th of November, 1808, in the River Tagus, by stabbing him in the belly with a dirk (dagger)!" Bodleian Library, Oxford, Document 501429746.

[92]*R.v. Gamage* (1812): Crook, op. cit., vol. 5, p. 150.

[93]Although the bulk of Admiralty's caseload was suits for payment of wages (in which he also showed a new leaning towards the complainants), its authority was expanded in 1799 to enable it to hear more cases of alleged violence, both civil and criminal [Henry J. Bourguignon, *Sir William Scott, Lord Stowell* (Cambridge, 1987), p. 29].

of being heard in his own defence."[94] Here Stowell introduced, apparently without precedent, a requirement of minimal due process aboard ship.

By the 1830s the military, like the maritime, no longer formed a legal world of its own, and in 1837 for the first time Burn's *Justice* discussed the justification and limitations of military "correction." "A military officer," it now noted, "may order a correction for disobedience of orders. But he must in no case be guilty of any unnecessary injury to the offender, or he would be liable [to criminal conviction for assault or assault and battery]."[95] The next edition of Burn in 1845 went further, adding the observation in regard to homicide that "persons on board a ship are necessarily subject to something like a despotic government, and it is extremely important that the law should regulate the conduct of those who exercise dominion over them."[96] By this time the anti-flogging movement had gained great strength, and particular cases of soldiers or sailors flogged to death roused public storms. When Frederick White, a soldier, was flogged to death after assaulting an officer in 1846, newspapers of all political persuasions covered the story. While the Chartist *Northern Star* had a field day with the case, observing that the persistence of flogging "is one of the disgraceful indications now left among us of the iron rule of the aristocratical classes," even the solidly middle-class *Illustrated London News* provided full coverage of the lengthy inquest. Although White had confessed his guilt and pled the influence of drink before his punishment, the coroner's jury, finding that he had died of the effects of the flogging, announced their "horror and disgust at the existence of any law . . . which permits the revolting punishment of flogging to be inflicted upon British soldiers" and urged petitions to Parliament to outlaw the practice. This call was supported not only by the *Northern Star* but by the *Illustrated London News*.[97]

Concern about excessive maritime discipline included merchant shipping. It was only by the Merchant Shipping Act of 1854 that an obligation was specifically placed on a shipping master to take legal action if death at sea had occurred through violence. Previously, according to the informal law of the sea it had been nobody's specific business, and much seems to have gone

---

[94]Ibid., pp. 101–102: "In *Enchantress* (Killock) (1825), 1 Hag. 395, 397, Stowell awarded £120 and costs to a seaman for the 'aggravated and unmanly cruelty' of the captain." ["On the other hand, where Stowell found that the punishment inflicted on a seaman was commensurate to the offense committed, that it was imposed only after a formal inquiry by the officers, that it was ordered by due authority and administered with proper moderation, Stowell decided that the seaman was not entitled to damages [*Lowther Castle* (Baker) (1825), 1 Hag. 384,385]."]

[95]Burn, *Justice*, 28th ed. (1837) 1: 281.

[96]Burn, *Justice*, 29th ed. (1845), 3: 804.

[97]Anne Baltz Rodrick, " 'Only a Newspaper Metaphor': Crime Reports, Class Conflict, & Social Criticism in Two Victorian Newspapers," *Victorian Periodicals Review* 29 (Spring 1996), 1–18.

unreported. Even before the Act, however, opinion-makers were urging prosecution and conviction of ship's captains. When in 1846 one captain, George
Johnston, won an insanity verdict at the Old Bailey after he ran through
two surly members of his crew, several important London newspapers declared the verdict a miscarriage of justice.[98] The Radicals John Stuart Mill
and Harriet Taylor, more concerned (surprisingly perhaps) about violence
than about rights of defendants, went even further: "The state of mind of
the jurors," they declared, "is a specimen of the tendency of the humanity-
mongering which has succeeded to the reckless brutality of our old laws, and
which has brought us to such a pass, that every man is now to be presumed
insane as soon as it is fully proved that he is a ruffian."[99] Judges were thinking similarly: after another jury, doubting the credibility of key prosecution
witnesses, convicted a captain only of manslaughter in 1849, Justice Williams
found it nonetheless necessary, for a crime "serious in its own nature, and
serious upon public grounds," to sentence the man at least to two years' hard
labor.[100]

One sign of the heightened official intolerance of personal violence was
that it frequently overruled race prejudice: abuse of black and Asian, as well
as of white British seamen, was prosecuted and often successfully. In 1845, the
captain of a ship trading with the coast of Africa who had personally beaten a
black seaman, who had several times fallen asleep on his watch, on the head
and shoulders with a paddle, with fatal results, was convicted at Liverpool
of manslaughter. He was apparently disliked by his crew, some of who gave
evidence that he had subsequently had the ship's log altered to record the
man falling and then receiving a short flogging, losing consciousness and
dying thereafter. That his victim was black did not prevent Baron Rolfe
awarding him the most severe sentence possible, transportation for life, and
denouncing him as a brutal tyrant. "You have numbers of persons under
your dominion," he declared, "and to your violence they are all more or less
obliged to submit."[101] Trial reports of prosecutions after deaths at sea fail to
show the racial discrimination we might have expected.[102]

[98] *Times*, 7 February 1846, p. 4; *Morning Chronicle*, 10 February 1846, p. 5.
[99] *Morning Chronicle*, ibid., p. 5.
[100] *R.v. Ford: Times*, 26 July 1849, p. 7.
[101] *R.v. Hill: Liverpool Mercury*, 29 August 1845, p. 2; see also HO18/158/48.
[102] Isaac Land has argued the reverse, that arguments by seamen and their sympathiz-
ers against brutal discipline built their case on a sharpened distinction between white
Britons, who had the full rights of Englishmen against such treatment, and other
races and nationalities, who did not, and thus that the eventual abolition of flogging
was inseparable from intensified British racism [Isaac Land, "Customs of the Sea:
Flogging, Empire, and the 'True British Seaman' 1770 to 1870," *Interventions* 3 (2001):
2, 169–185]. However, although his claims are for the nineteenth century in general,
Land's evidence does not extend beyond the very early years of the century, and even
then is highly selective. Indeed, the single incident to which he devotes the most space,

In the following decade sentiment against such captains hardened further. The year 1857 saw both Exeter and Liverpool greatly excited by murder trials of merchant captains. In Exeter in March Captain Hugh Orr was brought up for repeated beatings and floggings of his ship's cook, a black man from the United States, treatment that finally led to the man's death. "A case of such fearful cruelty and atrocity . . . was, perhaps, scarcely ever heard," was how the reporter for the *Times* began his account. At the close of arguments Justice Williams went so far as to instruct the jury that a murder verdict was reasonable, for while usually that required use of a dangerous weapon, lacking in this case, "the instruments of violence used [here] were used so often and so cruelly that the jury might come to the conclusion that they could not but infer that such a depraved and malignant spirit existed in him as would satisfy the imputation of malice." He continued that "although it was true . . . that the master of a merchant vessel had authority over all persons in the ship, and might administer reasonable correction, yet his authority in that respect was that of a parent over a child. He must take care that there was sufficient cause for chastisement, and that the chastisement was reasonable, or he would be criminally responsible. There did not appear to him to be any evidence of any occasion for such chastisement." The jury did not go as far as invited, but they did find the captain guilty of manslaughter and withheld any mercy recommendation; Williams then sentenced him to transportation for life.[103]

That summer murder charges were brought at Liverpool against Captain Henry Rogers and the two chief officers of the merchant ship *Martha Jane* sailing from Barbados to Liverpool, for killing a mentally unbalanced seaman by "persistent and vicious ill-treatment."[104] The Attorney-General himself took charge of the prosecution, indicating the degree of public attention it

a London magistrate's 1814 indictment of a Lascar supervisor for assault for the flogging of a Lascar seaman while berthed in London, is on balance evidence *against* his claim. Moreover, racial distinctions, while no doubt often made colloquially and also no doubt affecting treatment of seamen, never entered legislation or case law. In practice, also, as the likelihood of criminal prosecution of excessively violent shipboard discipline rose, cases with "colored" victims rose more or less proportionately.

[103] *R.v. Orr: Times,* 23 March 1857, p. 11. While this trial was going on in Exeter, at Liverpool an officer on an American ship was being tried for manslaughter, after an unknown man was taken unconscious from his ship and died in hospital of severe head injuries, kicks and lashings with a rope's end. Evidence showed that he had from the outset of the voyage been targeted by the bosun. The coroner's jury could not charge the captain with anything, but expressed their indignation that he should have allowed what they called "piecemeal murder." The bosun was convicted of manslaughter, though given only four months' hard labor; the judge stated that if he ever came before him again he "would receive the most severe sentence that the law would permit." *R.v. Lewis: [Liverpool Mercury,* 16 January 1857, p. 6; 30 March 1857, p. 3.]

[104] *Liverpool Mail,* 22 August 1857, p. 6.

had gathered. All three were convicted of the full charge of murder (even though Rogers had the services of a Queen's Counsel), largely on their "great brutality" rather than on a clear intent to kill.[105] The unusual verdicts were popular: as one newspaper reported with approval, "no sooner had the jury condemned them to the ignominy and agony of a public strangulation, that the vociferous applause of the grateful multitude went up to heaven like the cry of the blood of Abel."[106]

The *Liverpool Mail* saw the crime as a national humiliation: having on frequent occasions denounced brutalities occurring on American ships (one such trial having taken place in the city only a few months before) "we are constrained to admit that the wanton abuse of authority on shipboard is not peculiar to the mercantile marine of the United States." Indeed, the "savage ferocity" of this case had "not been outdone by horror by any American case which has ever come under our notice." However, the paper found the humiliation salved and national honor vindicated by the prompt and thorough prosecution of the malefactors. "Bitterly as we regret that such atrocities should have been possible on board a British ship, we find in the very fact of the trial, and in its result, abundant proof that they cannot, on board a British ship, be perpetrated with impunity. The Government did its duty, in directing a prosecution, and in taking care that it should be conducted without consideration of expense, and with the highest legal talent which the circuit bar could furnish, so that there might be no risk of a failure of justice. The jury did their duty, in convicting the prisoners." A lesson, the *Mail* hoped, had been taught to masters of merchant vessels that "invested, as they necessarily are, with vast powers, for the purpose of maintaining discipline, and enforcing due subordination, they must not go beyond the limits of reasonable correction; and that, if they exceed those limits, and are guilty of acts of cruelty, from which reasonable men would anticipate death as a consequence, and death actually ensues, they are guilty of WILFUL MURDER."[107]

[105]The trial also established the principle that, as the Attorney-General argued, "no one could plead the commands of a superior to injure life or limb, or do an illegal act." [*Liverpool Mail*, 22 August 1857, pp. 6–7.] The magistrate who committed them on the charge of murder suggested that the grand jury might reduce this to manslaughter; however, they did not. [*Liverpool Mail*, 20 June 1857, p. 6].
[106]*Northern Daily Express*, 26 August 1857, p. 2. The *Times* reported similarly, if with more restraint, that "the sentence was received by a very large crowd who were gathered in St. George's Hall awaiting the result of the trial, with loud cheering. His Lordship and all in court appeared much astonished at this very natural demonstration of popular feeling" [21 August 1857, p. 10].
[107]*Liverpool Mail*, 15 August 1857, p. 7. Baron Watson observed in passing sentences of death that "it is of the utmost importance in a maritime country like this, that the power with which you are armed to repress insubordination on board your ships should not be accompanied with too great severity, and the law should watch most

The jury had recommended the men to mercy, but one of their number dissented, and fervently wrote the Home Secretary:

> For a long period [he claimed] this port has been outraged with the arrival of ships on board of which not only cruelties, but actual murders which the law could not reach, have been of perpetual occurrence, and it is quite time that the majesty of the Law should be vindicated, that protection may be afforded (though at best but inadequately) to the unfortunate mariners whose life is held at the mercy of ruffianly captains and their equally, or more, ruffianly mates. The feelings of this place are almost daily outraged by cases of cruelty on shipboard, in which some [loopholes?] are ingeniously discovered by defence attorneys and the delinquents escape with an impunity that only increases the evil.[108]

Despite the jury recommendation, some uncertainties about the evidence expressed by the judge, and the plea for mercy made by even the prosecuting counsel, only the mates received reprieves, while Captain Rogers was left to hang before 40,000 spectators.[109] It was a dramatic and generally popular public statement that henceforth a new level of scrutiny would be applied to the exercise of shipboard authority. Even while supporting reprieves for all three one newspaper observed that "hitherto this class of men have had some reason to think that when they were out of sight of land they might do just as they pleased.... This has arisen, to some extent, from a reprehensible laxity in the execution of the law, and therefore its administrators are not altogether free from criminal responsibility."[110] This was now to change. In Liverpool itself the following year yet another captain and mate were charged with murder for kicking a Spanish seaman to death; convicted of manslaughter, the captain was given penal servitude for life and the mate one year's imprisonment.[111]

Other cases in other ports followed. At Newcastle-on-Tyne in 1859 an American officer on an American ship lying in dock was convicted of manslaughter and sentenced to penal servitude for life in the death of an American seaman.[112] Liverpool that year saw an even more celebrated trial,

---

carefully that that power is not too much extended" [*Times,* 21 August 1857, p. 10]. Rogers' clothes were sold by the hangman, Calcraft, to Allsop's Waxwork Exhibition in Liverpool.

[108] HO12/114/29217.

[109] After Baron Watson privately conveyed his doubts about some of the evidence against the men, Lord Chancellor Cranwell was consulted; his firm view was to reprieve the mates and hang Rogers, which was done. Ibid. The life sentences of the other two were later reduced to ten years.

[110] *Morning Star,* 10 September 1857, p. 2.

[111] *R.v. Anderson et al.: Liverpool Mercury,* 27 March 1858, p. 3 [for their committal for trial, see *Liverpool Mercury,* 30 November 1857, p. 6].

[112] *R.v. Moody: Times,* 9 December 1859, p. 11; *Standard,* 9 December 1859, p. 6.

which became known as "the case of the roasted sailor." The second engineer of a ship was convicted of aiding and abetting the first engineer in the murder of a sailor through a series of brutal "punishments," culminating in being (perhaps unintentionally) set on fire; the first engineer had been granted bail and had absconded. The Attorney-General again personally prosecuted. The defense was that he had only followed orders of a superior. "A ship could not be worked," the man's counsel argued, "unless there was perfect obedience and discipline on board it, and if the verdicts of juries were to be allowed to tamper with the long-established custom, and the idea that the contracts of seamen were to be governed by the new-fangled notions of what obedience was due, the days of the supremacy of this country on the sea were numbered." However, this argument was swept aside by Justice Willes, who argued that at the least the highest authority on board would have had to have issued the orders, which had not occurred: "There was no power to interfere with the liberty of a man on board a ship except by the direct command of the captain." Convicted of manslaughter, the second engineer, in spite of only having aided the absconded first engineer, was given fifteen years' penal servitude. The *Times'* correspondent reported that "public indignation at [the first engineer's] having been admitted to bail runs high."[113] Such cases fortified national pride when examples of other nationals' savagery came to light. In denouncing in 1860 "the cruelties for which the United States' merchant service has of late years become justly infamous" the *Annual Register* pointed out that the British authorities "have themselves shown what their view of this class of crimes is, by hanging a British merchant-captain and sending into penal servitude for life an American who had unadvisedly indulged in torturing a brother American to death in a British port."[114]

A series of naval mutinies between 1859 and 1865 shocked Parliament into passing Naval Discipline Acts in 1860, 1861, 1864 and 1866 that sharply limited the freewheeling authority traditionally allowed their captains and officers.[115] Despite the apparent re-emergence after the Indian Mutiny of

---

[113] *R.v. Mitchell: Times*, 2 April 1859, p. 11. A letter from "Vox Populi" called the crime "the most brutal and foul murder which has ever disgraced the annals of England," and argued that "the captain . . . and the whole ship's company should be tried for murder for allowing and not preventing such horrible brutality." [*Times*, 6 April 1859, p. 10] Two years later defense counsel in an Old Bailey trial of a black Caribbean seaman who had stabbed his captain in the hip, not life-threateningly, after he'd suffered much violence appealed to the jury that they "were perfectly well aware that these unfortunate black men were very frequently treated with great cruelty by these captains." His client was convicted only of a lesser charge and sentenced by Baron Bramwell to just one month's imprisonment. [*R.v. Manton: Times*, 29 November 1861, p. 9]

[114] *Annual Register for 1860*, Chronicle, p. 14.

[115] For accounts of naval discipline in this era, see Eugene Rasor, *Reform in the Royal Navy: A Social History of the Lower Deck 1850 to 1880* (New York, 1976) and Fredric

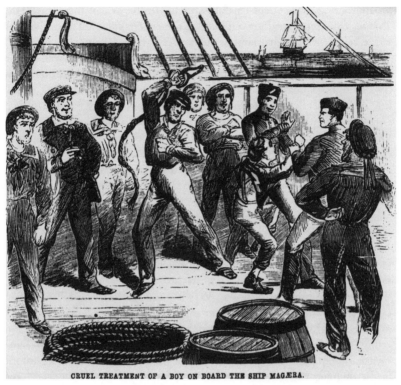

CRUEL TREATMENT OF A BOY ON BOARD THE SHIP MAGÆRA.

FIGURE 3. "Cruel Treatment of a Boy on Board the Ship Magera" (*Illustrated Police News*, April 27, 1867). The darker side of maritime life and of "Jack Tar" himself.

public support for a stronger hand over subject peoples in the Empire, the use of force against seamen (whether white or colored, British or alien) was increasingly hemmed in by law backed by strong public sentiment.[116]

New naval rules still left room for much unreported violence in the broader, and also almost entirely male "water world," including not only ocean-going vessels but thousands of fishing boats and coastal shippers. The law's reach, and the public's concern, also came to embrace this diffuse and little-supervised realm. In 1882, for instance, two men from two separate fishing smacks, a master and a seaman, were each hanged (with little public objection)

Smoler, "Emeute: Mutiny and the Culture of Authority in the Victorian Navy" (Ph.D. dissertation, Columbia University, 1994).

[116] Another black victim was John Francis, cook on the Cutty Sark. His first mate was charged at the Old Bailey in 1882 with his murder, and though the fact of Francis' disobeying orders was established, given seven years' penal servitude [*R.v. Anderson: Times*, 4 August 1882, p. 4; his inquest is recorded in PRO CRIM 1/16/1]. Other revealing trials are *R.v. Cocks* (1887): HO144/199/A47104B, and *R.v. Arthur* (1888): HO Printed Memorandum on Capital Cases.

for murdering apprentices by ill-treatment. In the first of these cases, the *Yorkshire Post*'s reporter observed that "as the prisoner was led from the dock to the cells [after adjournment to the next day] he was loudly hissed."[117]

Such cases form part of the context needed to understand the well-known 1884 trial of Thomas Dudley and Edwin Stephens who, after drifting many days in an open boat in the middle of the ocean, killed and ate their cabin-boy. Although their horrendous ordeal gained them much sympathy in their port of Falmouth, after their trial was transferred to the five-judge court of Queen's Bench in London they were convicted of murder. The universally expected lightening of their sentences was left to the Home Office, which indeed reduced them to six months' penal servitude. But the judiciary was firm in upholding principle. As Chief Justice Coleridge (speaking for all the five judges hearing the case) declared of their defense of necessity, a long-accepted one on the sea, "who is to be the judge of this sort of necessity? By what measure is the comparative value of lives to be measured? Is it to be strength, or intellect, or what? It is plain that the principle leaves to him who is to profit by it to determine the necessity which will justify him in deliberately taking another's life to save his own. In this case the weakest, the youngest, the most unresisting was chosen. Was it more necessary to kill him than one of the grown men? The answer must be, No . . . such a principle, once admitted, might be made the legal cloak for unbridled passion and atrocious crime."[118] This trial, a milestone in legal history for its discussion and ruling on the exculpation of "necessity," was at the same time also a milestone in the ongoing extension of the law's tighter restrictions on interpersonal violence by or against British subjects beyond the shores of Britain. As the *Spectator* noted during the proceedings, "the conviction that such murders are justified by the law of self-defence, and are not, therefore, illegal, is so general amongst seafaring men, and has so infected naval literature, that a solemn judgement to the contrary, pronounced by more than one judge, has become indispensable."[119]

At home also, other sorts of violence against subordinates – such as apprentices and servants – was being more roundly condemned. Prosecutions

---

[117] *R.v. Brand* (1882): HO144/95/A14575. Just before this case an MP had forwarded to the Home Office a newspaper report of a different trial before the Hull Stipendiary Magistrate, saying there were many deaths at sea that should be enquired into. Also, *R.v. Wheatfill* (1882): HO144/105/A21999.

[118] HO144/141/A36934. The story of Dudley and Stephens has been most ably examined and recounted by A.W. Brian Simpson [*Cannibalism and the Common Law: The Story of the Tragic Last Voyage of the Mignonette and the Strange Legal Proceedings to Which it Gave Rise* (Chicago, 1984)]. Simpson, however, does not put the case in the context described here. He does note, however, that earlier survival cannibalism had not usually been prosecuted (citing for example an 1837 case which judges had ignored).

[119] Quoted ibid., p. 251.

for acts of violence against servants, children, and wives – situations that had commonly escaped formal prosecution – became more frequent. Earlier, masters of all sorts had extensive discretion to use violence against their subordinates.[120] Although a new principle had been set out at the Old Bailey in 1776 in a case of a starved and beaten apprentice, when the Recorder of London declared that "if a master by premeditated neglect, or harsh usage, caused the death of his apprentice, it is murder," the jury nonetheless found manslaughter only, and the prisoner was simply burnt in the hand and released.[121] It was not until well into the next century that this principle won general assent. By the 1840s, a new public climate had come into being. The celebrated case of Thomas Wicks, a twenty-year old apprentice who murdered his master, was treated by the influential middle-class journal, the *Illustrated London News*, in 1846 more as a cautionary tale warning masters to treat their apprentices better than as the familiar old story of the untrustworthiness of servants.[122]

Three years before, Justice Cresswell set a "running-down" manslaughter trial of a wagon-driver (with a female victim) in the context of master–servant relations, enunciating the same requirement of "moderation" being established for shipboard force. "The law in these cases," he declared, "was this – it was not sufficient that the act upon which death ensued was a lawful act; it must be done in a proper manner, and with due caution, to prevent mischief. Persons having authority might give reasonable correction to persons under them, and if death ensued without their fault, it was accidental death; but if the correction exceeded *moderation*, it would be either murder or manslaughter."[123] In 1857 Cresswell was put in charge of the newly-created Divorce Court, where he became a well-known (and much-complained about) bane of bad husbands. The wife of one such husband, the former schoolmaster Thomas Hopley, was granted a legal separation in 1864 after alleging emotional and physical abuse; Hopley had only recently been released on license from penal servitude he had been serving for beating a pupil to death. That act had produced a leading case in 1860 establishing the limits of a teacher's rights of chastisement, even with parental consent. Despite having first gotten the father's written consent for his son's "severe beating," when the boy died

[120]See J.A. Sharpe, *Crime in Seventeenth-Century England: A County Study* (Cambridge, 1983), pp. 126–127; Paul Griffiths, "Masterless Young People in Norwich, 1560–1645" in *The Experience of Authority in Early Modern England*, ed. Paul Griffiths, Adam Fox and Steve Hindle (New York, 1996), pp. 146–186. It is useful to remember that the murder of a master by a servant, like that of a husband by a wife, had been legally defined as "petty treason" and liable to death by burning until 1828.

[121]*R.v. Self* (1776): 1 Leach CC 137 [in 168 ER 170].

[122]"A Master Shot by his Apprentice," *Illustrated London News*, 21 February 1846; HO18/179/23.

[123]*R.v. Ford*: see *Times* 28 March 1843, p. 7.

(after two and a half hours of beating) Hopley was convicted of manslaughter and sentenced to penal servitude.[124]

By 1865 one homicide case against a factory overlooker showed how the power of correction had been further delimited. The accused had strapped a sixteen-year-old worker who died several days later, but the prosecution was unable to establish the attack as the sure cause of death, and he was acquitted of manslaughter. However Justice Willes then made a point of declaring that "it ought to be well understood that no servant had a right to strike his underservant. There was a certain power of punishment placed in the hands of the masters, and in the exercise of that they would no doubt be closely watched; but no master had the right of delegating that power to any of his servants, even though that servant might stand in the position of overlooker."[125]

Another bastion of legitimate male violence that was undermined in this era was the use of violence in protection of one's home or property. An Englishman's home, even an English gentleman's home, was no longer to be his castle. A landmark case, for both the law and public opinion, was that of Captain William Moir in 1830. A man "of a family of the highest respectability," as he was described by his judge, Lord Tenterden, Moir fatally shot a trespasser on his land. The judge instructed the jury that he saw no evidence that the intruder have given him any reason "to think his own life was in danger," and, despite his rank, it returned a verdict of guilty of murder. At a time of rising social tensions this may have constituted too blatant an example of upper-class arrogance to be overlooked; a popular broadside displayed Moir on a horse shooting down an unarmed walking man. No mercy recommendation came from either jury or judge, and despite a strong appeal made afterwards by his friends claiming insanity, he was duly hanged.[126]

At a lower social level, a related legal rule was established in an 1837 conviction at Liverpool. When a man refused to leave a house, the occupant, in this case a woman, kicked him hard enough to get him out, but from which he died. "A kick," Baron Alderson declared (during the same session

---

[124] 2 F&F 202 [John Mews, *A Digest of Cases Relating to the Criminal Law from 1756 to 1883 inclusive* (London, 1884), p. 437]. On the separation, see *Times* 19 July 1864, p. 11, and the remarks on his wife-beating in the *Saturday Review*, 14, 21 July 1864. The limits of "correction" of children were also beginning to be examined; in 1869 a man was convicted of manslaughter for "correcting" his small child too severely, and Baron Martin set the broader precedent that "a father is not justified in correcting an infant of two years of age, and if he does so and the infant dies therefrom, he is guilty of manslaughter" [*R.v. Griffin* (1869):11 Cox C.C. 402].

[125] *R.v. Baxter: Times*, 4 April 1865, p. 13.

[126] *Annual Register for 1830*, Chronicle, pp. 344–50; Crook, op. cit., vol. 5, pp. 233–237; *Times* 31 July 1830, p. 1; "Trial & Execution of Captain Moir . . ." (St. Bride's Printing Library, broadside #168).

in which he dealt out tough sentences to a number of wife killers), "is not a justifiable mode of turning a man out of your house, even if he be a trespasser"; therefore, if the kick causes death, the perpetrator is guilty of manslaughter.[127] As Burn's *Justice of the Peace* put it in citing this case in 1845, "in no case is a man justified in intentionally taking away the life of a mere trespasser, his own life not being in jeopardy; he is only protected from the consequences of such force as is reasonably necessary to turn the wrong-doer out," and a powerful kick fell outside these bounds.[128]

In the nineteenth century legal condemnation and punishment of men's violence against other men continued on a path begun in the later years of the previous century. A continuing working-class tradition of settling disputes and establishing reputation by violence was gradually marginalized, while the use of force by men in authority was also subjected to new restrictions. In their work the courts gradually set out a more self-disciplined and pacific ideal of manhood than had prevailed in the eighteenth or earlier centuries. Male-on-male violence, while continuing, came to be strongly stigmatized and significantly curtailed by the law. However, such curtailment was selective: "fair fights," without weapons, still tended to be looked on leniently, and the amount of "chastisement" that could be given with legal safety to servants and apprentices continued to be quite large by later standards. Yet while judicial attitudes towards male-on-male violence continued to allow much leeway, a still sharper change was at the same time taking place in the realm of men's violence against women, to which the rest of this work will be devoted.

---

[127] *R.v. Wild* (1837): 2 Lewin, CC 214. The defendant was given three months' imprisonment [HO27/53].
[128] Burn, *Justice*, 29th ed. (1845), 2: 797. See also *R.v. Doyle* (1862): *Times*, 27 March 1862, p. 11, and *R.v. Daley* (1874): HO45/9374/39902; *Times*, 15 December 1874, p. 10.

# 3

# Sexual Violence

It is the "conventional wisdom" that sexual crimes against women were little regarded by the law until the re-awakening of the feminist movement in the last few decades of the twentieth century.[1] Any nineteenth-century changes in the patriarchal and misogynist status quo were, it has been argued, largely cosmetic, or installed as defensive measures in order to preserve the fundamentals of patriarchy in a changing world. This chapter takes issue with such a flattened view of Victorian treatment of sexual assault. Viewed from the beginning of the twenty-first century, it is easy to paint Victorian criminal justice as either uncaring or patriarchal in its treatment of rape claims. One can dip into the records and soon pull up a case like one that came before the Old Bailey in 1866, in which a twenty-one year old soldier was charged with attempted rape of a seventeen-year-old servant girl. Having gone out after dark near Hounslow to fetch supper beer she had been dragged into a ditch by the defendant and attacked; she hit him on the head with the jug of beer and screamed, bringing a policeman onto the scene. The defense admitted the attack but because the soldier had a good character and "the occurrence had taken place on the night of a merrymaking amongst the troops, when many of them were the worse for liquor," he was convicted only of indecent assault and sentenced to merely a month's imprisonment.[2] However, such cases can be countered by many others, which have tended to receive less notice, and more importantly, the presentist context by a more historically enlightening one. Viewed not from today, but from its own past, the Victorian era was a time of both heightened contention and major change in this realm. The nineteenth century saw sexual assault much more clearly defined in the courtroom as violence. The definition of the act altered to emphasize its violent character, the focus shifted somewhat away from the previous behavior of the prosecutrix, and the very notion of consent

[1] See Susan Brownmiller, *Against Our Will: Men, women, and rape* (New York, 1975); Susan Edwards, *Female Sexuality & the Law* (Oxford, 1981); Zsuzsanna Adler, *Rape on Trial* (London and New York, 1987), ch. 10; Sue Lees, *Carnal Knowledge: Rape on Trial* (London, 1997).
[2] *Lloyds' Weekly*, 23 September 1866, p. 4.

was reconstrued. These interpretative and procedural shifts, together with the removal of the death penalty, increased the likelihood of successfully prosecuting charges of rape and sexual assault, and indeed prosecutions and convictions did markedly rise. At the same time, to be sure, much of the older misogynist and patriarchal frame of mind continued, so that sexual assault trials, from petty sessions up to assizes, often became transcripts of cultural conflict. This story has only begun to be told.[3]

For centuries, rape figured only very slightly in the workings of English criminal justice.[4] In theory it was one of the gravest of crimes, carrying a mandatory death penalty, yet (in part because of this penalty) few were prosecuted for this offense, and many fewer still were found guilty. Local studies have agreed in the rarity of indictments for rape or other sexual crimes. For example, in all the Home Circuit assize trials calendared for the years 1558–1625, only fifty of 7,544 persons indicted were charged with rapes (no other sexual offenses, except buggery and sodomy, were dealt with at assizes).[5] In seventeenth-century Essex there were only twenty-eight cases of rape out of 2,255 felonies charged.[6] Even if a case came to trial, guilty findings

---

[3]Beginning in the 1970s, feminist scholars brought the issue of sexual assault out of the shadows, and showed how slow and partial change in legal conceptions and treatment of it had been. Since then valuable historical work has been done on it. Yet, in stressing the chasm between today's dominant values and those of the Victorians, most of this work has obscured or denigrated the change that was taking place during that period. It is quite insufficient to simply characterize this sixty-four-year period as an age of "patriarchy." Even more judicious recent scholarship, like Shani D'Cruze, *Crimes of Outrage: Sex, violence and Victorian working women* (London, 1998), certainly the best study that has been done on violence against women in this era, continues to make patriarchy its guiding theme.

[4]This chapter is based in part on the reports of rape trials at the Old Bailey occuring in sampled nineteenth-century years (174), and all reports of rape trials in England and Wales appearing in the *Times* between 1790 and 1905 (approximately 800), as well as about a hundred other English and Welsh cases, located in other newspapers or in official documents, and several dozen Scottish cases. These reports provide a great deal of evidence about attitudes and strategies of all the parties, very much including the judges, and sometimes the courtroom audience, the reading public and even the reporters themselves.

[5]J.S. Cockburn, ed., *Crime in England, 1550–1800* (Princeton, 1977), p. 58.

[6]James Sharpe, *Crime in Seventeenth-Century England* (Cambridge, 1983) pp. 79–80. Sharpe also examined indictments at other assizes, as well as drawing on other local studies, concluding that this very low level of rape indictments held generally true throughout England. One such unpublished study confirming this generalization is Sarah Anne Barbour-Mercer, "Prosecution and Process: Crime and the Criminal Law in Late Seventeenth-Century Yorkshire" (Ph.D. Thesis, University of York, 1988). On one very special seventeenth-century prosecution (and conviction) for rape, see Cynthia Herrup, *A House in Great Disorder: Sex, Law, and the 2nd Earl of Castlehaven* (London and New York, 1999).

were quite unusual: in the generation between 1589 and 1618 in Hertfordshire only seven men were indicted for rape and none were convicted.[7]

This rarity of rape indictments should not be taken to mean the act of rape itself was rare. As Cynthia Herrup has noted, the most comprehensive seventeenth century guide to legal matters concerning women (*Laws Resolution of Womens Rights*) "introduced the discussion of rape by lamenting men's proclivity to the crime." The anonymous author of this work claimed that " 'if the rampier [rampart] of laws were not between women and their harms, I verily think none of them [women], being above twelve years of age, and under a hundred, being either fair or rich, should be able to escape ravishment.' "[8] So many obstacles lay in the path of prosecuting a rape charge, as we shall see, that indictments can hardly be taken as any sort of guide to incidence.

Rape continued to be barely visible in the courts in the next century as well. Indeed, scholars have recently detected in that era not simply a continuation of traditional patriarchy but an actually "rising tide of misogyny," and in particular a new pressure upon (or encouragement of) men to be more sexually aggressive with women.[9] Whether actual sexual behavior of a significant number of men did become more aggressive has yet to be established, but we do know that rape continued to be only rarely prosecuted and even more rarely punished.

A sample of sixty-one years of Surrey assizes between 1663 and 1802 showed only forty-two indictments for rape, and a similar sample of Sussex showed a mere seventeen.[10] A year or two might go by without a single case being brought to assizes in either county. At the Old Bailey, which covered a much larger and more policed population, the seventy years from 1730 to the end of the century still produced only 203 indictments.[11]

Why should there have been so few rape trials (particularly if the incidence of sexual assault may have been increasing)? There were many reasons. First, to bring a felony charge was not an inexpensive process, costing during the

---

[7] Peter Lawson, "Patriarchy, Crime and the Courts: The Criminality of Women in Late Tudor and Early Stuart England," in *Criminal Justice in the Old World and the New*, ed. Greg T. Smith, Alyson N. May and Simon Devereaux (Toronto, 1998), 37n.

[8] Herrup, *House*, op. cit., pp. 26–27.

[9] Introduction by the editors to *English Masculinities 1660–1800*, ed. Tim Hitchcock and Michele Cohen (London and New York, 1999), p. 11; see also Randolph Trumbach, *Sex and the Gender Revolution: Heterosexuality and the Third Gender in Enlightenment London* (New York, 1998).

[10] J.M. Beattie, *Crime and the Courts in England 1660–1800* (Princeton, 1986) p. 131. This sample was simply those years for which complete records survived.

[11] Antony Simpson, "Masculinity and Control: The Prosecution of Sex Offenses in Eighteenth-Century London," (Ph.D. dissertation, New York University, 1994), pp. 811–813.

eighteenth century between ten shillings and a pound.[12] Since most victims were likely to have been servants or other lower-class young women, this cost could easily prevent legal action, unless a better-off patron was at hand. Beyond this, prevailing attitudes made it unlikely that a single woman over twelve, or certainly sixteen, could obtain vindication in court: the notion of rape as primarily a violation of some man's "property" still lingered.[13] In consequence of both attitudes coerced sex with any woman neither a child nor another man's wife tended to be viewed tolerantly.[14]

More specifically, many "filters" existed which successively reduced the number of such crimes that might reach the courts, and in particular the only courts that were empowered to try for the full offense of rape, the assizes, staffed by royal judges. Many – no doubt most – forced sexual encounters never made it to any legal venue, no charges ever brought. Except in the most outrageous cases, prosecution depended upon private action, especially difficult for women. If a victim was of low social position, if she were poor, if she lacked a protector ready to act on her behalf (a parent or a benevolent relative or employer), if she needed to keep her job, or if she simply feared the public ordeal a woman prosecuting such a charge faced, she would probably never appear before any legal forum. If her case did threaten to go there, it often was dealt with by the perpetrator by intimidation or bribery of witnesses or herself and her family.[15]

Those charges that did come before a magistrate (the first stage of criminal proceedings) faced further filters. The Justice might decide to simply dismiss the charge. When William Miller, a "member of a respectable family in Ireland," was charged at Bow Street in 1822 with raping the twenty-year-old daughter of his landlord, his solicitor told the magistrate that he was prepared to prove the accuser's bad character: "He held in his hand, he said, a list of 18 or 20 respectable persons, who were ready to prove that the prosecutrix was a most abandoned character, and that she had criminal intercourse with other persons – twice, thrice, fifty times!" He even was

---

[12]Beattie, op. cit., p. 41.

[13]See Nazife Bashar, "Rape in England between 1550 and 1700," in *The London Feminist History Group, The Sexual Dynamics of History: Men's Power, Women's Resistance* (London, 1983), 28–42.

[14]A wife, however, had additional reason not to prosecute, unless the rape was witnessed: to admit to sex with another man, however coerced she might claim to have been, laid her open to imputations of adultery (naturally, it was assumed, an unfaithful wife being discovered or fearing discovery, would cry rape, to save her reputation and her marriage). If such a prosecution failed, it might rebound back on her. Often, one must expect, such victims suffered in silence.

[15]Formally, the victims were always the prosecutor, even though typically the charges had actually been brought by fathers, husbands or other males "responsible" for the victims.

prepared to argue that this house in which the defendant lived was a house of ill fame. The magistrate threw out the charge.[16] If not dismissed, charges often were withdrawn after a private arrangement for compensation, or settled similarly at the magistrate's urgings.[17] The minority that survived these resolutions were sometimes simply tried by the magistrate or the more formal Quarter Sessions of magistrates as a lesser offence, usually attempted rape, sometimes merely common assault.[18] Conviction for these usually led only to fines in the former case, perhaps some months of jail time in the latter. On occasion magistrates acting alone even tried rape charges, though this was clearly illegal (all capital offenses were to go to assizes); such trials almost always produced acquittals. Then there was the further filter of the grand jury, drawn from men of social standing, which often failed to find a true bill, causing the case to be dismissed.[19]

At assizes also, many things occurred to reduce the chances of conviction. Fears of malicious prosecution for this crime were expressed with great frequency by jurists, judges, and magistrates, and defendants were quick to appeal to such fears, whether there existed any evidence of it or not.[20] Even

[16] *Times*, 1 March 1822, p. 4.

[17] Indeed, many charges brought to eighteenth-century quarter sessions, including those of sexual assault, were probably never meant to be proceeded with criminally, but were rather aimed at pressuring the accused to at least pay compensation. See Peter King, *Crime, Justice and Discretion: Law and Social Relations in England 1740–1820* (Oxford, 2000); also see Norma Landau, "Indictment for Fun and Profit: A Prosecutor's Reward at Eighteenth-Century Quarter Sessions," *Law and History Review* 17 (1999), 507–536. This was certainly claimed often by rape and attempted rape defendants in cases that did go to trial.

[18] The ubiquity of this practice was uncovered by Antony Simpson, in exploring all levels of adjudicating charges of sexual offenses in the City of London between 1730 and 1835. Simpson argued that "it is certain that more cases of this nature were dealt with summarily than ever reached a grand jury." Of a sample of seventeen allegations of rape or attempted rape reported to London magistrates between 1752 and 1795, he showed that only two ever reached the grand jury; all of the fifteen cases that didn't get beyond a magistrate resulted in discharges, either absolutely or after minor summary punishment [Simpson, "Masculinity," op. cit., p. 226]. Rebecca King ["Rape in England 1600–1800: Trials, narratives and the question of consent" (M.A. thesis, Durham University, 1998)] argues similarly for the difficulty of a rape charge getting to trial. Anna Clark has found that in the North-east circuit even by the later eighteenth century only one-third of men accused of rape of adult women were tried [Clark, *Women's Silence, Men's Violence: Sexual Assault in England 1770–1845* (London, 1987), p. 54].

[19] In the five years 1810–14, grand jury "no-bills" in rape cases almost equaled "true-bills": there were 66 of the former to 77 of the latter. [Parl. Papers 1819 XVII, pp. 306–312.] Even a true bill might never reach assizes; Simpson has found an instance where a case was "settled" after the grand jury's finding [p. 236n].

[20] The well-known dictum of the seventeenth-century Chief Justice, Matthew Hale, that "it is an accusation easy to be made and hard to be proved, and harder to be

at this level private accommodation, not only before but even after the trial was scheduled, persisted: in some cases the prosecutrix failed to show (sometimes, it is likely, after compensation had been agreed upon; other times perhaps out of fear), in others a compensation agreement or public apology or even marriage would be announced, stopping the case.[21] A prosecution could even be killed simply by evidence of a failed attempt, once the indictment had been lodged, to seek compensation, which, however common, was technically illegal.[22]

Thus, only a small fraction of the few rape cases that made it up to courts of assize produced convictions. In Surrey, the forty-two trials produced only five guilty verdicts, less than one-eighth, a lower rate than for any other charge. At the Old Bailey the outcomes were even starker: of the 203 prosecutions over the 70 years between 1730 and 1800, one-ninth – twenty-three – ended in convictions.[23] In the northeast counties of Durham and Northumberland, in the 82 years 1718–1800 of only 30 men accused of rape, attempted rape or being an accessory to rape, one was hanged, one reprieved for transportation, one pilloried, one imprisoned, and one fined.[24] Further, unless the victim was below the age of consent (for different purposes either ten or twelve),[25] prospects of prosecution or conviction were slighter yet. Out of forty-three men tried at the Old Bailey 1770–1800 for the rape of females over twelve

defended by the party accused, though never so innocent" was frequently cited. On eighteenth-century lawbooks' concern with this, see Rebecca King, op. cit., p. 30; Douglas Hay, "Prosecution and Power: Malicious Prosecution in the English Courts 1750–1850," in *Policing and Prosecution in Britain 1750–1850*, ed. Douglas Hay and Francis Snyder (Oxford, 1989), pp. 377–378. On Old Bailey practice in the late seventeenth century, see Bernard Capp, "The Double Standard Revisited: Plebeian Women and Male Sexual Reputation in Early Modern England," *Past and Present*, no. 162 (Spring 1999), and, in the eighteenth century, see Laurie Edelstein, "An Accusation Easily to be Made? Rape and Malicious Prosecution in Eighteenth-Century England," *American Journal of Legal History* 42 (1998), 351–390. Already in the late seventeenth century, Capp found, "defendants were likely to claim that the charge was founded on malice, conspiracy or extortion, and juries considered such claims very carefully." [93] Edelstein concluded that there were few actual malicious rape prosecutions, while the notion of them remained an effective defense weapon.

[21] For a case of marriage stopping an attempted rape prosecution, see *R.v. Stapleton: Times*, 3 September 1805, p. 2.

[22] For example, *R.v. Morris: Times*, 15 April 1793, p. 4. We know little as yet about the frequency of these; the nature of our sources resists such inquiry.

[23] Beattie, op. cit., p. 131; Simpson, "Masculinity" op. cit., pp. 811–13.

[24] Gwenda Morgan and Peter Rushton, *Rogues, Thieves and the Rule of Law: The Problem of Law Enforcement in North-East England, 1718–1800* (London, 1998), p. 230. They noted instances where "witnesses were seemingly rounded up to testify to prosecutrixs' previous sexual activity as a common prostitute" [p. 56], a tactic that continued to be used through the nineteenth century.

[25] It was a felony to seduce a girl under ten years, a misdemeanor if she were between ten and twelve.

years of age, only three were found guilty (and two of them had attacked girls of fourteen). In the Northeast Circuit in the same years only two of fifteen men tried for rape of adult women were convicted.[26]

Even the few convictions that were obtained were as likely as not to be followed by reprieves – three of five, for instance, in Beattie's Surrey sample.[27] Nor did reprieves from the gallows always mean transportation: in times of war, pardons were not infrequently granted to convicted rapists (as to other convicts) on condition of enlistment.[28] Even the misdemeanor charge of attempted rape, which demanded substantially less proof than rape, was only brought approximately twice as often as the charge of rape.[29] Still lesser sexual charges like molestation or indecent assault were rare, and dealt with, lightly, by magistrates on their own.

Thus, from an overview of what happened to rape complaints, we can safely say that in the absence of a child victim or, very rarely, an upper-class victim and a lower-class perpetrator, well into the nineteenth century this offense was not taken seriously by almost anyone who mattered in English society. Certainly, women over the age of twelve received from the law little protection against sexual assault.

This impression is supported and deepened by a look at how stringently rape was defined by law. Before anything else of course, the sexual act had to be established. If the accused man flatly denied it, as many – perhaps most – did, the woman had to present powerful evidence, such as a witness to the attack; her word against his, even supported by circumstantial evidence, was almost never sufficient.[30] Even if the existence of intercourse was established,

[26]Anna Clark, *Women's Silence*, op. cit., p. 58. Clark further noted [p. 41] that "no master was punished for rape in the eighteenth century records I have examined."
[27]Beattie, op. cit., p. 433. Many years ago Leon Radiznowicz, while observing that London and Middlesex saw 678 executions between 1749 and 1771, noted that only two of these were of rapists. [*History of English Criminal Law and Its Administration from 1750*, vol. I (London, 1948), p. 148.
[28]At least three men (and likely more) in the 1790s who were among the few convicted of rape as well as one man convicted of attempted rape were pardoned on condition of military enlistment [Bowell, Slater and Williams in 1793; Batho in 1797; HO 47/11, 17, 21].
[29]Simpson, op. cit., pp. 814, 822.
[30]Well into the nineteenth century, on the evidence of the cases either reported in the *Times* or in the Home Office petition files, a conviction in such cases was almost impossible to obtain without the minimum requirement of corroboration of the assault by a witness. The most common defense in the later seventeenth and through the eighteenth century was simple denial that any sexual act had occurred. [See S. Amussen, *An Ordered Society: Gender and Class in Early Modern England* (New York, 1988), on the later seventeenth century and R. King, op. cit., on the eighteenth century.] As Rebecca King [p. 15] has observed of this defense, "the accused men were able to rely on this flat denial of rape because contemporaries believed so strongly that women often lied about rape. The accused could then present himself as a non-fornicating innocent man, a victim of a false allegation of rape."

a narrow legal concept of rape (one not out of tune with popular notions) underpinned the low levels of prosecution and conviction. For one thing, not merely penetration (as in the Middle Ages) but emission also had by the close of the seventeenth century become necessary to constitute the act, something not easy to establish;[31] otherwise, it would be considered merely as an attempt. For another, the woman's consent (if she were not a child under the age of twelve, or if she were not a lady of standing) was in practice almost implied in the act. The burden of proof here was really on the prosecution, to disprove the presumption of consent. The kinds of evidence thought relevant to this task were physical injuries, immediate reporting of the attack to someone, speedy bringing of charges, *and* good previous character.

A virtual prerequisite for a rape conviction was a chaste victim. Characteristically, when it emerged in the 1791 trial of Robert Palmer that Palmer and the complainant, a fellow servant, had slept together consensually the previous night, Lord Kenyon observed that in general "it was expected that the person who complained of this offence, should produce an untainted and an unsullied character." Although he qualified this by noting that such a character was not strictly necessary, the prisoner was quickly acquitted.[32] If a prosecutrix had (or was generally believed to have had) a sexual history with anyone, a conviction was almost impossible to obtain. In two of the three rape trials at the Old Bailey in 1787 (selecting a year at random), the defense focused on the prosecutrix's "bad character" (i.e. sexual experience) and in both obtained quick acquittals; in the third case the victim was only seven years of age, and an acquittal was obtained on the more technical ground that evidence of penetration was lacking (although she had venereal disease).[33]

To establish resistance, which was almost always required for a successful prosecution (unless the victim was a child), demanded either direct witness of good repute, which was rarely available, or physical evidence. As prosecutrixes were not entitled to any examination by official persons, they had to furnish medical evidence themselves. If they failed to provide a surgeon's testimony of injuries, their case was almost invariably doomed.[34]

Nor did "reforms" in the trial process help women seeking to prosecute rapists; indeed, the reverse was more true. The most important "reform"

---

[31] The imposition of this new requirement, ironically, may have been fostered by the broader – and usually seen as enlightened – movement in the later seventeenth century to raise standards of proof, as with charges of treason and witchcraft.

[32] *Times*, 2 November 1791, p. 3. See the similar observations by Justice LeBlanc in the trial of Chapman, a police constable: *Times*, 19 September 1805, p. 3. The complainant in Chapman's case hadn't even slept with anyone; she had, however, worked as a servant in a house of ill fame, and "had acknowledged to one of the witnesses, that she had read books of a very vicious and profligate tendency, and the witness had frequently witnessed her using immodest language and actions."

[33] *OBSP*, 1786–87, #702 (Luston Vaughan) and #718 (William Wellen) (both on 12 September 1787); #890 (John Ince) (24 October 1787).

[34] See Simpson, op. cit., pp. 258–262.

in the late eighteenth and early nineteenth centuries was a growing judicial allowance of defense counsel, culminating in the 1836 Prisoner's Counsel Act establishing professional counsel as a right, and allowing counsel to directly address the jury. This of course afforded new assistance to those accused of rape, as of other serious crimes.[35] In rape cases particularly, the use of defense counsel had become common by the early nineteenth century, and they were much more capable than defendants alone of swaying jurors towards acquittal.[36] They could cite favorable precedents, cross-examine skillfully and aggressively, employ witnesses carefully, and, after 1836, address the jury; all these techniques could be used to powerfully attack the prosecutrix's credibility, which usually depended on her sexual character. The kind of gross slurs defendants had traditionally thrown upon prosecutrixes were now rephrased in more "respectable" language, professionally elaborated and driven home by barristers.[37] Indeed, part of the credit or blame for the intensified attention to the "character" of the prosecutrix which Anna Clark has pointed to in early nineteenth century trials likely should go to the expanding and assertive work of defense counsel. Their work reinforced the already very strong position of the defendant in rape trials. When a young woman brought a rape charge at the Old Bailey in 1798 against Abraham Ottey, a married man, his counsel called a long line of witnesses to establish her previous "loose" behavior; she did not even have a prosecuting counsel and could not make much of a legal case; Ottey was immediately acquitted.[38]

In these circumstances a rape conviction almost always required (in addition to some corroboration of the prosecutrix's story) either an encounter between strangers, in which the alleged victim was a highly respectable woman, usually of a higher social class, and the alleged perpetrator a lower-class man, more often than not on a deserted country path – or else violation of a child, which usually only came to light if the victim showed symptoms of venereal disease.[39] Almost all eighteenth-century rape convictions appear to have involved one of these two categories of victim. When in the spring of 1792 a Cambridgeshire laborer attacked from behind a hedge a "young Lady of respectable connections," only fourteen years of age, who was on a visit to her

[35]On this rise, see John Beattie, "Scales of Justice: Defense Counsel and the English Criminal Trial in the Eighteenth and Nineteenth Centuries," *Law and History Review* 9 (1991), 221–267; David J.A. Cairns, *Advocacy and the Making of the Adversarial Criminal Trial 1800–1865* (Oxford, 1999).

[36]On the aggressiveness of early defense counsel, see Allyson May, "The Old Bailey Bar, 1783–1834" (Ph.D. thesis, University of Toronto, 1997).

[37]In one summer, the *Times* twice described prosecutrixes undergoing "severe cross-examinations" and a barrage of defense witnesses on their sexual history: *Times*, 25 July 1831, p. 4 (*R.v. Reynolds et al.*) and 20 August 1831, p. 4 (*R.v. Garner and Davenport*). [One case ended in acquittals, the other in convictions.]

[38]*Times*, 25 May 1798, p. 3.

[39]For example, see *R.v. Murphy: Times*, 20 September 1794, p. 3; *R.v. Scott: Times*, 20 September 1796, p. 3.

grandmother, the prosecuting counsel called corroborating witnesses, while the defendant had no counsel. He was quickly convicted and hanged.[40] The other "classic" type of rape had a child victim. A typical successful prosecution of this sort was that of David Scott at the Old Bailey in 1796. His eleven-year-old victim, daughter of an innkeeper of good repute, was very ill with venereal disease (apparently syphilis), yet was able to give a clear and convincing account of her rape; Scott (also syphilitic) was unable to produce an alibi or impugn her character. Justice Rooke observed that "the only circumstance that could invalid [sic] the girl's testimony was that of her not immediately telling her parents what had happened to her. If she had been a full-grown woman, that omission would certainly have been favourable to the prisoner; but it was easy to account for it in a child."[41] "Adult" women of the working or even middle classes (a category that could start at 12, certainly 14) had little legal recourse, beyond the possibility of being "bought off" not to cause trouble. On occasion a married woman of good repute could successfully prosecute, but, as we have seen, single women (seen generally as very sexual beings, at least as dangerous to men as men were to them) were left by the law on their own to negotiate the world of sexual danger.

While violence between men was already being dealt with somewhat more seriously in the courts by the early years of the nineteenth century, there was little sign as yet of any significant change in attitudes to sexual violence against women. For some years into the nineteenth century the level of prosecutions and convictions for sexual assault remained low.[42] Even the combination of a victim whose screams had been heard, a surgeon's evidence of violence inflicted on her, her almost-immediate complaint, and a confession by the defendant might still fail to produce a conviction, as happened with Charles Dixon at Durham in 1821. His victim, a 19-year-old servant in a publichouse, was ordered by her mistress to go on an errand with Dixon, in the course of which, despite her repeated screams, he raped her. She reported this the next day to her mistress; Dixon, when apprehended after an attempt to escape, told the constable "I know I have been in fault, but I hope to get off with two years' imprisonment." At trial he offered no defense, but Justice Bayley stepped in to virtually offer one for him, casting some question over the victim's character (though there had been no testimony against it) and reminding the jury that a man's life was at stake. The jury returned an acquittal, after which the judge conceded that "it is likely that her evidence was quite true."[43]

[40] *R.v. Crosse: Times,* 28 July 1792, p. 3.

[41] *Times,* 20 September 1796, p. 3.

[42] For example, at the Old Bailey the twenty-five years 1800–24 produced only fifty-eight rape prosecutions; of these only ten issued in convictions – although this was indeed a higher conviction rate than had prevailed earlier, suggesting the beginnings of a change in treatment [Simpson, op. cit., table 2, pp. 813–814].

[43] *Times,* 27 August 1821, p. 3.

Yet by this time new sentiments were emerging in the courtroom. In 1829, the Radical *Morning Chronicle* strongly objected to what it saw as an increasing victimization of men. Complaining that growing numbers of men, though eventually acquitted, had to first undergo the humiliation of being charged and often jailed awaiting trial, it went on to declare that "Any girl who wishes a husband, and has no other means of obtaining one, is kindly invited to seek the aid of a Court of Justice, which will soften his heart by the fear of the rope which it suspends over his head."[44] The *Morning Chronicle*'s complaints suggest that the prevalent disregard of sexual violence may have begun to meet a new readiness by magistrates and judges, and other influential persons, to recognize this as an injustice needing to be addressed.[45]

In the 1820s the number of prosecutions for rape and also for lesser sexual offenses against women began to rise, increasingly so as the decade went on.[46] These trends suggest that magistrates and judges were shedding their indulgence towards sexual violence. The encouragement of private settlements between the parties was now increasingly frowned upon, and becoming associated with "less civilized" countries like Ireland. One provincial newspaper complained in 1829 of the same practice of which the *Morning Chronicle* had, but with a somewhat different take. Noting that in Ireland rape defendants were often allowed to escape conviction by marrying their accusers, it, like the *Chronicle*, objected that this practice "encourages depraved women to make false charges against men with whom they have been viciously familiar." Yet the paper's chief complaint against the practice was that it undermined the dignity of the law and its necessary deterrent power. Having just reported a rape trial in its county, fortunately from its view not settled, it emphasized that "it is a mistaken notion that the punishment of crimes is in the nature

---

[44] *The Morning Chronicle* (London), 31 July 1829, p. 2. Similar complaints appeared in this paper on a variety of occasions in this period (in 1829, for example, on 9 Jan., 7 Dec. and 29 Dec.).

[45] A sign of the shift in elite and "respectable" attitudes may have been the sharp increase in coverage by the *Times* of rape and attempted rape trials, from thirty in 1810–19 to eighty-eight in 1820–29 (and to 104 in the next decade).

[46] Rape prosecutions at the Old Bailey jumped from fourteen in 1820–24 to twenty-four in 1825–29, and convictions from two to five. In the single year 1830 there were nine prosecutions, although all ended in acquittal. [Simpson, op. cit., 813–814] Anna Clark noted this change setting in a bit earlier on the Northeast Circuit, where "54% of accusations of rape on females over the age of twelve resulted in trial between 1800 and 1829, as opposed to 33% between 1770 and 1799." [op. cit., p. 60] Nationally, rape prosecutions rose from about eighteen per year 1811–20 to about twenty-six a year 1821–28, and thirty-six and one-half a year 1829–30. [Simpson, op. cit., table 4, p. 818] Lesser sexual offenses against females – from the most serious, assault with intent to commit rape, to the least, indecent assault – from the later 1820s were being prosecuted more often in higher courts, and drawing sentences ranging from two months' to three years' imprisonment. [See Simpson, op. cit., pp. 277 and 826 and A. Clark, op. cit., p. 60.]

of redress for the wrongs of the individual – it is a debt due to public justice, which, however forgiving the sufferer may be, the offender is bound to pay."[47]

Yet at the same time, public revulsion against the death penalty for crimes other than murder was also rising, making juries even more reluctant to convict on the capital charge of rape.[48] Thus, while rape prosecutions were on the rise, convictions did not rise in proportion, and executions even fell, the last one taking place in 1836. Once, however, it was noticed that executions had ceased, the conviction rate began to rise, and when the death penalty for rape was itself abolished in favor of transportation for life in 1841, this rise accelerated, and again when that mandatory sentence was removed in 1845, the rate continuing to increase through most of the century.[49]

---

[47] *Monmouthshire Merlin*, 5 September 1829, p. 2. However, less drastic forms of settlement were still practiced in England. That year at the Old Bailey a man charged with "assaulting with a felonious intent" the wife of his employee, on the suggestion of the judge, "took a verdict of acquittal" upon paying the prosecutrix's costs and entering into his own recognizance to keep the peace towards her. [*Times*, 10 June 1829, p. 3.]
[48] Anna Clark has plausibly suggested that many of the increasing number of indecent assault prosecutions "were actually attempted rapes or rapes tried on lesser charges to increase the likelihood of conviction." [op. cit., p. 60]
[49] Rape convictions rose from six in 1837 and seven in 1838 to seventeen in 1839 and eighteen in 1840. [*Parliamentary Debates*, 3rd. S, 57 (1841), 52–53.] Lord John Russell argued successfully for repeal of the death penalty by pointing out the depressing effect executions had had on conviction rates. Committals to trial in England and Wales for sexual assault rose from an annual average of 189 for the years 1836–40 to 254 for 1841–45, 397 for 1861–65, 647 for 1881–85, 944 for 1886–90, diminishing somewhat after 1890, then rising again after 1906 and jumping to 1,246 for 1911–14. [Gatrell, "The Decline of Theft and Violence in Victorian and Edwardian England," in *Crime and the Law: The social history of crime in Western Europe since 1500*, ed. V.A.C. Gatrell, Bruce Lenman and Geoffrey Parker (London, 1980), p. 288 (from annual Judicial Statistics).] Even as prosecutions rose, the conviction rate also rose, that for rape (always the lowest of the sexual offenses) from 10% in 1836–40 to 33% in 1841–45, and then over 50% (through 1845: Clark, op. cit., p. 60, from annual Judicial Statistics). At the Old Bailey a sample of two years of every decade done by Judith Travers gave an average conviction rate for rape 1842–95 of 51%. [Judith Travers, "Cultural Meanings and Representations of Violence Against Women, London 1790–1895," (Ph.D. dissertation, State University of New York, Stony Brook, 1993), p. 153.] Travers found this quite low, certainly lower than the rate for all felonies, but since the rate for the 1840s was still well below that, the rate for the second half of the Victorian period would have to be higher than 51%. My reading of hundreds of trials around the country suggests a conviction rate close to 60% (far higher than today's UK conviction rate for rape {see Home Office Research Unit, *A Question of Evidence? Investigating and Prosecuting Rape in the 1990s* [London, 1999]}). As the number of prosecutions has risen, the conviction rate has fallen, from 24% in 1985 to 9% in 1997; Jennifer Temkin, "Prosecuting and Defending Rape: Perspectives from the Bar," *Journal of Law and Society* 27 (2000), 219–248. Moreover, combined with the rise in prosecutions, it reveals a striking increase in total convictions for rape over the century. My own sample of every tenth year at the Old Bailey shows a sharp upward

Such quantitative changes strongly suggest that sexual assault came to be taken more seriously by the courts (particularly as there is no reason to believe the Victorians witnessed an eruption of actual sexual assault). Yet statistics can only take us so far: if they are no reliable guide to the real numbers of sexual offenses, nor even their trends, neither do official statistics tell us directly of the meanings attached by participants and observers to these proceedings, verdicts, and judgments. One "meaning" was clearly drawn by the *Times*. In 1866 the paper, which had for years been urging stronger punishment of violent crimes, declared its concern that, at least in the case of rape, the pendulum had swung too far. It called attention to "a class of cases which become far too common" in which when men have been accused by women of "improper conduct" and in which juries "have shown a most unreasonable disposition to disregard improbabilities in the circumstances of the charge, and to interpret facts in the light most adverse to the person accused." It sympathized with the underlying "feeling for the weaker party," but pointed to the "danger lest the position [that once existed] should be reversed, and that women have at their absolute disposal the reputation of any man whom they may happen to meet." It concluded with the hope that "juries will cease to exhibit such an obvious bias in favour of feminine testimony."[50]

Whether or not the *Times* was accurate (the outcome in the case it cited does in fact appear unfair to the male defendant), its editorial suggests a major change in jury behavior had taken place.[51] An exploration of what was said in court and out about these offenses – which has been little attended to as yet by scholars – may reveal the contours and texture of such changes. This will be the task of the rest of this chapter.

The beginning of the rise in prosecutions in the 1820s was accompanied by changes in both the law of rape itself and the treatment of rape and rape charges in public discourse and in the legal process. Most important, perhaps, the law was being understood and applied in new ways in courtrooms, marking – and shaping – significant changes in Victorian conceptions of sexual violence. While effecting changes in legal interpretation, judges, magistrates, and other participants in trials of sexual assault were, if gradually

spike after the furor about child sexual victimization that led to the 1885 Criminal Law Amendment Act: in the single year 1890 sixty-one rape trials (more than the total there for the entire first quarter of the century) produced forty convictions, a rate of almost two-thirds (after this, prosecutions and conviction rates both eased; in 1900 thirty-one prosecutions yielded seventeen rape convictions, still a rate of almost 55%).

[50] *Times*, 16 July 1866, p. 9.

[51] It cited the case of *R.v. Toomey*, in which a man was convicted and sentenced to fifteen years' penal servitude after a household employee who had voluntarily stayed with him and had sexual relations several times over a period of some days eventually brought a rape charge. After much public protest nine months into his sentence he was released.

and inconsistently, setting out new expectations for men in their dealings with women (as we have seen in regard to men's dealings with other men). Changes were taking place in the definition of the offense and the kinds of evidence needed to legally establish it.[52] Indeed, by their rulings on definition, charges, and admissible evidence nineteenth-century judges (whether or not they had this end specifically in mind) made it less onerous than it had ever been to prosecute and convict for rape.

From one angle, this is surprising: now that defendants were typically employing professional counsel in such trials one would expect even fewer prosecutions to be won, and thus ultimately fewer brought. The defense side, as we have noted, was indeed strengthened in the late eighteenth and early nineteenth centuries. Yet as the Victorian era approached, just the opposite began to occur. Try as they might, even aggressive defense counsel could not prevent three traditionally powerful bulwarks against conviction from eroding or disappearing altogether, which suggests the force of new pressures rising against rape defendants.

First in time was a change in the definition of the act: the requirement of proof of emission of semen was abandoned, and the act came to be fully constituted by penetration of the penis into the vagina alone. Next, secondary charges came to be allowed to be brought together with the primary one of rape. Third, the legal relevance of the prosecutrix's previous behavior was narrowed, and with that the requirement of intense and sustained resistance on the prosecutrix's part eased; in the long run, the very notion of consent moved from the negative one marked by the lack of the strongest possible resistance towards the more positive one of some more explicit assent. The formal term "without her consent" gained prominence as against the term that had been more commonly used, "against her will"[53] – at first glance little more than a technical change, but one fraught with larger questions of the nature of individual liberty and the appropriate relation between the sexes. Along with these changes went a more expansive view of the kind of women who could qualify as rape victims, and the kind, therefore, about whom men were put on notice to constrain their behavior.

[52] There is evidence in the early nineteenth century of an increasing willingness of judges in rape trials to allow the testimony of children, without which a conviction would be most difficult. In 1823, for example, Daniel James was found guilty of raping a child after Justice Bayley had ordered his trial postponed for over half a year to allow time for the girl to be instructed "in the duties and sanctions of religion," so that she could testify against him, as she did when his trial was finally held. *Times*, 3 April 1823, p. 3.

[53] As the leading jurist James Fitzjames Stephen instructed a jury in 1888, in the definitions of rape from leading cases that had been cited during the trial, "the words 'against her will' must be taken to mean no more than 'without her consent'. . . ." He went on to explicitly define rape as "having connexion with a woman without her consent." [*R.v. Clarence*: 16 Cox C.C. 571.]

By the opening of the 1830s the offense had been redefined to no longer require emission. It became necessary for the first time to show only some degree of penetration to establish the physical basis for a prosecution. First stated in a 1777 case, though not taken up often in practice for several decades thereafter, this principle came into its own in the 1820s. In the 1823 trial at York of John Burrows Justice Holroyd gave a clear ruling that proof of emission was unnecessary, a ruling upheld by the Twelve Judges (all the High Court judges, meeting together), establishing it as case law.[54] It was then ratified by legislation in 1828[55] and confirmed again by that body (now numbering fifteen) four years later, this time citing the new legislation.[56] Differences of legal opinion continued, chiefly with child victims, over precisely how far "penetration" had to go: some conservative judges dragged their feet. Baron Gurney, for instance, declared, in the same year, 1832, in which the Fifteen Judges were confirming the sufficiency of penetration alone, that "if the hymen is not ruptured, the offense [of rape] is not complete."[57] However, this ruling was countered by at least two opposite ones, by Justice Williams at Gloucester in 1839 and by Baron Parke at Worcester in 1844.[58]

The leading text on medical jurisprudence, which had noted in 1844 that judges still did not speak with one voice on this, could observe eight years later that such differences had ended: "it is now . . . an admitted principle that a sufficient degree of penetration to constitute rape in law may take place without necessarily rupturing the hymen."[59] By this point a convicted offender was no longer liable either to death or to transportation for life; this easing of punishment no doubt greatly assisted the establishment of such a broadened interpretation.

[54] See the *Times*, 21 July 1823, p. 3 on the trial, and Russell & Ryan, *Crown Cases Reserved . . .* (London, 1825), pp. 519–520 on the Twelve Judges' ruling. [See also Simpson, op. cit., p. 179; V.A.C. Gatrell, *The Hanging Tree: Execution and the English People, 1770–1868* (Oxford, 1994), p. 472.] The fact that the victim was the daughter of a gentlemen no doubt encouraged judicial sympathy for the prosecution.

[55] 9 Geo. IV c.31, s.18 [Lord Landsdowne's Act].

[56] *R.v. Coulthart*, 168 *ER* 1044 [Carlisle Spring Assizes, 1832].

[57] *R.v. Gammon*, 172 *ER* 994 [Hereford Assizes, 7 August 1832]. In this case, however, the hymen was ruptured (the victim was a child) and the man convicted. Gurney admitted that "there have been cases in which a less degree of penetration has been held to be sufficient; but I have always doubted the authority of those cases. . . ."

[58] *R.v. Jordan* (1839), Carrington & Payne v.9, 118; *R.v. Lines* (1844), in Carrington & Kirwaun, *Reports of cases argued and ruled at nisi prius in the courts of queen's bench, common pleas and exchequer 1843–53* (London, 1845–55), 1:393. In the former case, the victim was a child and the defendant was convicted; in the latter case, the victim was not as young and against Parke's instructions the jury acquitted.

[59] A.V. Taylor, *Elements of Medical Jurisprudence*, 4th ed. (1852), p. 578, and 3rd. ed. (1844), p. 576, quoted in Louise Jackson, *Child Sexual Abuse in Victorian England* (London and New York, 2000), pp. 74–75. Jackson's book has much clarified the role of medical men in this and related issues of sexual abuse.

This change in the law had a double significance: practically, it made prosecution easier while, ideologically, it more clearly defined the offense as one of violence rather than of illegitimate taking, a crime against a woman as a person rather than as the property of her husband or father. Rather than a trespass on another man's property rights, rape was becoming seen as a violation of a woman's sphere of privacy and autonomy, an offense primarily against the woman and not her male protectors. It declared a woman's private parts a place where a man not her husband could not put his body, without permission, without the most severe sanctions.

This "progressive" implication of the 1828 provision has been minimized by the argument that it was not a desire to convict rapists but, as Anna Clark put it, "moral objections to women recounting explicit details in open court [which] seem to have provided the main impetus behind the 1828 legislation."[60] However, while one can readily grant that the rise of sexual prudery and an ideology of female purity were operating here, to see the change *only* as "silencing" women and not as at the same time stigmatizing and criminalizing their assailants, seems tendentious. For, as we have seen, the prosecution of sexual assault was rising, markedly so by the last quarter of the century (aided by the no-doubt puritanical Criminal Law Amendment Act of 1885, which among other things made it easier to prosecute molesters of young girls).

Yet before that point other legal developments also came into play. A second change was procedural. Before the 1830s, the crimes of rape and sodomy were unusual in that no lesser charges could be brought together with the full charge; thus, juries were faced with the stark choice of conviction on a capital charge or acquittal. No doubt many men owed their acquittals to the natural, and probably strengthening reluctance of jurors to condemn to hanging. The 1837 Act already discussed made a difference here also, as it now allowed secondary charges to be brought together with the primary one of rape (or sodomy), widening the jury's options. It encouraged more convictions at assizes of at least some crime, and at least some degree of punishment for sexual offenders.[61] A jury unwilling to convict of rape could

---

[60] Clark, op. cit., p. 63.

[61] 1 Vict. c.85, s.11 (1837) In 1838, Baron Gurney reminded a jury in a rape trial in which there was no evidence of resistance that before this statute "I should have had to direct you to find a general verdict of acquittal, but by that statute it is enacted that in any case of felony, when the criminal charge shall include an assault upon the person, it shall be lawful for the jury to find a verdict of guilty of assault against the person indicted, if the evidence shall warrant such finding." In this case Gurney practically demanded an assault conviction ("although in point of law this is not a rape, I consider it one of the most abominable offenses that can be committed.") The man was convicted of assault and sentenced to three years hard labor (a very harsh sentence for mere assault). Gurney reserved the point for the Fifteen Judges, who upheld it. [See *R.v. Saunders* (1838), 173 *ER* 488.] Even before the 1837 Act, judges

far more easily now be brought to convict at least of an assault. Though the penalties were far less, many convicted of assault would very likely have previously been simply acquitted.

A third change – less precise than these definitional and procedural modifications, not formalized by statute as they were, but ultimately perhaps even more important – was a narrowing of the notion of a woman's consent to sexual relations.[62] One indirect but important way the notion of consent narrowed was by the ending of judicial acceptance of the settlement of sexual assault charges before trial with a monetary payment, or even with marriage. This once-common practice had more or less ceased (in cases that had already come to judicial attention) by mid-century; implied in the practice was the notion that consent could be given retrospectively.

More directly, the restriction of consent proceeded by two paths. One course was to cease to take a complainant's possible previous unchasteness as virtually implying consent. Another, taking place somewhat later, was to take a less demanding view of the extent of resistance the victim had to have put up to establish lack of consent. Both of these legal journeys were fostered by the heightened importance, in the "Victorian" climate of opinion taking shape, of a woman's "character." This attention affected rape prosecutions in two opposite ways. On the one hand, as feminist historians have pointed out, such a focus (by no means absent even today) tended to put rape prosecutrixes themselves "on trial" perhaps even more than they had already been, as defense counsel continued, with more professional skill, the usual practice of smearing the complainant. It also denied women agency, and tended to "silence" them in court, since they were supposed to be either too ignorant or too modest to talk freely and explicitly about sexual matters in public.[63]

However, this preoccupation with "character" had opposite effects that were equally significant. If a woman could lay reasonable claim to chastity, she now possessed a new weapon to employ against male domination and a new way to use the law, while placing male defendants in a more difficult position. If a prosecutrix could successfully rebuff efforts at impugning her character, she now, even if poor, even if unmarried and over twelve years of age, stood in a stronger position in court than in earlier times. The new higher valuation of female character weakened class barriers, as well as enhancing the claims of women of all ages to protection against bodily assault. The "weaker"

were beginning to intervene this way. In *R.v. Smith* (1835), for instance, the judge directed that a man acquitted of rape be freshly tried on the lesser charge of sexual assault. [*Times*, 15 April 1835, p. 4.]

[62] Beginning in 1835, petitioners to the London Foundling Hospital were asked if they had consented to sexual connection; if they replied in the negative, their infant was more likely to be taken in, suggesting a greater sympathy for rape victims. [Clark, op. cit., p. 80.]

[63] Ibid., p. 58 on.

and de-sexualized image of women that went along with this "Victorianism" also reduced the requirements for a successful prosecution: more delicate creatures could not be expected to resist with great force; even more, their very willingness to engage in sex came to be more questionable, requiring greater "proof" on the part of the defense; and the typical probing by defense counsel into their sexual past was coming to upset judges and jurors, as an assault in itself, one on their social reputation, and which could raise sentiments of protectiveness among men imbued with the new gender ideals. Meanwhile, as more and more ordinary women laid claim to "respectability," men's sexual freedom narrowed; more and more women became "out of bounds" for sexual aggression.[64] Even more directly, the new importance of character (in which sexual restraint was becoming ever more essential, even to some degree for men) could rebound upon male defendants: the advance (if by no means triumph) of a single moral standard meant that the past of the defendant – if he had a reputation as a rake, or other kinds of bad character – could now come back to haunt him, and weaken his case.[65] In general, the "character" discourse so popular in the nineteenth century enhanced, for women who could meet its heightened behaviorial demands, their moral authority as against men, making women's evidence count for somewhat more, and men's (against women's) for somewhat less than previously.

Without doubt, greater sympathy for women in court had to work with an also intensified distaste for any sign of "coarseness" in an unmarried female. The public-house servant giving evidence of her rape in 1821 drew frowns by "stating," as a reporter put it, "the gross expression frequently in the mouths of sailors which [the defendant] applied to her" during the rape. In acknowledging the likelihood that her evidence had been true, Justice Bayley thought "it would [have] appear[ed] better if she had declined to repeat the coarse sailor terms."[66]

Still, if the prosecutrix conformed to the new rules of decorum and watched her tongue, her chances of winning her case were improving. As early as 1811, a sixteen-year-old servant girl, Harriet Halliday, helped set a legal precedent in winning a rape prosecution against one William Hodgson.[67] The defendant, it was claimed, had accosted and dragged her into a stable on a country road as she was returning to her master's house from a visit to her parents. Halliday struggled hard, "but at last fainted away." When her cries were heard, he threatened to kill her if she did not hold her "damned tongue."

---

[64]This may have had something to do with the flourishing of prostitution in this age, a development often noted by contemporary observers, British and foreign.

[65]As was discovered by Thomas Howard when he was tried for rape at the Old Bailey in 1867: despite being defended by two of the leading barristers of the time, his occupation as a pimp destroyed his credibility, and he was sentenced to fifteen years' penal servitude [*Times*, 20 December 1867, p. 9].

[66]*R.v. Dixon: Times*, 27 August 1821, p. 3.

[67]Russell & Ryan C.C. 211; *Times*, 14 August 1811, p. 3 & 15 August 1811, p. 3.

However, the overhearer of the rape was a most respectable witness, a surgeon, who after hearing shrieks from a stable at the back of his house, had gone out and found the girl "in a state of great distress," her shawl bloody, her hat and gown-front torn. The surgeon then financed the prosecution.[68]

Hodgson's counsel was aggressive.[69] First he called up a former mistress of Halliday's and established that she had discharged the girl after only two weeks; but when he then asked her why (to bring into evidence some discreditable behavior, hopefully sexual), Baron Wood barred the witness from answering it. Defense counsel then asked Halliday whether it had been the first time she had been connected with a man, but again the judge objected that it was an improper question, which she "had no occasion to answer." The next defense move (a most typical one) was to call two young men (Hodgson's friends) to impeach her testimony, swearing that they saw them together at that spot, with no sign of resistance on her part. The jury retired a long time and returned with a verdict of guilty, with a recommendation to mercy. As soon as the death penalty was pronounced, petitions for a mitigation to transportation were presented to the judge by the prosecutrix, her master, and the witnesses who had given evidence for the prosecution. But, despite "much discussion" in the county Wood was unbending: since this was the last case on the docket, he first dealt with seven other men convicted of property offenses by strongly suggesting that a commutation for them would be forthcoming from the Crown; he then turned to Hodgson, and in a fierce denunciation of his atrocious crime held out no hope for him. This produced great surprise among both lawyers and laymen, and demands for reconsideration immediately followed.[70] However, the Twelve Judges (to whom Wood had referred the case, after defense objections to his rulings) unanimously backed him up and declared that in cases of rape the character of the prosecutrix as to general chastity might only be impeached by general, not particular, evidence.[71] This circumscription on defense probings of the prosecutrix's life was only a partial one: it ruled out only references to possible

---

[68] Such interventions by respectable and affluent persons were not unusual in cases that came to trial; no doubt very many similar rape victims found no such benefactor, and never got to court, or even perhaps to a magistrate.

[69] Hodgson's social position is unclear, but it seems to have been higher than his victim's, in that he could engage counsel without a benefactor being mentioned. Even at this early date, in rape trials defense counsel was more the rule than the exception.

[70] "It was a decision," Sir Frederick Pollock observed years later, "that gave dissatisfaction to the whole Bar," for the girl's low moral character was apparent; for himself, he had no doubt that she had consented. [Royal Commission on the Criminal Law; 2nd report (P. P. 1836, xxxvi), 4–5), quoted in Gatrell, op. cit., 472n.]

[71] Russell & Ryan, C.C. 211. While the challenge to the new legal principle was crushed, efforts in favor of the convicted man did better: a year and a half later, he was pardoned on condition of serving in the army [*Times*, 10 May 1813, p. 3].

specific instances of sexual relations; the defendant and his witnesses might still, as one legal authority put it, "give evidence that the woman bore a notorious bad character for want of chastity and common decency."[72]

Of course because in this case the complainant was supported energetically by a witness of high status and had an unusually sympathetic judge, she fared better in court than most others in her situation. Baron Wood, a devout man, seems to have been particularly offended by the mistreatment of women. In another rape trial in 1821 he sharply stopped the attempt to question the complainant on her sexual history, causing the defense counsel to object that "this is the first time I was ever checked in this manner. At the Queen's trial [Queen Caroline], the questions were put much stronger." To this the judge only responded that "You are proceeding very wildly." Later, addressing the jury, Wood was more explicit: "suppose [he suggested] she did sleep with [another man than the defendant]; that has nothing to do with the prisoner at the bar; she has no right to be ravished on that account." He concluded that "such questions shall not be put to a witness. I will not suffer a witness to disgrace herself." He did not like, he went on, "the mode of hunting and terrifying witnesses when put into the box, and the whole history of their lives raked up, as a set-off against their evidence; for who amongst us, at one time or other, has not committed one foible."[73] The trial ended in a guilty verdict, though the man was thereafter pardoned by the Home Secretary.

Since Wood seems to have been thought of as something of a zealot on this issue, it is not surprising that other judges did not always follow the principle he set in *Hodgson*.[74] Feeling less strongly about the protection of women's reputations, other judges at times questioned or disregarded the *Hodgson* rule, but, even if personally unhappy with it, they nonetheless increasingly followed it. In George Gregory's 1827 trial, Justice Park stopped defense counsel from questioning the complainant "as to her former course of life."

[72]John Mews, *A Digest of Cases* (London, 1884), p. 522.

[73]*R.v. Hale, Star,* 27 August 1821.

[74]In Edward Frith's 1817 trial before Justice Dallas for raping a fourteen-year-old servant of his father's, his two counsel called (with no comment from the judge), among other witnesses seeking to "impeach the credit of the girl, and to show her of loose behaviour," a former servant in that household who "stated that the prosecutor at that time had frequently come unbidden to his bed." Such evidence was less persuasive now, however: the jury made clear its belief in his guilt, but reluctantly acquitted Frith in the belief that his attempt had not been completed. He was detained for a second trial on the charge of attempted rape [*Times,* 8 August 1817, p. 3]. As late as 1843 (in *R.v. Tissington*), Lord Chief Baron Abinger first cited Wood's decision in *R.v. Hale* (1821) in order to block evidence about the prosecutrix's previous behavior, but after defense counsel's strenuous complaints he withdrew his objection and allowed such evidence to be introduced, although then allowing the prosecution to call witnesses to rebut the defense witnesses. The defendant was nonetheless convicted [1 Cox C.C. 48].

He admitted "that for his own part he dissented from the doctrine thus laid down, but still they [the Twelve Judges] had been unanimously of that opinion."[75] In 1817 the rule in *Hodgson* had been reaffirmed and extended by Justice Holroyd to apply not only to rape but also to trials for *attempted rape*.[76] In an 1827 attempted rape trial Baron Vaughan observed that "it was a hardship in cases of this kind peculiarly afflicting to the sex, and certainly most distressing, that they had not only to undergo the wounded feelings and sufferings occasioned by the injuries they had received, but were obliged to come before strangers, and before a male audience, to disclose the details of the case." He characterized the case as one of "insulted virtue"; not surprisingly, a conviction was produced.[77]

In 1825, in the trial of John Pattern of Birmingham, Justice Holroyd, following his ruling eight years before, told the jury that even if they thought the prosecutrix, Ann Atkins, unchaste (the chief thrust of the defense), it would make no difference to their task; chaste or unchaste, a woman could not be taken against her will without the fullest legal liability.[78] After Pattern's conviction, a massive effort was mounted to persuade the Home Secretary to spare his life, including several petitions, letters from very influential men in the town, and many efforts to blacken the character of his accuser, claiming she accepted (indeed, negotiated) money from Pattern after the charge had been lodged with the local magistrate, and citing evidence no longer admissible at trial (for example, sworn statements by various men that they had known her sexually).[79] These efforts won a week's reprieve, to give time for an official sent down from Whitehall to re-examine the chief witnesses, including Ann Atkins. Yet the result was unchanged (particularly after the claim of her taking money, rather than weakening the charge as it usually had in the past, now was cited by Holroyd to Home Secretary Peel as "an attempt to suppress the evidence by compounding the felony"). Peel agreed with Holroyd about both the character issue and the offering of money and observed to his clerk that "if all that be alleged against her character be true, still if violence was offered to her under all the circumstances proved at the trial, and as I think confirmed by the subsequent inquiries, I am decidedly of opinion that the law ought to take its course."[80] It did, and Pattern was hanged.

---

[75] *Times*, 19 April 1827, p. 3.

[76] *R.v. Clarke* (1817): Mews, op. cit., p. 522 (2 Stark. 241): "Under an indictment for an assault to commit a rape, the defense may impeach the prosecutor's character for chastity by general, but not by particular, evidence."

[77] *R.v. Gyle*, *Times*, 5 September 1827, p. 2.

[78] *Warwick General Advertiser*, 13 August 1825.

[79] This effort included repeated attempts to get the prosecutrix herself to request mercy (a common practice in these efforts), including apparently the proffer of money and also, when that was turned down, threats.

[80] HO47/68. Peel also observed to his clerk that "I attach less importance to the public opinion and feeling in the town with respect to the character of the parties and

The line drawn in regard to the rape complainant's character between allowing general and disallowing particular evidence still gave the defense some room for maneuver. When John Noden went on trial in 1829, his counsel (besides arguing that the act had never been completed) managed, without ever clearly crossing the legal line, to indirectly probe damagingly the woman's past behavior with men. However, although Baron Vaughan permitted this tactic, in his charge to the jury he made clear his disapproval of this line, and summed up strongly against Noden, who was found guilty.[81] As with Pattern and some others, the conviction set off a substantial campaign for a reprieve, focusing on demolishing the complainant's reputation and credibility. It included no fewer than eight affidavits claiming sexual relations with the woman, as well as several from acknowledged former sweethearts. It also, unlike Pattern, included an apparently unpressured plea for mercy from the complainant herself.[82] Noden was spared the gallows but sent to a penal hulk in Bermuda for twenty years.

A similar intense effort failed to save William Reynolds and William Marshall. Charged with a joint rape on a Nottinghamshire country lane in 1831, they were convicted even though Justice Littledale allowed the defense counsel to ask her about previous sexual encounters with others, and some witnesses to be called to allege (against her denials) having previously had consensual sex with the woman. After conviction, with "public feeling . . . much excited," as one petitioner put it, letters asking for a reprieve hammered on the theme of her previous promiscuous behavior but to no avail: although the jury had recommended mercy for them on account of youth (one was eighteen), Lord Melbourne let both men hang.[83] Five years later another joint rape, this time of an old woman, produced at Durham another conviction, despite the prosecutrix's admission to previously having consensual sexual relations with one of the men. The two men were reprieved, perhaps because of her admission; perhaps simply because hanging for rape was no longer acceptable to the public.[84]

Even after convictions for offenses less than rape, the prosecutrix's character would often be subject to further attacks, particularly when the convict was of some status. When James Field, a former naval petty officer, was found guilty in 1839 at Norfolk Quarter Sessions of attempted rape and sentenced

---

guilt of the accused, than to the opinion which Stafford [his investigator] himself has formed; but the public opinion and feeling are not to be disregarded. Stafford I dare say heard something on that head while he was at Birmingham."

[81] With a recommendation to mercy, as was usual when men were convicted of raping women other than children.

[82] For a thorough and insightful exploration of this case, and the events leading up to it, see V.A.C. Gatrell, op. cit., ch. 17. Additional information can be obtained in the lengthy file on Noden in HO47/75.

[83] *Times*, 25 July 1831, p. 4; HO17/3 (Aq 1).

[84] *R.v. Urwin and Smith:* HO17/38 (Ew 36); *Durham Chronicle* 18 March 1836, p. 2.

to twelve months' imprisonment, his friends made strong efforts to reduce the sentence. A petition with about a hundred signatures from "respectable" men of his town, from lawyer and surgeon to butcher and baker, did not deny the assault, but made two claims – that as he had always conducted himself correctly "nothing but intoxication at the time could have induced him to be guilty of an offense of that nature," and that "since his trial it has been understood that the young female is a person of bad character" (but failed to support this charge with specific evidence). The chairman of the Norfolk Quarter Sessions began his reply to the Home Secretary's subsequent inquiry by observing that "nothing transpired [against the sixteen-year-old prosecutrix's character] at the trial, where her demeanor was modest and correct." The assault itself "was very brutal . . . carried to the utmost possible point, without actual violence, from which the poor girl was only saved by the approach of a carriage. It appeared probable that the man's passions had been excited by liquor, but he was by no means so unconscious, as not to be quite aware of the consequences of discovery, as upon learning the approach of the carriage he got off her body, exclaiming with an oath 'I cannot do it now.' The Bench, feeling it their duty to protect poor females from assaults of this description, and of which they do not consider excitement from liquor to be any justification, either as it respects the public or the individual, thought it their duty to pass the sentence" being appealed against. Home Secretary Lord Normanby did not interfere.[85]

Inventive defense counsel managed for a while to restore one avenue by which to discuss a woman's past sexual history – luring her under oath into a specific denial of sex with other men. In *R.v. Robins* (1843), even though the prosecutrix was the thirteen-year-old daughter of the defendant, this succeeded. Chief Justice Coleridge, overruling prosecution objections that called upon *Hodgson*, declared that once the prosecutrix, on cross-examination, had denied that she had had connection with other men than the prisoner, those men might be called to contradict her. They were, and deposed to "the grossest acts of lewdness and profligacy" by her, resulting in a speedy acquittal.[86] For years, if the prosecutrix was unwise enough to say anything to such questions, this defense option continued, but under growing challenge.

By the early 1870s this issue was settled. At Liverpool Assizes in 1870 Justice Willes sharply refused (repeating the similar refusal of Baron Martin in an earlier trial for the same offence) to allow evidence to be admitted contradicting a denial of previous sexual relations with men other than the defendant.[87] The official overruling of *Robins* came the next year. An 1871

---

[85] HO18/1 (22).
[86] *West of England Conservative*, 9 August 1843, p. 3; *Times*, 10 August 1843, p. 7; Mews, op. cit., p. 523 [2 M & Rob. 512]. Coleridge's summation, in eighteenth-century fashion, was confined to asking the jury "would you hang the prisoner upon this evidence?" – to which they immediately replied "no."
[87] *R.v. Cockcroft* (1870): 11 Cox C.C. 410.

conviction of two men in Surrey Quarter Sessions on the charge of indecent assault against a woman of apparent "loose" character produced a strong dispute between defense counsel and the presiding magistrate, and eventually to a hearing before the Court for Crown Cases Reserved (successor to the Fifteen Judges). There the defense counsel argued that the justices' refusal to allow him to call witnesses to contradict the prosecutrix's denial of prior sexual relations with other men went against the modern trend to allow counsel greater leeway in examining witnesses, particularly as to their credibility, vital in a rape trial. However, the appeals court unanimously upheld the magistrate. Chief Baron Kelly, presiding, went so far as to declare that "it seems impossible to entertain a serious doubt that the evidence tendered to contradict the prosecutrix was inadmissible." If it were, he went on, the intolerable specter would open up of an endless and unjust trial of the prosecutrix herself. Therefore, the Court concluded that "evidence cannot be adduced to contradict [a prosecutrix's denial of sexual relations with any other man than the defendant]."[88]

Evidence as to one kind of previous sexual relation of the prosecutrix remained admissible (and usually fatal to a prosecution) throughout the century: a "connexion" with the defendant himself.[89] In 1834, in the trial of Moses and Aaron Martin Justice Williams agreed with defense counsel that the prosecutrix might be asked the specific question of whether the prisoner had had intercourse with her, with her consent, before the offence.[90] This exception to the general rule was reaffirmed on several occasions down at least to 1973.[91]

---

[88] *R.v. Holmes & Furness* 1871: *Times,* 18 November 1871, p. 11; 12 Cox C.C. 137. This decision was reiterated in *R.v. Riley* (1887)[16 Cox C.C., 191]. Even as the Court of Criminal Review voided a conviction because evidence to contradict the prosecutrix's denial of previous consensual sexual relations *with the defendant* had not been allowed to be introduced, it was at pains to distinguish this from "the accepted principle of non-admissibility of evidence to contradict the denial of connection with other men." As Lord Coleridge observed, "it has been held over and over again that where evidence is denied by the prosecutrix with regard to acts of connection committed by her with persons *other* than the prisoner, she cannot be contradicted."

[89] Although not always: in William Lyon's 1845 trial, Justice Erle had even refused to permit witnesses to be heard claiming that the sixteen-year-old prosecutrix had previously had sexual relations with the defendant, her married employer, and then rebutted a petition the defense counsel had drawn up and gotten an MP to forward alleging just that; to the Home Office he insisted that he "saw no indication of a wanton or libidinous nature in the prosecutrix, but she appeared modest ... and respectable and I think she resisted and never encouraged the libidinous attempts of the prisoner." Lyon was transported. [*R.v. Lyon: Times,* 13 December 1845; Ho18/173 (37).]

[90] 172 *ER* 1364 [Moody, *Crown Cases Reserved . . . From the Year 1824 to the Year 1837,* London, 1837–44, 2 v, 2: 123–124].

[91] See Susan S.M. Edwards, *Female Sexuality and the Law* (Oxford, 1981), pp. 65–66. Yet even this sort of evidence could be overborne by other circumstances, such as a

For decades, the precise line between proper and improper questioning remained vague, and could move one way or the other according to the skill of defense and prosecution counsels, and the inclinations of particular judges. Indeed, as we have seen, the increasingly central place of defense counsel in court and a growing interest in securing to defendants the fairest possible trial constituted together a sturdy obstacle to any further protection for those bringing rape charges. Two "Victorian values" that guided many reforms through that era, and which would be widely seconded today – the protection of women from violence and due process for anyone charged with a serious crime – were here in conflict.[92] Moreover, by its nature, case law change is generally less clear and decisive than change through statutes, and everyday court practices were always subject to variation. Nonetheless, during the Victorian period clear lines of development did emerge, one of which restricted the admissibility and relevance of evidence about the rape prosecutrix's sexual history.

Certainly, much did not change, like the relevance of previous consensual sex with the defendant. Yet, much did change. The later Victorian rape trial was a rather different thing from the Hanoverian one. To be sure, changes in what kinds of evidence were allowable co-existed with strong class prejudices. The most difficult of cases in which to get a conviction were those where a domestic servant lodged a complaint against her married employer. When a husband and father was brought up to the Old Bailey in 1844 charged with raping his young servant, his counsel called a large number of witnesses and subjected the girl to "rigid cross-examination." He succeeded in showing the complainant to be "a girl of loose and demoralized habits." At the same time, the many witnesses testified to the defendant's excellent character. The subsequent acquittal drew some applause in the courtroom.[93]

---

group rape. In an 1830 case against three men, the prosecutrix admitted under cross-examination that she had had sex with two of them on previous occasions (and that she had consented to sex with one of them that night). Yet they were all convicted, though reprieved on account of youth (their ages ranged between seventeen and twenty). The judge in his summation focused on the third rapist, with whom the victim had never had sex, nor had shown any sign of consent. Justice Jervis observed in summing that though "sexual intercourse had taken place between the prosecutrix and two of the prisoners on two former occasions, yet, if she did suffer the embraces of [the third man] on this occasion, against her will . . . the circumstance of her having formerly fallen from the path of virtue with others did not shut her out from the protection of the law; nor was this altered even though she had submitted to [one] on this evening, under the circumstances detailed, for he, as well as the others, might then be equally aiding and assisting to the rape by [man number three]; for the commonest prostitute was protected by the law against brutal violence." [*R.v. Dakin et al: Times,* 20 April 1830, p. 3.]

[92] As they continue to be today, in, for example, ongoing arguments over whether defendants in rape and sexual abuse trials must be allowed, as in other criminal trials, to confront their accusers.

[93] *R.v. Wyatt: Times,* 6 February 1844, p. 8.

Domestic servants had always faced enormous obstacles to bringing and winning a prosecution for rape against their masters: their poverty, their employers' higher social position and the power they wielded over them, their relative lack of community and even family support close at hand all militated against their being able either to defend themselves against attack or to win justice in the courts. Most such assaults very likely never reached the authorities; of those that did, few reached trial. Convictions were almost unheard of.[94] Even a lesser charge of assault with intent to commit rape faced an uphill struggle in court. When it did produce a conviction, the defendant was often merely fined, really a form of compensation to the prosecutrix. An example was William Nicholls' case at the Old Bailey in 1825. Nicholls, a middle-aged family man, had trapped and attacked his house-servant, who managed to escape him, and complete rape, after a twenty-minute struggle. When, only probably because she was aided by two gentlemen friends of her family, she lodged charges at Bow Street, the magistrate advised her to go out and settle the case with the defendant. She refused, and, unusually, the charge went to trial, where a guilty verdict was returned. The judge "did not wish to hold out the encouragement of money to persons bringing forward charges of this nature," but called the prosecutrix "a most deserving young woman . . . entitled to some compensation for all she had undergone." He therefore sentenced Nicholls, a "very respectable man," to pay a fine of £40 "with liberty to speak to the prosecutrix." This last phrase was understood by all to mean that if he paid half to her, the other half would be remitted and he would be discharged, as indeed happened.[95]

Yet attacks on servants did begin to appear more outrageous over time. The second conviction surviving appeal for raping a servant noted in the *Times* occurred in 1839 at the Old Bailey and had several aggravating features. It involved a married publican, George Cont, who had drugged his middle-aged barmaid (who lodged in his house). She provided medical evidence that she had been a virgin before that night and, although the defendant produced a witness who swore that he and not the defendant had had sexual relations with her that night, and that she was willing, the jury brought in a guilty verdict, and the publican was transported for life.[96] Three years later, also at the Bailey, a married sawyer, Robert Snell, was charged by his

[94]The *Times* reported such a conviction in 1793 (a verdict strongly urged by the judge, Lord Kenyon), a tailor found guilty of raping his young servant; however after a post-trial investigation he was granted a free pardon. The first such conviction reported by the *Times* that was let stand was in 1815, and the second not until 1839; thereafter, they became less rare: from 1839 to 1899, the *Times* reported nine guilty verdicts in rape cases brought by servants [*R.v. Lavender: Times*, 13 April 1793, p. 3; HO47/17; *R.v. Cont: Times*, 29 October 1839, p. 6]. This sort of conviction would have been unusual enough early in the century to make a report in the *Times* likely, even in a period in which that newspaper did not cover most rape trials.

[95]*Times*, 14 September 1825, p. 3.

[96]*R.v. Cont: Times*, 29 October 1839, p. 6.

sixteen-year-old servant (it is not known who had intervened to bring the charge; she was most unlikely to have done it on her own). She was, as had become the rule with the prevalence of defense counsel, "subjected to a very severe cross-examination." But nothing very damaging was obtained, and she made a sympathetic victim, seeming younger than her age. The jury convicted, and Snell also was transported for life. Justice Erskine, in pronouncing sentence, denounced the convict for violating his strict "duty" to protect female persons in his service.[97] Another three years hence, another master was convicted of raping his sixteen-year-old domestic servant and also was transported for life, although the servant could show evidence neither of resistance nor of cries.[98] It would appear that the notion of childhood in the minds of judges and others was expanding – in Snell's case, the judge had referred to the sixteen-year-old prosecutrix as a "child"; in earlier years, girls of that age had been considered fully responsible for their own sexual behavior and only very rarely won rape prosecutions. Such ascriptions of young prosecutrixes as "children" were also being made in other cases from the 'forties onwards, preparing the way for the raising of the age of consent to sixteen a generation later.[99]

A new element that was to be increasingly important appeared in an 1855 case, which at the same time also exhibited the persistence of the traditional license over servants of masters and their male family members (especially if of high social status).[100] The public closely followed the trial of a rector's son, only fifteen years old, for raping his father's servant. On the one hand, he was, not surprisingly, acquitted; his youth brought a measure of indulgence, and cross-examination had "very much damaged" the prosecutrix's character, and Baron Platt observed that "a most essential ingredient for the consideration of the jury was the conduct of the woman who complained of the outrage, both before and after it occurred." On the other hand, that the case came to assizes at all was rather novel, and would appear to have happened only because of the intervention of a new organization, the Associate Institute for Improving the Laws for the Protection of Women.[101] The Institute's

---

[97] *R.v. Snell: Times*, 30 October 1842, p. 6; *CCCSP*, 1841–42, #2793.

[98] *R.v. Warland: Times*, 21 July 1845, p. 8. The young servant explained those lacks by the fact that she had fainted, and awoke to find herself naked in his bed, the act underway; at that point she was "afraid to cry out, as she feared he would murder her." She made an appealing female witness, fainting during her examination, and having to be carried out of court.

[99] On Victorian heightened interest in childhood and belief in its innocence, see James Walvin, *A Child's World* (London, 1982).

[100] *R.v. Elton: Times*, 29 March 1855, p. 9.

[101] It had been established in 1843 as a prostitute rescue charity. After the passage of the 1853 Act for the Better Prevention of Aggravated Assault Upon Women and Children, which increased the liability to criminal sanctions of violent men, its leader, William Shaen, shifted its focus to aiding female and child victims of physical and

representative brought the charges and conducted them through a magistrate into the assize court. The existence of this body afforded henceforth another and more generally available avenue of entry into the courts for an abused woman than the chance of having a determined parent or a respectable patron. This society was particularly dedicated to bringing prosecutions on behalf of poor women or children without patrons or strong families, for sexual offenses – not only rape but also lesser offenses like attempted rape and indecent assault. It not only succeeded in raising the number of prosecutions for such offences, it gave a new prominence to charges of sexual abuse leveled against men of all classes. Its activities both signified and intensified a new and more organized intolerance of male sexual license among at least the middle class public. Indeed, later that same year another man, this time not a youth, was not only convicted of raping his servant but sentenced quite severely. A 52-year-old married earthenware dealer in Liverpool had forced sex upon his fourteen-year-old domestic girl, claiming in court that she consented. The jury, after an hour's deliberation, found him guilty; Justice Wightman ignored their recommendation of mercy to sentence him to fifteen years' transportation.[102]

When in 1868 another alleged rape of a domestic servant, this time sixteen years old, brought a respectable married man, a tea dealer, to trial at Maidstone, the defense counsel expressed his regrets for the "seduction" [ignoring the many marks of violence on the girl] but argued that "in hundreds of other cases of similar character the prisoners had been justly acquitted . . . if [the jury] believed [her] statement, no man against whom a charge of that kind was brought would ever have the slightest chance." However, by this time the concept of "character" was being applied across the class divide. In this case "character" was made use of more effectively by the prosecuting counsel, who described the victim as the respectable daughter of respectable working people. With the Representation of the People Act having passed the previous year, the notion that many, perhaps even most, working people were "respectable" was becoming widely accepted. The judge also reminded the jury that the prosecutrix needed protection as well as the defendant: "if [he cautioned] they came to the conclusion that her evidence was false it would stamp her for life as a bad character." The jury brought in a verdict of guilty, and Justice Willes gave him penal servitude for ten years (which would have been longer, he announced, but for the jury's strong recommendation to mercy).[103]

sexual abuse, and to supporting criminal prosecutions. Its name was later changed to properly describe its new sphere of activity, to the Society for the Protection of Women and Children.

[102] *Liverpool Mail,* 15 December 1855, p. 6.

[103] *R.v. Hide, The Maidstone and Kentish Journal,* 26 July 1868. Despite the evidence of violence, the defense counsel argued that "the prosecution had unfairly insinuated

As Willes' cautioning suggests, even though the prosecutrix's (chiefly sexual) character has remained an important consideration into our day, the then-unusual concern Baron Wood had shown early in the century to protect prosecuting women's reputations against defense attacks came to be shared by more and more judges. As early as an 1842 Old Bailey case between two servants, even an old judge like Baron Gurney rebuked a weak defense effort to discredit the prosecutrix's character (she was but thirteen) as only aggravating the offense, and the man was transported.[104]

By the 1860s, defense counsel had to tread carefully in impugning character. In sentencing "a respectably-dressed lad of seventeen" at the Old Bailey in 1866, Justice Keating was mindful of the jury's strong recommendation to mercy on account of youth. However he also could not "altogether forget the line that was adopted in his defense, in attempting to question the character of the poor young girl on whom the outrage had been committed, who, he must say, had given her evidence in the most unexceptional manner, and she left the witness-box without the slightest imputation upon her." Observing that were it not for the jury recommendation he would award a much more severe sentence, he compromised on five years' penal servitude (transportation having just been abolished).[105]

The extreme case of bad character in the complainant was the prostitute, and it was long assumed that although in strict law even prostitutes could be raped,[106] it remained almost impossible to actually convict a man of raping one. Yet, like some other manifestations of eighteenth-century masculinity, this assumption was disrupted in the course of the nineteenth. Not surprisingly, prostitutes were slower to benefit from increasing sympathy for victims of sexual assault, but benefit they eventually did.

If developing reliable statistics on the incidence of rape generally is a forlorn aim, then doing so for the rape of prostitutes is surely impossible. Even in cases brought to trial the background or occupation of the victim is usually not noted in official criminal statistical tables or even in many newspaper or other accounts.[107] Nor is it clear from such accounts when defense claims that the prosecutrix was a "common woman" or a "woman of the streets" – so frequent a defense technique – were true. Moreover, of

because [the defendant] yielded to temptation and seduced a girl, he was guilty of committing a rape on her." This time-tested appeal failed to sway any jurymen.
[104] *R.v. Greenland: Times,* 16 June 1842, p. 6.
[105] *R.v. Watson: Times,* 17 August 1866, p. 9; *Daily Telegraph,* 17 August 1866, p. 2.
[106] The common law rule that a man could be prosecuted for raping a prostitute dates back as far as 1631, to Lord Audley's Case. [A rape conviction would stand, notwithstanding proof "that the party ravished was of evil fame, and of an unchaste life . . . for it is the enforcing against the will which makes the Rape." *State Trials* 3: 401 (1816).]
[107] The Old Bailey Sessions Papers, so useful a source for other offenses, fell silent on rape cases towards the end of the eighteenth century, for fear of "causing offense."

course, few prostitutes were likely to have brought such charges, not eager to become entangled in the often-unfriendly arms of the law. Here the "dark figure" of crime is in all likelihood especially large, and the trials that do take place hardly representative.

Thus, we deal here almost exclusively with non-quantifiable evidence, and examine particular cases for insights into evolving notions of rape. A case described by Anna Clark might stand as an exemplar of the long-accepted image of the prostitute as virtually "fair game" for sexual mistreatment. After a brutal gang-rape committed in public in Gloucestershire in 1824, only one man was tried. The complainant was a young woman "of loose morals," who had taken money in the past from men and who had willingly left a pub with the defendant. The charge was only brought, she admitted, under pressure from parish officers.[108] The jury without withdrawing instantly acquitted.

This attitude would seem to have been as prevalent in the metropolis as in the provinces. When three men (all married, and all fathers) were before the Old Bailey in 1830 for another such group rape, they were defended by counsel, but prosecuting counsel did not show up. Despite a respectable witness to their attack and her struggles, Mr. Justice Park focused on the complainant, noting that "it is highly necessary that we should know something of your former life." Under judicial request, the police reported that she was believed to be a common prostitute. Even the respectable witness admitted under cross-examination that her language before the assault had been "very gross." By this point "there appeared here an evident disposition on the part of the jury to stop the case," and as soon as it was, they acquitted all three.[109] Around 1830 the line remained clear in courtroom thinking between ordinary working-class women who might not have led a chaste life, yet who were beginning to receive more sympathy and support, and outright prostitutes.

However, by the close of the following decade of criminal law reform, the almost-always ignored legal principle, cited by Blackstone, that even a prostitute could be raped began to be taken more seriously – at least in the case of group rapes, which appeared to have been not unusual.[110] William Barker was charged at the Old Bailey in 1839 as one of two assailants by a lame former prostitute, who testified that she had accepted a lift in a wagon from the defendant and his escaped friend, and when they reached a deserted spot they raped her. A surgeon's report noted bruises upon her legs and arms, but "with reference to the violation of her person" he would give no positive evidence, since "the girl, by her own admission, had previously led an abandoned life in the streets of London." The defendant claimed that she

[108] *R.v. Witts: Times,* 30 August 1824, p. 3; see Clark, op. cit., p. 73.
[109] *R.v. Warren et al: Times,* 20 April 1830, p. 3; *OBSP* 1829–30 #835.
[110] It remained until very recent times almost impossible for a prostitute to win a rape prosecution against an individual.

had agreed, but several persons had heard her cry for assistance. This jury retired for an hour and returned a guilty verdict, though also, as was typical as long as rape was a capital offense, a strong plea for mercy on account of his youth (he was nineteen; she eighteen) and also on the ground that "the girl herself had afforded him an opportunity for the commission of the offense." The judge, Baron Vaughan, then denounced the prisoner at some length, describing the complainant as "a poor, unfortunate, friendless girl" and declaring that "if ever there was a case in which a judge would be justified in determining that the law ought to take its course, the present case is one of that description." However, the era of hanging for rape had in practice ended. Vaughan promised to forward the jury recommendation, though without his formal support, and not without openly questioning part of it: "I cannot quite understand," he observed, what was meant by her "affording him opportunity." "It may be said," he concluded, "that the prosecutrix is a female of abandoned habits, but it is not because she has not presented herself here today as a chaste and unsullied virgin that she is therefore to be assailed by any man that might think fit to gratify his brutal passion against her." Strong public protests – her own mother declared her "a very old bad character" – ensured that Barker wouldn't be hanged, and he was respited to transportation for life.[111]

Not surprisingly, most judges and juries continued to be ambivalent about the rape of prostitutes. In an 1841 case of a prostitute's gang-rape by no fewer than seven men, Chief Justice Coleridge (no friend, as we have seen, to "lewd women") clearly leaned towards only an assault verdict. Although he allowed that resistance was not always necessary,[112] he urged the jury to "consider what sort of person she was" and reminded them that a fellow prostitute had testified that the prosecutrix "herself told them that she should make no objection if they came one at a time." The jury duly returned a verdict of assault only.[113]

Another jury went further a few years later. In 1855, four men were charged with raping a young woman earning her living at the time as a prostitute, or, as the trial report put it, who "has for some years past pursued an abandoned career of vice and immorality." While she testified to struggles and screams, the defense maintained it had only been "a larking and romping." Nonetheless, they were found guilty of rape. Even though a mercy recommendation helped keep their sentence at the moderate level of two years' hard labor

---

[111] *R.v. Barker: Times*, 23 September 1839, p. 7; HO17/131 (Zz 33).
[112] This point seems to have been a settled one by then.
[113] *R.v. Hallett et al.* (1841): 173 *ER* 1036. However Coleridge by his own lights was no friend of "real" rapists: In an 1852 case tried by him at Leicester, the prosecutrix was "a respectable young woman," attacked by several men and "frightfully injured." The two men who raped her were transported for life [*R.v. Stone et al.: Times*, 23 July 1852, p. 7].

each, this case can be seen as a milestone, possibly the first full conviction for rape of a currently active prostitute.[114]

Indeed at a Liverpool assize that same year another such conviction took place, along with several others for rape. The prosecutrix, a beggar and a prostitute, under severe cross-examination "could not remember how many times she had been in the different gaols and before magistrates." The defense counsel, representing the four men charged, then addressed the jury, "begging them not to place any reliance upon the testimony of persons of such abandoned character." Here, as often, the stress was less on her previous ready acceptance of sexual intercourse as the unreliability of a witness from that walk of life. Mr. Justice Wightman was more receptive to the latter than the former argument. He reminded the jury that "the circumstance of the prosecutrix being a prostitute was no kind of justification for the conduct of the prisoners", while also allowing the jurymen to give her whatever credence they felt "reasonable." Still, three were convicted of the full charge, and given by Wightman a not insubstantial sentence of four years' penal servitude each.[115] At the same assize, Wightman sentenced another man who had tried to drown a prostitute to twenty-five years' transportation.

However, prostitutes continued to face an uphill struggle in bringing rape charges. Their occupation weighed heavily against their credibility and could not be kept out of court, for (as previously described) testimony was allowed as to the prosecutrix's "general" character. Though specific evidence of sex with other men was no longer admissible, "general evidence" of character was, and this usually was taken to include a public reputation as a prostitute. This point was argued at length in an 1851 Shropshire case, in which Justice Patteson at first refused to allow such evidence but was at last swayed by precedents cited by defense counsel and reversed himself. The two defendants were acquitted, even though the prosecutrix was not currently a prostitute. She was however, it emerged on cross-examination, cohabiting with a man and residing on and off in the workhouse; such a woman's credibility when bringing complaints of being sexually assaulted was easily questioned.[116] Similarly, in a Kent case four years later, despite Baron Pollock's having emphasized that following the occupation of a prostitute for fourteen years did not leave the complainant

[114] *R.v. Wright et al: Times,* 26 July 1855, p. 10. The recent passage of the "Women and Children" Act may have helped sensitize the members of the jury to such violence.

[115] *R.v. Leyland et al: Times,* 10 December 1855, p. 10. At the same assize, three other men were convicted in separate cases of rape, two of them being given the heavy sentence of fifteen years' transportation. The third convict received four years' penal servitude: his accuser had raised strong doubts, and the jury had only hesitantly convicted [*Liverpool Mail,* 15 December 1855, p. 6].

[116] *R.v. Clay & Stone* (21 March 1851): 5 Cox C.C. 146. For accounts of this trial, see *Eddowes' Journal,* 26 March 1851, p. 4 and *Shropshire Conservative,* 22 March 1851, p. 3 [the *Times* did not report it]. She failed to produce any corroboration of her charge, and thus the credibility/character question became central.

any less protected by the law, two soldiers were acquitted.[117] This uncertain situation continued through the century and well beyond;[118] in 1887, Justice Stephen made a point of noting that a reaffirmation by a unanimous appeals court (of which he was a member) of the inadmissibility of evidence as to prior sexual activity was not to be taken to rule out testimony as to general reputation as a prostitute.[119]

Still, in the second half of the century, with the increase in public orderliness, the danger of gang-rapes of prostitutes seems to have markedly diminished,[120] a social development to which the new intolerance of both Parliament and the courts probably contributed, for it was now clear to the entire public that such acts were no longer considered "sport" but would very likely be strongly prosecuted. A revived and intensified drive against violent crime that began in the late 1860s finished off any remaining tolerance for group attacks on prostitutes. At the Old Bailey in 1871, five laborers were convicted of raping a drunken prostitute. As not unusual, the jury recommended mercy. However, Justice Blackburn not only denounced the offense, but particularly upbraided the entire neighborhood in which this took place, where many "seemed to have looked on as though it was no concern of theirs to interfere and endeavour to rescue the woman." He sentenced the two men who had been proved to have committed rape to the heavy sentence of fifteen years, and the others to a range of five to nine months.[121]

The change in legal treatment of rape against prostitutes remained carefully delimited. As long as they acted *alone* and not in groups, and in *private* not public, men forcing themselves on prostitutes were most unlikely to get into trouble with the law. Hardly any cases in which a prostitute brought rape charges against an individual ever came to trial during the century.[122] Here

---

[117] Cited by C.A. Conley, *The Unwritten Law* (Oxford, 1991), p. 90, from *Maidstone and Kentish Journal*.

[118] Indeed, at least as late as *R.v. Bashir and Mansur* (1969), and in practice at times still today: see Edwards, *Female Sexuality*, op. cit., p. 64.

[119] *R.v. Riley*, op. cit., Stephen's dismissive attitude towards the notion of women's rights in his *Liberty, Equality, Fraternity* (London, 1871), which drew critical replies from Millicent Garrett Fawcett and from Lydia Becker, throws some light on his unwillingness to convict men of raping prostitutes.

[120] At least hardly any were reported in the *Times*.

[121] *R.v. Hornsby et al.*: *Times*, 8 June 1871, p. 11. The same fifteen year sentence was pronounced four years later by the new Chief Justice Cockburn on three soldiers who had violently raped a drunken woman of low repute and then claimed to have been so drunk themselves as not to be able to recall any of it. Cockburn explained to the court that he "must pass a severe sentence, which would serve as a warning against the idle and silly belief that intoxication could afford any defence or palliation for such conduct" [*Times*, 22 March 1875, p. 11]. [On the increasing disallowance of a defendent's drunkenness as mitigation for violence, see Chapter 7.]

[122] A partial exception is the 1860 case of William Jones, convicted at Worcester Assizes of raping a fellow hop-picker who until that year had been a prostitute; he received

of course, very difficult evidentiary questions intruded; there were rarely witnesses, and little to go on beyond the competing stories of the two parties, one of whose credibility was automatically in question. Justice Coleridge's observation in an 1841 trial in which a prostitute had accused a client of shooting at her with intent to kill was still widely accepted: "Although," he had there cautioned, "the evidence of women who led a dissolute course of life was not on that account wholly disentitled to belief, still justice required that their testimony should not be received with the same implicit credit as that of a modest woman; because when a female threw off her modesty she generally threw off a great deal more."[123]

In general, Carolyn Conley has found in mid-Victorian Kent that "when a victim was a prostitute or a drunkard, the conviction rate dropped to ten per cent."[124] Nonetheless, compared to the opening years of the century significant changes affecting most situations were undeniable: even with prostitutes, the legal contest over rape revolved less around the character of the complainant and more around the nature of the act; even active sexuality of the prosecutrix ("immoral behavior") no longer precluded examination of the behavior of the defendant. Men were no longer practically at liberty to take their pleasure with women whose reputation was dubious or could be made to appear so.[125]

The second route by which a woman's consent was being reconceived was that through the requirement of resistance. Forms of resistance less than total began to be accepted, while courts also began to show a correspondingly expanded view of what constituted "force" by the perpetrator. This important change in the treatment of rape prosecutions arrived somewhat later than others, becoming evident only in the second half of the century. In the later eighteenth and early nineteenth centuries, as we have seen, the lack of testimony of injuries from a surgeon almost invariably doomed sexual assault prosecutions. A small breach in this requirement had been opened in 1807,

---

from Baron Wilde the fairly stiff sentence of ten years' penal servitude [*Times*, 13 December 1860, p. 11].

[123] *R.v. Eden: Times*, 15 July 1841, p. 7.

[124] Conley, op. cit., p. 90. Of course, all discussions of conviction rates must keep in mind first, that this kind of offense, when against a prostitute was especially likely to lack witnesses and be particularly difficult to prove; second, that defendants of course have rights that must be respected; and third, that not *every* defendant was in fact guilty: there were times when women (particularly if married) did have strong motives for charging rape after consensual sexual intercourse. A 100% conviction rate would hardly inspire confidence in the fairness of the law.

[125] For example, in 1852 at Worcester two men were convicted of attempted rape and each given the very stiff penalty of eighteen years' transportation despite the facts that there was no eye-witness and that the complainant was a common field-worker who admitted that she had been drunk at the time [*R.v. Shepherd et al.: Times*, 10 March 1852, p. 7].

when the Twelve Judges affirmed a conviction for common assault (a misdemeanor only) in which the young victim could show no injuries of any
kind; indeed, she had apparently not offered any physical resistance. While
reaffirming the general principle that proof of violence was a necessary ingredient in the crime of rape, the judges agreed that under certain circumstances
resistance was not necessary in an assault case, even a sexual assault, if its
absence could be accounted for by such factors as the authority and influence
of the attacker combined with the "tender years" of the victim.[126] While this
applied only to the charge of common assault, and thus did not affect rape
trials, it was novel, a straw in the wind.

However, to satisfy themselves that a rape had occurred judges continued to demand evidence of full-fledged violence and all-out resistance. Even
when Thomas Wright was charged in 1808 with raping his own granddaugh-
ter, aged 13, Baron Graham observed that the child had neither cried out
nor offered resistance. Granting that the grandfather's conduct had been
"abhorrent . . . to every sense of humanity and justice . . . in the present indictment it must be positively proved that the prosecutrix had made every
possible resistance . . . and therefore he could not recommend to the jury to
convict the prisoner." Despite this instruction, a jury enraged at this violation
of family bonds did convict.[127]

In 1830, skeptical looks at "resistance" that failed to leave injuries were
still the judicial norm. At the York Spring Assizes that year Baron Parke
warned the jury in a charge of rape of an unmarried woman that "it sometimes happens, that a person, who with more or less reluctance has given
her consent, will afterwards, for the purpose of protecting her character, be
ready to deny it." Even, he went on, "when the desire of the woman goes
along with that of the man . . . there is some degree of resistance generally."[128]
However, as fear of working-class (male) violence and more passive and sex-
less notions of female nature simultaneously gained sway among the middle
classes, Parke's observation gradually came to seem less commonsensical. In
court, the required amount of both force applied and resistance put up began
to diminish, particularly if there were aggravating factors present. Already a
year before this last case, a man was convicted of the full charge and went to
the scaffold even though his frightened victim, accosted by him on a country

---

[126] *R.v. Nicholl:* Russell & Ryan 130–132.

[127] *R.v. Wright: Times,* 2 December 1808, p. 4.

[128] He did separate this situation before them from attacks on children: "In cases of
extreme youth, and absence of passion, consent is not to be presumed. Where there
are marks and scratches, they are proofs of resistance" [168 *ER* 1045]. However, in this
case not surprisingly an acquittal was returned. In another trial the same day, a man
was convicted of attempted rape; in his case, lacking witnesses as had the previous
one, the prosecutrix was a married woman, and she showed evidence of vigorous
resistance; the man received twelve months in the House of Correction [*York Chronicle,*
8 April 1830, p. 4].

path, had not resisted. A thirteen-year-old servant told the defendant that "she would be quiet if he would not hurt her," which she was; nonetheless, he did injure her.[129] His unusual conviction was no doubt aided by his being an outsider to the local community and by the active intervention of the girl's former employer, who personally apprehended the rapist; it would take decades more for strong resistance by the prosecutrix to cease to be normally insisted upon.[130]

One of the first situations where resistance ceased to be insisted upon was if the prosecutrix had been drunk. Until 1845 the prosecutrix's alcohol intake seems to have made no difference, and defendants in such cases were almost invariably acquitted.[131] In the *Camplin* case that year at the Old Bailey, a young victim had been deliberately plied with alcohol until she was hardly conscious. Here, after being out for an hour, the jury convicted, and the middle-class defendant was sentenced to transportation for life. The judge sent on the case to all the Judges on the point of consent. They affirmed the conviction by 10-3, after Chief Justice Tindall, along with Baron Parke, observed that the statute of Westminster which created the offense of rape described it as "ravishing a woman 'where she did not consent,'" and not ravishing against her will." The highest court declared that "if the victim was insensible through intoxication, she was in no position to exercise free will, and evidence of force in this situation did not have to be presented." This decision went beyond the occasional recognitions of extreme youth or family relation or sheer terror as negating the need for strong resistance, and directly began to reshape the concept of free will. "Against her will" as a stock legal phrase began here to share the spotlight with the phrase "without her consent."[132] In this latter phrase lay the seeds of the modern insistence upon explicit evidence of consent.

---

[129] *R.v. Radnor: Times*, 27 August 1829, p. 4; *Monmouthshire Merlin*, 29 August 1829, pp. 2–3 and 12 September 1829, p. 3.

[130] Social class, not surprisingly, particularly in the sensitive matter of rape, could override legal presumptions and requirements. William Lyon was convicted at York in 1845 of the rape of the sixteen-year-old daughter of the farmer he worked for, despite much evidence that sexual intercourse had taken place between them on two occasions and that she had been willing, even eager. On the judge's advice, the Home Office rejected a petition, forwarded by an MP, that strongly argued that point, and Lyon was transported for life. If the victim had been a farm servant instead of daughter of the master, Lyon would have stood an excellent chance of acquittal. [*Times*, 13 Dec. 1845, p. 8; HO18/173 (37).]

[131] A. Simpson, op. cit., p. 156 (on the period to 1830).

[132] Susan Edwards argues that the *Camplin* decision played merely a "fanciful" role in the history of English rape law, being often ignored in latter cases [Edwards, *Sex and Gender in the Legal Process* (London, 1996), p. 337]. Yet it entered law books and guidebooks for magistrates, became well known and was cited during many trials. [*R.v. Camplin: Morning Post*, 8 March 1845; 169 *ER* 163.] In 1852 three men were convicted and sentenced to 15 years' penal servitude although their victim had been drunk, and indeed "guilty of light and improper conduct." [*Times*, 20

The ruling was quickly extended to weak-minded victims as well. Another case that came to be cited thereafter was an 1846 Old Bailey rape conviction against a man named Ryan where he had encountered no resistance whatever. The victim was an "idiot" girl, and Baron Platt told the jury, more broadly than required by the facts of the case, that it would be rape "if the connection took place during a state of unconsciousness, whether produced by the act of the prisoner or otherwise." This point became a precedent with implications beyond idiot victims. It suggested, as had *Camplin*, that "consciousness" in a victim was intellectual as well as physiological.[133]

These principles, though not always followed, were reiterated and extended in 1859, when the Court for Crown Cases Reserved unanimously upheld the rape conviction of Richard Fletcher in Liverpool. His victim was weak-minded, and the defense had argued that the act had not been proved to have taken place against her will, since she had offered no objection or resistance, but both Justice Hill and the jury considered that the girl was "incapable of giving consent." At appeals, the point at issue was whether "against her will" or "without her consent" was the operative term. As Chief Justice Campbell put it, "the question is, what is the proper definition of the crime of rape? Is it carnal knowledge of a woman against her will, or is it sufficient, if it be without the consent of the prosecutrix?" The five-member court unanimously found for the latter term, citing both *Ryan* and, especially, *Camplin*.[134]

The rape of drunken women was, as would be expected, a more frequent situation in trials. In 1864, a prosecutrix who had been drinking at three pubs in one night nonetheless won a conviction against three pitmen who had taken advantage of her intoxication to take her outside and rape her. Although defense counsel argued that "her conduct had been such that the prisoners might have inferred her assent," Justice Keating pointed the jury to her injuries (inferring resistance), and the jury (although only after two hours

---

July 1852, p. 7.] In an 1856 trial Justice Willes observed that "some doubts were entertained whether the offense of rape could be committed upon the person of a woman who had rendered herself perfectly insensible by drink so as to be unable to give any signs of resistance. His own impression was that that the condition of the woman could not be alleged as an excuse by the man." [*R.v. White: Times,* 6 December 1856, p. 11]. As Chief Justice Campbell remarked in the 1859 *Fletcher* case, specifically citing *Camplin*, "it would be monstrous to say that these poor females are to be subjected to such violence, without the parties inflicting it being liable to be indicted. If so, every drunken woman returning from market, and happening to fall down on the road side, may be ravished at the will of the passers by" [8 Cox C.C. 131].

[133] *R.v. Ryan:* 2 Cox C.C. 115 (26 September 1846). Although even here the judge first inquired about her previous behavior, and issued his ruling only after being assured that it had been proper.

[134] Campbell's conclusion was that "Camplin's case settles the definition of the offence, and the ten judges concurred in that." [*R.v. Fletcher:* 8 Cox C.C. 131.]

of deliberation) brought in "guilty" verdicts against all three. They were all given the stiffest possible sentence, penal servitude for life.[135]

Four years later, an Old Bailey prosecutrix "much addicted to drinking" and able to show little evidence of resistance nonetheless won an instruction from Baron Bramwell to the jury to convict for attempted rape. Bramwell observed that "however little an object of sympathy the woman was who was in the habit of spending her husband's earnings in drink and neglecting her children . . . the woman appeared to have been violently ravished by three men, and no question as to consent on her part could be raised in such a case." At the same time, he ruled out a conviction for rape itself, even while acknowledging that it seemed to have taken place. Here her bad character seems to have produced a judicial compromise. The man charged was duly convicted of the attempt, and given the maximum sentence for that offense, two years at hard labor.[136]

If intoxication was shown (and particularly if the prosecutrix were not unrespectable) even a defendant from above the working classes could be convicted in the absence of resistance by his victim. In 1887, Henry Harbert, a clerk, was suspected of drugging a girlfriend's drink (though this was never established); even though the prosecution was only commenced after he re-neged on a promise to marry her (a fact which would have killed a prosecution dead a half-century before), he was found guilty and sentenced to five years.[137]

Other situations were also becoming recognized as obviating the need for resistance. The most important of these was where the prosecutrix was a child, a situation in which a conviction had always been, and continued to be, somewhat easier to obtain.[138] In this circumstance also, leading cases expanded the notion of force beyond purely physical acts. In 1848 Jabez Day was found guilty of raping a child under ten; though he used no violence and she offered no resistance, her youth rendered the question of consent moot. This case was frequently cited thereafter as establishing that "there was a great difference between consent and submission." In the case of an adult, submitting quietly to an outrage of this kind would go far to show consent, but the same expectation could not be applied in the case of a child (a concept being extended in practice, if not yet in formal law, upwards in age). The notion of "consent through terror" now entered the common discourse of the courts.[139] Several convictions for the lesser charge of indecent

[135] *R.v. Rainshaw: Times,* 8 December 1864, p. 11.

[136] *R.v. Naylor: Times,* 28 February 1868, p. 9.

[137] *R.v. Harbert: Times,* 30 March 1887, p. 4.

[138] Louise Jackson (*Child Sexual Abuse in Victorian England,* op. cit., p. 90) has noted that of a sample of 1146 trials of sexual assault in several counties at five-year intervals from 1830 to 1900 "only 45 per cent of cases known to have involved adult victims ended in conviction compared to 69 per cent of cases involving child victims."

[139] *R.v. Day: Times,* 5 August 1848, p. 7; 9 C&P 722. Day received fifteen years' transportation. For "consent through terror," see Mews, op. cit., p. 526. This case was cited in Burn, *Justice,* 30th ed. (1869), 1: 309: see below.

assault in 1850 and 1853 were based on judicial instructions that up to the age of sixteen, a girl was not really capable of consenting to sex.[140] If such instructions restricted the sexuality of young girls, they also provided these girls new protection against kinds of coercion against which they had hitherto had no legal recourse. They clearly differed from statute law, which put the age of consent at twelve. Although statute law was not to be changed until 1875 (when the age of consent was raised to thirteen) and again 1885 (when it rose to sixteen), a more elastic notion of incapacity to consent was already being employed in some courts.

Terror was cited again as negating consent in an Old Bailey trial in 1870 for carnal knowledge (accomplished without violence or resistance) of a girl above ten and under twelve (the defendant's own daughter). This produced a conviction and formalized for law books two kinds of qualifications to consent that had long been gaining ground: "Although [as one law book summed up this case's significance] consent would be a defence, consent extorted by terror, or induced by the influence of a person in whose power she felt herself, is not really such consent as will have that effect."[141] Three years later, a full rape conviction was obtained at Worcester with a non-resisting victim a half-year over twelve.[142]

The upward extension in practice of the concept of female childhood was illustrated at the Kingston Spring Assizes in 1863, when a rape conviction was obtained against a man "of very respectable appearance" in the absence of evidence of resistance by the victim beyond some face scratches, because so many other usual requirements were present. Though defense counsel "felt bound to profess his disbelief in rapes, unless the woman resisted to the utmost," Justice Wightman pointed out that "the girl was young [she was sixteen], the attack was at dusk, the place was lonely, and no doubt she was under the influence of terror"; moreover, her screams had been heard, and a surgeon confirmed her account. The jury "without any difficulty" convicted.[143] Thus, as Burn's *Justice* informed magistrates for the first time in 1869, "there is a great difference between submission and consent; consent

---

[140] *R.v. Kipps* (1850): 4 Cox C.C. 167; see also 6 Cox C.C. 143 (1853). While this view has often been interpreted as restricting the sexual freedom of adolescent girls, it also gave them a new power to complain of unwanted advances and for criminal charges to be brought on their behalf. For example, in 1857 a sixteen-year-old girl who had been a house-servant charged her former employer, a schoolmaster, with having twice attempted to rape her a year before. In spite of her having said nothing at the time, her continuing to work there for some time, and her lacking evidence of having offered resistance, she obtained a conviction on the second charge of indecent assault; the schoolmaster was sentenced to imprisonment for eighteen months [*R.v. Mackay: Times*, 5 March 1857, p. 12].

[141] *R.v. Woodhurst* (1870): 12 Cox C.C. 443.

[142] *R.v. Coles: Times*, 21 July 1873, p. 13.

[143] *R.v. Baldwin: Times*, 31 March 1863, p. 11.

involves submission, it by no means follows that mere submission involves consent."[144]

A variety of relationships, including employer–employee (both inside the home – as seen above – and also outside), were similarly being recognized in court as making resistance very difficult. Even an affluent man could now be found guilty of rape of a working girl, whether she clearly resisted or not. Lewis Thomas, a manager of the Gadlys Ironworks at Aberdare and a man of considerable property, found himself on trial at Cardiff in 1872, after having used his authority to sexually assault a fifteen-year-old employee at the works. His Queen's Counsel managed to shake the prosecutrix "as to the amount of resistance she had offered" her boss, and a doctor found "no marks on her person when he examined her which were inconsistent with consent on her part." Despite this evidence, Thomas was convicted and given ten years' penal servitude.[145] Unlike most rape prosecutions, this case roused strong class as well as gender sentiments: his counsel had suggested there had been no need to rape, since a man of his position could easily have seduced such a girl – a suggestion that seems to have not gone down well with the public or the jury.[146]

In the courts even trickery, long a tolerated weapon in the perennial war of the sexes, was coming under closer scrutiny and sanction. As the century proceeded, judges and juries began to allow deception to stand in for force, and explain away the failure to resist. The worst such case, it was felt, was the abuse of the high moral standing and personal authority adhering to the clerical or medical professions. In 1859 the Rev. Henry John Hatch, late chaplain to the Wandsworth House of Correction, and at the time running a private school, was convicted of the indecent assault of two female pupils, aged eleven and eight, while assuring them that he was merely checking their health. The girls, despite their tender ages, were subjected to a very severe cross-examination, and a long line of character witnesses, some of them of social distinction, spoke for Rev. Hatch. Nonetheless he was found guilty, and

---

[144]Burn, *Justice*, 30th ed., I, 309. It went on to: "Thus the submission of a child, when in the power of a strong man, and probably acted upon by fear, does not amount to a consent so as to preclude the idea of an assault in law. Nor can the non-resistance of a female scholar of thirteen years [above the age of consent] to acts of indecency on the part of the master, whose wife kept the school; or of a female patient suffering from fits, to a medical man, who on pretence of treating her medically unnecessarily stripped off all her clothes; or of a female patient of fourteen years of age suffering from suppressed menstruation, under the belief that he was treating her medically to a medical man's having connection with her, be said to amount to a consent which will prevent the commission of an assault."

[145]*Times*, 31 July 1872, p. 11.

[146]Although it seems to have won the sympathy of Justice Channell, who in his summation quoted the well-known line, ". . . And saying she would ne'er consent, consented." *Cardiff Times*, 3 August 1872, p. 7.

Baron Bramwell, declaring that "it was impossible to conceive a worse crime than for a man to take advantage of his position and act in such a manner towards two poor little children who had been placed under his protection," gave him the strongest allowable sentence, two years' hard labor on each charge, a total of four years.[147]

A leading case in 1850 made clear the suspension of the force/resistance requirement in cases where a medical man took advantage of his unique position of authority over bodies. A physician had apparently "interfered" with a fourteen-year-old, without resistance, after saying he needed to do a procedure to cure her. He was tried at Quarter Sessions (the court one level beneath assizes) for assault and convicted; the Court for Crown Cases Reserved unanimously upheld both the Recorder's instruction that force or resistance was not necessary to convict and the verdict itself. Indeed, speaking for the court, Chief Justice Wilde went even further than had the Recorder, declaring the case to be "free from doubt. . . . It is said that as she made no resistance she must be viewed as a consenting party. That is a fallacy. . . . The prisoner disarmed her by fraud. . . . where consent is caused by fraud, the act is at least an assault; and perhaps amounts to rape." Justice Patteson added the observation that the defense argument quite wrongly "entirely confounds active consent with passive non-resistance." In concluding the deliberations the Chief Justice let his indignation boil over, announcing that "the notion that a medical man might lawfully adopt such a mode of treatment is not to be tolerated in a Court of Justice."[148]

This ruling was not only cited thereafter but was extended two decades later to permit not just assault convictions but convictions for rape itself. The Chief Justice's "perhaps" was now made into a "certainly." In 1877 the Court for Crown Cases Reserved unanimously voided a number of precedents by ruling that a medical man named Flattery had indeed committed rape against a patient, and declared that "a man, who by fraud and falsely pretending to give medical advice to a female patient, and in pursuance of such advice to perform a surgical operation upon her, procures her submission to his medical treatment of her, under colour of which he has carnal connection with her, she believing all the while that she was undergoing medical treatment, is guilty of a rape."[149]

Sex obtained by deception by laymen was less liable to felonious prosecution, but it too was coming under closer scrutiny and could constitute rape. Beginnings of judicial relaxation of the literal interpretation of force that had prevailed for centuries can be perceived as early as the 1822 *Jackson* case, of a man who had gotten into the bed of a married woman, and induced her

---

[147] *Times*, 2 December 1859.
[148] *R.v. Case* (1850): 4 Cox C.C. 220.
[149] *R.v. Flattery* (1877): 13 Cox C.C. 388; see also *Times*, 25 December 1876, p. 9.

to suppose he was her husband. He was convicted at the Lancaster Spring Assizes of burglary with intent to commit a rape, and Mr. Justice Bayley reserved the point of whether this could constitute rape for the Twelve Judges. Although eight of twelve replied in the negative, several in the majority displayed restiveness with the state of the law, "intimat[ing] that if the case should occur again, they would advise the jury to find a special verdict."[150] Another sign of shifting attitudes, this time from the popular side, came three years later in an attempted rape trial at Westminster Quarter Sessions. Here, again, the defendant had crept into the prosecutrix's bed while she was sleeping. The jury ignored magisterial instructions to acquit and convicted.[151]

The 1837 Act that permitted convictions on lesser charges for accused felons also specifically allowed those obtaining sexual intercourse by deception, not yet accepted as convictable for rape, to be convicted for assault.[152] Immediately thereafter such convictions began to be brought in. In the 1838 trial of Bernard Saunders, another creeping-into-bed case, Baron Gurney now could direct the jury that the offense was not rape but that it did constitute assault, which verdict was duly given. He then awarded the prisoner the comparatively stiff sentence of three years' hard labor.[153] Thereafter, it was not unusual for rape prosecutions that could not get convictions on the full charge to convict on a lesser charge of attempt or of assault.[154]

---

[150] *R.v. Jackson* (1822): 168 *ER* 911. Another such case of sexual intercourse by deception did recur before Justice Bayley later that same year, and he told the jury that if they "thought themselves warranted in convicting the prisoner, he should direct them to return a special verdict, so that the point might be raised before the Twelve Judges. The jury, however, acquitted [*R.v. Pearson, Times*, 21 December 1822, p. 3].

[151] *R.v. Charles: Times*, 24 October 1825, p. 3. In general, magistrates tended to be more lenient to accused rapists than High Court judges. This case would appear to mark a watershed: Simpson noted that it was "the only case" of a conviction for rape or attempted rape while the victim was unconscious, either through drink or sleep, that he had found in rape or attempted rape trials at the Old Bailey or in the many such trials examined at Westminster Quarter Sessions between 1740 and 1830. [op. cit., p. 155].

[152] Burn, *Justice*, 29th ed. (1845), 1: 686.

[153] Gurney apparently was not as sure as he made out to the jurors, for he reserved the point. The Fifteen Judges affirmed the verdict. [*R.v. Saunders* (1838): 173 *ER* 488.]

[154] For example, in a sex-by-deception trial in 1863 at the Old Bailey, Justice Keating directed an acquittal on a rape charge (the only charge on which the defendant had been indicted) but then immediately had him arraigned again on a charge of assault, of which the jury found him guilty. Keating regretted that he had escaped conviction on the original charge, for "there could be no doubt that, although in point of law the prisoner had not committed a rape, yet morally he was guilty of that crime, and he should therefore pass upon him the heaviest sentence he had it in his power to award" – which was, with the ongoing diminution in sentence lengths for most offences, by then only a year's hard labor [*R.v. Rackstraw: Times*, 22 August 1863, p. 11].

It would have been unrealistic to expect rape convictions for such behavior as long as the possibility of death or even transportation for life for those so convicted remained. Only after repeal of the capital sanction in 1841 and four years later of the mandatory sentence of transportation for life that replaced it, could this become possible, and even then juries and judges could still be very hesitant in this imprecise area. Not until 1853 did the *Times* report a rape trial (again in which a married woman prosecuted a man who had entered her bed under pretense of being her husband) in which Justice Erle now declared his opinion that "if the woman had been deceived, though force had not been used, that constituted a felony." His immediate acknowledgment that this view was his own and not shared by the majority of his brethren no doubt made it easier for the jury to ignore it and acquit. The jury action is understandable: unlike most previous such cases, this woman had been wakened before the beginning of intercourse and presumably should have realized he was not her husband.[155]

However, change on this question was nearing. In 1854 a York jury convicted a similar defendant, Richard Clarke, of rape.[156] The judge reserved the point for consideration by the Fifteen Judges, "as in the opinion of some learned persons that offense could only be committed either by violence or against the will of the person against whom it was committed." The higher court remained conservative on this, and quashed the conviction, citing as its precedent the 1822 majority judgment in *Jackson*. However, it is notable that the prosecuting counsel made a vigorous argument that that decision was no longer clearly ruling and cited the expressed doubts of several of the majority in that case.[157] Five years later, the Scottish High Court of Justiciary found "great difficulty" with this point. Each judge gave a lengthy opinion, and the majority affirmed that this act was not rape: as Lord Neaves concluded for them, "to the crime of rape by our law the element of violence has always been essential." But two judges vigorously disagreed, one of them the Lord President of the Court, holding (in a surprisingly "modern" manner) that "the force essential for the crime of rape is relative to the resistance offered, and where there is not resistance to be overcome, it is not necessary to prove the use of force."[158]

As in *Clarke* four years before, in 1868 a rape conviction was obtained in a deception but then quashed. In *R.v. Barrow*, consent obtained by slipping

[155] *R.v. Wood: Times*, 18 July 1853, p. 10.
[156] But it recommended mercy on the grounds that "that they did not believe he intended to commit it by violence if he could not accomplish it by fraud."
[157] *R.v. Clarke: Times*, 22 July 1854, p. 11; 169 *ER* 779. Nonetheless, *Jackson's* reign continued: a reluctant Justice Keating advised the jury in *Rackstraw* (above) that the judges had held that personating a husband to obtain sex could not be rape as long as the wife, however deceived, consented to the sex.
[158] *R.v. Sweenie* (1858): 8 Cox C.C. 223.

in the dark into a married woman's bed and pretending to be her husband did produce both a judicial instruction for a rape conviction and such a verdict by the jury. Yet while Chief Baron Kelly thought of *Fletcher* and advised the jury that the case for rape was made out, he reserved the point, and the appeal court again quashed the conviction. It was a weak case for changing prevailing practice: the woman's husband was also in the bed and, as Chief Justice Bovill observed, "it does not appear that the prosecutrix was asleep or unconscious at the time when the first act of connection took place."[159]

Judicial change here, as on many other matters, tended to come slowly, for the publication of leading cases and the extensive printed discussion of principles and rules that accompanied such publication within the profession, together with the steady rise in the authority of Parliament and the Civil Service, would appear to have increased the already traditional judicial reluctance to interfere with precedent. Yet change did come. By 1872, Chief Baron Kelly's views were being echoed on the bench. In a leading case, Justice Lush (again citing *Barrow*) rejected a strong challenge from defense counsel to his direction that if a man had or attempted to have connection with a woman while she was asleep, "it is no defense that she did not resist, as she is incapable of resisting. The man can, therefore, be found guilty of a rape, or of an attempt to commit a rape." The prisoner was so convicted (the charge in this case was attempted rape). The next time this issue went to the appeals court, in 1877, a different outcome took place; in the *Flattery* case a rape conviction of a medical man was unanimously upheld. While defense counsel unsuccessfully cited both previous favorable rulings on sexual assault cases against doctors, but also cases like *Barrow*, judges now vigorously challenged him. That the judges were thinking of a much wider range of cases than only those involving medical treatment is clear from their reported discussion, in which the point was made and agreed with that nonresistance cannot be taken for consent. Four of five judges expressed their desire to see the *Barrow* decision reconsidered. "I lament," Chief Baron Kelly declared, now supported by other judges, "that it has ever been decided to be the law of England that where a man obtains possession of a woman's person by fraud that it does not amount to rape."[160]

Such appeals-level reconsideration of fraudulent sexual possession did come, sooner for Ireland than for England. In 1884 the Irish Court for Crown Cases Reserved ruled very clearly, in another case of sex obtained by getting into a woman's bed and pretending to be her husband, that there was no difference in law between possession of a woman without consent by violence or by fraud. Force, they noted, could mean more than physical

[159] *R.v. Barrow* (1868): 11 Cox C.C. 191.
[160] *Flattery*, op. cit.

violence, and consent had to be "rational." As Chief Baron Palles explained,

> Consent is the act of man, in his character of a rational and intelligent
> being, not in that of an animal. It must proceed from the will, not
> when such will is acting without the control of reason, as in idiocy or
> drunkenness, but from the will sufficiently enlightened by the intellect
> to make such consent the act of a reasoning being.

In the present case, he pointed out, "the consent of the [woman's] intellect,
the only consent known to law, was to the act of the husband only, and of
this the prisoner was aware." Thus the act was without the woman's consent,
and was rape. *Flattery* was held to rule, and *Barrow* to be no longer law in
Ireland.[161]

Ironically, the reconsideration of *Barrow* in English courts was delayed by a
section of the major reform legislation on this subject passed in the same year
the *Dee* case was being heard, the well-known Criminal Law Amendment Act.
In the 1884 committee stage of the bill, Lord Bramwell moved an amendment
that would allow for the possibility of rape by threats and intimidation, by
false pretenses and by fraud. After a lengthy debate in the House, Charles
Hopwood, a leading Liberal crusader for sentencing and penal reform, a
civil libertarian known for concern with the rights of defendants, and a
champion of the workingman against class justice, succeeded in defeating
that amendment and having the Act of 1885 state that a man obtaining sex
by fraud "shall be guilty of a misdemeanour."[162]

Thus did the vigilance of civil libertarians ensure that Englishmen, unlike
Irishmen, would be protected still for years more against rape conviction in
most such circumstances. The Criminal Law Amendment Act consequently
had both facilitating and restricting effects on the prosecution of sexual offenses. Predominantly, it made it easier to convict and award significant
punishment to a man charged with indecent assault and did in fact stimulate
a further rise in such prosecutions, as well as for rape itself. On the other hand
because of the Hopwood amendment it was cited by astute defense counsel
to block rape convictions in cases of sex obtained by fraud. For example, in
the leading case of *R.v. O'Shay* (1898) defense counsel succeeded in convincing
Justice Ridley that the Act made evidence of fraudulently obtained consent
an argument for reducing a charge of rape to one of indecent assault. Such

---

[161] *R.v. Dee* (1884): 14 Cox C.C. 579. Even the defense counsel noted a "tendency in
the judgements [in leading cases over the century] to extend the definition of rape,"
while arguing that that extension did not apply in the case at hand.

[162] Even so, the same clause excluded the case of "a man who induces a married
woman to permit him to have connexion with her by personating her husband";
"every such offender," it specifically declared, "shall be deemed to be guilty of rape."
[48–49 Vict. 69 s.4]

arguments were by no means unchallenged, and a period of legal uncertainty, with conflicting opinions being issued, ensued.

By 1909, it was generally agreed in legal circles that *O'Shay* had been wrongly decided. The authoritative *Russell on Crimes* flatly declared in its edition of that year that "consent or submission obtained by fraud is not a defense to a charge of rape."[163] It took until 1923 for a case to appear that ratified this at the highest level, when the Court of Criminal Appeal affirmed the 1922 rape and indecent assault convictions of a music teacher who under pretense of improving the voice production of two students, aged sixteen and nineteen, was "permitted to have carnal connection with one and to indecently assault the other." Lord Chancellor Hewart, speaking for the court, pronounced the defense argument, drawn from *O'Shay*, "absolutely untenable," and the judges in *O'Shay* as having misread the 1885 Act.[164]

Throughout the century traditional acceptance of male sexual aggressiveness certainly persisted, as did skepticism about the testimony of any but "pure" women.[165] Women's charges of rape continued to face more of a struggle for acceptance than most other kinds of criminal complaints. As the influential jurist Edward Cox, publisher of the *Law Times* and himself a one-time magistrate, argued in 1877, a woman's "natural defences" were usually sufficient to prevent a rape. If a woman were not overmastered by drink or drugs, multiple attackers, or an unusually strong single assailant, "there might be an *attempt* at rape; but actual rape is so nearly impossible that it should be accepted only on the most conclusive evidence." He went on to note that "all who have had experience in the trial of these cases are aware of how unreliable often is the evidence of the woman."[166] Nonetheless, even in the face of such attitudes, prosecutions and convictions for rape and other sexual assaults rose. By the later years of Victoria's reign, and even more by the beginning of World War I, a greater proportion of a larger number of prosecutions for sexual assaults were resulting in convictions than ever before.[167] Thereafter, however, as "Victorian" prudery retreated, so apparently did public and official concern about punishing and deterring sexual violence. Only in the last three decades of the twentieth century, with the rise of the modern feminist movement, did such concern revive, with greater force

[163] *Russell on Crimes*, 7th ed. (1909), 1:934.
[164] It was "perfectly clear" to Hewart's court that the Act "did not override common law, but made an addition to it" [adding the possibility of convicting for indecent assault]. *R.v. Williams*, 27 Cox C.C. 350. The appellant had been convicted of both rape and indecent assault at Liverpool Assizes on 10 November 1922 and sentenced to seven years' penal servitude *and* 12 months imprisonment with hard labor.
[165] For examples particularly at lower legal levels, see D'Cruze, op. cit.
[166] E.W. Cox, *Principles of Punishment* (London, 1877), pp. 82–3.
[167] Moreover, the Incest Act 1908 statutorily criminalized another form of nonconsensual though usually non-resisted sex.

than ever before. From today's standpoint, it is easy to forget the foundations laid during the nineteenth century for the treatment of sexual assault as a most serious criminal offense. The Victorian reconstruction of masculinity and femininity, however much rejected today, had been central to the laying of these foundations. Acting together with a diminishing tolerance of most forms of interpersonal violence and with an ongoing democratic trend that brought a growing acceptance of the full personhood of all women, it helped proscribe and punish an increasing amount of men's violence against women.

# 4

# Homicidal Women and Homicidal Men: A Growing Contrast

Another form growing sympathy for "women's wrongs" took in the Victorian criminal courts was a fading of the powerful fears and horror earlier evoked by female killers, in contrast to the hardening attitudes towards violent men. When Thackeray fictionalized in 1839 the early eighteenth-century life of the burned husband-murderer Catherine Hayes, he intended a rebuttal to "Newgate novel" romanticization of criminals; nonetheless he treated her far more gently and sympathetically than her contemporaries had done. In Thackeray's novel, her fall starts with being seduced by a wicked aristocrat and is entrenched by being forced into loveless marriage and then by poverty: he admitted to his mother that "you see the author had a sneaking kindness for his heroine, and did not like to make her utterly worthless."[1]

Even the far most common mode of women's violence – against their own, often illegitimate, newborns – increasingly came to be blamed on men. In representations of infanticide between the mid-eighteenth and the mid-nineteenth century there was a marked increase in the use of what Christine L. Krueger has called "cover stories of natural innocence and melodramatic

---

[1] Quoted from his *Letters* in Micael Clarke, *Thackeray and Women* (DeKalb, Ill., 1995), pp. 51–52. Hayes' treatment in 1726 was unimaginable by Thackeray's age. Within a few years of marrying the son of her master, a wealthy farmer, she apparently persuaded two lodgers, with both of whom she had become intimate, to kill her husband and cut off his head (it was claimed that she planned to boil it away, but one of the murderers buried it instead). She claimed her husband had gone away, and wrote letters supposedly by him. There was a good deal of sympathy for the male killers, who confessed and publicly repented, as having been good men until succumbing to her blandishments and promises of wealth. For Hayes, however, no one came forward; nothing was said on her behalf either in broadsides or at the trial. Hostile crowds, including both men and women, gathered outside the Old Bailey, and on her entrances and exits, it was observed, "a more than ordinary number of persons were set to protect her from the insults of the populace, who were desperately exasperated against her, and would, in all appearance, have done her some mischief, could they have got at her." ["A narrative of the barbarous and unheard of Murder of Mr. John Hayes by Catherine his wife, Thomas Billings, and Thomas Wood . . . at night. . . ." (London, 1726) (British Library, hereafter BL)]. The two men were hanged, but she was burned.

seduction" derived from fiction to save murdering mothers from the harsh fate decreed by the law.[2] The early nineteenth-century popularity of the scenario of bad men seducing and abandoning naïve women encouraged magistrates, judges, and juries to look for an evil man behind the poor un-married girl discovered with a dead newborn. Not even an 1825 newborn murder he termed "barbarous" (the infant's head was battered in) prevented a broadside author from putting in a plea for its killer: "Let the frailties of human nature be what they may, and in an unguarded moment a female be led astray and wander in the paths of illicit intercourse; it is much to be regretted that the laws operate so severely against them, and that the finger of scorn is for ever to be pointed at the despised victim of man, and drive them to commit acts at which human nature shudders, rather let us follow the example of him who said on a similar occasion, 'Let him that is without fault cast the first stone at her.'" Indeed, jurors may have taken this exhortation to heart, for she was convicted only of concealing the birth and sentenced to six months in prison.[3] The last hanging of a woman for mur-dering her own newborn appears to have taken place in 1832, and the last of a woman for murdering her own infant under the age of one occurred in 1849, already an anachronism: this woman went to the gallows only because she confessed to poisoning not one but seven of her children.[4] The previous such hanging in 1842, with only one victim, was greeted even by the *Times* as a disgusting "judicial strangulation of a woman."[5] During the Victorian era newborn murder charges against mothers almost always ended in either acquittal (sometimes by reason of insanity) or conviction on the far lesser charge of concealment.[6] In fact, at the Old Bailey between 1840 and 1880,

[2] See Christine L. Krueger, "Literary Defenses and Medical Prosecutions: Represent-ing Infanticide in Nineteenth-Century Britain," *Victorian Studies* 40 (1996–97), 271–294. See also Margaret Arnot, "Gender in Focus: Infanticide in England, 1840–1880" (Ph.D. thesis, Essex University, 1994).
[3] "A full and particular account of the apprehension and taking of Ann and Mary Brinkworth, for the willful murder of the infant child of Ann Brinkworth" (BL); *Times*, 11 April 1825, p. 6.
[4] See Patrick Wilson, *Murderess* (London, 1971), pp. 72–75; Roger Smith, *Trial by Medicine* (Edinburgh, 1981), p. 147; Judith Knelman, *Twisting in the Wind: The Murderess and the English Press* (Toronto, 1997), pp. 151–152.
[5] *Times*, 8 August 1842, p. 6.
[6] In an 1845 editorial the *Times* [17 March 1845, p. 4] described how Justice Erle strained his instructions in a recent case to enable a jury to acquit such a defendant: "to constitute the offense of murder," he had told them, "they must be satisfied that the child was *completely* born, and had a *complete* independent existence of its own;" he had concluded by urging that if they had any doubts they should certainly acquit of murder and find only concealment, which they did. The newspaper argued that a change in the Poor Law would make such crimes far less common and such contorting of the law unnecessary.

out of sixty indictments not a single woman was convicted of the murder of a newborn child, whether her own or anybody else's.[7]

If a woman murdered her children who were beyond infancy she could still without much difficulty be seen as a victim. When Emma Aston was tried at the Old Bailey in 1888 for the murder of her two children, after being deserted by her husband, she was found insane, a verdict which the *Times* published an editorial in order to applaud. "Seldom," it declared,

> has a more distressing tale been told. . . . The cowardly selfishness which betrays its victim and abandons the helpless fruit of its own misdeeds, seems to be brought more frequently than ever before the public eye. The same melancholy theme, with slight variations, has lately furnished the plot of a terribly large number of the tragedies of the criminal court. . . . In this particular case the merciful view taken by the jury was unquestionably correct. The heartless conduct of the father of the little victims was too cruel a weight for a brain already deranged by deception, anxiety, and want, and it is not to be doubted that the murderer was irresponsible for her actions at the time the deed was done. Considering all that she has had to bear, we hope that the Home Secretary will agree with the opinion of the jury, suggested by the judge, that the poor woman is now recovered of her madness, and that it will be "Her Majesty's pleasure" not to detain her in custody as a criminal lunatic longer than the fulfillment of the necessary formalities requires. She has suffered enough for an act, the real guilt of which, assuredly, is upon another head than hers.[8]

Of course in the right circumstances such a female killer could be judged as harshly as a man. When in 1853 Honor Gibbons poisoned her little girl to collect burial insurance she was found guilty at Chester of murder, and Justice Wightman thundered that "for the basest motives of gain, [she] had unnaturally violated one of the deepest feelings of human nature." Even Gibbons, however, was recommended to mercy and reprieved from the gallows; it is safe to say this would never have happened if she had been a father, as convicted male poisoners were almost invariably hanged.[9] Overall, the

---

[7] Arnot, op. cit., p. 138. Even the minor charge of concealment was becoming less successful: At the Old Bailey 1840–80 convictions on this charge fell each decade from 34 to 26 to 18 to 12%. When they pled guilty, most received less than two weeks' imprisonment [Arnot, p. 139].

[8] *Times*, 21 March 1888, p. 11. Here was a case of "temporary insanity" which jury, judge, *Times* and Home Secretary had no trouble in accepting. The judge in this case was the normally merciless "hanging Henry Hawkins," who however, one barrister later recalled, "was a most lenient judge in the case of women who had been deceived." [Evelyn Burnaby, *Memories of Famous Trials* (London, 1907), p. 58.]

[9] *Times*, 11 April 1853, p. 7.

*Times* reported 431 English homicide trials of parents accused of killing minor children over 24 hours old. Although the great majority of these involved mothers only, only two women were hanged, as against nine men.[10]

The murder of a former lover by a jilted woman, of which nineteenth-century France provided many examples, was far rarer in England. When it did occur, a standard tactic of the defendant's counsel was to "try the victim," to paint the man as the real villain, seducing and then abandoning a woman to a miserable fate. In February 1848 in St. James' Park Annette Myers, a lady's maid, shot at point-blank range the Guardsman who had loved and then jilted her; he died instantly. Her trial naturally drew intense public interest, as horror at her deed vied with outrage at his behavior. It became clear that after he had won her by promising marriage, he used her callously, continually extracting money from her quite small stock, which he spent gambling and carousing, while also seeing another woman. He indeed seems to have embodied most of the vices often feared from soldiers. In court Myers, as the *Times* sympathetically reported, "looked very pale, and was evidently suffering severe mental distress. She was seated in the dock during the trial, kept her handkerchief to her face nearly the whole time, and appeared to be crying." Her counsel read a portion of some of the love letters she had written him. "My happiness in this world," he quoted from one, "depends upon you – my very existence is bound up with your wellbeing and prosperity." "God help her, poor creature," said her counsel, "she was little aware how that expression would be realised." The deceased, he declared, "after having polluted and destroyed the wretched girl at the bar, had basely deserted her, because, having made use of all her wages to supply his cravings for money, she refused to comply with an odious suggestion which he had made to her as a means of raising more money for him" (the suggestion that she should go on the streets).[11] Even without corroboration (indeed, the fellow servant and close friend to whom she had shown the pistol testified that Annette never mentioned his having suggested this) it was a most effective claim. The jury had no choice but to find her guilty of murder but accompanied their verdict with a very strong recommendation to mercy on account of the "extraordinary provocation" she had received. This recommendation was seconded in public meetings – one in the City was addressed by the leading Radical, John Bright, who depicted her as "a victim of systematic and atrocious villainy. Every feeling in her woman's heart was wronged and outraged by the man who had fallen by her hand." The press also took up the cudgels for her, even the eminently respectable *Morning Post*, which published an editorial to praise her and to call her victim "the vilest of the vile." "Surely never," it concluded, "was murder committed under more

[10] I owe this information to Carolyn Conley.
[11] *Times*, 4 March 1848, p. 8.

palliating circumstances."[12] Myers won her reprieve, an "heroic criminal" as
Jane Carlyle ironically called her, to much of the public.[13]

A few months before Myers' crime Hannah Williams had also been in the
Old Bailey dock for violence against a jilting lover. In revenge for his breaking
off with her and engaging himself to another woman she cut him in the neck
with a knife. The wound was not a dangerous one, but its recipient brought
charges, and she was tried for wounding with intent to do grievous bodily
harm, the charge one notch below that of attempted murder. The prosecutor
had to admit that she was of good character and that he'd seduced her under
promise of marriage; moreover (again like Myers' case) when he had been out
of work, she had given him money and clothing. He certainly appeared a cad;
she was found guilty of misdemeanor assault only, with a recommendation to
mercy on account of provocation, and Justice Cresswell "quite concurred" for
"there was no doubt that the conduct of the prosecutor had been most base,
profligate and disgraceful." Feeling that he had to give her some sentence,
for "it was impossible to overlook entirely the use of a deadly weapon," he
sentenced Williams to one month's imprisonment, without hard labor; this
at a time when the use of knives was being cracked down upon.[14]

The presumption of female innocence and weakness helped save women
in other situations as well. When Elizabeth Humbler was charged at the Old
Bailey in 1862 together with her lover and employer Samuel Gardner in the
murder of his wife, Chief Baron Pollock, over the strenuous objections of
Gardner's counsel, chivalrously ordered the charge against her dismissed.
The jury went on to convict Gardner.[15]

In the murder of husbands, women similarly benefited from newly established stereotypes. When in 1832 Mary Ratcliffe was charged at Lancaster
with having incited and aided her lover to murder her husband, no expressions of horror were made at the trial or in the press. Whereas her lover
was separately convicted and left for hanging, Ratcliffe's judge declared the
case against her weak, and she was set free.[16] In 1843 Sarah Westwood was
convicted of murdering her husband by poison, but even though she had a
lover and in addition her method, poisoning, was especially abhorred, her
jury still recommended her to mercy, on the simple ground that she was a
woman.[17] Such a ground for reprieving had rarely been explicitly cited before

[12] *Morning Post*, 8 March 1848.

[13] *The Collected Letters of Thomas and Jane Welsh Carlyle* (Durham, N.C. and London,
1970–2000), 23:224. For a fuller account of Myers' story, see Wiener, "The Trial of
Annette Myers," in *On Murder 2: True Crime Writing in Australia*, ed. Kerry Greenwood
(Melbourne, 2002), pp. 125–131.

[14] *Times*, 28 October 1847, p. 6.

[15] *Times*, 1 November 1862, p. 11.

[16] *Times*, 23 August 1832, p. 3.

[17] Judith Knelman, in her account [op. cit.] fails to mention this. Westwood nonetheless
did go to the scaffold [*Times*, 30 December 1843, p. 7]. Interestingly enough, it was

this time.[18] The execution in Bury St. Edmunds four years later of another husband-poisoner with a lover, Catherine Foster, was very unpopular: "Her youthful appearance," a local newspaper observed, "created the most awful sensation amongst the assembled multitude, and in a moment all seemed to be struck with awe . . . the drop fell. Her struggles were painful in the extreme, and a thrill of horror ran through the crowd, voices being heard in many places, crying 'shame, shame! murder, murder!' It must have been a couple of minutes ere life had ceased."[19]

One marker of altered sentiment (as in the case of Foster) was the way newspaper and broadside accounts of murderers of husbands (or, rarer events, of fathers) came to focus less on the crime and more on the female criminal's state at the trial and on the scaffold. The sufferings of the accused woman were coming to compete with the murder itself as the center of public interest. When they came to hang the poisoner Ann Barber in 1821, it was related that she became "violent and clamorous. Her shrieks were bitter and piercing, beyond any thing that is possible to imagine. . . . The heart-rending cries that announced her approach [to the scaffold] filled almost every face with dismay." Her last words were "God bless my children" – a very maternal picture of womanhood, quite different from that broadside accounts had presented of Mary Channing or Catherine Hayes in the previous century.[20] Fainting

---

in this year that the Home Office began keeping a record of the sex of convicted murderers.

[18] Very few mercy petitions for women in cases of murder have so far been found in the eighteenth-century pardon files. See Peter King, *Crime, Justice and Discretion* (Oxford, 2000).

[19] "Execution of Catherine Foster," *Bury and Norwich Post*, 21 April 1847. The paper noted that no woman had been executed in the town since 1800. On her trial, see *Times*, 29 March 1847, p. 7 and 31 March 1847, p. 7. One broadside announced that "Under the authority of the Secretary of State for the Home Department this day . . . A YOUNG GIRL is to be PUBLICLY STRANGLED in front of the county jail, Bury St Edmonds . . . and if the neck of the wretched victim be not by this shock broken, the said MORAL TEACHER will pull the legs of the miserable girl until by his weight and strength united he Strangles Her." ["Grand Moral Spectacle!" (Chelmsford, 1847 {BL})] After Foster's hanging, it became even harder to convict a woman. Three other wives were tried later that same year: one, Elizabeth Johnson, was convicted but reprieved, and the other two, Mary Lennox and Anne Mather, were acquitted.

[20] "A particular account of the trial and execution of Ann Barber. . . ." (1821) (BL) One broadside noted that no woman had been executed in York for husband murder since 1776 ["A brief account of the trial and execution of Ann Barber. . . ." (1821) (Bodleian Library, Oxford, John Johnson Collection)]. Patrick Wilson, *Murderess*, op. cit., provides much useful information on the sixty-eight women hanged since 1842. Knelman, op. cit., has interesting observations about the public image of female murderers in the nineteenth century, although she concentrates overmuch on horror and repulsion (traditional sentiments in cases of murder, and equally present in accounts of murders by men) and neglects the more novel growth of sympathy for the female defendant and discomfort with subjecting her to severe punishment.

seems by the nineteenth century neither to have been unusual for female defendants, nor limited to "ladies." Even the tough Sarah Polgrean, who poisoned her husband in 1820 in order to remarry, appeared overwhelmed at her trial and fainted repeatedly.[21] Five years later, Hannah Read in her murder defense emphasized her husband's brutality and her own weakness, claiming that she had wanted to leave but was too afraid of him to do so. In court she appeared to be "pale and agitated, she could hardly stand," and pleaded for herself on behalf of her six children.[22] This tactic evoked a good deal of sympathy from her judge, who scolded the prosecuting counsel for seeking to introduce into evidence a confession wormed out of her. Nonetheless, not surprisingly given the clear evidence, she was convicted (upon which she fainted), and hanged.

Although she too was hanged in 1831, the domestic killer Mary Ann Higgins, in spite of committing what was considered the basest of crimes, stirred still more sympathetic feeling among spectators. She had fed her uncle, with whom she lived, doses of arsenic until he died, with the aim of gaining his considerable wealth and going off with her lover. The *Times* observed that she was "rather a good looking girl [and had] an appearance of modesty and innocence about her which, in despite of the general belief in her guilt, excited strong feelings of interest and compassion towards her." Against usual practice, she was allowed to sit down in the dock. A reporter noted that "the male prisoner [her lover], although his case was involved in much more doubt, was an object of a very different feeling."[23]

After the law was amended in 1836 to allow time after murder convictions for appeals for mercy to be considered, these sentimental feelings had scope to produce greater results, and the hanging of women immediately became highly exceptional. Whereas six women were hanged in the two years 1835 and 1836 for murdering their husbands, thereafter in the following two-thirds of the century only another eighteen went to the scaffold for this offense, five of these occurring in the six years, 1847–52, in which there reigned something of a "poisoning panic."[24] Apart from this panic, therefore, only thirteen

---

[21] *Times*, 15 August 1820, p. 3. See the observations on this case in R.M. Short, "Female Criminality 1780–1830" (M.Litt. thesis, Oxford University, 1989). Short's chief argument – that a significant amount of female aggressiveness and violence existed in the early nineteenth century, but was underplayed in press coverage – though aimed elsewhere (at uncovering "hidden" female assertiveness and agency) supports the argument here, that the old fear of female violence was waning, submerged under a sharpening image of woman as victim of male violence and brutality. Even if much female violence survived into the nineteenth century, as Short maintains, fears of it are ever harder to find in popular literature.

[22] *Star*, 6 August 1825.

[23] *Times*, 11 August 1831, p. 6.

[24] On this panic see Judith Knelman, "The Amendment of the Sale of Arsenic Bill," *Victorian Review* 17 (1991), 1–10; Peter Bartrip, "A 'Pennurth of Arsenic for Rat Poison': The Arsenic Act, 1851 and the Prevention of Secret Poisoning," *Medical History* 36

husband-killers hanged during Victoria's entire reign, as compared to several hundred wife-killers.[25] Poisoning was the only category of spouse murder for which more women than men were convicted, yet even here, while every single man found guilty of poisoning his wife (and no one else) from 1840 to the end of the century (thirteen in number) hanged, only six (of eighteen) women similarly convicted went to the scaffold. This disparity would have been even greater, but for the fact that many more wife-poisoners than husband-poisoners killed themselves afterwards (a gender disparity repeated in all spouse murders): a very incomplete search between 1860 and 1905 turned up seven wife-poisoners who thus evaded trial, but *no* husband-poisoners.[26]

Juries came almost invariably to recommend that the lives of female defendants be spared, virtually the only exceptions being when there were multiple victims. In 1848, the accused husband-poisoner Ann Fisher even won acquittal despite powerful evidence against her. A young woman, rumored to have a lover her own age, married only three months to an older man, she had gotten her husband to change his will to leave her all he had, about £5000. A medical man testified with confidence to the presence of a lethal amount of arsenic in the deceased, and a fellow woman prisoner claimed under oath that Fisher told her she did it. Yet it took the jury only ten minutes to acquit her.[27]

Even a sudden wave of apparent husband-poisonings in the summer of 1849 failed to bring back the old horror of what once had been the offense of petty treason.[28] Despite having spent a week deliberately poisoning her well-respected Somerset husband in order to marry a rich old man, and getting for a judge Mr. Justice Cresswell, who was developing a reputation as one of the most severe members of the bench, Charlotte Harris escaped the noose. Her trial lasted nearly two days, and the jury was out for an hour before finding her guilty. "They were all," it was reported, "extremely affected, and it was with much difficulty that the foreman could deliver his verdict." The *Times'* reporter observed that "the prisoner fainted away and was unconscious several times during her trial, and was in a most pitiable state when taken out of court."[29] She was found to be pregnant and respited

---

(1992), 53–69; George Robb, "Circe in Crinoline: Domestic Poisonings in Victorian England," *Journal of Family History* 22 (1997), 176–190: Ian Burney, "A Poisoning of No Substance: The Trials of Medico-Legal Proof in Mid-Victorian England," *Journal of British Studies* 38 (1999), 58–92.

[25] Wilson, op. cit. Cases between 1835 and 1842 are drawn from my spouse murder database. These numbers exclude multiple murders, such as familicide.

[26] This is the same gendered pattern of homicide followed by suicide noted by contemporary criminologists: see M. Cooper and D. Eaves, "Suicide Following Homicide in the Family," *Violence and Victims* 11 (1996), 99–111.

[27] *Times*, 27 March 1848, p. 7; *Bell's Life*, 2 April 1848.

[28] A crime that had been formally abolished by the 1828 Offenses Against the Person Act.

[29] 1 August 1849.

until she gave birth, allowing time for public interest to build. And build it did, drawing many mass petitions specifically from "the women of..." a number of different localities, as far away as Dublin. These petitions were mostly addressed to the Queen, as "the first woman in this great empire," and "as reverencing in your person the virtues which, while they belong to our common nature, grace your Majesty in a peculiar manner – pity and maternal love." While the Queen probably never saw them, they won Harris a reprieve to transportation.[30] Henceforth, a new mother was never to be hanged.

Later that same year, Mary Ball, an adulteress convicted of poisoning her husband near the fashionable town of Bath, did hang, but only after a reluctant jury deliberated a very unusual two hours, and was then pressured by the judge, Lord Coleridge, a man well known for his severity, to withdraw a recommendation to mercy.[31] Two other women similarly charged that year were acquitted, while one other was hanged. The last, however, had poisoned not only her husband but also her two adult sons and collected death benefits on them all – a weak case for portrayal as a "wronged woman"![32]

Press coverage of these women's cases (all rural) made more of their rustic primitiveness than of the threat to gender hierarchies they might have symbolized. By the mid–nineteenth century even women killers, unless their victims were multiple, were able to draw from the increasingly dominant cultural motif of the "helpless woman," the woman as much sinned against as sinning. Consequently, it was ever harder for their deeds to evoke general fear, and ever easier to marshal sympathy for them, even when their guilt was acknowledged.

While men who captured the sympathy of the court after killing their wives sometimes got off lightly, such an outcome was much more likely when the shoe was on the other foot. Jane Colbert received a mere one week's

---

[30] HO18/274/1. This despite the thundering of the *Times* about "a specimen of murder which, in its sublimated atrocity, transcends anything we have yet recorded" [8 August 1849, p. 4]. Similarly, one disgruntled male correspondent to the Home Office sourly dissented to the reprieve: "What reliance," he asked the Home Secretary, "can a man place in his wife on whom he depends for comfort, tenderness and affection in sickness and sorrow when perhaps she may take that as the opportunity of terminating his existence?" Writing also to the *Times*, he complained there about the female petitioners: "It is very probable, from the part they are acting, that the ladies of Somersetshire and Devonshire think that murdering a husband in cold blood, and for a sordid purpose, were not a crime...deserving of extreme punishment – a source, no doubt, of satisfaction to their husbands...." However, the Home Secretary did not reply, and neither the *Times*' leader nor his letter to it drew any further correspondence.

[31] *Times*, 31 July 1849, p. 7.

[32] Mary Ann Geering [see *Times*, 2 August 1849, pp. 6–7]. She was, as the *Times* noted, "a woman of masculine and forbidding appearance."

imprisonment in 1854 for her husband's death, when she responded to a beating by seizing a knife and throwing it at him, piercing his lung. He had apparently been in the habit of beating her.[33] Four years later Harriet Webster claimed self-defense and was acquitted after killing her abusive husband with a poker. "There was no doubt," the court report noted, "that the deceased was a man of drunken habits, and addicted to fighting."[34] Both women were saved by acting in hot blood, and in a situation in which a claim of self-defense was plausible. Such a defense was not open to Ellen Rutter in 1859, a battered wife who cut her husband's throat while he slept. She was convicted of murder, though even here the jury urged mercy "on account of her husband's cruelty," and the foreman went so far as to state they "trusted their recommendation would be taken into consideration." Her sentence was commuted.[35]

The same year Ellen Rutter was convicted of murder, Susan Trotter fatally stabbed her husband with a table knife. However, "threats and violence had been used towards her by her husband, who, as well as she, was intoxicated at the time. . . . Her contrition afterwards was most touching." She received a mere three months in prison.[36] In 1888 Mary Ellen Coleman was sentenced to one day's imprisonment for killing her abusive husband. She had been attempting to get him home from a pub after he had gotten quite drunk; he kicked her violently in the chest, to which she responded by seizing a poker and striking him. Four days later he died from the blow. His history of abusing her was cited, as was the fact that she was suffering from consumption, and that "she was likely to die from the shock if she were sent to prison." Her sentence of one day allowed her immediate discharge.[37]

Similarly, in non-fatal cases of violence against husbands, Victorian courts were often surprisingly indulgent. Mary Ann Willey was acquitted of all charges in 1849 after stabbing her husband in the neck during a drunken quarrel. Her counsel successfully argued that "she had committed the act in a moment of desperation brought on by wretchedness and starvation and that, without imputing actual insanity to her, they would be justified in coming to the conclusion that she was in such a state of mind as not to be aware of the effect of the act she was about to commit."[38]

Within a few weeks of each other in the spring of 1853, a man was tried at Huntingdon and a woman at the Old Bailey for the same act, that of throwing acid on a former lover who had spurned them. In neither case was

---

[33] *Times*, 22 September 1854, p. 10.
[34] *Times*, 18 December 1858, p. 10.
[35] *Times*, 15 August 1859, p. 12.
[36] *Times*, 15 December 1859, p. 10.
[37] *Times*, 30 July 1888, p. 3.
[38] *Times*, 6 March 1849, p. 7.

there any doubt of the act having been done by the defendant. The man, John Mason, received twelve months' imprisonment while the woman, Elizabeth Hodges, was acquitted. Such behavior might be forgivable in a seduced and abandoned woman but was hardly "manly."[39]

Even when a judge called for a conviction against a woman, he was not necessarily heeded. After her husband came home drunk and beat her, as he had often done before, Eliza Ward, daughter of the verger of St. Albans Abbey, dug out a knife and stabbed him. The wound was not serious, but he brought charges and in 1871 she was prosecuted for wounding with intent to cause grievous bodily harm. Justice Blackburn found the more serious charge unproven, but told the jury that "he could not see the evidence which showed that the wound was inflicted in self-defense, and unless the jury could see their way to that conclusion, they must convict the prisoner of unlawful wounding." Nonetheless, the jury found her not guilty, a verdict which "met with the approval of every one in court."[40]

The second half of the century saw a decline in the prosecution of women for serious crimes, a larger decline in their conviction, and a still larger decline in the length of their prison sentences.[41] As for the number of women executed, it fell almost to nothing. The one figure that did rise for women (even more than for men) was that of insanity verdicts.[42] If it was easier to see men as bad, it was correspondingly easier to see women as mad. Over the Victorian period as a whole women were twice as likely to be acquitted on the ground of insanity, even when women and men were charged with similar crimes. Paying little attention to the M'Naughton rules, later Victorian juries increasingly concluded that a woman who committed a heinous crime must have been insane. As the Edwardian superintendent of Broadmoor claimed, "had the M'Naughton dictum been rigidly insisted upon, it would have been the means of hanging more than half the women who are

---

[39] *Times*, 10 March 1853, p. 7; 9 April 1853, p. 8. Similarly, Annie Lovesay was acquitted in 1897 after throwing acid at a man for whom "she had provided food and lodging [and herself], but [who] had treated her cruelly." Justice Grantham called the prosecutor "a brute" and essentially dismissed the case. His remarks "were received with manifestations of approval in Court" [*Times*, 6 May 1897, p. 12].

[40] *Times*, 12 July 1871, p. 11.

[41] See Lucia Zedner, *Women, Crime, and Custody in Victorian England* (Oxford, 1991), tables drawn from the annual judicial statistics, pp. 304–327; Wiener, *Reconstructing the Criminal* (Cambridge, 1990), p. 309 [from annual reports of the Prison Commission].

[42] Out of a sample of more than a thousand cases over the Victorian period, Jill Ainsley has found that overall 7% of women charged with a violent crime received insanity acquittals. "By the end of the 1880s, however," she noted, "the proportion had climbed to 11%, and in the 1890s increased to 17%." [Jill Newton Ainsley, " 'Some mysterious agency': Women, Violent Crime, and the Insanity Acquittal in the Victorian Courtroom," *Canadian Journal of History* 35 (April 2000), 37–55.]

now in Broadmoor, as criminal lunatics, for the murder of their children!"[43]
The same re-imagining of gender that made men more vulnerable to the
sanctions of the criminal law had made women less so. Of course, this does
not at all mean that women became freer from social control overall, or even
that criminal justice was necessarily favoring women over men[44] – as has
been noted by Lucia Zedner and others, the ready ascription of insanity to
lawbreaking women denied them the agency granted to men put on trial for
their acts. It does mean, however, that severe criminal punishment of women
was becoming ever less acceptable to "respectable opinion." As a result, at
least in the area of crimes against the person, the criminal law focused its
regulatory work increasingly on men and decreasingly on women. It was
a trend that depended upon, and reinforced, the cultural reconstruction of
manhood and womanhood that took place in the nineteenth century.

The relaxing treatment of homicidal women in nineteenth-century courts
was accompanied by a hardening of the treatment of homicidal men, particularly when the victims were women. Most such killing was spousal, but the
killings that provoked the greatest horror were those of the most vulnerable
of all women, the "seduced." Indeed, the form of femicide that first leaped
into public attention early in the century was the murder of a sexual partner
not married to the killer. The victim of this crime was almost always a young
woman, for this was perhaps the most gendered of all crimes. Such killing
was already being regularly given the maximum penalty of the gallows, but
in the early Victorian years it received much wider and more thorough publicity than ever before, and seemed to evoke greater anxiety.[45] Sometimes this
murder was committed in the act of rape; sometimes more cold-bloodedly, to
prevent the victim of either rape or seduction making it known or because the
woman had become pregnant and importunate to marry or for financial support.[46] Changing social conditions may have contributed to anxiety about

[43] Quoted in *Roscoe's Digest of the Law of Evidence,* 13th ed. (London, 1908), p. 814.
[44] Since the actual circumstances of men's and women's violent crimes may well
have differed sufficiently to justify differential treatment, even perhaps treatment
*more* "favorable" to women than was the case [as argued for recent years in Susan
Edwards, *Sex and Gender in the Legal Process* (London, 1996), pp. 371–72]. For one thing,
almost all violence against husbands was retaliatory in nature, and arguably meriting
substantially less punishment than violence against wives. As previously pointed out,
this study is not concerned with rights and wrongs, but with historical developments
and their explanation.
[45] An upsurge of interest in this kind of homicide has also been found in America in this
period; see Daniel Cohen, "The Beautiful Female Murder Victim: Literary Genres
and Courtship Practices in the Origins of a Cultural Motif, 1590–1850," *Journal of
Social History* 31 (Winter 1997), 277–306.
[46] Local authorities would indeed press a presumed father for child support or marriage; examples of such pressing abound in David Vaizey, ed., *The Diary of Thomas
Turner* (Oxford and New York, 1984).

such dangers: with the control exerted by small local communities yielding before increasing individual freedom and possibilities for social rise, the specter loomed of ambitious men freeing themselves of inconvenient lovers by this ultimate violation. The press coverage of such men, both factual and fictional, served to shape a vivid negative archetype, which functioned as a cultural indictment of the possibilities of unchecked aggressive masculinity. The greatest "villain" of the Victorian public imagination was the sexual predator who was also a "man of blood."

Particularly from the end of the Napoleonic Wars, crime broadsides and chapbooks describing the murder of women became more numerous and ever more widely selling, most of them carrying illustrations of such acts.[47] The first great such public sensation, drawing crowds to the vicinity of the trial, was a case that combined both fears – that of Abraham Thornton, prosecuted for the rape and murder of Mary Ashford, a poor but virtuous young woman of twenty, in 1817.[48] Thornton admitted they had sex, though he claimed consensually, but maintained he knew nothing of the murder. His acquittal, as a local newspaper reported two weeks later, "in this atrocious rape and murder ... has excited the most undisguised feelings of disappointment in all classes of people, from one end of the country to the other."[49] The strong public feeling against him enabled subscriptions to be raised to defray the not-inconsiderable cost of a new prosecution, and Thornton was re-arrested through the archaic method of a private appeal of murder (by Ashford's brother). This time the case was dismissed after Thornton successfully claimed another archaic right in private appeals, to trial by combat! Yet, as one author observed,

> though the rigid application of the letter of the law thus a second time saved [Thornton] ... nothing could remove the conviction of his guilt from the public mind. Shunned by all who knew him, his very name became an object of terror, and he soon afterwards attempted to proceed to America, but the sailors of the vessel in which he was about to embark

---

[47] I have found (in the British Library, the Bodleian Library, and St. Bride's Printing Library) only a bare handful of such publications for eighteenth-century England, as compared to dozens apparently for the first half of the nineteenth century. I have not been able to arrive at a precise figure for the pre- and post-1800 broadsides, since quite a few are undated and without sufficient other markers to locate them chronologically. Even allowing for the greater likelihood for survival of more recent broadsides and the increasing market for them with urbanization and population growth, the contrast is notable.

[48] See *Times*, 11 August 1817, p. 3 and 25 August 1817, p. 3. This case has been discussed at length in Anna Clark, "Rape or Seduction? A Controversy over Sexual Violence in the Nineteenth Century," in *The Sexual Dynamics of History: Men's Power, Women's Resistance*, The London Feminist History Group (London, 1983).

[49] *Times*, 25 August 1817, p. 3, quoting verbatim from a Lichfield paper.

refused to go to sea with a character on board who, according to their fancy, was likely to produce so much ill-luck to the voyage and he was compelled to conceal himself until another opportunity was afforded him to make good his escape.[50]

After the Thornton–Ashford case both the fictional and the "factual" literature of seduction-and-betrayal took off, exemplified in an efflorescence of broadsides (some describing real cases, others concocted ones) featuring the seducer-turned-murderer. Always there was the warning to young women: "So all pretty maidens," a typical sheet of this type concluded, "wherever you be, Beware of enticements and false perjury; For fear, like young Mary, you're mind full soon, Like a rose in the summer you're plucked in your bloom."[51]

The fictional literature emphasized class themes, the gentleman seducing and betraying a girl socially beneath him. George Caddell, cutting the throat of a lover who wanted to marry and threatened to expose their affair, was an archetypal fictional villain: he lured the girl to an isolated country spot and cut her throat. Her great mistake, a broadside remarked, was to think herself "an equal match for one of Mr. Caddell's rank of life."[52] Other stories had the seduced woman pregnant. In 1835 a broadside account of the seduction and murder of a farmer's daughter by a gentleman appeared in two widely separated versions. The factuality of either is dubious, while their fit with the melodramatic plays of the time is perfect. Like those, both versions exhibit a most popular plot line of the era: a beautiful young woman, seduced and impregnated by a young gentleman of "large fortune," has nowhere to turn: when her father discovers her pregnancy, "being a strict moral man," as a broadside put it, he beats her severely and throws her out of the family

---

[50] Crook, *Complete Newgate Calendar*, vol. 5, p. 170.

[51] "A full and particular account of a most barbarous and cruel MURDER committed upon the body of Mary Thomson, by her sweetheart David Gaston, who seduced her under pretence of marriage, and how she became pregnant – showing how the Villain murdered her, and threw her body into a pond. . . ." [London, n.d.]. Another example among quite a few extant is "An account of a most horrid, barbarous and cruel murder, that was committed by Henry Cummins (a respectable farmer's son residing near Wells) on the body of Mary Price (a servant in his father's family) . . . given in the following affecting copy of verses." Anne Rodrick has found that "a large proportion" of the cases printed in both the Chartist paper the *Northern Star* and the more middle-class and less explicitly political *Illustrated London News* in the typical early Victorian year of 1846 "were murders of young women by their lovers, many of whom were men married to other women and who sought to avoid exposure of an unexpected pregnancy." [" 'Only a Newspaper Metaphor': Crime Reports, Class Conflict, and Social Criticism in Two Victorian Newspapers," *Victorian Periodicals Review* 29, no. 1 (Spring 1996), 1–18.]

[52] "Horrid Murder, committed by a young gentleman on the body of his sweetheart, by cutting her throat," London, n.d. (BL1888.c.3).

home. She then goes to her seducer and pleads with him to fulfill his many fervent promises of marriage; he fears social ruin and instead takes her into the woods and stabs her repeatedly through the heart.[53]

However, real cases rarely followed this cross-class script, instead more typically describing a predatorily ambitious man seeking to advance himself socially through sexual alliance; a "normal" social scenario given a horrific outcome. In either scenario, however, pregnancy could doom a woman. At just one Essex assize in 1821, two murder cases with pregnant young women as victims, from different parts of the county, were heard. Both James Emery and William Akers were convicted of murdering their pregnant lovers and were hanged. Emery's motive was probably not homicidal; he gave his girlfriend arsenic, but apparently to procure an abortion, from which dosage she died. Akers more villainously strangled his pregnant secret lover, the daughter of his landlady. He nearly escaped justice by claiming that she had hanged herself and by getting the body quickly laid in a coffin. However, just before burial a suspicious relative had the coffin opened and the corpse examined, and the truth came out. Such close calls only further stoked the fires of fear: one might well wonder how many like deeds had passed undetected.[54]

In 1823 John Radford stood trial at the Exeter assizes for another such killing. His lover's pregnant body was found in the river, and incriminating evidence was brought against him. A friend related his confession, in which he attributed it all to a drunken impulse. Yet in court he seemed more the classic villain: "The whole court," it was reported, "was deeply affected, and the ladies who crowded the galleries were dissolved in tears; but the prisoner listened with a steady countenance, only a slight convulsion agitating his features on quitting the bar." After the jury delivered its verdict of "guilty," Justice Best told Radford that "if any case of murder can be capable of aggravation, yours is that case; for it appears, from what passed early in the evening, that you led her to suppose you would make her your wife – one cannot doubt you were the father of her child; and thus, by one wicked act, you deprived one human being of existence whom you ought to have protected, and prevented another from coming into life with a similar claim upon you."[55] Judges themselves took to issuing warnings to young women.

---

[53] "A most horrid and dreadful murder" [by John Anson], (Gloucester, 1835 [BL]). The same account was given in "The Richmond Tragedy" (BL), published the same year.

[54] *Suffolk Chronicle*, 18 August 1821, p. 1.

[55] *The Alfred – West of England Journal – General Advertiser*, 29 July 1823, p. 2. On the similar case of Sam Fallows (whose "very respectable relatives" were unable to save him from the gallows) in the same year, see *Chester Courant and Anglo-Welsh Gazette*, 15 April 1823, pp. 1–2; "Trial, Conviction and Execution of Samuel Fallows, aged 24 years" [Bodleian Library, Harding Collection].

After a man was found guilty at Chester in 1824 of the rape of a woman he had first enticed, the judge pronounced a sentence of death, telling him that "the treatment this girl has received from you will be a warning to others, not to enter into that familiarity with, and form an acquaintance with persons so unknown to them as it appears you were to her."[56]

In the next national *cause celebre* of a predatory man, the trial of William Corder for the murder of Maria Marten in 1828, a kind of pre-trial media feeding frenzy excited the judge to denunciation: he complained "that drawings and placards have been dispersed, not only in the neighbourhood of this town, but also in the immediate neighbourhood of this very hall, tending to the manifest detriment of the prisoner at the bar. Such a practice is so indecorous and so unjust, that I can with difficulty bring myself to believe that any person, even in the very lowest class, will so far degrade himself as to think of deriving gain from the exhibition of this melancholy transaction."[57] However, the judge's view was not shared even by the "respectable" press: The *Times* congratulated the public "on a manifest improvement in the condition of its moral feeling, since the sickly sensibility of the press, and of the multitude to whose foul taste it ministered, was wont to declare itself on the side of ruthless and treacherous murderers, and to stifle at once every movement of honest compassion for the victim. . . . Corder has united in this one deed of horror – if it be his only one – whatever the heart revolts at most in the conduct of man to woman. He seduced – then betrayed – then massacred the wretched creature, in cold blood."[58] In fact, Corder did even more: he had placed matrimonial advertisements in the press, and had drawn many scores of responses, some of which were read out in court; in this sense, his female victims were legion.

Corder was convicted and hanged before a crowd of perhaps 7,000. The story became the basis of many popular plays, one of which, *Maria Martin; or, the Murder in the Red Barn* (1840) may have been the most performed nineteenth-century criminal melodrama.[59] These plays generally portrayed Corder as a demonic monster for whose extinction all creation cried, also, in the process, de-emphasizing or omitting the moral slips of the victim. Her two children by

[56] *Times*, 16 September 1824, p. 3.

[57] 9 August 1828, p. 3. For an example of the intense coverage, see the lengthy pamphlet, "The trial of William Corder, for the wilful murder of Maria Marten, by shooting and stabbing her, and afterwards burying her body in the Red Barn, at Postead, in the county of Suffolk. Containing a full account of every particular connected with the awful catastrophe, the evidence of the witnesses, the prisoner's defense, and behaviour before, at, and after his trial. His conviction, sentence, confession, and execution. Together with a copy of the advertisement, by which he obtained his wife" (London, 1828); this is only one of several different pamphlets that have survived.

[58] *Times*, 11 Aug. 1828, p. 3.

[59] Michael R. Booth, *English Melodrama* (London, 1965), p. 139. See also Beth Kalikoff, *Murder and Moral Decay in Victorian Popular Literature* (Ann Arbor, Mich., 1986).

Corder tended to disappear from the plays, as Maria Marten was made over, like Mary Ashford, into a hitherto-virginal maiden walking unknowingly to her doom.[60]

Another predatorily ambitious man was Samuel Thorley, a Cheshire nurseryman who in 1834 courted a young lady possessing an inheritance of £2000. When her family broke off the relationship, he cut her throat in a rage and ended on the gallows. Catnach, the printer, knowing his market, turned Thorley into a butcher and claimed that he "ate the calf muscle of his victim, out of professional curiosity."[61] Further events fueled the image of villainous men at large and women at risk. In 1837 a "respectably connected" Londoner, James Greenacre, secured his place in the gallery of great villains by not only fatally stabbing his fiancee, Hannah Brown, but also mutilating her body (here the printers were relieved from the need to embroider). When he discovered she had tricked him into believing she had property, he killed her, cut up her body, and burned parts to avoid detection. After his conviction and death sentence, the jury leaving the courtroom were cheered by a crowd of thousands.[62] One of the many broadsides published noted that "like the case of [Gov.] Wall [hanged in 1802 for having a soldier flogged to death], the crime of Greenacre has engendered the bitter resentment of society.... It was not alone a wish that justice should have its due course, but the desire of vengeance which his malefactions had excited; and, actuated by this sentiment, thousands were seen, ere the sun had emerged from the horizon, directing their eager steps to the spot where an act of retributive justice was to terminate the career of one of the most sanguinary monsters that ever disgraced the name of man...."[63]

As the Greenacre drama was playing out in the press, Charles Dickens was creating, in *Oliver Twist* (1838), the characters of Bill Sikes and Nancy. The terrifying scene of Sikes' murder of her was to be re-enacted many times in the years following by stage adaptors and by Dickens himself in enormously popular public readings. Although Dickens insisted on its realism,

[60] Another case of this kind, but with a working-class defendant and taking place in a Northern locale, failed to become a national sensation like Corder's (most likely because it took place away from London; moreover, the man was undefended and the trial was much shorter): William Shaw, near Huddersfield in 1830: see *York Herald, and General Advertiser*, April 3, 1830, p. 3 and *York Chronicle*, 8 April 1830, pp. 3–4. Like the others, Shaw hanged.

[61] "Particular account of a most dreadful Murder" (London, 1834) (St. Bride's Printing Library, S607); *Times*, 7 April 1834, p. 6.

[62] *Times*, 13 April 1837, p. 5.

[63] "Greenacre, or the Edgeware-Road Murder" (Lilly Library, Bloomington, Ind.). See also Crook, *Complete Newgate Calendar* (London, 1926), vol. 5, pp. 286–290. Mary Poovey has noted Caroline Norton's repeated rhetorical use of Greenacre, in writings from the early 1850s into the 1870s on women's wrongs [Poovey, *Uneven Developments: The Ideological Work of Gender in Mid-Victorian England* (Chicago, 1988), p. 87].

FIGURE 4. "The full account and latest parts of the awful, inhuman and barbarous MURDER OF A FEMALE, by cutting off her head, arms, and legs, and burning them...." One of the numerous broadsides on James Greenacre's killing of Hannah Brown. Courtesy of the British Library (1881.d.8 {22}).

his delineation of these characters – the brutal burglar and the helpless fallen woman – was as much ideological as realistic. The less palatable aspects of Nancy's profession were left out, and Nancy became a sentimentalized and archetypal victim of brutal men and a callous society, an "unfortunate" whose life was horribly cut off just as (indeed, because) she was struggling towards redemption.

In 1842 a London coachman, Daniel Good, secured his place in the gallery of evil men by following Greenacre's example of murdering and then mutilating the body of his lover. Having enticed Jane Jones into intimacy and then having found a new girlfriend, he killed her and dismembered her body parts, burning the head and burying the less incriminating parts. He was prosecuted by the Attorney-General himself and readily convicted, to the cheers of the large crowd outside. Lord Denman observed in pronouncing sentence that "perhaps a case more abhorrent to the feelings of human nature than the present was never presented to a court of justice.... There is no doubt that it is the owing to the indulgence of your inclinations for one woman after another, that being tired of the unhappy deceased, and feeling that you could not enjoy to its fullest extent the fresh attachment you had formed, that you resolved upon destroying the unhappy

# APPREHENSION OF GOOD
## For the BARBAROUS MURDER of JANE JONES.

GOOD CUTTING THE HEAD OFF.

DANIEL GOOD IN THE ACT OF MURDERING JANE JONES.        GOOD CUTTING THE BODY IN PIECES.

FIGURE 5. "Apprehension of Good for the Barbarous Murder of Jane Jones."
Courtesy of the British Library (1888.c.3 {26}).

woman who was the former object of your affection."[64] Like Corder's and
Greenacre's before him, Good's deed and trial set new records in broadside
sales.

Three years later, a less gory but even more diabolic killing furnished
another occasion for public horror and excitement. A married and prosperous Quaker, John Tawell, stood charged of poisoning his pregnant mistress,
a former servant, with prussic acid (Tawell had once worked as a druggist).
Though there were real doubts as to whether the girl had not taken the poison
on her own volition, he was convicted, after a three-day trial, very long for the
time. It was widely expected that, notwithstanding his post-conviction confession of guilt, his respectable history and many strong character witnesses
would gain him a reprieve, but it was not to be. Perhaps as a demonstration
to Chartists and other dissidents of the class impartiality of English justice,
Tawell hanged.[65] The case was given extensive coverage in the *Annual Register*
and *Punch* observed with regret that it was "a very powerful rival to the makers
of Newgate volumes [novels]."[66]

[64] *Times*, 16 May 1842, p. 6; as with Corder and Greenacre, a large number of broadsides on Good survive.
[65] *Times*, 13, 14, 15, 18, 27, 29, 31 March 1845 (pp. 5, 6, 5, 7, 4, 4, 6); HO18/153/49; "Life,
Trial & Execution of John Tawell. . . ." (Bodleian Library: John Johnson Collection).
[66] *Punch*, vol. 8 (1845), p. 68. This journal went on to complain of the excessive media
attention given to a criminal from the respectable classes, concluding that "it may
almost be questioned whether the assassin may not be considered as a sort of public
player – an heroic victim self-doomed – for the agreeable excitement of a most civilised
nation."

The following year, 1846, a Manchester married factory foreman was tried for drowning his lover, a "good girl" who taught in a Sunday school and was employed in the mill under his supervision. Rumors, devoid of any medical support, immediately began circulating that she had been pregnant (the popular "script" demanded it). Continuing over four months from her death through his trial, the Chartist paper the *Northern Star* played this case, with its overtones of class sexual exploitation, for all it was worth, in highly melodramatic terms. In the end, however, unable to rule out either accident or suicide, the jury acquitted him, surprising the paper's readers, and perhaps others.[67] Perhaps unexpectedly, the *Northern Star* did not confine its murder interests to cases with clear class implications: in that same year it covered several other murders of young women by their lovers, who were neither of a higher social class nor in positions of authority over them. A number of these men were married and seemed to be seeking to avoid exposure of an unexpected pregnancy. The subject itself fascinated great numbers of people, whether or not class differences were present, and the emerging popular press, including even Chartist papers, was quick to respond to that mass interest. By contrast, no woman murderer received such notoriety in these decades until Maria Manning in 1849, and then she had to share the stage with her husband.

When in 1851 another seducer-murderer, Thomas Drory, was hanged at Chelmsford together with a husband-poisoner, Sarah Chesham, the *Essex Herald* spent nearly all its account sermonizing on Drory's "fearful" crime, scarcely mentioning Chesham, although that was the year a poisoning panic crested and the Arsenic Act was passed, and one might have expected some expression of this panic.[68] Drory, a farmer's son who had seduced a servant girl and when she became pregnant had murdered her, fulfilled most of the requirements of sentimental melodrama, being as well of previously good reputation and ultimately repentant before the scaffold. However, by his insistence on his innocence at the trial he deprived the public of a sufficiently romantic conclusion. Though he apparently lured his victim to an appropriately dark and deserted spot and there strangled her (much better for broadside sales than say, a quick bullet), the terrible act failed to leave a clear mark on his nature. After his execution The *Times* reflected that "in the commission of the crime there must have been some incidents of a very touching character, such as the last words of the poor girl, the delusion under which she lay as to his intentions in making the appointment, and her dying struggles; yet Drory seems to have been quite as possessed and quite as stupid

[67] *Times*, 2 April 1846, p. 8. See Anne Baltz Rodrick, " 'Only a Newspaper Metaphor': Crime Reports, Class Conflict, & Social Criticism in Two Victorian Newspapers," *Victorian Periodicals Review* 29 (1996), 1–18.
[68] *Essex Herald*, 25 March 1851; *Times*, 19 October 1850 & 8 March 1851, p. 7; I have seen five different broadsides on this case.

after the act as before. Thus a man who seemed the last to do an unkindness really felt no abhorrence at murder. . . ."[69]

After mid-century, lover-killings seemed to become less common, or at least less noticed. As the *Times* observed in 1855 about the case of Abraham Baker, who had murdered his sweetheart after she broke off with him, "the facts of this case were such as we have read of, but are not now very frequently heard."[70] Fewer broadsides appeared, even while overall broadside production did not falter for some years yet, and newspaper accounts were uncommon.[71] It was not until 1860 that such a case again attracted wide attention, and then only because of its exceptional cold-bloodedness and multiple intimate victims. In that year a London tailor, William Youngman, having successfully wooed a "respectable young woman," persuaded her to use his money to take out an insurance policy of £100 on her life, he being the beneficiary. Soon after that had been accomplished, he cut her throat. Finding that he'd been observed, he then killed his own mother and his two brothers. He insisted throughout on his innocence, and maintained at his trial what was noted as "the most extraordinary coolness and self-possession." His hanging attracted what was described as upwards of 30,000 persons, the largest audience for an execution since that of the celebrated Mannings eleven years before. "He seems," the *Annual Register* observed, "to have inspired a general horror in the public mind.[72]

Youngman's case was followed by a fifteen-year interval until the next sensation of this kind, again in London – that of Henry Wainwright, a once highly respectable man who had taken a mistress and in 1874 cut her throat. Her body was found, cut into thirteen pieces, a year later as he was transporting the parts in black satchels. Wainwright had once been a prosperous brush maker in the East End, but was now bankrupt. He had been a school manager and a churchgoer, as well as a father of five children. As he presented it, he had been ruined by his obsession for a woman who had been a prostitute, a woman who had pursued him with threats of exposure and demands for ever-increasing amounts of money. Yet his tale of ruination by a fallen woman fell on deaf public as well as judicial ears. His trial, the prosecution

[69] *Times*, 26 March 1851, p. 7.
[70] *Times*, 21 December 1855, p. 9.
[71] Broadsides on twenty-one English seducer–murderers in the eighteen years running from 1828 to 1845 (which appears to have been the "peak season" for this crime, at least in public attention) exist at the British, Bodleian, and St. Bride's libraries, but only nine from 1846 on, although broadsides continued appearing through the seventies, and later broadsides have survived better than earlier ones. On the other hand, the rapid growth of cheap newspapers from mid-century ate ever more into the broadside trade, finally extinguishing them.
[72] *Annual Register for 1860*, Chronicle, p. 540; *Times*, 17 August 1860, p. 11; HO12/127/42058; "The Life, Character and Execution of William Youngman" (Bodleian Library: Harding Collection).

assumed by the Solicitor-General himself, took an unprecedented nine days, and the press throughout the country had a field day with a gentleman fallen into such evil. Indeed, his case produced one last burst of broadsides.[73] As L. Perry Curtis, Jr. has observed, "the total space assigned to the case by the *Times* and *Telegraph* amounted to almost twice that devoted to the entire Ripper saga."[74]

Utterly evil characters like Wainwright were, however, uncommon, and far outnumbered by more prosaic murderers. Alongside occasional larger-than-life popular villains came to stand apparently growing numbers of usually less melodramatic wife-murderers. Indeed, fortunately for broadside-publishers, already in 1851, the year of Thomas Drory's hanging, the *Annual Register* was moved to observe that "cases of wife murder have lately become shockingly numerous."[75] Henceforth, they served the public in the lengthy hiatuses between the appearance of more exciting seducer-killers. A transitional case had perhaps been that of John Holloway in 1831, the first famous wife-killer of the century. Having been forced by Sussex parish officials to marry a girl he had gotten pregnant, Holloway left her for a new woman after several years of unhappy marriage. Enraged at then having to send money to her for their two children, he strangled her and also cut her throat, afterwards cutting the corpse into many pieces and burying it. He was reviled by the crowd as he came to gallows, but then he made an impressively repentant gallows speech. All in all, his trial and execution seem to have produced the largest outpouring of broadsides and chapbooks for a wife-killing in English history up to that time, from many parts of the country.[76]

Holloway's case was all the more shocking because he had been a Sunday-school teacher. During his brief unhappy marriage he seduced several other women; his effort during the trial to blame women for being so easily seduced was reprimanded by several chapbook authors. Holloway was described as a "dark, designing, treacherous villain [who] commenced his guilty designs on the virtue and innocence of a credulous, confiding girl, with all the systematic tact of the most accomplished seducer."[77] Here was a classic seducer-killer, who ended at the gallows for murdering his wife. In him two forms of woman-killing were blended. After Holloway, the public had to make do generally with wife killers who were less purely villainous, but as both broadside and

---

[73] *Times* 14 September, 23 November through 2 December 1875; *Illustrated Police News*, 18 September 1875, 1 January 1876. Wainwright's appears to have been the last murder case covered by broadsides, several of which survive.

[74] L. Perry Curtis, Jr., *Jack the Ripper and the London Press* (New Haven, 2001), p. 104.

[75] *Annual Register for 1851*, Chronicle, p. 416.

[76] At least eight different broadsides on Holloway survive. See on some of these and other murder broadsides, Robert Collison, *The Story of Street Literature: Forerunner of the Popular Press* (London, 1973).

[77] "An Authentic and Faithful History of the Atrocious Murder of Celia Holloway" (London, 1832).

# Sorowful Lamentation
## OF
# WILLIAM LEES,
### NOW UNDER SENTENCE OF DEATH AT NEWGATE.

*Copy of a Letter from the Prisoner to his Mother.*

Newgate, Dec. 3rd, 1839,.

Dear Mother,

I scarcely dare presume to adress you and I wonder that I have sufficient nerve to Write, being fully inpressed with the knowledge of the dreadful Crime that I've commited and the shame and disgrace which must 'for ever be a stain on the character of my Family and Friends; Oh

how do I wish that the Sinful World knew what I now suffer, knowing well that I shall shortly die an ignomicious Death, which I sincerly pray may be a warning to all others, do my dear Mother compasve yourself endeavour to see me soon as possible, remember me to all my relations and beg of them to forgive me tell them all to abhor Jealousy and intemperance as the last Dying wish of your unworthy and Unhapyy Son,

Wm. LEES.

On *Monday* Nov. 18th, the eastern district of the metropolis was in a state of great commotion, in consoquence of a *Dreadful Murder* commited in the house at No. 1, Lower Chapman Street, St. George's East. The unfortunate victim is a young Woman named Lees, the Wife of a Hair-dresser, who has carried on Business in the above House for about Twelve months. The parties have been on bad terms for some time and have frequently quarrelled *Monday afternoon,* between Three and Four o'Clock, William Lees, the murderer, closed the Shop and proceeded to the House of some Relations at Islington.

He seemed in a very perturbed state and communicated to his Relatives that he had murdered his Wife, by nearly servering her Head from her body with a Razor, They were horror-struck at this intimation, and for some time disbelieved him, but he repeated the tale so often, and his manner appeared so strange that they were induced to accompany him to his house, where they found his Story to be too true. On entering the shop they found the Young Woman lying stretched on the ground, which was covered with Blood. There was several gashes on her face, and a deep wound on the throat seperating the jugular vein, there was also a bruise on the right eyebrow, which appeared to have been inflicted by same blunt instrument, from which it appears that the murderer, after striking his hapless victim with a stick or piece of wood and rendering her perfectly senseless, completed by cutting her throat, and that in her struggles he cut her about the floor, The relations of the unfortunate deceased immediately secured Lees, and sent off to the Denmark Street Station House for assistance. The divisional Surgeon of Police soon afterwards attended, who said the woman had been dead more than two Hours.

### INQUEST.

Yesterday, Mr. Baker, held an inquest on the body of the unfortunate woman.

Rhode Hall, examined, She said that I have known Mr. and Mrs. Lees during the 8 Years they have been married, I have seen Mr. Lees drunk, I have heard that he was very jealous of her.

Other witnesses were examined, after which the Coroner adjourned the Inquest until Thursday next.

On Thursday the inquest was resumed. The first witness called was Elizabeth Fraser, who resided next door to the deceased, and who stated that she had seen the deceased and her husband come home together and go into the house. Juror—Did you hear any noise ! Witness I heard a sort of rumbling noise, but as I keep a school and the children present, I could not hear very distinctly.

Mr. Garratt, Surgeon, No. 3, New Road, deposed that about half-past 5 on Monday evening he was called to the house of the prisoner, and on examining the body he found about the throat, face and head eight different wounds, but the deepest and most extensive was on the left side of the throat, and caused instant death. Other witnesses were examined at some length, the Jury returned a verdict of Wilful Murder against William Lees.

### OLD BAILEY SESSIONS.

This Morning William Lees was placed at the Bar, charged with the Wilful Murder of his Wife Elizabeth Lees.

The first witness examined was Elizabeth Fraser who stated that she kept a school next door, at 9 o'clock on monday morning she saw the prisoner and his wife pass her door on very good terms, at three in the afternoon of the same day she was standing at her door when she saw the prisoner leave his house, lock the door and put the key in his pocket. The prisoner appeared to be very fond and attentive to his wife when sober, but when tipsy they very often quarrelled.

Mrs. Rhoda Hall said she kept a shop opposite to the prisoner and had been intimately acquainted with him and his wife.; about Half-past 2 on Monday week the prisoner sent a boy for her, and on going into the shop he said his wife was very ill, and desired her to go up and see her. She went up stairs and found Mrs. Lees lying on the floor crying, and appeared as if recovered from a fit. Witness saw no more of the prisoner until 5 o'clock, when an alarm was given that she was murdered, and on going into the shop saw her on the ground covered with blood

The next witness called was Mrs. Sarah Bailey, sister to the prisoner stated that she resided at 33, York Street, Saint Luke's, that about 4 o'Clock on the even-

ng before, the prisoner came to the house and said he was a Murderer, and wished her to accompany him to his house.

John Lees, a brother to the prisoner stated that he has at the house of the last witness on the evening before, when the prisoner came, and on entering the back parlor, the prisoner caught hold of Benjamin Bailey's hand and kissed it and said " I'm a Murderer," but did not say who he had murdered.

Other witnesses were examined whose evidences corroborated the above.

The Judge having summed up the evidence, tho Jury retired, and after a short deliberation, eturned the following Verdict **GUILTY—DEATH**

### LAMENTATION

Come litten to my mournful tale,
You tender christians all,
And kindly shed one pitying tear,
Unto my sad downfal,
My name is William Lees,
In Chapman Street did dwell,
And there the horrid deed was done,
As you all know full well.

My parents dear, with tenderness,
Endeavour'd but in vain,
To keep me from all wickedness,
But their souls I've filled with pain ;
I followed sin as you do know,
Which brought me to this place,
Thro' drinking, and bad company
I'm cover'd with disgrace.

O how, could I so cruel be,
To a wife I loved so dear,
To take her precions life away,
And cut her throat from ear to ear ;
Twas jealousy that prompted me
To take away her life.
Fulwell I know, she was to me
A most endearing wife.

When I had done the wicked deed,
I was filled with fear and dread,
I unto my relations went,
Told them my wife was dead.
And that, I was her murderer
But that they'd not believe,
But when with me they did come home,
Their minds were undecieved.

Then listen all, who now are gay,
Unto my dreadful fate,
For the dreadful crime that I have done,
I alas repent too late ;
Twas jealousy and drunkedness,
Caused me her life to take,
I hope you'll all shun wickeness,
And ne'er meet my sad fate.

Good people all, a warning take,
Before it is too late,
For if you dont repent in time,
You'll surely meet my fate ;
Ne'er give your mind to jealousy,
Intemperance, quick give o'er,
Or else like me you soon may be,
In the prime of life "so more".

Printed and Published by *J. MARTIN*, 18, Little Frescot Street, Goodman's Fields.

FIGURE 6. "Sorrowful Lamentation of William Lees, Now Under Sentence of Death at Newgate." As was common with broadsides, his "lamentation" was provided by the publisher, with warnings to other men to avoid his sins of "jealousy and drunkenness." Courtesy of the British Library (1881.d.8 {14}).

newspaper publishing expanded rapidly, they responded. In 1839, between the cases of Greenacre and Good, a London barber, William Lees, by using his razor to cut his wife's throat became the first wife murderer who was not otherwise a villain (like Holloway) to become a celebrity and broadside best seller.[78] Henceforth, wife murderers came to fill the space of public horror in the widening gaps of time between the apprehension of lover murderers.

In the course of the Victorian era wife killing appeared to be particularly resistant to the "civilizing offensive." Recorded killings and serious assaults of men by other men steadily diminished per capita, as did even cases of serious violence against men committed by women, but recorded assaults and homicide committed by husbands against wives did not diminish.[79] In an increasingly "civilized" society, the home seemed to have become the "last retreat" of men's violence.[80] In recorded homicide a new, more "modern" social pattern developed of fewer total cases overall, but with a substantially higher proportion of them taking place within the family, or within intimate relations, and thus with women rather than men as typical victims.[81] Yet the rise in the domestic proportion of homicide prosecutions was not only the result of diminution elsewhere; it also reflected the increasing readiness of the law to "invade" the home, as indicated by the new inclination to prosecute child killing through mistreatment or neglect.[82]

The proportion of officially recognized homicides that were spousal rose in the course of the nineteenth century: James Cockburn has found that in the county of Kent, the percentage of recorded spousal killings suddenly rose from four per cent of all homicides in the 1810s to fourteen per cent in the 1820s and sixteen per cent in the 1860s, jumping to twenty-eight per cent in the 1870s, falling to twenty per cent in the 1880s and then rising to thirty per cent in the 1890s.[83] Limiting ourselves to the killings considered

---

[78] See the discussion of Lees in Chapters 5 and 7.

[79] For example, even as the total number of prosecuted assaults declined in Northampton in the later nineteenth century, the proportion that were wife assaults rose [Mary Beth Wasserlein Emmerichs, "Five Shillings and Costs: Petty Offenders in Late-Victorian Northampton" (Ph.D. thesis, University of Pennsylvania, 1991)].

[80] On current knowledge about domestic violence, the most useful work is Neil Websdale, *Understanding Domestic Homicide* (Boston, 1999).

[81] Most "ordinary" spousal violence, of course, did not end in death. The chief subject of this book are those atypical cases which had fatal outcomes. Legally, they existed on the other side of a chasm from the much larger number of cases of domestic violence without fatal results, which either never reached the courts or when they did yielded far lighter punishments. Yet socially, many times the cases examined here arose out of "ordinary violence" that went beyond the usual limits, and thus formed one pole of a continuum of marital violence.

[82] See George Behlmer, *Child Abuse and Moral Reform in England, 1870–1908* (Stanford, 1982); Louise Jackson, *Child Sexual Abuse in Victorian England* (London, 2000).

[83] J. Cockburn, "Patterns of Violence," *Past and Present* no. 130 (1991). It continued to rise to thirty-eight per cent in the 1900s, then declined through the 1940s before rising

most serious, those prosecuted as murder, I have found that spouse victims similarly formed larger proportions of the total, making up sixteen per cent of all murders tried in England and Wales in the 1860s, twenty-three per cent in the 1870s, twenty-four per cent in the 1880s, and twenty-seven per cent in the 1890s.[84] At the Old Bailey, the largest and most important criminal court, there were two convictions for spouse murder, manslaughter or attempted murder in 1830, but *eighteen* in 1880.[85]

The term "spouse" is misleading here: only one kind of spouse killing was rising, that of wives. Among manslaughters (killings thought to be without lethal intention) wives always greatly outnumbered husbands as victims: at the Old Bailey, in the seven decadal years 1840–1900, sixteen husbands were so tried, but only two wives, one in 1850 and one in 1880.[86] Certainly among killings prosecuted as murder, the form of homicide normally requiring evidence of intent, most evoking of horror, and punishable with death, wives were increasingly more likely to be victims than husbands. In the sixty years 1841–1900, there were seventy-eight trials in England and Wales for husband murder, but at least 701 for wife murder.[87] The disproportion greatly increased during the period: in the first thirty years of the period, trials for husband murder numbered fifty, sharply falling to twenty-eight in the second thirty years. Meanwhile, despite a slight decline in murder prosecutions overall, wife murder trials rose in number from 254 to 447. In other words, while the absolute number of wives on trial for murder fell by about forty-five per cent, that of husbands rose by three-quarters, causing the ratio of officially recorded murderous husbands to wives to almost triple between the

again. Anne Parrella has found a similar nineteenth-century rise in the proportion of recorded domestic murders in northern France that were spousal ["Industrialization and Murder: Northern France, 1815–1904," *Journal of Interdisciplinary History* 22 (1992), 627–654].

[84] My database of spouse murder trials reported in newspapers compared with totals from Annual Judicial Statistics.

[85] This court in 1880, to be sure, covered a somewhat larger area and markedly larger population. In that same year of 1880, it saw one conviction for husband manslaughter, and none for husband murder or attempted murder.

[86] Official statistics on spousal manslaughter (as on spousal murder) do not exist, but from extensive if unscientific sampling it would appear that there were somewhat more wife manslaughter trials than wife murder trials, comprising very approximately sixty per cent of all wife homicide trials. Since there were approximately three times as many manslaughter as murder trials overall in the Victorian period (the ratio reached a maximum of about four to one in the 1860s and then declined to a bit over two to one in the Edwardian decade), this would mean that the killing of wives was more likely than other killings in general to be charged as murder rather than manslaughter.

[87] Information on these trials has been obtained from press reports, chiefly in the *Times* (which began to thoroughly cover assizes by the early 1840s, as railways began to cut travel times and costs), supplemented by Home Office records.

two periods, from five to one to fourteen to one. Even more remarkably, the ratio between them rose from less than 4:1 in the 1840s (eighty-two wife murder and twenty-one husband murder trials) to more than 22:1 in the 1890s (158 wife murder and seven husband murder trials). As wife-murderers were becoming apparently more numerous and certainly more visible, husband-murderers were becoming, so to speak, an endangered species.[88] A similar trend appears in trials for attempted spouse murder, at least as reported in the *Times*.[89] The number of trials described there for attempted wife murder totaled 154 in the first thirty years, but 279 in the second thirty.[90] Comparable totals for attempted husband murder are twenty-six in the first half, falling to nine in the second.[91] At the Old Bailey, in the five decadal years 1810–50 only three charges of attempted murder of a wife were tried; the next five such years, 1860–1900, saw twenty-one such charges.[92] Attempted murder trials with male victims at the Old Bailey rose far more moderately, in line with population growth, from fourteen to twenty-three. Seventeen of the eighteen convictions there in 1880 for spouse murder, manslaughter, or attempted murder were of husbands.

The only type of prosecuted homicide that was increasing in number in the second half of the nineteenth century was wife murder; by contrast, husband murder seems to have been the most sharply declining category. The most pronounced change in recorded murder and attempted murder (and perhaps manslaughter as well) in the Victorian era was thus the increased prominence of wives compared to husbands as victims. What might this change mean? Perhaps women were indeed less often killing or attempting to kill their husbands, while the same was not true of husbands; possibly the 1857 Divorce Act saved a few men's lives (though not women's, since it tended to be much easier for husbands than for wives to simply leave). Yet it is difficult to believe there was in actuality such a large shift in the gender ratio of

---

[88]Prosecutions at the Old Bailey show a similar trend, the number for homicides of wives (both murder and manslaughter) rising in decadal years: none in 1830, one in 1840, six in 1850, none in 1860, two in 1870, nine in 1880, six in 1890 and six in 1900. In comparison, only four wives were prosecuted there in these years for husband killing (vs. the 31 husbands prosecuted): one in 1820, two in 1850, and one in 1880. For murders only, nine husbands and one wife were charged in these years.

[89]On occasion (perhaps out of constraints of space) such trials were unremarked on by the *Times*, even when it was covering an assize and reporting on capital trials there.

[90]Rising from forty in 1841–50 to forty-six in the decade of the 1850s, to sixty-eight in the 1860s, to 113 in the 1870s, then falling to eighty-one in the 1880s and eighty-five in the 1890s.

[91]Eight in the 1840s, eight in the 1850s, ten in the 1860s, falling to three each in the following three decades.

[92]There were none in either 1810 or 1820, one each in 1830, 1840, 1850, three in 1860, five each in 1870 and 1880, six in 1890, and two in 1900.

spouse homicide. Also playing an important part would seem to be prosecu-
torial discretion: some defensive husband killings that might have led to trials
earlier would appear now not to be reaching that stage (perhaps because of
a growing reluctance on the part of the authorities to bring prosecutions that
were unlikely to win convictions), and, even more, some wife killings that
in the past would very likely have been charged only as manslaughter, or
even escaped prosecution altogether, were now coming before the courts under murder charges. Hardening attitudes towards violence against women,
against wives in particular, and within the home, it is suggested here, increased the readiness to charge men with the capital crime of murdering their
wives.

In early modern England violence within the home had been common,
familiar to all in a culture in which home life was little separated from the rest
of life. Such violence was sometimes restrained by community sanctions but
rarely, unless death ensued, formally prosecuted.[93] For example, *none* of the
579 assaults indicted at Essex quarter sessions between 1620 and 1680 involved
violence between spouses, even though such violence certainly existed.[94] The
problem of violence may have even worsened for wives in the eighteenth century, as community controls weakened without any corresponding increase
in legal sanctions.[95] Non-fatal domestic violence only occasionally entered
eighteenth-century court records, and when it did, it was almost always at
the lowest level, that of petty sessions. There it was usually dealt with by
mediation rather than punishment. As with violence between men but more
so, magistrates sought to reconcile wives and husbands, often by extracting
the wife's "forgiveness" and then dismissing the charge; when that could not
be obtained, offenders were typically chided and bound over to keep the
peace. Even as mediation was giving way more often by the early years of the
nineteenth century to punishment for many violent acts perpetrated by men
upon other men, it continued to flourish in domestic cases, handled by one or
two magistrates acting on their own.[96] Even at quarter sessions, magistrates
continued into the nineteenth century usually to prefer mediation to a criminal punishment.[97] Peter King found only "a handful" of husbands indicted
for domestic violence by the Essex quarter sessions during the last third of the

[93]Susan Amussen, " 'Being Stirred to Much Unquietness': Violence and Domestic
Violence in Early Modern England," *Journal of Women's History* 6 (1994), 70–89.
[94]James Sharpe and Roger Dickinson, "Violence in Early Modern England, Research Findings, Initial Results" (2000) [report to the Economic and Social Research
Council].
[95]Margaret Hunt, "Wife Beating, Domesticity and Women's Independence in
Eighteenth-Century London," *Gender and Society* 4 (1992), 10–33.
[96]Peter King, "Punishing Assault: The Transformation of Attitudes in the English
Courts [1748–1821]," *Journal of Interdisciplinary History* 27 (1996–97), 54.
[97]See Charles M. De Motte, "The Dark Side of Town: Crime in Manchester and
Salford 1815–1875" (Ph.D. dissertation, University of Kansas, 1977), pp. 302–303.

eighteenth century.[98] Much the same was true in Bedfordshire, as Clive Emsley has noted, and in London, as Greg T. Smith has discovered, well into the nineteenth century.[99] One Glasgow magistrate as late as the 1830s was cited by Anna Clark as deciding in one wife-beating trial that "if [the accused] had so beaten any other person than his wife, he would have been punished most severely, but as it was only his wife" he bound him over to keep the peace under penalty of a £5 fine if he beat her again.[100] For centuries a man had been allowed wide discretion in exercising his proper authority within his household, particularly among his wife and children, and even if such "disciplining" resulted in his wife's death, criminal charges did not always follow. In Wiltshire over nearly the entire second half of the century there were but three homicide prosecutions of husbands for killing their wives (and one of a wife for killing her husband), out of 126 prosecuted homicides.[101]

When criminal charges were brought, many ended only in acquittal. This was true not only of the charge of murder, a capital offense, but even of less common manslaughter prosecutions, which entailed upon conviction only the minimal punishments of branding on the hand, or a fine, or perhaps a few months in jail. When in 1790, for example, William Cooper was so charged by the parishioners of Enfield for the death of his wife after she suffered his

---

[98] King, "Punishing Assault," op. cit., p. 54.

[99] Clive Emsley, *Crime and Society in England 1750–1900* (2nd ed., London, 1996), p. 45: the indictment rate in Bedfordshire for assaults against wives brought to magistrates 1750–1840 was lower than for assaults generally; Greg T. Smith noted that "the number of cases of domestic violence coming before the [Middlesex] quarter sessions 1760–1835 was small. They account for only 1.3 per cent of the total number of assault cases in my sample. [61 of 4578 indicted cases] The low prosecution numbers might suggest that judges and magistrates tended to encourage a peaceful reconciliation rather than an exemplary punishment for the abusive husband, a point suggested also by the proportion of unknown outcomes in such cases." He went on to observe that "domestic assault was not seen as a simple sub-category of assault. The fact that it was a wife rather than a stranger being assaulted appears to have been an important factor in determining how some magistrates decided to settle the issue and work towards a solution to the problem of violence that would not upset the broad conventions and duties of marriage" ["The State and the Culture of Violence" (Ph.D. thesis, University of Toronto, 1999), pp. 267–8, 275].

[100] Anna Clark, *The Struggle for the Breeches: Gender and the Making of the British Working Class*, (Berkeley and Los Angeles, 1995), p. 73. Lack of attention to violence against women in this era is also suggested by the lack of significant or general change in the gender proportions of the accused in crimes of violence at quarter sessions between the 1770s and 1815 (in Essex they shifted slightly towards men, while in London slightly towards women). Nor did the proportion of female victims rise; indeed, in Essex it noticeably declined (from 26 per cent in the 1770s to 17 per cent in 1818–21).

[101] Emsley, op. cit., p. 42. In eighteenth-century France, wife killing was similarly treated more leniently than husband killing. [Benoit Garnot, "L' 'Uxoricide Feminin' au XVIIIe s.: Du Particulier au Général," in *Histoire et Criminalité*, ed. Garnot (Dijon, 1991).]

enraged assault, Baron Hotham, while denouncing his extensive beating and kicking of her as "very much unlike a husband and a man," found insufficient evidence that that brutality was the direct cause of her death, which only took place some days later. No one had bothered to examine her body at the time of death, despite two medical men being in attendance. Cooper went free.[102]

It was only in the years around Victoria's accession that a second phase in the restriction of men's violence opened, one in which attention turned to violence against wives. This turn was facilitated by the expanding reach of the state. Each year there was a greater number of increasingly trusted professional constables walking their beats available to answer domestic calls, often from neighbors, making more feasible some degree of surveillance of disordered families. At the same time the increased activity of coroners was intended to have effects inside the home, as the pioneering coroner Thomas Wakley specifically noted. Even more important for his office than detecting crimes, Wakley argued, was preventing crime by making inquests expectable and he cited the hypothetical case of the unexplained sudden death of a highly respectable man's wife. If that were publicly inquired into, other men, perhaps a "ruffian who has been assaulting and brutally treating his wife and children, will be warned, knowing that if anything happens to his wife or children, there's sure to be an inquiry."[103]

Religious change also played its part. While the fading of assertive and interventionist religion in the first half of the eighteenth century probably diminished public intervention inside the family,[104] the revival of such forms of religion at the end of the century helped set the stage for a turn back towards such intervention. The idealization of women, the suspicion of men, and the making of the home more central to religious life that characterized nearly all of the growing forms of Christianity in the first half of the nineteenth century all increased the importance of seeing that women were encouraged to carry out their spiritual and moral duties and were at the same time protected from harm at the hands of un-Christian husbands.[105] Indeed, even before the impact of Evangelicalism, prescriptive marriage literature was increasingly setting out a more caring and self-disciplined ideal for husbands, and the literature of "sensibility" heightening sensitivity to suffering caused women by men.[106]

---

[102] *OBSP* 1789–90 #720.

[103] Quoted in Burney, *Bodies of Evidence* (Baltimore, 2000), p. 53.

[104] On this diminution in colonial America, see Cornelia Hughes Dayton, *Women Before the Bar: Gender, Law and Society in Connecticut 1639–1789* (Chapel Hill, N.C., 1995).

[105] See Leonore Davidoff and Catherine Hall, *Family Fortunes: Men and women of the English middle class 1780–1850* (Chicago, 1987); Callum Brown, *The Death of Christian Britain* (London and New York, 2001).

[106] See G.J. Barker-Benfield, *The Culture of Sensibility* (Chicago, 1992) op. cit. and Elizabeth Foyster, *Manhood in Early Modern England* (London, 1999).

Of course, the consequences of this rising idealization of the home were neither simple nor direct. In one way, such a picture of home as the great refuge from life's cares worked against public intervention, reinforcing the existing reluctance to bring the rough arm of law into the heart's sanctuary. Characters like Charles Dicken's Wemmick, in *Great Expectations* (1859), with his imaginary drawbridge to his little suburban house, brought to life the old notion of a man's home as his castle, free from invasion. And yet, the home did begin to be so entered, more and more as the century went on, and in no small measure precisely because of its very idealization. Dickens himself could not resist, as he famously put it, "pull[ing] the roofs off houses" throughout London to reveal private lives. The very heightened importance placed upon the family unit, its new centrality to the maintenance of moral order in an age of weakened traditional authorities like church and community and of unsettlingly rapid change, made any perversions of its "proper" functioning appear ever more intolerable and dangerous to society. As illustrations of happy families gathered at supper or by the fireside began to circulate in enormous numbers, evidence of the gap between such an ideal and reality could only cause increasing concern. Fears of social disorder joined with hopes for social improvement, the energies of evangelical religion with those of utilitarian reform to stimulate schemes for state and private intervention in the domestic relations of the poor (that part of society traditionally subject to regulation by their betters). Much of the social legislation of the 1830s and 1840s (and beyond) – whether hated poor-law reconstruction or popular factory regulation and Corn Laws repeal – was in part conceived in domestic terms, as measures towards moving the family life of the poor towards the new ideal.[107] The evil of family violence came to share in this new attention. The increased emphasis on the wife's moral and spiritual duties, and the husband's duty of support and protection, made wife-abuse (chiefly to be found among the poor and working classes) ever more outrageous.

Fears of cruel and even violent husbands were not however confined to those of the lower classes. Much early Victorian fiction took up these fears within the higher classes. One best-seller along these lines with real-life as-sociations was Lady Lytton's *Cheveley; or, The Man of Honour* (1839), written to pay back her estranged husband, Edward Bulwer-Lytton, for his mistreat-ment of her. In it, a thinly-disguised Lord Lytton seduces and bullies his way through life, behaving worst of all to his beautiful and long-suffering wife. His downfall comes through his seduction and betrayal of the daughter of one of his tenants. Disguised as a Norfolk farmer, he woos her, and goes through

---

[107]See Dror Wahrman, " 'Middle-Class' Domesticity Goes Public: Gender, Class, and Politics from Queen Caroline to Queen Victoria," *Journal of British Studies* 32 (1993), 396–432; Mary Poovey, *Making a Social Body: British Cultural Formation, 1830–1864* (Chicago, 1995); George Behlmer, *Friends of the Family: The English Home and Its Guardians, 1850–1940* (Stanford, Calif., 1999).

a mock ceremony of marriage with her. When she finds herself with child, he writes a letter brutally renouncing all responsibility and advising that she take herself off to a House of Correction. However, his victim eventually gets to denounce her oppressor in front of a full courtroom. He flees the room, leaps on to his horse, and falls to his death a few hundred yards down the road (an event she had foreseen in a trance).

Bad husbands in the higher classes were criticized in novels of all three Brontë sisters – in *Jane Eyre* (1846), *Wuthering Heights* (1847), and, most directly, in the less renowned but well-received novel by Anne Brontë, *The Tenant of Wildfell Hall* (1848), which describes with intense feeling a heroine suffering under and eventually fleeing from a drunken, callous and unfaithful husband. Anne Brontë in her preface made clear her didactic aim: "If I have warned one rash youth from following in [the steps of the villain and his friends], or prevented one thoughtless girl from falling into the very natural error of my heroine, the book has not been written in vain."[108] From such works, the "victimization" tradition flowed into many of the now much-studied sensation novels of the 1860s,[109] placing men's treatment of women in the dock.[110] In one of the most popular of these novels (read avidly by Gladstone himself), Wilkie Collins's *The Woman in White* (1860), a violent and cruel husband – "a mean, cunning and brutal man"[111] and an even more frightening and sexually predatory Italian Count dominate and terrorize the two female heroines.[112]

Consensus on the salience of this evil crossed the class and political spectrum, embracing the Chartist, Ernest Jones, who produced in 1851–52 a collection of fiction, *Women's Wrongs*, with melodramatic accounts of working-class female victimization. One of the four stories in that volume, "The Labourer's Wife," depicted a workingman who had been blacklisted for union

---

[108] *The Tenant of Wildfell Hall* (Haworth edition: London, 1900), xxiii. This melodramatic novel was an immediate success, going into a second edition soon after publication [Mrs. Humphrey Ward, introduction to the Haworth edition, xiv–xv].

[109] In such widely-read novels as *Adam Bede, Sorrow on the Sea*, and *Lady Audley's Secret*, Jill Matus notes, "the aberrant mother was readily conceived of as a victim." [*Unstable Bodies: Victorian Representations of Sexuality and Maternity* (Manchester, 1995), p. 188.] One might add here the immensely popular *East Lynne* (1864) by Ellen Wood. For an introduction to the sensation novel, see Lyn Pykett, *The "Improper" Feminine: The Women's Sensation Novel and the New Woman Writing* (New York, 1992).

[110] In a related vein, Elizabeth Gaskell's *Ruth* (1853) was only the best-known of early Victorian novels about prostitutes as victims of men; see Tom Winnifrith, *Fallen Women in the Nineteenth-Century Novel* (New York, 1994), and Jill L. Matus, *Unstable Bodies: Victorian Representations of Sexuality and Maternity* (Manchester, 1995).

[111] Wilkie Collins, *The Woman in White* (New York, 1985), p. 274.

[112] Collins was also to write a novel explicitly concerned with wife abuse: *Man and Wife* (1870) offered, in addition to a fervent attack on the "muscular" ideal of manliness, two women from two social classes, both trapped by the marriage laws with evil and physically threatening husbands; the poorer woman finally kills her batterer.

activities descending to drink and wife-beating, thus both highlighting the evil (the chief subject was the wife and her travails) and, unlike the Brontës, fixing the ultimate blame on capitalism. While as a committed Chartist who had renounced his comfortable position and potential income as a barrister Jones denounced society's mistreatment of the workers, he put aside any political inclination to idealize the workingman in his description of the husband. "On the whole," Jones introduced him, "he was not by nature a bad man. Sunk in utter ignorance, his principal pleasure was the satisfaction of his appetites – society had done the best to make a brute out of a man – yet he was capable of a sudden generous impulse, though devoid of that gentleness and feeling which smoothes the intercourse of home, and wins domestic sympathy. A machine of flesh and bone, he could be good or bad according as the hand of circumstance might push him." Towards his wife, he was increasingly bad.[113]

Such new cultural discourses of gender, morality and violence could now call upon new administrative capabilities of more extensive policing and punishment to make social policy. The drunken and brutal husband had become a "problem" and the way was open for domestic violence to enter the expanding public sphere in the 1840s. In 1846 a series of newspaper attacks broke out on brutal mistreatment of wives and the failure of the law to deal with it. On April 21 the *Times* in a leader cited a case just heard before a Clerkenwell magistrate as "an illustration of the fact that offenses against the person are not visited by the law with anything like adequate punishment." A "drunken ruffian" was charged with having brutally assaulted his wife, who appeared with "a face one mass of contusions." It was a classic melodrama: the "poor creature had merely asked for money to get food for herself and her three children, as her husband was going out to spend what he had at a public-house." Her entreaties were greeted with savage blows and kicks. The magistrate denounced the "atrocity" of the offence, but "the law would not allow him to mark his sense of the enormity of the crime by a sufficiently severe sentence." He decided not to send the case up to quarter sessions but himself gave Reece three months imprisonment at hard labor. The *Times* sadly accepted his judgment, since in its view "the judicial authorities at Clerkenwell are . . . so generally distinguished for making comparative light of offenses against the person when placed in competition with offenses against property, that it is very possible the ruffian, if convicted, would hardly have got as much as two months' imprisonment." It went on, likely referring to one or

---

[113] *Chartist Fiction Volume 2*, ed. Ian Haywood: Ernest Jones, *Women's Wrongs* (Aldershot, 2001 [originally published London, 1852]), p. 4. Like those to his political right, Jones accepted the centrality of the home. Somewhat surprisingly given his sharp indictment of society, Jones concluded his introduction to these stories by exhorting his readers, once they had read his portrait of life today, to "go! try to alter it, and BEGIN AT HOME" [p. 1].

both of two trials for wife killings reported in the *Times* several weeks earlier, that "when we see instances, as we did not very long ago, of femicide being treated in a criminal court as little more than a venial exuberance of animal spirits, we must expect that semi-femicide will experience a proportionate reduction in the severity of the punishment assigned to it." In the first of those cases of femicide a man found by his wife drinking and gambling at a pub struck her in the head with a brick, from which a few days later she died. He was most contrite, "sobbing very heavily in court," and the jury returned a recommendation to mercy. The judge gave him three months hard labor. In the second, a wife drunk in the street had so provoked her husband that he knocked her down and then kicked her around, from which she died a few days later; although the jury did not return a recommendation here, the defendant had been given "a good character" and was sentenced to twelve months.[114]

The *Times* called for "a few wholesome examples made of brutal husbands," and warned that "for one case of domestic ruffianism which comes before the world, there are thousands in which the unhappy victims suffer without making their ill-treatment known."[115] Meanwhile, *Punch* refused to spare the magistrate from its scorn in the above case, noting that the man had previously served one month for assaulting his wife and that the magistrate could have awarded him up to six months' hard labor. Thus, "the decision – judgment in any sense we cannot call it" to give a "half-punishment" showed a sad lack of will to enforce the law.[116]

A few months later another Clerkenwell case roused the *Daily News*. In this case a man threw the woman with whom he lived out of a window, after nearly fracturing her skull with a brick. She survived, and he got off with a light sentence, leading the paper to conclude that "it seems as if a man intending to murder his wife or paramour, has only to go about it openly enough, get up a mock passion, and then beat out the woman's brains in the presence of the assembled neighbors, to escape the extreme punishment of the law."[117] The following month it took aim at the Old Bailey, where one man who murdered his common-law wife had been acquitted and another who had cut his wife's throat had been given merely one year's imprisonment; by contrast, it noted, at the same time a young servant who wrote a check for a larger amount that he was supposed to and pocketed the difference was sentenced to transportation for seven years. "How much safer it is to stab one's wife than to defraud one's master!"[118]

---

[114] *R.v. Showell: Times,* 2 April 1846, p. 8; *R.v. Bridger: Times,* 6 April 1846, p. 5.

[115] *Times,* 21 April 1846, p. 3.

[116] *Punch, 26* (1854), 224.

[117] *Daily News,* 10 July 1846.

[118] *Daily News,* 24 August 1846. The first was apparently that of Benjamin Gibbons. Despite medical tests showing blood on his sleeve, injuries consistent with blows from

Even the severe sentence of transportation for life now seemed to many
unjustly lenient for a deliberate, savage and prolonged wife killing in Liverpool, tried at the same time as the Old Bailey cases. Both the *Examiner* and
the *Daily News* denounced the failure of the Liverpool jury to find murder. "If
it was not murder," the *Examiner* declared, "no case of beating to death can
amount to murder. The violence . . . was as resolutely and ruthlessly continued till the sufferer was in the agonies of death . . ." It noted "many similar
verdicts" recently, and that "the frequency of crime and outrages against
women has been the subject of much indignant remark lately."[119]

Among those indignantly remarking were John Stuart Mill and Harriet
Taylor, who began that year to write leaders in the *Morning Chronicle*, continuing through at least 1851, exposing similar cases illustrating judicial leniency
towards male brutality.[120] In that latter year Harriet Taylor could refer to
"every newspaper, every police report teem[ing]" with cases of "hideous maltreatment of their wives by working men," and, with Mill, urge Parliament to
pass legislation declaring such maltreatment to be grave crimes, and increasing their penalties.[121] That year also Charles Dickens co-authored an article

---

an iron bar found nearby, and witnesses that she had previously told them of beatings
from him, the defense claim that her death was caused by a fall downstairs led Baron
Platt to stop the trial and the jury to return an acquittal. [*Times*, 22 August 1846,
p. 6; see also PRO, CRIM 1/5/13 (coroner's inquest).]

[119]*Examiner*, 29 August 1846, reprinted immediately by the *Times*, 31 August; p. 5; see
also *Daily News*, 28 August 1846.

[120]*Morning Chronicle:* 28 October 1846; 17 November 1846; 13 March 1850; 29 March
1850; 31 May 1850, 28 April 1851; 24 August 1851; 28 August 1851. Ironically for such
radicals, they even blamed the escape from due punishment of men who kill their
wives on the fact that "juries are composed of men in a low rank of life" [29 March
1850]. Despite the existing property qualification for jury service apparently juries
were still not sufficiently socially elevated enough for Mill and Taylor.

[121]Harriet Taylor, "The Enfranchisement of Women," *Westminster Review* 55 (July 1851),
154n; Mill and Taylor, "Wife Murder," *Morning Chronicle*, 28 August 1851, p. 4. It is
frequently argued that, as Louise Jackson has put it, [*Child Sexual Abuse* (London,
2000), p. 108] "references to men as essentially aggressive were disappearing fast as
they were replaced in the courtroom with a racialised discourse of class/respectability.
Sexual [or physical, as argued by other scholars] abuse was increasingly delineated
as a heinous offense committed by 'brutes' and 'savages' – in other words, by social
deviants – rather than by 'normal' men. This construction firmly placed the male
abuser in the category of male 'otherness'; the abuser was the vicious, idle slum-
dweller who represented the antithesis of the 'normal,' respectable breadwinner."
However, Jackson's argument, that the new sensitivity to violence against women
was diverted away from threatening the middle and upper classes to anti–working-
class purposes (not to mention that it became racialized), though containing a truth,
misses a crucial facet of this development. As long as physical and sexual violence
towards women was seen as somehow within the range of normal male behavior
it was accepted, or at least tolerated. It was only when its "normality" was denied,
when it became identified as the behavior only of "brutes," that it could be attacked

in his journal on a recent case of man murdering his sweetheart in a lonely rural spot. This familiar seduction-and-betrayal scenario served for Dickens as a starting-point for a riff of outrage on a recent "frightful harvest" of "domestic poisonings, violent murders, and other barbarities in the country," which he and his fellow author argued outdid the supposedly evil Metropolis. Several of their cited examples of this harvest of evil were murders of women by men (along with burglars murdering a clergyman and a mother murdering her child). They denounced rural juries for their tenderness towards men who killed their wives: "The fact of a woman being the lawful wife of a man, appears to impress certain preposterous juries with some notion of a kind of right in the man to maltreat her brutally, even when this causes her death; but, if she be not yet married, the case assumes a different aspect in their minds – a man has then no right to murder a woman – a verdict of murder is found accordingly."[122]

Now highly visible in the rapidly expanding press (one with a growing proportion of female readers), violence against wives was ripe for Parliamentary attention. In 1853 the first piece of legislation specifically addressed to the problem passed, the 1853 Act for the Better Prevention of Aggravated Assault Upon Women and Children.[123] This measure set the first clear ceiling on the degree of "chastisement" permitted husbands and fathers, by allowing magistrates to summarily punish attacks on all females and on males under fourteen that resulted in actual bodily harm by up to six-month imprisonment with hard labor (raised in 1868 to one year). Wife-beating now joined the ranks of other newly discovered and officially recognized social evils in the "age of reform."

Four years after the passage of this act, the Associate Institute for Improving the Laws for the Protection of Women, now titled the Society for the Protection of Women and Children, began to send observers into police courts to encourage and assist prosecutions of brutal husbands and fathers. With the prodding of such voluntary bodies and of newspaper leaders, this trend to criminalize violence against women continued through the rest of the nineteenth century, with prosecutions for assaults on females rising even as total prosecutions for assault (most of which were male-on-male) began

---

by public opinion and by law. The rise of this quasi–"racialized discourse" was the sign that such behavior was no longer acceptable, and thus marked the beginning of serious efforts to eradicate it.

[122] Richard J. Horne and Charles Dickens, "Cain in the Fields," *Household Words*, 10 May 1851, p. 148. Dickens periodically continued these complaints about such brutality; as late as 1867, his magazine *All The Year Round* noted that a reading of current newspapers found "records of violence and bloodshed – more especially of violence inflicted on women – reported on every page" ["Rough Doings," 23 November 1867].

[123] 16 and 17 Vict. c. 30.

to fall.[124] Every decade produced new legislation – in 1861, 1878, 1886 and 1895[125] – providing increased legal recourse, both criminal and civil, for victims of marital violence. Such measures reflected two desires, inter-related but distinct: to better protect women and to reform men. As one M.P. observed in introducing a bill in 1856 to make such violence punishable by flogging, the issue was at root not a woman's but "a man's question.... It concerned the character of our own sex, that we should repress these unmanly assaults; and he believed that upon the men who committed them they had a worse and more injurious effect than they had upon the women who endured them."[126]

On the other hand, as Dickens had noted in his exasperation with rural juries, such "respectable" condemnations had to struggle against persisting attachments to customary definitions of manliness that included the readiness to be violent when circumstances called for it, including against the vicious tongues and bad behavior of wives. This was a struggle both between new and old notions of masculinity, to some degree between town and country, and also a class struggle, between the "respectable" middle and upper classes and the largely "unrespectable" working classes. Yet its lines were not drawn quite this simply: many "respectable" men, not just in the working classes but in the middle classes who staffed juries and sometimes even upper-class judges frequently themselves held aspects of these customary conceptions of manliness, or if not, at least sympathized with the men who held them. Indignation at physical maltreatment of women was often moderated by sympathy for hard-working men cursed with shrewish or, worse, dissolute wives and a willingness to "understand" a degree of violence even if it were not ultimately acceptable. It was common to distinguish between "brutal" and lesser violence. If such "respectables" rarely endorsed outright

[124]V.A.C. Gatrell, "Decline of Theft and Violence," in *Crime and the Law*, ed. Gatrell, Lenman and Parker (London, 1980), p. 291. Several local studies bear out and illustrate this national trend: see C.A. Conley, *Unwritten Law* (Oxford, 1991), pp. 80–81, and Emmerichs, "Five Shillings and Costs," op. cit. After studying Manchester newspapers, Charles De Motte concluded that "concern for the victims of family violence appeared to be much more widespread after mid-century, judging from the number of cases of wife beating that were brought to trial." (De Motte, "Dark Side of Town," op. cit., p. 303.)

[125]The 1861 Offences Against the Person Act made such violence easier and swifter to prosecute by classifying "aggravated assaults" on women and children under 14 as non-indictable offenses to be dealt with at a police court level (while maximum punishment was raised from six months to one year). The later acts helped battered wives win legal separations, child custody and maintenance. On these, see Mary L. Shanley, *Feminism, Marriage, and the Law in Victorian England, 1850–1895* (Princeton, 1989).

[126]Lewis Dilwyn, M.P.: *Hansard's Parliamentary Debates*, 3rd series, House of Commons, 7 May 1856, 142, col. 169.

A WIFE BEATER LYNCHED NEAR ROTHERHAM

FIGURE 7. "A Wife Beater Lynched Near Rotherham." This was not an American-style lynching, but an example of "rough music," a ritual humiliation and roughing-up (*Illustrated Police News*, January 23, 1869).

older notions of manly behavior, they often allowed them to influence their judgment of the heinousness of a particular killing.

Moreover, even respectable condemnation of violence could work in favor of violent husbands, by increasing the reluctance to see even a "man of blood" hang. One sure way of preventing that outcome was to convict of manslaughter rather than murder; another, much less sure but often employed, was to add a recommendation to mercy. Defense counsel naturally frequently appealed to such dislike of the gallows, and if they failed to prevent a death sentence could still hope for strong efforts to win a reprieve. One facet of the ideology of "civilization" itself – the revulsion against state violence – might in this way war with another – intolerance of violence by the strong against the weak. So rather than a simple struggle for civilization, or for "class control," the treatment of wife killing was shaped by cross-currents of ambivalence and contradiction.

Indeed, the treatment of wife killing was complicated still further by another tension, this time within Victorian respectable gender ideology itself. New ideals of domesticity embodied new expectations for *both* genders: while they raised new expectations for husbands, not only to support but to protect and, increasingly, to care for their wives (and children), they did the same for wives. A wife's behavior and character became more crucial than ever to the happiness and viability of the home, and thus it was liable to come under stricter scrutiny even than in past times. Industry, sobriety and of course chastity became indispensable attributes of a good wife. As with men, for poorer women such expectations could be unrealistic. When husbands became violent with wives, these two linked sets of expectations could pull in opposite directions: on the one hand, such violence was now more condemned, and more likely to be moved against by the law; on the other, such prosecution opened the door to excusatory explanations of "provocation" by bad wives, who had failed in their now-heightened domestic responsibilities. If wives had greater claim to considerate treatment, this claim rested largely on their own "goodness" – when they failed to live up to these expectations, violent husbands could appeal to juries of respectable men for, if not justification, at least understanding.

Both these heightened sentiments – dislike for the gallows and disgust at "bad" wives – were given increased influence by the growth of public petitioning as a factor in the disposition of those convicted of murder. While petitioning had long existed in the aftermath of criminal trials,[127] it was only after the 1836 act extending the time between sentencing and execution that petitions became feasible for those convicted of murder. Moreover, by this time the "people," not just persons of some standing, were becoming involved in the process, and mass petitions, with hundreds or thousands of signatures, begin to appear. "Democratic" tendencies in Victorian political life impinged also on criminal justice, as public petitions became more frequent and larger. At first ignored by Home Secretaries, when provoked by sympathetic cases petitions became longer and more pressing. By 1860 they began to have an effect; in that year an Edinburgh excise officer who killed his drunken and "depraved" wife was saved from hanging after petitions totaling thousands of signatures were presented to the Home Office, along with the urgings of local officials fearing the public disorder that a hanging might provoke.[128] Similarly in 1866 another killer of a drunkard wife was reprieved by a reluctant Home Secretary after a flood of petitions, including one to which the mayor of Liverpool put his name.[129] Two years earlier another reluctant Home Secretary yielded to a petition with the remarkable total of nearly 70,000 signatures and issued a reprieve to a Birmingham workman who had killed his unfaithful wife.[130] In this way, the advance of democracy itself was providing yet another obstacle to the drive to punish more seriously violence against wives.[131]

---

[127] Peter King, *Crime, Justice and Discretion* (Oxford, 2000), pp. 315–325.
[128] *R.v. Salt:* HO12/125/39772.
[129] *R.v. Reid:* HO45/9370/38104; see also *Times,* 22 December 1866, p. 8; *Liverpool Mercury* 24 & 25 December, 3 January 1867.
[130] See Chapter 7.
[131] The increased determination of judges to get murder verdicts from juries itself helped increase the use and effectiveness of mass petitions; with more murder verdicts, struggle over a prisoner's fate shifted more to the post-trial phase and to influencing the Home Secretary. By 1875 it had become common practice for defense solicitors to ask jurymen and grand jurymen to sign petitions for mercy [as Home Secretary Cross complained in that year (HO45/9389/47114: *R.v. Morris*)]. Yet this "obstacle" was always limited by the receptivity of the Home Secretary; despite agreeing to a

Yet at the same time the advance of democracy was also strengthening this punitive drive. As popular political activity revived and became ever more effective, anxieties among the respectable classes intensified about the growing size in great cities of a "demoralized" lower stratum, constituting an "underworld" – "those vast, miserable, unmanageable masses of sunken people," as Matthew Arnold saw London's East End in 1868.[132] Once the "leap in the dark" of the 1867 Franchise Act had been taken, social policymakers felt it increasingly urgent to "moralize" the masses advancing towards political power, and social policy (in regard to poverty as well as crime) drew ever sharper distinctions between "respectable" working families and the "residuum."[133] The *Manchester City News* was typical in 1869 in its editorializing on a recent wife killing. It was hard to say, it observed in a leading article, whether the perpetrator "was a savage by nature or a savage by education. It was enough to know that he was as savage as any of the naked Iroquois, who roamed the wilderness."[134] A decade later the *Times* reflected that "in most respects our lower classes will compare favourably with the corresponding orders in other countries. . . . But one clear difference to their disadvantage is in regard to the treatment of their wives. Some Englishmen have not yet learnt the elementary fact that their wives have a few rights, and may not be beaten as they in their supreme pleasure think fit."[135] And a few years after this Chief Justice Coleridge observed that "in some classes of society a wife seemed to be regarded as a kind of inferior dog or horse."[136]

These sorts of comments were no doubt conservative in stigmatizing the lower reaches of the populace, but perhaps paradoxically, they also eased the advance of democracy by providing an Other against which ever-growing numbers of increasingly "respectable" working-men could be distinguished and admitted into an extending political (and social) nation. Kindly treatment of one's wife, and children, became an important qualification for full citizenship. The spread of such respectability made the growth of democracy acceptable to the existing holders of power, allowing an ultimately more deeply rooted transition to democracy in Britain than occurred in most other European nations at the time. In this sense, moralistic social policymakers were the midwives of British democracy. One of their obstetrical instruments was a harsher treatment of wife killing. For not only violence in general, but

reprieve in the particular case of Morris, Richard Cross prided himself on not being so swayed, and if others in his position were not so adamant, they often did not feel it necessary to bend to popular pressure: even the largest petition I have located, one with 150,000 signatures for Joseph Jones in 1909, failed to prevent his execution.

[132] Quoted by Gareth Stedman Jones, *Outcast London* (Oxford, 1971), p. 241.

[133] See Lynn H. Lees, *The solidarities of strangers: The English poor laws and the people, 1700–1948* (Cambridge and New York, 1998).

[134] *Manchester City News*, 17 April 1869.

[135] *Times*, 1 November 1879, p. 4.

[136] *R.v. Little: Times*, 6 May 1886, p. 7.

the specific form of it represented by wife-beating and wife-killing were increasingly identified with the worrisome "underclass." Never to raise one's
hand against one's wife was one mark of respectability that growing numbers
of working men could and did claim.

As the *Times'* reflections hint, yet another aspect of democratization was
also now working to increase attention to wife abuse – the emergence of the
women's rights movement as a political force. Publications like Lydia Becker's
*Women's Suffrage Journal* reported in graphic detail examples of violence
against women, and, roused by such reports, in 1878 Frances Power Cobbe
published in the *Contemporary Review* a highly influential article, "Wife-torture
in England." This article greatly helped pass the Matrimonial Causes Act
of that year, which provided legal separations for abused wives in summary
courts.[137]

Under this dual influence, the courts more and more took on the role of
denouncers and "educators" – through deterrent punishment – of lower-class
men, in the process marking off wife-beating as a practice incompatible with
any sort of respectability. If this stigmatized workingmen as the characteristic
perpetrators of such uncivilized behavior, and thus stiffened resistance to their
further advance to suffrage, it also recognized the right of all women, married
as well as single, to be secure in their persons and thus marked an important
step in the dismantling of patriarchy. Moreover in the working class itself, as
growing numbers of men sought respectability, continuing physical abuse of
wives began to evoke complicated psychological tensions. If their behavior
was slow to change, many workingmen's feelings about such behavior did
seem to alter: after mid-century, working-class dialect poetry and prose, A.J.
Hammerton has pointed out, exhibits a tone of "guilt" over their treatment
of their wives.[138]

With all these contending attitudes potentially coming to bear upon each
instance of spousal violence, particularly those with fatal outcomes, the mix of
discourses surrounding such cases could be highly complex, simultaneously
performing many different forms of cultural work, and legal outcomes could
vary a good deal. Not infrequently trials found juries and judges at odds,
and this tension was often re-played after trial, when a conviction set large
numbers of the public and the civil servants at the Home Office in opposition
to each other.

A majority of wife killings continued to be prosecuted as manslaughter
(usually cases of beating or kicking deaths, or deaths caused by thrown

---

[137] See Shanley, op. cit., ch. 6; Laurel Brake, *Subjugated Knowledges: Journalism, Gender
and Literature in the Nineteenth Century* (New York, 1994). Similar melodramatic stories
of abused working-class wives also helped pass the Married Women's Property Acts
of 1870 and 1882, as Ben Griffin has recently noted ["Class, Gender and Liberalism
in Parliament, 1868–1882: The Case of the Married Women's Property Acts," *The
Historical Journal* 46.1 (2003), 59–87].
[138] A.J. Hammerton, *Cruelty and Companionship* (London, 1992), p. 32.

objects, where intent to kill was dubious),[139] and these cases produced more acquittals and of course much lighter sentences than did murder trials, as several scholars have observed.[140] A.J. Hammerton cited as "instructive" the case of Robert Knowles, a Preston butcher who kicked his wife to death and received a sentence of merely one month's hard labor. Hammerton noted how at both inquest and trial Knowles was characterized as a hard-working and affectionate husband, deeply remorseful, while his wife was pictured as a provoking drunkard, "a scandal to her sex."[141] Carolyn Conley comparably called attention to the Drought case in Kent in 1879. In that instance, a shoemaker, whose wife refused to hand over some money, beat and dragged her across a road, fracturing her skull. He was described by witnesses as industrious, sober and long-suffering of a wife prone to drink. After declaring that "had [Drought] been guilty of habitual and unprovoked ill-usage [of his wife], he should have passed a much more severe sentence," Justice Cockburn sentenced him to six months' imprisonment. Lenient, yes, but, as Conley herself added, after being sharply criticized by the London press, Cockburn took the unusual step of publicly justifying his sentence, saying that " 'There can be little doubt that the wife wished to spend the money on drink, or that her refusal to let her husband have it was accompanied by foul and abusive language habitual to her. Exasperated he struck her, but no doubt under great irritation.' " "That Cockburn felt obliged to defend the sentence," Conley observed, "reflects some change in attitudes," as sentences in domestic homicides in Kent had been growing more severe.[142]

And indeed, such light sentences for wife-killing can readily be matched by others more severe, even in manslaughter trials, where light sentences for all defendants were common. By Knowles' time, his very light sentence was quite exceptional; by then even light sentences were more like the six months awarded Drought or Timothy Sullivan in 1882. Sullivan had come home drunk and, enraged by his wife's rather obscene insults, threw the fireplace tongs; they struck her in the head, and she died from the blow. His trial went very well, as female neighbors testified to the lack of any previous abuse on

---

[139]Although, as with murders, no official tabulation of manslaughter cases by type of victim was ever compiled, from samples it would appear that during the Victorian period something in the range of sixty per cent of recognized spouse killings were prosecuted as manslaughter.

[140]See Hammerton, op. cit., Conley, *The Unwritten Law* (Oxford and New York, 1981); Shani D'Cruze, *Crimes of Outrage* (London, 1998).

[141]Hammerton, op. cit., pp. 34–5.

[142]She noted that "at the [Kent] assizes between 1859 and 1866 five men were convicted of beating their wives to death. The maximum sentence given was three years. Between 1866 and 1880 nine similar cases were heard in Kent and seven of the men were sentenced to more than five years' penal servitude." Conley, op. cit., p. 80 (quoting the *Maidstone and Kentish Journal* of 8 Nov. 1879); see also *Times*, 1 November 1879, p. 3.

his part, and it was convincingly argued on his behalf that the throwing of the tongs, near at hand, was a moment's impulse, from which a fatal outcome could hardly have been anticipated.[143] Even Sullivan's six-month sentence was more lenient that most convicted wife killers received. More typical was the fifteen months given John Longhurst at the Old Bailey in 1880. Longhurst and his wife had frequently quarreled, with her throwing things as well as his landing blows; on this occasion she had been drinking, and he gave her several kicks in the groin; he immediately fetched a doctor, but soon after the doctor's arrival she bled to death from a laceration in the vagina.[144] When there were few factors in his favor, a husband was likely to receive reasonably severe punishment, as in the case of William Sutton, whose solid middle-class status did not seem to help him much. A Birmingham edge-tool manufacturer, Sutton had repeatedly kicked his wife, sending her into premature labor, from which she died. Justice Hawkins denounced his behavior as "brutal and inhumane" and gave him twelve years' penal servitude.[145]

Overall, the later nineteenth century saw an increase in the level of punishment of wife killing, particularly as compared with other killings.[146] Of

---

[143] *CCCSP* 1881–2, #649; CRIM 1/15/2; *Times*, 8 June 1882, p. 8; 28 June 1882, p. 12.
[144] *CCCSP* 1879–80, #535; CRIM 1/10/10.
[145] *Times*, 5 August 1890, p. 10.
[146] Conley found that in Kent 1859–80 seventy-six per cent of the seventeen cases of wife killing resulted in convictions, as opposed to sixty per cent of all homicides (190) (even though a somewhat higher percentage of wife killers – 5.9 vs. 4.7 – were found to be insane), and twenty-three per cent of these convictions were death sentences (for murder), as opposed to twenty per cent of the lower proportion of convictions for all homicides [private communication]. Moreover, in her book she observed that from midway through the period she studied treatment of violence against wives began to toughen, which leads one to believe that if the last two decades of the century were included the disproportion between the treatment of homicide of wives and other homicides would be found to increase. The two cases of husband killing she found led to one conviction, for manslaughter.

More recently, Conley has found that in both Scotland and Ireland in the quarter-century 1867–92 homicide convictions were more likely when the victim was a spouse, but that wives who killed husbands were treated less harshly by judges than husbands who killed wives. Half of the wife convicts in Scotland and a third in Ireland served less than two years and no woman in either country was executed in this period for killing her spouse. In fact, only one woman in either country was convicted of the full offense of murder, and she was reprieved. Not only were husbands treated more severely than wives, they were also treated more severely than men who killed persons not their wives [" 'Innocent life and weak and feeble women': domestic violence in late Victorian Ireland and Scotland," unpublished paper 2001.] Conley's recent study also highlights the role of expectations in shaping perceptions of how much of a problem wife abuse was: while she found the rate of spousal homicides to be almost identical for the two countries, she noted that the Scottish authorities "complained that the high number of such cases was quite appalling while the Irish authorities boasted that whatever sins the Irish may commit, they were not cruel to their wives."

the sixteen wife manslaughter trials held at the Old Bailey during the seven decadal years 1840–1900, three (in 1880 and 1900) resulted in sentences of penal servitude for ten years to life, while *none* of the sixty-nine manslaughter trials there with an adult male victim produced a single sentence that long. Even sentences between one and ten years were given in only three of those sixty-nine trials, compared to two of the sixteen wife killings. The two husband manslaughter trials in those years produced one acquittal and one sentence of six months imprisonment.

The large minority of wife killings prosecuted as murder drew especially toughening treatment.[147] In the handling of wife murder not only did prosecution increase, so did punishment. Between the decade of the 1850s and that of the 1870s, while total murder prosecutions in England and Wales remained fairly stable,[148] (and the already-small number of prosecutions for husband murder actually fell), prosecutions for wife murder almost doubled (from seventy-two in the '50s, to 100 in the '60s, to 142 in the '70s), continuing thereafter to rise more modestly. As total charges of wife murder doubled, convictions tripled, and acquittals (apart from insanity) diminished. Even executions, contrary to what might have been expected, rose, both in absolute terms and as a proportion of prosecutions. Even per capita, more wife-killers were being hanged at the close of Victoria's reign than in its early years. Only insanity was gaining as a ground for reprieve from execution; other traditional grounds were less and less persuasive [see Table 1].[149] In no way was husband murder treated more seriously than wife murder, as has sometimes been suggested, although their rarity ensured trials of wives for the murder of their husbands great attention and thorough prosecution, and the greater likelihood in such cases of demonstrating intent to kill should have greatly facilitated conviction.[150] In the last four decades of the century men who murdered their wives were slightly *more* likely to be found guilty than the

[147]All statistics, unless otherwise noted, are for England and Wales; Scotland, with its separate legal system, and Ireland, with its distinctive political situation and legal administration, are not a systematic part of this study.

[148]From 612 in the 1850s to 646 in the 1870s, a slight per capita decline [Annual Judicial Statistics, England and Wales].

[149]Old Bailey experience would also suggest increased prosecution of attempted wife murder: there were none in that court in 1810 or 1820, one in 1830, none in 1840, one in 1850, two in 1860, five in 1870, five in 1880, and six in 1890. There were only two trials for attempted husband murder, one in 1870 and one in 1890. It is also perhaps significant that in the last hanging for an attempted murder, in 1861, the attempt had been against the defendant's common-law wife: *R.v. Doyle: Times*, 9 August 1861, p. 9; see also Wilson, *Murderess* (London, 1971), p. 129; J.F. Stephen observed in passing two years later that "his execution produced general satisfaction": "The Punishment of Convicts," *Cornhill Magazine*, 19 February 1863.

[150]Roger Chadwick, *Bureaucratic Mercy: The Home Office and the Treatment of Capital Cases in Victorian Britain* (New York, 1992), p. 313.

TABLE 1. (Virtually) All Wife Murder Prosecutions, England and Wales [Wiener Database]

|  | [n = 701] | | | | | |
|---|---|---|---|---|---|---|
|  | 1841–50 | 51–60 | 61–70 | 71–80 | 81–90 | 91–00 |
| NG | 19 | 13 | 8 | 19 | 7 | 15 |
| NG Insane | 10 | 6 | 14 | 12 | 12 | 23** |
| MS | 31 | 25 | 34 | 41 | 42 | 50 |
| M Reprieved | 0 | 5 | 19 | 16 | 23 | 13 |
| M Insane* | 0 | 0 | 1 | 5 | 7 | 6 |
| M Executed | 22 | 23 | 24 | 49 | 56 | 51 |
| Total | 82 | 72 | 100 | 142 | 147 | 158 |

*M Insane = certified insane & committed to Broadmoor after conviction
**1901: 7 not guilty on insanity verdicts in one year.

far fewer women who murdered their husbands, and much more likely to be hanged.[151] They were also substantially more likely to be convicted and almost twice as likely to be hanged than all others who were charged with murder [see Tables 2 and 3]. Once charged with murder, they were certainly not treated leniently.

The Victorian era saw both continuity and change in the handling of men's lethal violence against their wives. Customary attitudes held on tenaciously and were even reinforced in some ways by newer sentiments and ideals. Yet significant change nonetheless occurred, as public discourse and legal treatment toughened towards such offenders. The contestations produced by the clash of "custom" vs. "civilization," and by the conflicts within "civilizing discourse" itself led to a variety of compromises, the most notable as will be seen being the increasing allowance for insanity, both before, at, and after trial.

Once a homicide had been committed, and particularly once a perpetrator was brought to the bar of justice, the discourses that surrounded wife killing were rich and informative about both Victorian criminal justice and Victorian culture. Such discourse developed through several stages and venues. Coroners' inquests, magistrates' hearings, grand jury considerations, trials, and, if a murder conviction resulted, deliberation at the Home Office over whether to issue a reprieve[152] all afforded opportunities for "wife killing

[151]The conviction rate 1861–1900 was 46 per cent for husband murder (seventeen of thirty-seven) vs. 49 per cent for wife murder (270 of 547). The execution rate was 24 per cent for husband murder (nine of thirty-seven) vs. 33 per cent for wife murder (180 of 547).
[152]Once a murder verdict had been reached, the character of the discourse changed: the decisive locus of decision-making moved from the public sphere to behind closed

TABLE 2. Disposition of Wife Murder v. of Husband Murder [Wiener Database]

| | Wife Murder | | | |
|---|---|---|---|---|
| | 1861–70 | 1871–80 | 1881–90 | 1891–1900 |
| Trials | 100 | 142 | 147 | 158 |
| Guilty of Murder | 44 [44%] | 70 [49%] | 86 [58.5%] | 70 [44%] |
| Reprieved | 20 [20%] | 18 [14%] | 30 [18.5%] | 19 [12%] |
| Executed | 24 [24%] | 49 [35%] | 56 [40%] | 51 [32%] |
| | Husband Murder | | | |
| | 1861–70 | 1871–80 | 1881–90 | 1891–1900 |
| Trials | 9 | 10 | 11 | 7 |
| Guilty of Murder | 4 | 3 | 6 | 4 |
| Reprieved | 2 | 1 | 3 | 2 |
| Executed | 2 | 2 | 3 | 2 |

TABLE 3. Disposition of All Murder Other Than of Wives [Annual Judicial Statistics][153]

| | 1861–70 | 1871–80 | 1881–90 | 1891–1900 |
|---|---|---|---|---|
| Trials | 578 | 507 | 524 | 444 |
| Guilty of Murder | 199 [34%] | 200 [39%] | 195 [37%] | 167 [38%] |
| Reprieved | 93 [16%] | 94 [19%] | 100 [19%] | 77 [19%] |
| Executed | 106 [18%] | 103 [20%] | 92 [18%] | 77 [19%] |

doors at the Home Office. There officials confidentially deliberated whether or not to grant a reprieve from the mandatory death sentence. In this arena, the Home Secretary, his "faceless bureaucrats," and the trial judge, who presented them with his report and sometimes answered further queries from them, were the central actors. However, even here members of the public had several parts to play: juries could if they wished recommend mercy, and even go beyond that to write the Home Office, while public petitions were becoming more frequent, more organized and more numerously signed.

[153] This category of course includes infanticides prosecuted as murder [a separate criminal charge for these did not exist until 1923], which numbered about 32 in the 1860s and declined thereafter to 14 in the 1900s. The rate of murder verdicts for these was quite low, and of execution almost zero, so they lower the total rate somewhat. On the other hand, it also includes murders committed in the act of robbery, or of policemen – particularly aggravated kinds of murder which were punished more severely than "simple" murders such as those of spouses, and their inclusion raises the total conviction (and execution) rate. The effects of these two types tend to cancel out.

FIGURE 8. "Dreadful Murder Near Bolton" (*Illustrated Police News*, October 2, 1869). After killing his wife with an axe James Schofield, 58, fatally cut his own throat. Many Victorian wife murderers similarly killed themselves, and thus never came to trial.

discourse." The following chapters focus particularly on the latter t
which have left very large and rich archives of documentation,
analyze such discourse as a way of understanding types of "ratio
wife killing and their reception. First we will look at the rationa
justification, of a husband's right of "chastisement." This did not lo..ᵧ ---
nineteenth-century scrutiny. Of the less thoroughly justificatory rationales
put forward as excuses or mitigations of an acknowledged crime, by far the
most common was that of provocation. It however fell into more than one
category. Most typical was that offered a husband by a drunkard wife, who
was thereby failing her wifely duties (or much less often, a wife who failed
in her household duties, even though sober). The most heinous provocation
of all was, not surprisingly, wifely infidelity, to which a chapter of its own
is devoted. Finally, there were excuses of lack of intention, usually through
the man's own drunkenness, or as the century went on, his insanity or other
mental disability; these will be looked at in the final chapter. But first, the
provocations of "bad wives."

# 5

# Bad Wives: Drunkenness and Other Provocations

The killing of "good wives" had always been viewed harshly (though now even more so).[1] The real Victorian battleground was over the killing of "bad" wives. Despite the general condemnation of wives who failed to maintain a proper home, overall the excusable range of a husband's use of physical force, even on a "bad" wife, was being significantly restricted.

In the increasing amount of prosecution of domestic violence can be seen a rising revulsion against physical abuse in itself: when it issued in death, "mere" kicking, if prolonged or otherwise carried out with some deliberation, became in the second half of the century liable to a murder charge, as urged in 1846 by several newspapers (as well as the Mills and Dickens, among others), and even could lead to the gallows. Murder charges for this kind of killing rose even faster than the total wife murder caseload: from 5 in the 1850s to 18 in the 'sixties to 34 in the 'seventies. One can also see in these trials a class fear of the persisting "brutality" to be found among the lower classes now approaching a share in political power. The defendants in these trials were overwhelmingly working class: only twelve of the 141 prosecutions for wife murder in the 1870s had middle-class defendants, and in only one of these twelve was beating or kicking the cause of death; when a "respectable" man killed, then as now, it was usually with a weapon – poison, a gun – which required less directly and sustainedly "violent" action. "Brutality" was to a very high degree class correlated.[2]

---

[1] John Manion's trial for the manslaughter of his wife at Lancaster in 1830 was perhaps a harbinger of changing attitudes. While Manion claimed his wife had fallen down stairs in a fit, neighbors testified hearing him beating her. Her character was unimpeached, and he was not only convicted but given a surprisingly harsh sentence of transportation for fourteen years. *Times,* 27 August 1830, p. 4.

[2] The often-heated issue of whether murders in the "respectable classes" were to an important degree hidden is beyond the scope of this work, which relies on accounts of cases that reached public attention. Almost surely there were a significant number of fatal poisonings that went undetected, and these are likely to have had a higher proportion of "respectable" perpetrators than other kinds of killings. Thus, the profile of Victorian spouse killers based on officially recorded cases is probably to some unknown degree class-biased. Yet it should also be kept in mind that poisons were far from unknown among the working classes as well, and even after the 1851 Arsenic Act

However, we must go behind numbers to reach some understanding of these developments. What did domestic homicide mean to Victorians? How was wife murder construed as opposed to wife manslaughter, what kinds of excuses and defenses were made by wife killers once in the hands of the law, and what did judges, jurors, the press and public, and the Home Secretary and his officials think of these excuses and defenses? In this chapter, we will be looking at such questions, first through the notion of "chastisement" of one's wife, and then, with its disappearance, through provocations that were claimed, the most important being that of a wife's drunkenness.

Physical assaults upon wives, and of course children, were endemic before and during the nineteenth century and largely accepted popularly (certainly by most husbands and many wives). As one man declared while giving evidence in an 1859 murder trial of another man who had stabbed his wife in jealousy, "seeing her bleeding at the mouth, I naturally thought it was like most men's and wives' quarrels, and that he had been hitting her."[3] Yet we shall see courtroom tolerance for such violence evaporating, beginning well before this man spoke his piece.

Even before the nineteenth century opened, husbands' use of force was coming under challenge, most immediately from wives themselves. By the last years of the eighteenth century, for example, even as the total amount of men's homicidal violence was falling, at least one woman a week was appearing before the Middlesex Justices to prosecute her husband for assault.[4] At the same time, magistrates and judges seem to have become somewhat more sympathetic to these complaints (which no doubt would have contributed to their increase). They responded by stigmatizing such behavior and providing some form of punishment, in both criminal and civil courts. In the 1790s,

were not very difficult to obtain. Another issue besides class raised when considering the likelihood of undiscovered poisonings is gender: if all of these were known, the proportion of wives among the perpetrators of spouse murder would no doubt rise. But again this is speculative.

[3] *CCCSP* 1859–60, #700.

[4] On the overall decline in homicide during the eighteenth century, see Beattie, *Crime and the Courts in England 1660–1800* (Princeton, 1986); Cockburn, "Patterns of violence," *Past and Present*, no. 130 (February 1991); Shoemaker, "Male Honor," *Social History* 26 (2001). Shoemaker shows the construction of masculinity already changing in the course of that century for the upper class and for much of the middle class. The nineteenth century saw these new expectations of masculine self-restraint extend to *all* classes, and also extend to self-restraint in regard to women, an area hardly affected in the eighteenth century. On women and the Middlesex magistrates, see Anna Clark, "Humanity or Justice? Wifebeating and the law in the eighteenth and nineteenth centuries," in *Regulating Womanhood: Historical essays on marriage, motherhood and sexuality*, ed. Carol Smart (London and New York, 1992), p. 192. Needless to say, these represented only the proverbial tip of the iceberg, given the great disincentives to such prosecution. It is not clear from Clark or anyone else what kind of success these women had.

these magistrates even sometimes found such husbands guilty on the sole evidence of their wives – a break from legal tradition, which had been highly reluctant to allow a wife to testify against her husband, and which looked more generally with suspicion upon testimony uncorroborated by either material evidence or other testimony.[5]

### Rights of "Chastisement"

As attitudes hardened against abusive husbands, this problem began to attract juristic attention. The strongest traditional defense for violent and even, in the right circumstances, homicidal husbands, the "right" of "chastisement," was only now challenged and repudiated. A signal that change was impending may have been sent by the *Quarme* case in 1791. Bartholomew Quarme and his wife had left a pub, and a drunken quarrel in the street ensued, in which he knocked her down and then repeatedly kicked her, treatment from which she died a short time later. The jury at Ely, noting that he had "expressed great sorrow" after she died, could not decide whether to find murder or manslaughter, and gave a special verdict that was then brought up to the Court of King's Bench. The judges there acknowledged the existence of the right of chastisement, cited in Quarme's defense, but set sharp new limits upon its exercise. They ruled unanimously, all delivering their opinions in turn, that a prolonged kicking of a drunken wife leading to her death, even though that had not been intended, could be, and in fact in this case was, murder. Justice Ashurst, speaking for the court, declared that "chastisement, wherever that right exists, must be done in a reasonable manner; but where it is exercised in so violent a manner as in the present case it shows the heart to be regardless of social duty, and deliberately bent on mischief," and pronounced death upon Bartholomew Quarme, who, as then required by law, was hanged within 48 hours.[6] The right of "chastisement" remained, but the meaning of "reasonable" was narrowing.

Too much should not be read into one case; *Quarme's* more restrictive interpretation of "reasonableness" in chastisement left a good deal of room for excusable violence particularly when no death ensued: great leeway continued to be allowed for marital chastisement, especially when not exercised in public. In an 1811 wife-beating trial in Yorkshire that happened to be covered by the *Times*, a man's counsel claimed he was simply exercising his right to

---

[5] Clark, ibid. In the eighteenth century, John Beattie observed, "normally a parent or master who used 'moderate' methods and a 'reasonable' instrument in chastising those over whom they had natural authority would have been acquitted of both murder and manslaughter." [Beattie, op. cit., p. 86]

[6] *Times* 7 February 1791, p. 3; see also Crook, *Complete Newgate Calendar*, vol. 4, pp. 184–86. *Quarme* would appear to be the first higher court reconsideration of the principle, at least for other than aristocrats.

chastise his wife. The Wakefield quarter sessions magistrates accepted this and merely bound over both of them to keep the peace.[7] In such non-fatal cases, far more numerous of course than fatal ones, such a right continued to be accepted well into the century.

Even when beaten wives died, a notion of reasonable chastisement survived, though no longer explicitly articulated as such. In the Old Bailey trial of William Leadly, who repeatedly struck his habitually drunken wife with a stick in 1825, inflicting serious wounds that probably caused her death ten days later, the degree of his violence was carefully evaluated: after a witness made a damaging claim that he had powerfully kicked the deceased in several parts of her body while she was down (the kind of excess that had helped hang Bartholomew Quarme in 1791) but then retracted it, Justice Gaselee, an older judge notably sympathetic to harassed husbands,[8] expressed his relief that "that the prisoner had not been guilty of the very gross and unmanly conduct [at first] attributed to him." Refraining from "gross" violence would have ensured him conviction of manslaughter only, but a lack of certainty about the precise cause of his wife's death (she was already in poor health from alcoholism) led to Leadly's acquittal (a common outcome at the time in killings of wives "addicted to drink"). The medical man who had treated her opined that she died chiefly from the "extreme heat of the weather, added to the quantity of spirits [she] was in the habit of drinking."[9]

Yet legal recognition of a husband's right of chastisement was in retreat in the 1820s, particularly at assizes. In 1828, in a case where an old man, suspecting his wife's fidelity, beat her to death with a large stick, Mr. Justice Park made it very clear he rejected any notion of chastisement, however "reasonably" exercised, as a legal right: "I shall certainly not," he remarked, "lay it down as the law of England that a man may *at all* chastise his wife. I am rather of opinion that a man does not possess that power."[10] The defendant (whose wife does not seem to have been a notably "bad" one) hanged.[11] A watershed in regard to chastisement came in 1831, when a new editor of Burn's *Justice of the Peace* removed the last phrase of the statement that had been in it through many editions, that a charge of assault and battery would not be sustained in the case of a parent chastising a child "in a reasonable

[7] *Times*, 21 October 1811, p. 3.

[8] Only one of the eight wife-killing trials reported in the *Times* between 1825 and 1832 that Gaselee presided over ended in any sort of conviction; that one was the last, in 1832. Even then, Gaselee deferred sentencing "in order to see whether, consistently with the public safety, he could pass any less judgment than that of transportation." *Times*, 6 August 1832, p. 3.

[9] *Times*, 23 September 1825, p. 3.

[10] *R. v. Baker: Times* 25 July 1828, p. 3.

[11] Both probably would have escaped the gallows if their wives had more clearly fallen down in their domestic duties.

and proper manner" or "a master his servant being actually in his service at the time, or a schoolmaster his scholar, or a gaoler his prisoner *or even a husband his wife.*"[12]

Thereafter, any claim to a right of chastisement of wives disappeared from courtroom argument, at least the assize courtroom. It cannot be found in any wife murder trial reported in the *Times* through the rest of the century, or even in any trial for wife manslaughter sampled.[13] However, the view widely survived, at least in the working classes, that it was only to be expected that a husband might with some justification, physically beat or kick a "bad" wife (though not of course to death). Men in court for such behavior often indignantly recounted their wives' misdeeds as justification. One man, brought by his wife before a London magistrate in the same year of 1828 in which Justice Park was rejecting the supposed right of chastisement, declared that he "had a right to govern in his own house," and the magistrate agreed, while criticizing the extent of the violence used.[14] Later trials however saw judges following Park in explicitly denouncing such beliefs. When the navvy John Vickery beat his drunkard wife to death in a Sussex village in 1867, Baron Bramwell told him that "it appears that you have been an honest, hardworking man. But it is necessary that *people in your class should be taught* – what I fear they don't understand – that they have no right to beat their wives."[15] Similarly, when a Lancashire laborer, William Bradley, pushed his drunkard wife into their fireplace and held her there in 1872, Justice Willes, saw the prisoner's act as "aggravated" by being directed against his wife;

---

[12] Burn, *Justice of the Peace* 25th ed. (1830), 1: 223 (italics added); compare the 26th ed., which had a new editor: (1831), 1: 271. Another, less widely used, manual, Bacon, *A New Abridgement of the Law,* [orig. pub. 1736], kept through its final edition in 1832 its traditional wording: "The husband hath, by law, power and dominion over his wife, and may keep her by force within the bounds of duty, and may beat her, but not in a violent or cruel manner; for, in such case, or if he but threaten to beat her outrageously, or use her barbarously, she may bind him to the peace by suing a writ of *supplicavit* out of chancery."
[13] Newspaper reports of 283 wife manslaughter trials between 1830 and 1905 have been examined.
[14] *Times,* 2 January 1828, cited in J.C. Wood, "The Shadow of our Refinement" (Ph.D. dissertation, University of Maryland, 2001), p. 162.
[15] *Times,* 28 March 1867, p. 11 [my italics]. In the 1866 murder trial of a London laborer, George Crane, for beating his drunkard wife to death, testimony showed that he had been in the habit of beating her. Justice Willes reminded the court that "where a man had the misfortune to have a bad and provoking wife he must try to put up with her; but he *had no right* to beat her within an inch of her life because she misconducted herself." [*Times,* 1 February 1866, p. 11; *CCCSP* 1865–66 #245.] However, the jury returned a manslaughter verdict, with a recommendation to mercy because death was unexpected and (a frequent reason up to this time for refusing to convict) because "the woman's system was liable to be injured by violence because she was intoxicated."

never, he insisted, would he "permit the idea to prevail that men had a right to maltreat their wives as they liked."[16]

If chastisement of a wife could no longer be openly claimed as an Englishman's right, it continued to be alluded to indirectly. In deaths at the hands of a husband a wife's alleged prior misbehavior was very important, to mitigate if no longer to excuse. From a legal standpoint, such misbehavior became relevant insofar as it constituted a kind of "provocation," which, allowing for the frailties of human nature, the law had long recognized as a mitigating factor in homicides. Trials for wife killing after the later 1820s (years, as we have seen, in which "lover murder" was creating public sensations, and in which rape also began to be treated more seriously) ceased to explore whether and to what extent "rights" were properly exercised and came to focus on whether either significant provocation from the victim, or a lack of intention to kill, had existed, and whether they were sufficient to mitigate the perpetrator's subsequent loss of self-command.[17]

The lack of any such provocation ensured Daniel Goulding's 1830 manslaughter conviction, without any mercy recommendation, at the Old Bailey. Goulding's beatings led to his wife's miscarriage and then nine days later to her death. Critical was a female neighbor's evidence that the deceased had been "a very good quiet woman," and that he had beaten her on earlier occasions. Despite the time lag between beating and death (such time lags, raising doubts about the proximate cause of death, had often allowed acquittals), both jury and judge ignored the defense argument that without the miscarriage she might well still be alive, as well as its unsupported claim that she had syphilis. Though the finding was manslaughter rather than murder (since there was no evidence of intent to kill), Baron Parke made a point by giving Goulding the toughest possible sentence, only made possible eight years before, of transportation for life.[18] In similar circumstances at Lancaster two years later Justice Park gave Benjamin Halliwell the same stiff sentence for fatally beating and kicking his pregnant wife.[19] In both these cases the crime was aggravated by the victim's pregnancy and the resultant loss of fetal life. Fatal beatings or kickings of wives who were not clearly "bad" (and not in notably poor health) nearly always produced manslaughter convictions, and when the defendant was seen to be a bad character, either repeatedly beating

---

[16] *Times*, 29 July 1872, p. 11.

[17] At least in the more serious cases heard at assizes; a thorough study of lower courts is needed to decide just how far the fairly unanimous judicial line was followed by magistrates; one suspects a good deal less so.

[18] *Times*, 21 April 1830, p. 3; *OBSP* 1830, #892. Earlier practice appears more lenient: Richard Griffin, who had killed his wife with a razor in 1810, had received at the Old Bailey only one year's imprisonment, as had Joseph Lowton, fatally throwing a poker, in 1825 at Durham.

[19] *Times*, 17 August 1832, p. 4.

his wife or giving her a particularly brutal beating, the most severe sentence
for that offense, transportation for life, was now more often employed.

Even if a wife had failed in some way in her domestic duties, such failure
might no longer go as far as it once had towards excusing her killer, however
unintending he had been to end her life. When in 1825 a London workingman, Cornelius Sullivan, came home to find supper not prepared and his
common-law wife out talking in the street, he beat and kicked her there,
then dragged her back into the house, where he continued the beating. She
died two days later. Sullivan had been tried and acquitted at the Bailey three
years before this for the murder of his previous wife, though mention of it
was excluded from the trial; given that, the jury's manslaughter verdict was
not surprisingly found inadequate by the audience, and the Recorder, also
not surprisingly, sentenced him to transportation for life, making him one of
the first to receive that sentence for this offense.[20]

There were three main ways, in rising order of seriousness, in which a
wife might provide sufficient provocation to her husband for the question to
be raised in criminal proceedings: by verbal abuse or blows (as men might
provoke other men), by habitual drunkenness and the neglect of her domestic
duties that usually went along with it, or by sexual infidelity (provocations
specific to wives). The last, not surprisingly considered the most serious –
"the unexpiable wrong," as Justice Day was to call it – will be the subject
of the following chapter. Here we will explore how the first two types of
provocation were treated by the criminal justice system.

### Wives' Words

In earlier centuries, when honor, which might be somewhat simplistically
thought of as one's public image, was central to the social standing and
self-respect of both men and women, words, especially if uttered in public,
carried power. Words could damage, perhaps irreparably, that public image.
This type of power, unlike physical force, was open to women as well as
men, allowing women in unquestionably hierarchical "traditional" English
society to exercise some social power.[21] Yet such power had its price: While
affording women a way of asserting their will, its very potency provided excuse
for male violence against them. As Laura Gowing, studying the Tudor–
Stuart church courts, noted, "men's blows were figured as, most justifiably, a
response to women's words." "Shrews" were an accepted problem, and their
"chastisement" by blows a familiar theme in popular literature, married life,

[20] *Times*, 19 September 1825, p. 3; *OBSP* 1824–25, #1306.
[21] See Amussen, *An Ordered Society* (New York, 1988); Foyster, *Manhood in Early Modern
England* (London, 1999); Tim Meldrum, "A Women's Court in London: Defamation
at the Bishop of London's Consistory Court, 1700–1745," *London Journal* 19 (1994),
1–20.

and the courts.[22] As long as women's tongues were feared, they remained in great danger of violent response, with little remedy open to them.

In the course of the eighteenth century, it appears that words lost some of their potency. The defamation suits Gowing had examined for the earlier period moved from church to secular courts, there joining assault charges, and changing their character in the process. In quarter sessions defamation cases, Robert Shoemaker has found, the physical acts accompanying slanderous words received increasingly frequent mention; in general, there was a decreasing sensitivity to words alone along with an "increasing intolerance of physical molestation."[23] Blows were replacing words as chief sources of harm for those seeking legal redress. Such a shift, which was accompanied by a growing proportion of male defendants, suggests a decreasing fear of women and their verbal weapons, and a complementarily increased fear of men and their physical threat.

Such a change held both loss and gain for wives, as, in opposite measure, for husbands. On the one hand, women were losing a weapon; on the other, as wives' power to harm seems to have lessened, their consequent increased vulnerability to men began to incline magistrates, judges and, more hesitantly, juries to protect them and to punish their abusive spouses. Thus, the decline of the fear of the "shrew" paved the way for increased proscription of the use of violence by husbands against wives.

Although the legal principle that words were insufficient to constitute provocation that would reduce murder to manslaughter had been established in the late seventeenth century, it was very often ignored in practice; only when fear of the "shrew" had sufficiently faded – a point arrived at only in the nineteenth century – did it truly become a governing rule. Even then, it was not infrequently a point of tension between judges and juries, as the latter often gave greater weight to a wife's provoking words than did the former;

---

[22] Laura Gowing, *Domestic Dangers: Women, Words, and Sex in Early Modern London* (Oxford, 1996), p. 209. In the London church courts she found that "a relatively high proportion – 42% – of complaints sued by men, centering on women's adultery, were sentenced. Suits alleging men's violence, sued by women, were much less successful, and only 26% received a final sentence." [p. 181]

[23] Most of these suits were not domestic, and involved both male and female plaintiffs and defendants. "Whereas," Shoemaker noted, defamation recognizances in the late seventeenth and early eighteenth centuries "tend to focus on words and their scandalous and defamatory nature, later recognizances increasingly focus on the physical acts which accompanied the words, as if it was the pushing, beating, mobbing and spitting that was as much the source of complaint as the actual words used. . . . The increased intolerance of physical molestation can be seen in the growing frequency with which defendants bound over by recognizance for words were accused of real or threatened violence. Whereas in the late seventeenth century only 9% of recognizances mentioned violence, between 1730 and 1760 this figure was 53%." [Shoemaker, "The Decline of Public Insult in London," *Past and Present* #169 (November, 2000), p. 117.]

this was particularly the case (as shall be seen later) when such words related to a wife's unfaithfulness.

In an 1852 murder trial, Mr. Justice Cresswell (soon to become the legal arbiter of Victorian marriage in the Divorce Court created in 1857), reiterating the old legal principle often ignored, firmly rejected the relevance of defense evidence of the wife's taunting language.[24] Nonetheless, the jury found only manslaughter (understanding the man's rage and entertaining some doubts about intent, as the fatal stab wound was delivered in a confused scuffle).[25] In a case like this, if provocation by the victim was not by itself sufficient, it could be supplemented by questions about intent to save the defendant (though, as we will see, intent too was coming to be more readily found by judges).

Again and again, judges now informed juries that a wife's words, however provoking, could not reduce a murder charge. In an 1859 case in which a wife had been killed after a quarrel spiraled out of control, Justice Willes convinced Monmouth jurymen to return a murder verdict. "No doubt women could be exceedingly provoking," he assured them. Women had, he continued, "the power to excite a man's passions, and by laughter and insult to excite and irritate him." But, Willes concluded, "provocation by mere words and gestures" was not sufficient in point of law to reduce the crime of murder to that of manslaughter. At the same time Willes further increased the chances of conviction by stressing that intent should not be too narrowly defined. "It did not matter whether the impulse to kill her came into his mind on a sudden, or whether the intention was deliberately formed; for if the man gave way to the impulse he was guilty of murder." He told the jury he could see no way that they could find manslaughter only. They convicted of murder; the man hanged.[26]

In 1869 during an Old Bailey trial Chief Justice Bovill similarly insisted that "language, however provoking or long-continued, is not enough to justify taking life," all the more when a lethal weapon (in this case a gun) was employed. However, the wife in this case was not only a fierce verbal abuser but a drunkard – "I am sorry for it," the middle-aged defendant said, "but

---

[24] John Mews, *A Digest of Cases* (London, 1884), used this case as authority for the rule that "when in a contest, the law makes great allowance for blows and a personal encounter, but not for words." [p. 435]

[25] *R.v. Noon: Times* 20 July 1852, p. 7; 6 Cox C.C. 137. Cresswell may not have been pleased with this verdict: a few months later in another case he publicly vented his frustration that an obvious wife-murderer was escaping justice because of the difficulty of firmly establishing the cause of death [*R.v. Parrot: Times* 4 February 1853, p. 7].

[26] *R.v. Francis: Times*, 8 August 1859, p. 11. The Home Office generally shared (or exceeded) judges' lack of sympathy towards such provocation claims: an 1860 murder conviction for a fatal wife-stabbing brought forth many petitions for mercy; on one of them, from the man's daughter alleging provocation, George Cornewall Lewis observed dismissively, "an altercation between the husband and wife and angry words passed – this is what is meant by provocation" [HO12/127/42050 (*R.v. Gallagher*)].

she drove me to it." He himself was (uncharacteristically, according to witnesses) drunk at the time – enough mitigations to lead the jury to find only manslaughter and append a strong recommendation to mercy "on account of the excessive provocation under which the crime was committed and of the prisoner's uniform good conduct" up to then. Bovill took account of this recommendation and gave the man only five years' penal servitude.[27]

In the celebrated London murder trial three years later of the Rev. John Selby Watson, neither his wife's sharp tongue nor his social position saved this eminently respectable clergyman, schoolmaster, and scholar from a full murder conviction. They did, however, help the post-conviction argument that his distinguished mind had cracked under a series of strains, the final one being his wife's insults, and won him a reprieve from the gallows.[28]

If words were no longer acceptable as provocation, blows could be. There were occasions when women did use physical force, and if a husband charged with his wife's death or serious injury could prove her prior blows, especially if they were repeated or inflicted some damage, this evidence could provide mitigation or even excuse for his offense. Yet women's physical violence was generally seen, at least by judges, as rarely very threatening – all the more so as notions of female helplessness became ever stronger: a single blow, for instance, would not help a husband with the Bench very much. In the Cornishman John Rusden's 1839 wife murder trial, the defense that he had been struck first by his wife allowed the jury to convict him of manslaughter rather than murder, yet Justice Coleridge, agreeing with the jury that her blow had removed the killing from the category of murder, nonetheless sentenced him to transportation for life. Since questions had been raised at the trial as to whether her drawn-out death had been primarily caused by his beating, an effort was mounted for a pardon or at least a reduction in sentence. Upon being queried by the Home Office, Coleridge (a recent arrival on the bench, eventually to become Lord Chief Justice), observed that "*as this was a case of husband and wife,* and one in which not one or two, but according to the evidence a great many brutal blows were struck on the head... it seemed to me one which required very severe punishment." The verdict and

[27]*R.v. Midson: Times,* 15 July 1869, p. 11. Even in 1877 Fitzjames Stephen had to rebuke one jury for taking taunts as sufficient provocation to reject a charge of attempted murder for a non-fatal stabbing and return a verdict of "wounding with intent to inflict serious bodily harm," with a recommendation to mercy. "Whatever the provocation in mere *words* might have been," Stephen told them, "it could not possibly excuse the cruel and cowardly act of stabbing her in the throat, and inflicting a wound which the jury had found was intended to be serious, and which very nearly caused her death. Besides, whatever the provocation might have been, it had passed hours before, and the prisoner had ample time to get over it. Under such circumstances, the sentence must be twelve years' penal servitude" [*R.v. Janes: Times,* 23 July 1877, p. 8].
[28]For a fuller account of Watson's case, see Chapter 7.

sentence were not interfered with.[29] From a lesser form of violence, wife-beating was becoming, for a growing number of the new generation of judges like Coleridge, an aggravated form. Many other kinds of homicide were dealt with much less severely. In the same week as this case, Coleridge sentenced another man in a prizefight death to one year, which, after protesting petitions were collected, he recommended reducing to four months.[30]

In the same year William Lees, the London barber who cut his wife's throat and became a celebrity, also claimed his victim had struck the first blow (and then threatened further violence). On the stand he "pointed to a deep scar on his head, which he said was produced by her flinging a bottle at him, and he also exhibited two other wounds produced by her violence." However, where Rusden had simply beaten his wife until her death, Lees's use of a weapon (one he was professionally familiar with) invalidated this argument, and he was convicted and hanged.[31]

Similarly, when in 1843 a Liverpool-area workingman, Wilmot Buckley, fatally stabbed his wife after she had viciously insulted and then struck him, his use of a lethal weapon (even if only with his bad hand) ensured that he would be drawn no slack for these provocations. Baron Parke explicitly warned the jury away from a possible manslaughter verdict, insisting that "the law was clear." After strongly reiterating the principle that words alone were not a sufficient provocation to reduce the offense, he added that neither were "even blows," if they were not deliberate, but merely the product of the wife's "passions of anger." The jury duly returned with a murder verdict, though appending a mercy recommendation on the ground of provocation. The recommendation fell on deaf ears, and Buckley was hanged.[32]

This new provocation threshold was confirmed the following year in a similar case, that of a Sunderland army pensioner, Mark Sherwood, who had responded to his wife's obscene verbal and gestural abuse, combined with a slight blow, by cutting her throat. Chief Baron Pollock told this jury that "every provocation by blows will not reduce to manslaughter, particularly when, as in this case, the prisoner appears to have resented the blow [a box on the ear] by using a weapon calculated to cause death." Pollock conceded, in an aside that was recalled by defense counsel in future cases (but not however with great success), that it was possible for words and blows, neither by themselves sufficient to mitigate, in *combination* to be sufficient to reduce the verdict to manslaughter; however, he made clear, that did *not* apply in the present case. The jury brought in a murder verdict reluctantly, only after being

[29] *R.v. Rusden:* HO18/6/1; see also *Times*, 8 August 1839, p. 7. My italics.
[30] *R.v. Rudge:* HO18/6/1 and 2.
[31] *Times*, 17 Dec. 1839, p. 7; HO18/9/17; see Chapters 4 and 7.
[32] HO12/102/24; see also *Times*, 10 April 1843, p. 6 and "Life, Trial and Confession of Wilmot Buckley for the murder of his wife, aged 22 years, at St Helen's...." [BL 1888.c.3].

confined for six hours without food or drink.[33] A vigorous reprieve campaign insisted that a manslaughter verdict had been generally expected in court, after much had been heard of the wife's longtime querulousness; the verbal abuse that Sherwood had received impressed petitioners more than it did the judge and certainly seemed to them to amount to legal provocation. Still, the judge (perhaps having in mind, as the petitioners did not, the interesting fact that Sherwood's first wife had died under suspicious circumstances, burning to death without witnesses other than him present) advised the Home Secretary against mitigation, and Sherwood, like Buckley, hanged.[34]

When in 1866 James Fitzjames Stephen, as a rising defense counsel, called upon Pollock's concession in *Sherwood* as a precedent, he was put in his place by Mr. Justice Byles. Stephen significantly acknowledged that "the ordinary meaning [of 'malice aforethought'] had been greatly extended by successive decisions of courts of law" (thus reducing the scope of legal provocation). But, he claimed, "still many kinds of provocation were undoubtedly sufficient to raise in the mind of the person provoked that 'short madness' which may cause him to kill the provoker without malice aforethought." For instance, Stephen argued, it had been held "that when a person is assaulted under circumstances of personal indignity, and the person assaulted kills the other, the offense is only manslaughter." But Byles, while allowing that in a conflict between military officers a provocation defense based upon insult was possible, placed husband–wife conflict "at the other extreme" of conflicts, where such a defense could never be admitted. In those (and indeed most) situations, "mere words are not sufficient provocation; a serious assault may be, but a slight assault [in this case spitting] cannot." Furthermore, he reminded the jury that the law did not require "that any malice was cherished before the act was done, or that death was intended; it is sufficient if, a deadly instrument being used, mischief was intended at the time."[35] In another case tried by Byles, witnesses in William Cogan's Old Bailey trial in 1861 established that

[33] One mercy petition observed that "the jury had great difficulty in being brought to deliver a verdict of murder."

[34] *Times*, 5 Aug. 1844, p. 4; 174 ER 936; HO18/146/2; several different broadsides have survived, in the British Library.

[35] *R.v. Smith:* 176 *ER* 910 and *Times*, 15 December 1866, p. 11. Like *Sherwood*, this case has been misunderstood by modern commentators: because both Graeme Coss ["'God is a Righteous Judge, strong and patient: and God is provoked every day': A Brief History of the Doctrine of Provocation in England," *Sydney Law Review* 13.4 (Dec. 1991). 570–604] and Norman J. Finkel ['Achilles Fuming, Odysseus Stewing, and Hamlet Brooding: On the Story of the Murder/Manslaughter Distinction," *Nebraska Law Review* 74 (1995). 742–803] relied solely on the *English Reports*, neither, in citing Byles' concession here and the subsequent manslaughter verdict as evidence for a wider view of provocation, seemed to be aware that the judge had summed up strongly *against* reducing the offense to manslaughter. The very traditional sympathy with Smith for putting up with his wife's apparent infidelity, and not the technical point argued between judge and defense counsel, led the jury to rebuff the judge.

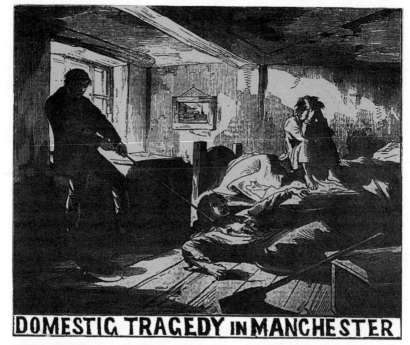

FIGURE 9. "Domestic Tragedy in Manchester" (*Illustrated Police News*, August 27, 1870). Patrick Durr's murder of his wife.

"the deceased was a violent woman" (against whom he had brought assault charges) and that on the night of her killing she had been in "a very drunken and excited state." Nonetheless Cogan, who had cut her throat, was found guilty of murder. Byles and the Home Secretary ignored the jury's mercy recommendation, and Cogan hanged.[36] Similarly, "the bad habits of the deceased," dwelled upon by a Manchester workingman's counsel in 1870, did nothing to mitigate for the jury Patrick Durr's strangling of his wife with a rope: they, like the judge, refrained from recommending him to mercy, and he too had a fatal encounter with a rope.[37]

In an 1872 trial of an Irishman from a mining district, the defense claimed that he "had been greatly provoked by the words and threats of his wife." Justice Denman told the jury that legal provocation required a clear "act of violence" to have been perpetrated on the defendant – "If the jury, on the evidence, thought there had been mere words of abuse and threats by the wife, the blow which caused her death was murder. If they saw anything

[36] *Times*, 27 September 1861, p. 8; *CCCSP* 1860–61, #783; HO12/133/47378.
[37] *Times*, 7 December 1870, p. 11; *Illustrated Police News*, 27 August 1870; HO12/195/94760.

in the circumstances which led them to suppose that the prisoner's act was caused by hot blood, *resulting from violence used to him,* they might find him guilty of manslaughter." The jury still found manslaughter (probably grasping the speculative defense suggestion that given her abusive behavior, while they were struggling she may well have used violence to him), but Denman, more skeptical or less sympathetic than the jury, gave the man the maximum sentence of penal servitude for life.[38]

Wifely blows would now have to be truly damaging to be taken seriously by either judges or most of the press. In a knife murder of a drunkard wife in Newcastle in 1875, after lecturing a jury to obtain a conviction, Lord Denman had little difficulty urging a like-minded Home Secretary Cross not to block execution. Denman complained of what he saw as a "growing disposition, especially in these Northern Counties, [to believe that the slightest] provocation however feeble in the nature of a defensive blow given even by a woman to a man is enough to reduce the crime to manslaughter." A growing mass-circulation press may have been making such sentiments more visible, but courtroom trends were moving in the opposite direction, towards more murder and fewer manslaughter verdicts in such cases. What the judge said in confidence to the Home Office, the *Newcastle Daily Journal* said in its leading article, declaring that "it is necessary that helpless women should be preserved, as far as the law can preserve them, from the sudden fury of passionate husbands; and the provocation involved in the administration of a 'smack,' in retaliation for being forcibly dragged from the street into the house, is no excuse or even palliation for so ruthless an assault."[39] Thus after the London gardener Charles Revell cut his wife's throat in Epping Forest in 1878, even her repeated blows did not constitute provocation to Justice Thesinger, who instructed the jury that even physical assault by a wife would not necessarily reduce her murder to manslaughter. His "retaliation" did not appear to be "the effect of passion under a sudden provocation" but rather "a deliberate act of a malignant and cruel mind." Revell received no recommendation to mercy and hanged.[40]

## Drunkard Wives

A worse wifely provocation than words or blows was drunkenness. Frequent drunkenness in a wife had always been deplored and used as a justification

[38]R.v. Grant: *Times,* 18 December 1872, p. 11 [italics added].

[39]*R.v. Anderson* (1875): HO45/9395/49945. The jury deliberated a long time and asked the judge for clarification as to the difference between aggravated manslaughter and murder; indeed at least one member claimed afterwards that he had never agreed to a "murder" verdict. Nonetheless, the man hanged. See the similar comments of the nation's largest-selling paper, *Lloyds' Weekly Newspaper,* 5 April 1874, condemning the finding of manslaughter in *R.v. Buckley.*

[40]*Times,* 9 July 1878, p. 4; HO45/9463/75390.

for "chastisement," but newer ideals of domesticity were if anything adding to its condemnation. As the symbolic importance of the home mounted, the "breadwinner ideal" that the husband should be able to support his wife and children by his own efforts spread and the maintenance of domestic harmony, order and economy was more thoroughly made the wife's responsibility. In such a climate, an addiction to drink in a wife was ever more repulsive. Persistent drinking undermined virtually all facets of a married woman's essential roles as wife, mother and housekeeper. A husband's addiction to drink, as long as it did not prevent him from holding a job, was seen as less serious. Even apart from the practicalities of family survival, drunkenness clashed far more with the womanly ideal increasingly accepted lower and lower in the social scale than with the manly ideal, it too becoming more widely accepted through the social scale. Ironically therefore, the cultural democratization that led to ideals hitherto applied chiefly to "genteel" women to be held up even for working-class women may have made drunken wives even more repugnant to jurors and even judges as the century went on, and thus induced greater sympathy for a man so afflicted. The jurist Edward Cox, whose skepticism about rape charges we have noted, also expressed his sympathy for husbands trapped with such bad wives. In the vast majority of wife-beating cases, he observed in 1877, "the suffering angel of the sensation 'leader' is found to be rather an angel of the fallen class, who has made her husband's home an earthly hell, who spends his earnings in drink, pawns his furniture, starves her children, provides for him no meals, lashes him with her tongue when sober and with her fists when drunk, and if he tries to restrain her fits of passion, resists with a fierceness and strength for which he is no match."[41]

The combination of old and new forms of condemnation of bad wives continued through the century to help wife killers in court, particularly when they were charged only with manslaughter, as Robert Knowles' one-month sentence in 1888 illustrates. Even judges did not necessarily oppose this defense: when James Palmer, a Kent laborer, was charged in 1863 with the manslaughter of his wife, the jury recommended him to mercy and Justice Pigott observed that "human nature is human nature and he was provoked because she was drunk," and sentenced him to just three months in prison.[42]

Yet despite the long life of such attitudes, they were nonetheless increasingly on the defensive against the growing strength of other attitudes less favorable to such defendants. If "civilizing" sentiments could shore up older

---

[41] Edward W. Cox, *The Principles of Punishment* (London, 1877), p. 101.

[42] See Conley, *Unwritten Law*, p. 79 [*Times*, 19 December 1863]. At his Old Bailey trial in 1865 for killing his wife by kicking her in the head, witnesses praised Henry Rickman's care for his wife's two children by her former husband and his persistent patience in the face of her perennial drunkenness; although the judge told him he had committed "a very unmanly assault," he gave him a sentence of only nine months [*Times*, 23 September 1865, p. 11].

patterns, they also challenged them: the democratization of "ladylike" behavior standards was matched by a similar democratization of "gentlemanly" behavior standards which made husbands' brutality all the more repellent. Thus, a husband's violent response to wifely dereliction was, like the dereliction itself, coming to appear even more intolerable than formerly. The spread of these parallel yet contending sets of standards produced heightened condemnation of *both* victim and perpetrator, and often legal outcomes for violent husbands depended on which evil most impressed jury and judge.[43] While wifely misbehavior could evoke sympathy, most judges were ever less inclined to let husbandly brutality pass lightly through their courts.

Unless a lethal weapon was used, the killing of a wife failed to produce any murder convictions at all for almost two decades into Victoria's reign. However, wife manslaughter verdicts, if sometimes light, could in other cases be quite heavy, even when the deceased had been a drunkard. In 1837, the first year of the new reign, Baron Alderson (raised to the bench in 1830) tried three killers of drunkard wives, two laboring men and a local innkeeper, one after the other at the same Liverpool assize, along with a fourth wife killer, who had merely in a quarrel pushed his wife downstairs with fatal results. As only one of the men had used a weapon, and he only incidentally, their juries found manslaughter in all cases. Despite evidence as to the three wives' habitual drunkenness, Alderson was as severe as the law allowed. One wife was described by the *Times*' reporter as "an habitual and inveterate drunkard, [who] sold anything that she and her husband had for drink, till she made him quite destitute." The leading Liverpool newspaper's account of that trial was especially sympathetic to her husband's "exasperation."[44] Nonetheless, in the face of both sorts of mitigation – wifely drunkenness and the lack of use of deadly weapons – Alderson awarded all three men, who had repeatedly punched and kicked their victims, transportation for life. In

---

[43]In a little over 100 of the 701 located wife murder trials, the victim's habitual drunkenness had been noted.

[44]*R.v. Culberson: Times*, 3 April 1837, p. 3; *Liverpool Mercury*, 7 April 1837, p. 110. "The prisoner is a sailor [the *Mercury* wrote], and had purposed to have gone a voyage on the 3rd of November, and had provided necessaries for the journey. On coming home on the evening preceding the morning he was to have started, he found his wife, who was a woman of most dissipated habits, lying on the floor, in a beastly state of intoxication, and discovered that she had disposed of the whole of the articles he had provided, and that he should be unable to prosecute his voyage. He became exasperated, and began to beat his wife, after which he turned her out of the house, but at the request of the neighbours, he was induced to take her in again. On returning she behaved in a very indecorous manner, and lay herself upon the floor, when the prisoner, in a passion, stamped on her stomach, which occasioned death. The only evidence to convict the prisoner was his admission to the surgeon, that he had beaten his wife rather heavily."

at least one of the trials Alderson averred his belief that the extent of the wife's injuries, drunkard or no, made it "a case of murder."[45] For Alderson, husbandly "brutality" trumped the provocation of wifely drunkenness.[46]

Alderson, though perhaps stricter in these matters than most, was by no means alone among high court judges in this priority. In the same year at the Old Bailey a man who had beaten and kicked his wife to death was sentenced by Baron Vaughan to the same maximum penalty as Alderson had used (in this case, however, the victim was no drunkard).[47] However, sentences varied with the particulars of each case, and with judges' attitudes, and similar killings might find quite different degrees of understanding in court. A year later another Liverpudlian, John Davies, received from Justice Patteson only eighteen months' imprisonment for beating and kicking his drunkard wife to death – in his case even though she was pregnant. The defendant's counsel told an affecting story of social ruination, from "a very comfortable house" to a cellar, because of her spending his ample wages (he was a pilot) on drink. Even the wife's mother acknowledged that her daughter had pawned her husband's property, though, she maintained, not for drink. As the counsel concluded, the victim "had reduced him from comfort to beggary, and his children to want and a cellar, and when he came home from his dangerous toil, instead of comfort and solace, he found every thing to disgust and provoke him, and under that provocation he had unfortunately inflicted the injury which had caused her death." The jury, their own fears of falling from their comfortable situation perhaps touched, readily convicted him of manslaughter only. Justice Patteson described how this particular story had also softened him: After reading the depositions, he had "thought the offense would have turned out to be murder" and had advised the grand jury to bring in such a bill. Yet by the close of the trial, he concluded that a short term of imprisonment at hard labor would be sufficient punishment. Lest this leniency have the wrong effect, he went on to denounce such violence and warn of harsher sentences for others: "It was true that the prisoner had endured very great provocation, and had been reduced to a state of poverty and misery by his wife's conduct, and that of his mother-in-law. His mind must, he had no doubt, have been strongly embittered against the deceased; but the fact of a man striking a woman under any circumstances was indefensible and cowardly, and betokened a very brutal character, more especially when that woman was his wife and five months advanced in pregnancy. . . . He would impress upon all who then heard him, that, if violence were used towards a woman, it was very probable that [transportation] might be inflicted. In this particular case he did not deem it necessary."[48]

[45] *R.v. M'Kenna: Liverpool Mercury*, 7 April 1837, p. 110.
[46] *Times*, 3 April 1837, p. 3. The fourth man received four years' imprisonment.
[47] *R.v. Hennessey: CCCSP* 1836–37, #2163.
[48] *Times*, 3 April 1838, p. 3.

Similar tensions were making themselves felt north of the Tweed as well. Although this study is generally limited to England, it would appear that Scotland was following a comparable trajectory. Indeed, when in 1840 a Glasgow bookbinder, Thomas Templeton, dashed his drunken wife's head against their wall and floor and casually left for a pub, his murder conviction set off a major confrontation between official and popular conceptions of provocation. Templeton had certainly intended harm, but probably not intended his wife's death, for he told a friend when he arrived at the pub that "I have given her as much as she will not trouble me for two or three days." In the event, she was not to trouble him ever again. Lord Cockburn firmly declared his opinion that it was nothing less than murder, and the Scottish jury then found him guilty of that by 14 to 1, while unanimously recommending him to mercy on grounds of "the repeated provocation which the prisoner had received from the deceased."[49] More impressed by what he called the "brutal nature of the crime,"[50] Lord Meadowbank pronounced the sentence of death without further remark. Glasgow public sentiment was quickly mobilized, and a petition with 12,000 signatures arrived within the week at the Home Office, which decided reprieves for Scotland as well as England and Wales. Feeling against the death penalty was rising, particularly in Scotland. However, the strongest source of support for a reprieve came from sympathy for Templeton's troubled marriage. As a letter to the Home Secretary from a bank clerk, himself plagued with a dissolute and quarrelsome wife, observed,

> ...when a husband has to earn his bread, by the sweat of his brow, and feels that toil and torment are his earthly lot, and that torment too, springs from her who of all others should be his comfort, becoming moderation is more perhaps than can reasonably be expected. ... I am aware that Lord Cockburn seemed to lay less stress on the provocation than [did] the jury. This rather grieves than surprises me, because from his very circumstances he cannot be supposed to know the provocation spoken of, but it seldom, in my opinion, happens that fifteen men of various professions and from different quarters meet without including some, who know and feel this worst of earthly evils.

A new more democratic voice can be heard here, unafraid to point out lack of worldly understanding in august judges; a voice speaking for ordinary

---

[49]The implied "negotiations" that may often have shaped jury verdicts like this one are suggested in the aftermath of another Scottish wife murder case, *R.v. Salt* (1860), in which the jury foreman, pleading for a reprieve, argued that the murder verdict had been given in expectation that the prisoner's life would be spared; had they known their recommendation would be ignored, he suggested, they might well have found "not proven." [HO12/125/39772.]

[50]And the prisoner's lack of moral standing to be provoked: he later noted to the Home Secretary that "neither the husband nor the wife were of very temperate habits, but he was the worst of the two. ... He was habitually violent on Saturday night."

husbands (though hardly for their wives). Yet it failed to have an effect. Cockburn, seconded by Meadowbank, argued confidentially that "I do not hold intoxication, not accompanied by violence ... to be provocation, in reference to such a charge, and by such a husband."[51] For a wife's drunkenness to mitigate her murder her husband would have to possess a "good character" and a nature not "brutal." Moreover, to a growing number of judges (and "respectable" observers) an angry blow was one thing, a prolonged and fierce beating quite another; similarly, a hitherto "good" husband might merit consideration not to be extended to "bad" ones. If Templeton had merely struck one or two angry blows, however fatal, or if his explosion had been a "one-off" thing, the Scottish judges might likely have relented; but not only was Templeton's violence repellent, he had, as he was to admit only after reprieve was denied, "once been in the habit of giving his wife a good beating." He consequently went to the scaffold.[52]

Although in both nations the gallows were to remain a rare destination for a wife killer who used no lethal weapon, beginning in the 1840s coroners' juries and committing magistrates became readier to charge murder, not merely manslaughter, in bad examples of such cases, even for men burdened with drunkard spouses.[53] Even though these cases for years always ended in manslaughter verdicts, if there were aggravating circumstances a maximum sentence could ensue. As the century went on, a growing number of cases in which the deceased wife's drunkenness was cited as provocation were charged as murder, and a growing number of these ended in convictions and even executions.[54]

When in 1844 Thomas Donahoo "knocked the b——h" – his frequently drunken wife – around with fatal results, he was (even without using a weapon) charged with murder, and while convicted only of manslaughter was soon on

[51] Lord Justice Clerk Boyle agreed, warning the Home Secretary that "it would be most dangerous doctrine, were it to be held, that the egregious drunkenness either of the deceased or the survivor can alter the nature of the crime."
[52] HO18/22/25; *Times*, 14 May 1840, p. 6. Another Scot had just hanged a few weeks earlier for murdering his drunkard wife: see HO18/16/29; *Times*, 21 April 1840, pp. 5–6 (*R.v. Weymss*). This case is discussed in Chapter 7.
[53] For example, *R.v. Lilburn: Times*, 11 March 1843, p. 8 or *R.v. Swanston: Times*, 26 August 1844. A heightened sensitivity to wife abuse is suggested by the report of an 1839 inquest near Manchester, in which a jury was only very reluctantly brought by its only witness, a medical man, to a verdict of death by disease in the case of a woman known to have been beaten in the past by her husband [*Manchester Times*, 30 November 1839, p. 4].
[54] Murder prosecutions in such circumstances rose from six in the 1840s and five in the 1850s to thirteen in the 1860s, twenty in the 1870s, nineteen in the 1880s, and twenty-nine in the 1890s; murder convictions from none in the 1840s and one in the 1850s to four in the 1860s, seven in the 1870s, seven in the 1880s, and eleven in the 1890s (executions rose from none in the '40s or '50s to one in the '60s, three in the '70s, four in the '80s, and six in the '90s).

his way to Van Diemen's Land for life.[55] On a single day at the Old Bailey in 1847, Chief Justice Wilde and Justice Patteson heard two similar murder trials of drunkard wives being beaten and kicked to death and similarly sentenced both defendants, convicted of manslaughter, to transportation for life.[56] In 1850, a 47-year-old London baker, Alexander Moir, who had beaten and kicked his drunkard wife over a period of years – "a long continued course of brutality," as the *Times* described it – was charged only with manslaughter by the inquest jury, since her death could not be attributed to a specific act of his. Despite this the magistrate to whom their finding passed upgraded the charge to murder, and Moir was so tried at the Old Bailey, where one witness told of the defendant speaking "of cheating the law by killing her by inches." Even the jury, returning a manslaughter verdict, called it an "aggravated" one, and the judge, Baron Alderson, then characterized it as "very little short of murder." Alderson went on to comment that the prisoner's counsel's claim "that he had been induced to act towards the deceased in this manner by reason of her drunken habits, he considered as no excuse or palliation whatever for his brutal conduct" and had him transported for life.[57] And two years later, a Devon man who had fatally beaten and kicked his drunken wife was, despite several favorable circumstances – he was described by a female neighbor as "a very quiet sort of man" who "never quarreled with anyone," and he had shown immediate remorse upon her death – also charged with murder and dispatched overseas by Justice Erle for life.[58] Declaring that violence against women "must be punished as crimes of the deepest dye," Justice Wightman in 1855 (at the same assize in which he sentenced three separate rapists to a total of fifty-five years' transportation) gave a man who had beaten his drunken wife to death fifteen years.[59]

English courts through the century saw continuing contention over the treatment of these cases, as a variety of developments exerted their influences for and against severity. One external development working against long sentences was the rapid economic and political development of Australia, which was closing off the punishment of transportation, for wife killers as for other convicts. In 1853 Tasmania (Van Diemen's Land) ceased to receive convicts, leaving only Western Australia, and in the following decade transportation gradually gave way to imprisonment in special institutions

[55] *Times*, 21 February 1845, p. 7. An inhabitant of Ulverstone, Lancashire, he had long been in the habit of beating his wife. He tried to conceal his role by placing her at the bottom of the stairs and instructing his son to say that she had fallen down; the son did as he was told when the policeman came, but recanted and implicated his father once he was at the police station. No doubt Donahoo's attempt to deceive the authorities increased his sentence.

[56] *R.v. M'Donald, R.v. Lamson: Times*, 18 June 1847, p. 7.

[57] *Times*, 10 May 1850, p. 7; *CCCSP* 1849–50 #922.

[58] *Times*, 3 April 1852, p. 7.

[59] *Liverpool Mail*, 15 December 1855, p. 6.

meant for long-term prisoners in Britain. This was a form of punishment now generally considered to be harsher than transportation, since penal conditions in Australia had eased over the years, release on license had come ever sooner, and economic opportunities there had greatly improved. Consequently, judges became less likely to impose life sentences to this new form of penal servitude than they had to award transportation for life. A sentence of at most ten years penal servitude was more equivalent in perceived and probably actual severity to what transportation for life had become by mid-century.

Internally, the contemporaneous widening of the public sphere was providing another kind of check to the increasing judicial determination to put down domestic violence. Severe sentences issued to defendants who did not appear to be such bad men as Moir was were becoming more likely to produce public protests – especially of course murder verdicts, with their capital penalty, but also sentences of transportation for life. In a time of growing "popular" political influence, these were emerging as a factor that neither judges nor Home Secretaries could completely disregard. In this area, strengthening "humane" sentiments also encouraged disapproval of capital punishment (particularly in the public form it then took) and unhappiness with transportation, as well as sympathy for "provoked" husbands, as evident in the unsuccessful agitation to save Thomas Templeton. Even when, as most often, the husband's life was not at stake in wife killings, sensitivity to public expectations encouraged judges to award less than maximum sentences.

Newspaper circulation and popular political activity rose together, aided by the national integration brought by the new railways, both expanding the space for "public opinion" to be brought to bear from the 1830s on – a space encouraged and utilized by now ubiquitous and newly empowered defense counsel. Tough judicial rulings were more often meeting public response, often organized by solicitors and barristers for the defense. When in 1839 Justice Coleridge sentenced John Rusden to transportation for life for fatally beating his wife (who, though not a drunkard, was thought to be "a quarrelsome woman"), widely-signed public protests to the Home Secretary forced him to defend his sentence on the grounds that "a [homicide] case of husband and wife," particularly when a great deal of brutal violence was inflicted, decidedly merited more severe punishment than most others. Nonetheless, he did allow privately that he would not object to earlier release than usual for Rusden.[60]

---

[60] *Times*, 8 August 1839, p. 3; HO18/6/1 [this case is more fully discussed in Chapter 7]. Coleridge was setting himself against any special allowance for wife-killers; as he had observed to the grand jury in opening the assizes, "there is a dangerous laxity growing up in the country as to the question of murder or manslaughter. . . . I cannot but think that the practice of limiting murder to one or two particular sorts of cases induces an allowance in dangerous ferocity which, otherwise, people would have the

Sometimes now, public intervention was organized even before trial. Benjamin Owen, a gasfitter tried in 1859, was well-liked in his town of Wednesbury and "bore a fair character as a peaceable, well-disposed man," while evidence was given of his wife's drunkenness. His defense counsel, while accepting that he had at least struck her with his fists several times and thrown her out of their house, argued that she had died of apoplexy, "brought on by a fall in the drunken state she was in." This claim was not accepted, but he was prepared: as soon as a manslaughter verdict was returned, this counsel "handed up two documents in favor of the prisoner," signed by nearly five hundred inhabitants of Wednesbury. Justice Willes responded sympathetically – "from the character given of the prisoner, he was sorry to pass any sentence upon him at all" – but felt it necessary ("for the protection of women and to put a stop to such brutal assaults by men on their wives") to give him six years' penal servitude.[61]

Such proactive defense behavior was often not necessary. On occasion inquest juries, whose prescribed role was only to find a cause of death and if indicated charge someone with murder or manslaughter, might in doing so make a case for lenient treatment. An inquest jury charging Abraham Pembrook with the manslaughter of his wife in 1860 declared his provocation to be "peculiarly aggravated . . . the deceased having run her husband extensively into debt; having left her home and cohabited with another man without any apparent cause." It continued, noting also "as it appeared from the medical test, that the deceased for some time previous to the influence of the injuries had been suffering from chronic disease of two vital organs." This statement was read in full at trial. The judge agreed with its points, although then telling Pembrook that "however great the provocation, nothing could justify the cruel and merciless beating you gave her." He sentenced the defendant to a year's hard labor.[62]

Juries, especially the inquest jury but even the more economically select trial jury,[63] lived much closer than magistrates or judges to the social situation of most defendants. Perhaps for this reason they held to "customary" notions longer and more intensely than did their superiors. Indeed, many

---

wit and prudence to restrain." *Cornwall Royal Gazette*, 9 August 1839, p. 4. The protests had been based first on the fact that Rusden's wife didn't die for over a month after her beating, second on his claim that she struck him first, and third on his previous good character.

[61] *Times*, 9 December 1859, p. 12.

[62] *Times*, 9 March 1860, p. 11.

[63] By an act of 1825, trial jurors were required to be householders with a minimum annual value of £10, if freehold, or £20 if leasehold; in Middlesex, with its higher property values, the latter value was £30 and in the City of London, £100. This did not change until the twentieth century. By contrast, almost any man might serve on an inquest jury; however, their role was in law restricted to simply finding suspicious circumstances in a death.

jurymen could understand all too well the pressures acting upon men of the "lower classes," pressures that were merely abstract to the elite of judges and Home Office bureaucrats. Other times skilled defense counsel could win over jury and judge alike, and obviate the need for a petition. In his 1860 trial at Carlisle, William Usher's Queen's Counsel was "listened to with profound attention in court" as he declared that "there, perhaps, could only be one source of misery more irritating for a man placed in such a situation. Next to conjugal infidelity surely [a wife's drunkenness] was the next provocation he could receive. What if he yielded to the passions of the moment – if he struck one blow, or more than one blow? If the prisoner yielded to passion it was provoked by most exasperating circumstances, and was soon repented of." Several witnesses attested to Usher's general repute as a "sober and industrious man," and Justice Hill observed in sentencing him to a mere fifteen months' imprisonment that "he had been grievously provoked." Regardless of provocation, "had he used any weapons, or exhibited any malice toward her, in the violence which had caused her death, he would have been guilty of murder . . . [ but] he was willing to believe he intended nothing of the kind."[64]

Even if judges thought a beating death of a drunken wife were indeed murder, as was increasingly happening from the 1860s, juries were reluctant to agree. In 1863, Joseph Howes, a Sussex labourer, came home drunk and, as he later claimed, found his wife also drunk. He beat her, keeping on even after neighbours complained and urged him to stop, and she died that night. Howes' counsel, taking up a long-established line, questioned whether the woman would have died if she had not already had a weak constitution due to her drinking.[65] He also emphasized that Howes had used no weapon but his fists, strongly indicating the lack of any intent to kill, and provided witnesses testifying to his character as "a peaceful and well-conducted man." Nonetheless, Baron Channell, in his summation, virtually urged the jury to convict of murder, regardless of the non-use of any but what were often called a man's "natural" weapons. Channell distinguished between an angry outburst of violence and a prolonged attack: "If a man used such brutal violence towards a woman," Channell concluded, "and continued to do so, after having been warned and cautioned not to kill her, it was difficult to see that he could have meant anything else than to cause her death." However,

---

[64] *Times,* 27 February 1860, p. 11.
[65] One of the chief practical obstacles to convicting for the killing of a drunkard wife (in the absence of weapons) was the difficulty in proving beyond reasonable doubt the proximate cause of death. Often a victim lingered for days, sometimes weeks, allowing time an already weakened physical state due to illness or "addiction to drink" to be a factor; it was common for heavy drinkers to suffer a variety of ailments and debilities. This difficulty could, of course, be seized upon by jurors already somewhat sympathetic to the defendant.

the jury convicted him only of manslaughter. The judge then gave him ten years' penal servitude.[66]

A similar compromise emerged from the trial of the Surrey navvy, John Vickery, four years later. Vickery had killed his wife in circumstances comparable to Howes's. Provoked, as we have seen, by her spending his money on drink, he had beaten her to death with much brutality. Probably because of the absence of a weapon, the grand jury had thrown out the coroner's jury's finding of murder and charged Vickery only with manslaughter. But again the judge, Baron Bramwell, served as a back-up prosecutor, telling the jury that "if they believed her death was the result [of the beating], then they must find him guilty [of the manslaughter charge]. Could they really doubt that it was so?" Bramwell went on to note that the prisoner's "having been in a passion at the time was no defense; if it were, we should all be at the mercy of passionate men." The jury convicted of manslaughter, but even for this reduced charge added a recommendation to mercy. Bramwell sentenced Vickery to five years' penal servitude, more it appears than the jury wanted but less than he would have given on his own.[67]

In an 1872 case of a drunkard, William Bradley, pushing his drunkard wife into the fire and holding her there until she died, the jury similarly found manslaughter with a recommendation to mercy. Justice Willes, after having told the grand jury that the case should have been charged as murder, when sentencing Bradley and another man convicted of manslaughter in the death of his aged housekeeper, echoed Bramwell: "You are the two prisoners who have made assaults of an angry and violent character upon women, and brought them to their graves. In one respect the case of Faulkner is decidedly preferable to that of Bradley, though on grounds which I am afraid I shall have to answer at the bar of some people who hold a different opinion – on the ground that the woman whose death you caused was your wife, whom you were bound to cherish and protect, and to whom you owed a duty far beyond that which was merely imposed by human law. Persons had been let off lightly because of the notion that a man might do what he liked with his wife, and it was thought than an offense of that kind was more easily atoned for and forgiven than when committed upon others, but it is a doctrine which, so far as I am concerned, I feel bound to protest against; it is revolting to my feelings, and runs counter to my judgement, and I think it most necessary to check the notion that husbands may maltreat their wives by only imposing on them such a sentence as will show men they must not abuse the women they are bound to protect.... but for [the jury's] recommendation I should have passed a heavier sentence than that I am about to give. The sentence of the court is that you be sent to penal servitude for ten years." The case of the other man, who "kicked or tread upon [his old housekeeper], and left her

[66] *Times*, 6 August 1863, p. 8.
[67] *Times*, 28 March 1867, p. 11.

helpless to die as she might," still had "less aggravation about it than that of Bradley," and he gave him five years' penal servitude.[68]

By the turn of the 1870s, the press was an increasingly important player in these cases. However, if the press could provide a forum for criticism of judicial harshness against homicidal husbands, it also afforded a public space in which to publicize their crimes. Vickery's arrest in 1866 had been heralded as a "Shocking Wife Murder," and newspapers noted the bloody details, the "circumstances," as the *Times* put it, "of great brutality."[69] Thereafter, perhaps influenced by the abolition of public hangings in 1868 which made capital punishment less offensive, and by the rise of the movement for women's rights, which hardened public opinion against domestic violence, many papers shifted the direction of their shafts from hanging judges to soft juries. In Bradley's case, the *Pall Mall Gazette* backed up Justice Willes, also complaining of the lack of a murder charge, but especially attacking the jury for adding a mercy recommendation on the ground that "the wife's state of drunkenness might have provoked him." "It would seem," the paper sarcastically observed, "that a new mode of correcting wives – by placing them on the fire – is growing into favour among husbands. Nay, it would even appear from a verdict recently given by a Lancaster jury that the punishment in question is felt to have so peculiar an appropriateness under certain circumstances that a husband must not be too severely judged for resorting to it on such occasions." As for the jury's view of provocation, the paper went on to "agree" that "no grosser provocation can present itself to an intoxicated man than the discovery that his wife is intoxicated also; and when once his passions are fully aroused by this discovery the idea of putting her on the fire would suggest itself so naturally and with such irresistible force that to refrain from this act would demand a larger measure of self-control than can be reasonably expected from our weak and erring humanity."[70]

By this time "mere" kicking, if issuing in death, was a good deal more likely to yield a murder charge and even lead to the gallows. Murder charges in such cases rose even faster than the total wife murder caseload: from 5 in the 1850s to 18 in the '60s to 34 in the '70s. As we have seen, the defendants in these trials were overwhelmingly working-class; indeed, only one of the 34 such murder trials during the '70s had a middle-class defendant. Thus, the rise in murder charges for killing one's wife (whether legal or common-law)

---

[68] *Lancaster Gazette*, 27 July 1872, pp. 4, 5.

[69] *Times*, 26 November 1866, p. 7.

[70] *Times*, 29 July 1872, p. 11 and 1 Aug. 1872, p. 4 (reprinting from the *Pall Mall Gazette*). Jurors could indeed stretch the meaning of provocation considerably. In the case of Thomas Edwards, a butcher who in 1862 stabbed to death a prostitute with whom he had been living, the jury recommended to mercy on the "provocation received, caused by his previous intimacy with deceased." The judge did not bother to hide his scorn of this recommendation [*Times*, 18 Dec. 1862, p. 10].

by beating or kicking also meant intensifying the pressure of the criminal law upon working-class men in particular – or, viewed from another angle, the extension of the sword of the law to more strongly condemn and deter serious violence against working-class women.

Although the Home Office's attitude was already hardening, the Conservative Home Secretary Richard Cross soon after assuming office in 1874 took a further step by requesting information from magistrates and other local officials throughout the country on how "brutal assaults on women and children" were being handled. The request stimulated public discussion of the subject, and the Home Office's ensuing publication of the responses of officials and statement of its position put the central government on record, along with many magistrates, as favoring sterner punishment for such acts.[71]

Changing public and official attitudes took some time to penetrate the minds of the men who killed their wives. Henry Bradshaw, a Sheffield saw-grinder, declared in 1871 to his neighbor as it became apparent that his wife had died from his kicking, "let the – cat do a stiff 'un [die], I can do a 'twelver' f her." However, Bradshaw's judgment was as flawed as his impulse control: he was a returned convict, and he committed the act in public. Bradshaw was given twenty years' penal servitude.[72] When in the fall of 1874 John Bishop, in lodgings near Leicester Square, gave his drunken wife a beating prolonged enough to break six of her ribs and finally kill her, his neighbors trooped through the witness box to vouch for him, calling his wife "a great drunkard," who was "known to be very violent when in liquor"; him, on the other hand, they praised as a model husband. Nonetheless, the defense counsel reminded the jury that in the new official climate they could no longer expect to keep him from hanging by recommending mercy: "By recent experience," he warned, "it was plain that their verdict would not be interfered with by the authorities... with them consequently rested the prisoner's fate." This reminder had its intended effect: after deliberating for three hours, the jury found manslaughter only. However, Justice Denman gave Bishop penal servitude for life, to "mark [his] sense of the extreme brutality of such brutal conduct." Indeed, Denman added, as if to confirm the defense counsel's point, "if [the jury] had thought fit to return another verdict, which the evidence would have warranted, he should have been compelled to sentence him to death, and that without hope of mercy."[73]

A month later a Liverpool bargeman, William Worthington, added a poker to his boots in dealing with his drunken wife. Although she did not

[71] See "Reports to the Secretary of State for the Home Department on the State of the Law Relating to Brutal Assaults, etc." *Parl. Papers* lxi (1875).

[72] *Times,* 7 December 1871, p. 11.

[73] *CCCSP* 1873–74, #455; *Times,* 29 October 1874, p. 11; also, *Lloyds' Weekly* 27 September, 4 October, 1 November 1874. *Lloyds'* report was headlined "Brutal Murder of a Woman."

die for some days, and then of pneumonia (aggravated by her injuries), he went all the way to the scaffold. In part because of the poker and in part because of the evil reputation of Liverpool's "kicking districts," the jury's mercy recommendation was disregarded. The chief civil servant at the Home Office noted that "the prevalence of these kicking cases requires an example. This is a bad case of the sort and brutal violence must have been used without any apparent provocation."[74]

In 1879, when another fatal kicker of a drunkard wife, John Whelan of Manchester, was convicted of murder, with the usual recommendation to mercy, at least as much attention was paid at the Home Office to *his* character as to that of his wife. Her drunkenness was offset by his own, a consideration not often taken into account earlier. As one official observed, "she does appear to have been a drunken woman, but he was not a sober man"; another called him "a rough coarse brutal man." Yet in this case the jury's mercy recommendation was heeded, after Permanent Undersecretary Liddell decided that he had probably not meant to kill.[75] The next year John Walker, charged only with manslaughter for kicking his drunkard wife to death, favored by testimony that "he had always borne the character of a peaceable, sober man," and receiving a strong jury recommendation to mercy, still drew a severe response from Justice Hawkins. The judge acknowledged that "it was a painful sight for a man to witness his wife in a state of drunkenness, and in this condition, there was reason to believe, the prisoner had seen the deceased woman upon many occasions before," but observed that "when he had knocked her down he was heard to make the remark that he thought he had given her enough to last her a considerable time" and then continued knocking her about, helpless as she was, for hours. Such behavior could not be tolerated, and "notwithstanding the recommendation to mercy the sentence upon him would be one which would teach men that brutal and unmanly violence might not be used towards women, though in a state of intoxication." He gave Walker ten years' penal servitude, more than had been expected.[76]

"Brutality" (associated with men of "the residuum") was increasingly cited as a factor aggravating a killing, by reflection on the character and the intent of the defendant. A classic struggle between horror at brutality and sympathy

---

[74] HO45/9375/40027; *Times*, 18 December 1874, p. 9.
[75] HO144/49/188446; *Times*, 6 November 1879, p. 11.
[76] *Times*, 30 November 1880, p. 11; *CCCSP* 1880–81, #94; PRO CRIM 1/11/2. Juries were not always more merciful than judges. At Liverpool in 1881, Joseph McEntee's jury not only found him guilty of murder but failed to add any recommendation, despite the fact that his wife "had spent his wages and pawned his watch" to buy drink. Even Justice Mathew was convinced that McEntee had been "a good husband who always provided well for his wife." Yet, perhaps because McEntee himself was a heavy drinker, he received no recommendation and no reprieve [*Times*, 7 April 1881, p. 8].

for a man afflicted with a bad wife had taken place some years earlier in the Scottish case of Edwin Salt, an Edinburgh excise officer who had gone beyond use of his "natural" weapons of fist and foot.[77] In March 1860, Salt horrifically killed his "dissipated" wife by thrusting a hot fireplace poker into her vagina. Convicted of murder, he was reprieved after a strong jury recommendation followed by a vigorous petition campaign that focused on her "desperate" addiction to drink and her consequent neglect of her children and her husband's "domestic peace and comfort." The leading local paper, the *Scotsman,* supported reprieve, calling the victim a "depraved" woman. The foreman of the jury assured the Home Secretary that they had brought in a verdict of guilty only in the expectation that Salt's life would be spared. However, Lord Justice Clerk Inglis, more impressed by the savagery of the act than the character of the victim, took issue with the jury's recommendation. He doubted, he wrote the Home Secretary, that "it would be safe to admit that the irritation produced by the drunken habits of a wife can be accepted as a palliation of such a [brutal] crime." Home Secretary George Cornewall Lewis agreed with the judge, but, under heavy public pressure, he eventually issued a reprieve, for which he was thanked by no less than the Lord Provost of Edinburgh: it would be, he observed, "a great relief to the authorities in Edinburgh," fearful of an indignant public.[78]

In a case with similar circumstances to Salt's eighteen years later [1878] however, the defendant went to the Liverpool gallows. This later defendant, James Trickett, who had stabbed his wife, was of a lower class than Salt, though his defenders described his character highly. Apart from the possible influence of class bias, hardening official attitudes towards wife killing in the interval probably played a role. Upon the murder verdict, the prisoner, who had used a knife as well as his boots against a "dissipated" wife, delivered an impassioned and lengthy speech, in which he summed up his grievance: "When my wife was a sober woman I had a heaven of a home and had my meals regular and the rooms kept clean. I had no meals when she turned to drink; it was always the opposite way."

Trickett, like Salt, drew sympathy from his jury (who recommended mercy) and from the audience and wider public (who petitioned in numbers and with vigor). Indeed, several of the jurors got up their own petition. One petition complained that the neighborhood "cannot reconcile the sentence with that of fifteen years passed on Hugh Lennon, who killed his father – in the same street, and tried at the same assize – the case of Lennon being considered much worse in the neighborhood both as regarding provocation, premeditation and the habits of the two men, one being a drunken young fellow and the other a striving, industrious, and generally a well conducted man." That

---

[77] Such sympathy in this case was reinforced by the man's own drunkenness, which was seen as diminishing his responsibility.

[78] HO12/125/39772. See *Times,* 1 and 6 March 1860, for an account of his trial.

killing a wife could be treated more harshly than killing a father seemed un-just to most of Trickett's neighbors. However, not to his judge, Baron Pollock. In his confidential letter to the Home Secretary, Pollock observed that "there was no provocation except the woman being an habitual drunkard," which for him had no bearing in a murder case. Moreover, he continued, "the stab removes all doubt about the case to my mind. It was a deliberate murder." The Home Office agreed.[79]

As these cases suggest, employing a weapon in killing one's drunkard wife, as in other killings, racheted up the seriousness of the offense. Sometimes jurors still would find manslaughter, but since weapon use was readily seen as a marker of intent to kill, a murder conviction was increasingly likely.[80] Not always, however, for by the nature of the jury system verdicts were not uniform, even in similar circumstances. William Moore was convicted only of manslaughter at the Old Bailey in 1859 even after the Recorder described his stabbing of his drunkard wife as murder. Here male fellow feeling may have played a part: the witnesses lined up by gender, women citing his previous beatings of his wife and recounting his threats against her, while male neighbors gave him an excellent character – one called him "as good, affectionate and kind a man as ever walked England's ground" – and could recall nothing bad about his behavior. When the jury returned manslaughter, Justice Wightman confessed that he "could not understand" why they had not found murder, declared it "one of the worst cases of the kind within his experience" and sentenced Moore to penal servitude for life.[81]

As it became apparent by the 1890s that recorded serious violent crime had been declining for some time, both public and official concerns about the level of violence in society eased.[82] With that easing a general relaxation in the treatment of criminal violence set in. Public and official attention shifted from the dangers of violence and barbarism in the lower classes to the severities of penal servitude, which were now publicized and denounced, bringing about by the Edwardian era a major overhaul and reform of all prisons and the shortening of prison sentences,[83] trends which continued down to the Second World War. Prisons became less purely punitive, and sentences of penal servitude for life became very rare, except as the usual form of reprieve from execution.

[79] HO45/9454/70764; *Times*, 26 January 1878, p. 11.
[80] The subject of weapon use is discussed more fully in Chapter 7.
[81] *Times*, 14 May 1859 [recorder's charge]; 7 July 1859, p. 11 [trial]; *CCCSP* 1858–59, #700.
[82] The official homicide rate began to clearly fall after 1870, and declined drastically from 1.5 in 1871 to 0.3 in 1931, a rate that then held through 1951 before beginning a half-century rise to the present. J. Briggs, C. Harrison, A. McInnes and D. Vincent, *Crime and Punishment in England: An Introductory Survey* (London, 1996), p. 178.
[83] See Wiener, *Reconstructing the Criminal* (Cambridge, 1990), Chapter 8.

Nonetheless, the shortening of sentences in the 1890s and 1900s was less pronounced for wife killers. Such men, when not showing previous good character, continued to be dealt with severely. Once murder was found, the character of the prisoner – how "bad" a man he was – remained probably the most important single factor in determining his fate. Such a man might hang or not, and much depended on the kind and strength of support for a reprieve. Two men tried in 1902 in Manchester met different fates because of this: a Salford laborer, Peter Howarth, won a reprieve despite battering his drunkard wife's head in with a shovel he had gone outside to get and then in addition cutting her throat, while a man from Oldham, Harry Mark, went to the gallows for having killed his drunkard and promiscuous wife without any weapons beyond his boots. Howarth had held the same job for eighteen years and was known as an excellent workman and workmate; a petition for him gained 20,000 signatures (including that of the Mayor of Salford), and the *Manchester Evening News* editorialized in his favor.[84] Mack, on the other hand, had many previous criminal convictions and apparently was living on his wife's earnings as a prostitute. The jury made no recommendation to mercy, no petition was gotten up, no newspapers editorialized, and he hanged.[85]

Looking over the Victorian era we can see that as the notion of acceptable physical "chastisement" of bad wives was dismissed from courtroom discourse, argument focused on mitigations rather than excuses. Those claiming provocation, the most common mitigation claim made by those on trial for killing their wives, often continued to find sympathy from juries but a narrowing path to acceptance by judges and the Home Office. Provocation by means of words and even light blows now rarely succeeded. Provocation by a "dissipated" wife, attached to drink and neglectful of her domestic duties, was a more effective claim. This position however was strongly contested, both between the voices of an advancing respectability and the many outside its boundaries and between competing strictures of respectable ideology itself. Such contestation, often resulting in compromises – between judges and juries, or between the Home Office and "public opinion" – in the treatment of these crimes, set a limit on change. Yet change did take place. Over the century provocations came to mitigate less or not at all, and wife killing moved up the scale of comparative seriousness, prosecuted and punished more often and compared to many other homicides more severely.

---

[84] *Times*, 3 February 1902, p. 11; HO144/577/A63168. The head of the Home Office Criminal Department, less influenced by "character" and public reputation, was reluctant to reprieve, until a letter from the trial judge in favor of the prisoner tipped the balance.

[85] *Times*, 17 November 1902, p. 7; *Manchester Evening Chronicle*, 14 November 1902; HO144/681/102278.

If the wifely provocations to husbands' violence examined in this chapter elicited both contention and change in the processes of criminal justice, the greatest wifely provocation of all – infidelity – evoked, not surprisingly perhaps, the greatest contention of all and also a decided change in legal treatment.

# 6

# Bad Wives II: Adultery and the Unwritten Law

In the sixty years 1841–1900, covering almost Victoria's entire reign, forty-three trials for murders motivated by a legally married spouse's established infidelity took place, and all but one of these placed men in the dock.[1] At least twenty-three more murder trials took place in which the chief motive had been a legally married spouse's unsubstantiated belief in the other's infidelity, all these being of men.[2] Possibly, as evolutionary psychologists have suggested, this sort of violent sexual possessiveness is, more than simply violence in itself, a biologically male-linked trait.[3] Here was "a man's crime" *par excellence,* akin perhaps in its gendered character to the murder of newborn infants, a crime almost invariably perpetrated by women.[4] Always of great interest, this male-linked crime brought forth particularly strong and conflicted responses in Victorian England.

[1] The one exception was that of Elizabeth Gibbons, who shot and killed her husband in a jealous rage in 1884. She was convicted of murder and after an active press and public effort for her life, reprieved. Her rarity merited her a place in Madame Tussaud's gallery. [*Times,* 19 December 1884, p. 12 and 20 December 1884, p. 11; HO144/146/A38012/72]

[2] One other case in which female sexual possessiveness was alleged was really more complex. Elizabeth Martha Brown, tried in Dorchester in 1856 for killing her unfaithful husband, had obvious additional reasons for dissatisfaction: her husband was a drunkard and beat her harshly when she would complain about his other women. Although she denied jealousy, the prosecution focused on that rather than her other motives (even the judge, Baron Channell, privately doubted that jealousy was the motive). Her hanging was witnessed by a fifteen-year-old Thomas Hardy, whose *Tess of the D'Urbervilles* owed much to the experience. [*Times,* 23 July–19 August 1856; HO12/108/23372; Patrick Wilson, *Murderess* (London, 1971), pp. 124–127.]

[3] Margo Daly and Martin Wilson, *Homicide* (New York, 1988); idem., "An Evolutionary Psychological Perspective on Male Sexual Proprietariness and Violence Against Wives," *Violence and Victims* 8 (1993), 271–294.

[4] Phillippe Chassaigne's study of Old Bailey homicide trials 1857–1900 corroborates this point: of victims of killings he labeled "crimes of passion," 90 per cent were women, 5 per cent men, and 5 per cent children. "La Meurtre à Londres à l'Époque Victorienne: Structures Sociales et Comportements Criminels, 1857–1900" (Thèse de Doctorat, University of Paris, 1991), p. 301.

A closely related crime was the killing of a sexual rival, one's spouse's lover, also virtually a purely male offense. Women almost never killed either their husbands or other women out of sexual possessiveness.[5] Killing a wife's sexual partner was not exonerated in Victorian courts but was dealt with comparatively leniently. Men were seen as generally more responsible, and certainly so in sexual matters. As "natural" sexual aggressors they were in most cases more obviously to blame; the scenario familiar in popular lore of a naive man seduced by a licentious and scheming woman, while without doubt still part of the culture's repertoire, was less plausible than in previous centuries. Moreover, fighting and other use of violence were viewed as almost a normal part of men's lives, and the fact of a man killed by another was less shocking than that of a murdered woman.[6]

As long as a man was legally married to his woman, and the adultery with another man was accepted as true, if he killed the other man he was normally treated with some indulgence. Of the six English cases I have encountered that met both these criteria,[7] none ended in a hanging. More characteristically, Justice Grantham observed after sentencing Isaac Hazlehurst to only one year's imprisonment for murdering his notoriously unfaithful wife in 1887 upon finding her in his bed with another man, that if Hazlehurst had instead killed the man, he would never have been even charged with murder.[8] If however, the adultery was not clearly established (just as with murder of an "unfaithful" wife herself), judges set themselves against leniency. As Baron Bramwell pronounced in Albert Turner's 1858 trial, "no doubt a husband would be justified in killing any man whom he detected in the act of committing adultery with his wife. It was a very different case, however, where a man only entertained a suspicion, however strong the grounds of that suspicion might be, that his wife was unfaithful."[9]

---

[5] They did, however, on rare occasions wound them in jealousy, either in a fight or by throwing acid on their faces, as did Harriet Minton to her former common-law husband who had left her in 1876; he was nearly blinded, and she was given six months' hard labor [*Times*, 17 July 1876, p. 11].

[6] Similarly, a wife's rare killing of her husband's lover was punished less severely than a man's killing of a woman, whether his wife or not. If the fact of a murdered woman was highly shocking, so too now was that of a woman's execution; not only juries but even judges bent over backwards to avoid hanging a woman [see Chapter 4]. A petition from Dumfries, Scotland, for the reprieve of Mary Timney for murdering a woman neighbor in 1862 stressed the "shame" that would be brought down on their town by "a public execution of a woman." In this case, however, a reprieve was refused, and the *Manchester Guardian* reported that "the scene was harrowing in the extreme, and affected many to tears" [13 April 1862 ; HO12/136/50441].

[7] No doubt there were others; unlike spousal murders, no systematic trawl for these kinds of killings was made.

[8] *Barnsley Independent*, 14 May 1887.

[9] *Times*, 31 July 1858, p. 11.

In lesser cases, doing violence to one's wife's lover was not often regarded as worthy of much punishment at all. James Johnson's 1881 attempted murder trial ended in a wounding verdict and immediate release. Johnson broke into the man's house and discovered him in the act of adultery with Mrs. Johnson; he then "struck [him] violent blows on the head with a cleaver . . . and so seriously injured him that he was in the infirmary for five weeks." Nonetheless, Justice Kay declared the provocation "one of the greatest a man could receive. . . . I would not punish him further." The release was received with applause.[10] However, the killing, or serious injuring, of an unfaithful wife was a more serious matter.

The greatest literary work to deal with the killing of a wife for her supposed unfaithfulness, Shakespeare's *Othello*, was especially popular but also especially difficult to stage in this era. Its powerful evocations of sexuality and of intimate violence stirred audiences but at the same time discomfited them.[11] Most of all, its hero's fusion of sensuality and brute violence with nobility of character was now almost impossible to sustain. Productions tended to either "purify" Othello or "primitivize" him. Already in 1836 John Forster could declare that "jealousy is not the grand feature of Othello's passion." A few decades later the great actor Edwin Booth was outraged when a friend told him that Shakespeare had intended Othello for a "beast": "did you ever?!!! [he wrote to another friend] I cannot possibly see the least animalism in him – to my mind he is pure and noble; even in his rage . . . I perceive no bestiality."[12] Something of a culmination to this purification came in 1861 with the celebrated actor–dramatist Charles Fechter's production of the play. It capped several decades of efforts already made by other directors to soften character traits of the hero with which respectable audiences could no longer readily identify, such as his sensuality, impulsiveness, and violence (however central they were to Shakespeare's conception). Fechter's Othello was calmer, more reflective, and generally less expressive – less "Mediterranean," more reminiscent, perhaps, of Hamlet than of the Moor of Venice as he had previously been known. The "advanced" critic G.H. Lewes missed the passion and complained that Fechter's Othello was merely "an affectionate but

---

[10] *Times*, 8 November 1881, p. 10.

[11] It was staged in many forms, from popular melodrama to more refined tragedy, and was familiar to many. In a wife manslaughter trial in 1840, against the defense's reliance on the dying wife's denial that her husband had harmed her, Baron Alderson cited the play to show the plausibility of suspecting such a denial: "When Desdemona was discovered to be dying from the effects of the violence inflicted upon her by her husband, Shakespeare . . . the great painter who drew his matchless pictures from nature . . . represents the dying wife as falsely accusing herself instead of him . . . [thus] showing the opinion of one who knew human nature well, that the circumstance was not so improbable as the learned counsel had argued." [*R.v. Mayo: Times*, 10 August 1840, p. 7.]

[12] Julie Hankey, ed., *Othello* [Plays in Performance] (Bristol, 1987), pp. 65, 85.

feeble young gentleman."[13] When a reaction to this theatrical "milding" of the more dangerous passions came with the arrival of the actor–director Tomaso Salvini and his Italian production of the play, quite successful commercially in England, even stronger critical reactions were provoked. Salvini's fierce 1875 Othello was perceived as a primitive savage. The *Athenaeum* described his character as the "barbarian whose instincts, savage and passionate, are concealed behind a veneer of civilization so thick that he is himself scarcely conscious he can be other than he appears. . . . In the end the barbarian triumphs. . . ."[14] Such responses suggest that the figure of the jealous wife murderer was a powerfully repelling one for respectable Victorian audiences.

Sexual infidelity, it was generally agreed, was the worst kind of provocation a wife could offer her husband and aroused the greatest sympathy for the wronged husband (particularly as men in the dock who had suffered this wrong were generally older than other wife killers and thus all the easier for the predominantly middle-aged jurymen to empathize with). Indeed, the Victorian obsession with female chastity had made the blow to the husband even more horrifying than formerly, and cuckolds had changed from figures of malicious humor into figures of tragedy. Justice Kay, in the attempted murder case mentioned above, was moved to literary quotation and called it "the unexpiable wrong, the unutterable shame that turns the coward's heart to steel, the sluggard's blood to flame."[15] Such a sentiment was shared by at least the male members of the public. Indeed, when the Home Office confidentially listed five cases between 1860 and 1895 where "popular feeling" had to be taken into account in granting a reprieve, four were of killers of unfaithful wives.[16]

Yet at the same time, as we have seen, violence against women, and particularly their killing, was being regarded with ever greater repulsion. And legally, the clearly motivated basis of this sort of killing made a murder charge for an unfaithful-wife homicide almost inevitable and a murder verdict hard to avoid: the act was usually deliberate and often intended to kill, and the law had for centuries specified "malice aforethought" as the key constituent of murder. The grey areas of intention involved in many other wife killings[17] were rarely present here. Moreover, since there was often an intent to kill, weapons were more often employed than in more common homicides. Killings on the basis of sexual unfaithfulness thus presented a unique and stark situation for the criminal justice system: a confrontation between the worst provocation and the clearest intent to kill. The first consideration called

---

[13]G.H. Lewes, *On Actors and the Art of Acting*, quoted in Marvin Rosenberg, *The Masks of Othello* (Berkeley and Los Angeles, 1961), p. 75.
[14]Quoted in Rosenberg, ibid., p. 103.
[15]*Times*, 8 November 1881, p. 10.
[16]The fifth was of a poacher [HO347/15/47286].
[17]See Chapter 7.

out for stretching the law to find a lesser crime, or at the least for mercy to the offender,[18] while the second consideration demanded the death penalty. It is not surprising that such cases not only drew much public attention but often called forth intense feelings and argumentation, both during and after trials, putting a strain on the criminal justice system and in so doing providing an especially revealing window into Victorian attitudes and sentiments about male and female nature and the relations between them.

Given all this, it is not surprising that jealous wife killing generated more conflict between judges and jurors, and between legal officials and members of the general public, than most other homicides.[19] The representatives of the state – magistrates, judges and the civil servants at the Home Office – tended (and increasingly so) to take a harder line than most people were comfortable with. Murder convictions in such cases usually (once time was allowed, from 1836, between sentence and execution) were accompanied by jury recommendations to mercy, and followed by public petitions for the same, together with other efforts to win a reprieve. English juries normally tended to follow the thrust of their judge's summation; but in these cases they often showed greater independence. Yet as the century went on, such resistance weakened; English juries and English public opinion seemed to be less inclined to excuse the lethal responses of men to their imagined or actual cuckolding, however tragic. Acquittals, other than on grounds of insanity, disappeared. Full murder convictions became more common, and in cases of men merely acting out of unsubstantiated belief in their wives' infidelity, almost invariable, and in these cases executions became the likeliest outcome [see Tables 4–7]. Thus, heightened tension and argument coexisted with a legal trend in the later nineteenth century towards diminished tolerance for the killing of even an unfaithful wife.

The general belief that Victorian men who killed their wives while claiming this provocation were treated a good deal more leniently than other

---

[18]As Justice Hannen instructed a jury in 1869: of the claim that the deceased spent the prisoner's money in drink, "He need not say that that would be a provocation utterly inadequate, not to excuse, but even to extenuate the crime of such an attack as this [kicking her to death with miner's clogs]. But a provocation of a different and more serious nature had been referred to. . . . If the jury were of opinion that, whether rightly or wrongly, but upon grounds not unreasonable, the prisoner acted on the belief that there had been improper conduct between the deceased and [the husband's work-mate], and immediately after its discovery, that was a ground which would entitle them to return a verdict of manslaughter" (which they did) [*R.v. Tracey*: *Times*, 16 July 1869, p. 4].

[19]Of the sixty-five legally married wife murder trials 1841–1900 in which the claim of the deceased infidelity was made, judges and juries differed in the amount of punishment they apparently wished to inflict (with the jury being more lenient) in twenty-three, over one-third, a substantially higher incidence than that for all murder trials.

TABLE 4. Unfaithful Wife Murder Trials – Legally Married [and adultery claim accepted as at least likely] [England and Wales] [$n = 17 + 25 = 42$]

| Dates | Not Guilty | Not Guilty: Insanity | Man-Slaughter | Murder: Reprieved | Murder: Executed |
|---|---|---|---|---|---|
| 1841–50 | | | 2 | | 1 |
| 1851–60 | | | 1 | 1 | 0 |
| 1861–70 | 2 | | 7 | 3 | 0 |
| 1871–80 | 1 | | 2 | 4 | 3 |
| 1881–90 | | | 2 | 6 | 1 |
| 1891–00 | | | 1 | 3 | 2 |
| 1841–1870 | 2 | 0 | 10 | 4 | 1 |
| 1871–1900 | 1 | 0 | 5 | 13 | 6 |

TABLE 5. Murder Trials with Unsupported Claim of Unfaithful Wife – Legally Married [England and Wales] [$n = 8 + 15 = 23$]

| Dates | Not Guilty | Not Guilty: Insanity | Man-Slaughter | Murder: Reprieved | Murder: Executed |
|---|---|---|---|---|---|
| 1841–50 | | | 1 | | 1 |
| 1851–60 | 1 | | 1 | 1 | 1 |
| 1861–70 | | | | | 2 |
| 1871–80 | | | 0 | 1** | 1 |
| 1881–90 | | 1* | 3 | 1* | 4 |
| 1891–00 | | | | 1** | 3 |
| 1841–1870 | 1 | 0 | 2 | 1 | 4 |
| 1871–1900 | 0 | 1 | 3 | 3 | 8 |

*to Broadmoor
**one reprieved solely because of disability, to avoid "repellent spectacle"

TABLE 6. Percentage of Murder Charges Resulting in Murder Convictions [England & Wales]

| Dates | Unfaithful Wife | Unfaithful Claim/ No Evidence | All Murder Charges |
|---|---|---|---|
| 1861–70 | 25 [3 of 12] | 100 [2 of 2] | 36 |
| 1871–80 | 70 [7 of 10] | 100 [2 of 2] | 41 |
| 1881–90 | 78 [7 of 9] | 56 [5 of 9] | 42 |
| 1891–1900 | 83 [5 of 6] | 100 [4 of 4] | 40 |
| 1861–1900 | 59 [22 of 37] | 76 [13 of 17] | 40 |

[total dispositions for all murder charges: Judicial Statistics England and Wales 1861–1900]

TABLE 7. Percentage of Murder Charges Resulting in Executions [England & Wales]

| Dates | Unfaithful Wife | Unfaithful Claim/ No Evidence | All Murder Charges |
|---|---|---|---|
| 1861–70 | 0 [0 of 12] | 100 [2 of 2] | 19 |
| 1871–80 | 30 [3 of 10] | 50 [1 of 2] | 24 |
| 1881–90 | 11 [1 of 9] | 44 [4 of 9] | 23 |
| 1891–1900 | 33 [2 of 6] | 75 [3 of 4]* | 21 |
| 1861–1900 | 16 [6 of 37] | 59 [10 of 17] | 21.5 |

*one reprieved solely because of disability, to avoid "repellent spectacle"

murderers is, for the latter half of that era, not really true. By then such defendants were in fact much more likely to be found guilty of murder (and no less likely even to be hanged) than other male murder defendants.[20] As general penal severity passed its peak in the 1880s and sentences of penal servitude and imprisonment began to shorten, and as criticisms of capital punishment revived, treatment of these killers diverged from that of killers more generally: not only did these men fail to share in the punitive easing, their chances of conviction and even execution, absolutely and relative to others charged with murder, rose.

From 1841 through 1900, then, sixty-five men were charged with murder for killing their legally married wives out of belief in their infidelity. At least another eleven (and no doubt more) cohabiting or in common-law marriages were similarly charged, but without a marriage license a man's claim to having been "inexpiably wronged" by his partner's infidelity lost much of its force.[21] When Frederick Hinson went to the Newgate gallows in 1869 for killing his apparently unfaithful common-law wife, the author of a printed circular asking for his reprieve acknowledged, while decrying, this distinction: "Had Hinson been married to the woman he murdered, thousands of people would have commiserated with him, and have considered him partially justified. It is, therefore, a morbid caprice to say he ought to be hanged because he was not married to the woman. He considered her his wife, she had children by him, and it appears that he had used her well."[22] However,

[20] Nineteen of the twenty-five murder trials 1871–1900 in which the deceased was legally married and the defense claim that she was unfaithful was generally accepted nonetheless resulted in murder convictions, a rate of 78 per cent; by comparison, 41 per cent of all murder trials resulted in murder convictions [see Tables 4 and 5].
[21] It cannot always be ascertained from reports of a murder of a woman by a man not described as her husband if they had been living together for some period of time. Even if that information were always obtainable, the very imprecision of the term "common law marriage" makes definitive totals impossible.
[22] HO12/189/89255; see also the *Times* 5, 11, 28 October, 27 November 1869 (pp. 7, 5, 9, 11).

this "morbid caprice" did matter, increasingly. A man tried in 1862 for the murder of a prostitute he had lived with for eleven years after her romantic involvement with another man did gain a mercy recommendation from the jury on the grounds of his "long intimacy" with her, but this was ignored by the judge and the Home Office.[23] In an 1894 trial of a baker who had lived as man and wife with his victim for four years, Justice Day explicitly instructed the jury that "her unfaithfulness was a matter which it would be their duty to discard in this case."[24] Of the eleven men definitely charged in these years with murdering, after their "infidelity," the women with whom they had cohabited for some time, all were found guilty of murder, and seven were hanged, five of them in the second half of the period.

Even as the total number of murder trials slightly declined, the number of men charged with murdering their unfaithful legal wives rose from twenty-five in the first thirty years of the period to forty in the second. More strikingly, murder convictions rose much faster, tripling from ten in the first thirty years to thirty in the second, as almost did executions, from five to fourteen. Further, of the five men executed in the first period, two had added another level of heinousness to their crime by killing, or attempting to kill, others besides their wives; all the fourteen executions of the second period were of killers of wives only.

Cases in which a legal wife's infidelity was claimed as mitigation divided into two types: those in which the claim had good evidentiary support and those without such support. Naturally enough, the first was treated with much more sympathy. In forty-two of the sixty-five trials convincing evidence of a wife's adultery was presented in defense. These cases rose over the period from seventeen to twenty-five. Three of these trials produced outright acquittals, in 1862, 1864 and 1872; thereafter there were none. Manslaughter verdicts diminished by half (from ten in the first period to five in the second) while murder verdicts almost quadrupled (from five to nineteen). One man hanged in the first period, six in the second.

Yet these outcomes were comparatively merciful compared to those murder trials in which a legal wife's infidelity was asserted but no credible evidence was produced. Five of the eight such men charged in the first period and eleven of fifteen in the second period were convicted of murder, with four in the first and eight in the second going to the gallows. Two of the three men reprieved in the second period were done so on the ground of

---

[23] *R.v. Edwards:* HO12/139/53852; *Times* 18 December 1862, p. 10; *Annual Register for 1862*, Chronicle, 200–201.

[24] *R.v. Langford: Times*, 7 May 1894, p. 3; HO144/259/A55879. Justice Montague Smith similarly explained to the Home Office in 1892 why he did not support the jury recommendation of mercy to John Noble: "the issue of provocation was irrelevant because the prisoner was not legally married to the deceased, and therefore had no authority to prevent her from doing as she liked." Noble hanged [HO144/245/A53737].

insanity, and were removed to Broadmoor Criminal Lunatic Asylum; the life of the third was spared only because his bad physical state (he had lost an arm in the army, and had as well other disabilities) would have turned the hanging into a "repellent spectacle."[25] In this type of case, not only were convictions increasingly the rule but executions as well. Stricter evidentiary standards had come to be applied to provocation claims. Mere belief in a wife's infidelity, however sincere, had become of no avail in escaping either the noose or the asylum.

These numbers suggest a previously unnoticed development in the courtroom, which a closer look at actual cases bears out. Judges in these trials were increasingly directing juries away from both acquittals (which disappear in this type of offense) and manslaughter verdicts, and towards findings of murder. By contrast, in non-spousal murder trials the proportion of convictions was quite stable [see Table 6]. It would appear that Victorian judges found it increasingly necessary, in wife killings like these where husbands' stories might evoke strong sympathies, to obtain a murder verdict. To accomplish this end, a judge might not only sternly lay down the law to the jury, but at the same time signal that after the verdict was delivered, he might be inclined to support a recommendation from it to mercy. Once such a man had been publicly stamped a murderer, his life might be saved (and where there was good evidence of a wife's misbehavior, reprieves were more likely than not),[26] but the principle was upheld that without important mitigating factors (which did not embrace a wife's infidelity) such a killing was murder. It was a principle held strongly by members of a Bench who had now all grown up in the nineteenth century – and more strongly still by the somewhat younger civil servants in the Home Office, born after the beginning of the reign, and they joined in trying to impress it upon the public.

This toughening of the law's response defied developments that, as already noted in regard to rape trials, should have yielded an opposite, relaxing, trend. After legislation in 1836 defense counsel not only became universal in murder trials but were for the first time permitted to address the jury and put their clients' cases in the most eloquently heartrending form. By the second half of the century "celebrity counsel" like Montague Williams and, after him, Edward Marshall Hall often dominated a trial.[27] In addition, by a separate act also of 1836 the requirement that execution be carried out within forty-eight hours of pronouncement of sentence was repealed, and time was allowed

---

[25] The case of Harry Grant: HO144/935/A58368 (1896).

[26] Twelve, as opposed to six executions in 1871–1900, a higher proportion of reprieves to executions than overall.

[27] See Montague Williams, *Leaves of a Life* [2 vols.] (London, 1890); Charles Kingston, *Famous Judges and Famous Trials* (London and New York, 1923); Herbert Stephen, *The Conduct of an English Criminal Trial* (London, 1926); N.W. Warner and T. Gilbert, *Marshall Hall: A Biography* (London, 1966).

for consideration of appeals from murder verdicts; one result of that was the increasing frequency of popular petitions urging reprieve, often supported by local newspapers as well as local notables – popular agency that with the advance of democracy should have been ever more influential. Finally, a growing use of and receptivity to insanity arguments encouraged jury recommendations to mercy and sometimes similar judicial or Whitehall inclinations.[28] All of these developments should have favored verdicts of manslaughter rather than murder and reprieves instead of hangings – yet they were it seems neutralized and more by a drive among judges and bureaucrats (and perhaps beyond that tight elite) towards more serious treatment of this offense.

If a closer look at individual cases does much to bear out such an interpretation of judicial (and bureaucratic) behavior, it also helps answer the more general question that arises when viewing the range of possible verdicts: what determined the particular verdict and the outcome of appeals for remission of execution? The legal definitions of guilt of murder and of manslaughter did not change significantly in the nineteenth century, but their application to particular situations did. In practice, they were reinterpreted to narrow the "escape routes" for a husband from a murder conviction. In the courtroom, if a wife's adultery could be solidly established or, even better, if the defendant had witnessed it and if he had not previously seriously ill-treated her, and, moreover, had not used such an obviously lethal weapon as a gun, he continued to stand a chance of a manslaughter verdict (although such verdicts might still lead to a sentence of life imprisonment). If any of these mitigating conditions did not apply, however, a murder finding was increasingly likely. Not only a murder verdict but even possibly a hanging; while the number of hangings for all non-spousal murders taken together were gradually diminishing, spousal murders (and here particularly are meant wife murders) defied this trend, hangings for them rising until the 'nineties. One consequence, as fewer of these cases ended in manslaughter verdicts and more in murder verdicts, was the increase in the number of situations of conflict, or at least tension, between judges and juries and the increase in the number of jury recommendations and large-scale petition efforts for mercy. Cases that formerly might have been found to be manslaughter were now reaching the Home Office, for consideration for the exercise of the royal prerogative of mercy, thus increasing that Department's importance in evaluating the heinousness of wife murder, particularly of adulterous wives. As in so many areas of national life, changing attitudes and changing political relations were combining to further centralization, even in decisions of individual life and death. When reprieves were then issued by the Home Secretary, public sympathies and "feelings of humanity" could be recognized without a formal public condoning of such barbarous behavior. The Law could in this way spare the lives of the majority of these homicidal husbands and yet still

[28] On the growing use of insanity arguments, see Chapter 7.

declare its full condemnation of such acts by having death sentences publicly pronounced over their perpetrators (with all the intimidating ceremony of the judge donning his black hat, kept solely for this purpose), keeping the majority imprisoned for much or all of their lives, and sending a substantial minority of them all the way to their deaths.

These punitive trends only gradually emerged and always intertwined with strong tensions between the language of condemnation and that of sympathy, increasingly colored by sentiments of dislike of penal severity. Before the nineteenth century, as we have seen, a jury finding of manslaughter instead of murder entailed little punishment – only a branding in the hand and either a whipping or a fine, and towards the end of the century, perhaps some months of jail time. After the act of 1803 that provided the option of tougher sentencing for manslaughter, jail time came to be awarded more frequently, and tended to lengthen, but (even when served) seems to have remained quite short for some years.

When in 1810 the Londoner Richard Griffin cut his wife's throat, he presented a sympathetic figure at trial. He painted his wife as "a woman of vicious habits," and in particular, one who "had brought men under his nose, and supplanted him in his bed, and threatened that her lovers should chastise him" – a claim supported by his character witnesses. In spite of his unwithdrawn satisfaction in the deed (he told the watchman who took him into custody that "I shall be happy if she is a dead woman, and I shall die a happy man"), his jury found manslaughter only. His judge, Baron Wood, who had helped the jury find a way to avoid a murder verdict (by instructing them that "if he had killed her purely out of revenge for her infidelity it was clearly murder [but] if a quarrel had ensued, and he had perpetrated the deed during this quarrel and under the sudden impulse of the moment, this would only amount to manslaughter"), initially sentenced Griffin to pay a fine and serve a year in Newgate, but afterwards dispensed with the jail sentence, accepting payment of the fine as full punishment.[29]

Early signs of stiffening in the legal treatment of unfaithful-wife killing (as for wife killing more generally) appeared in 1819. In that year Justice Best urged another Old Bailey jury to convict a butcher, Henry Stent, of the newly capital felony of *attempting* to kill his wife.[30] The jury, somewhat reluctantly, complied, appending a strong recommendation to mercy, which was, as expected, attended to by Justice Best. Best sentenced Stent to two year's

---

[29] *OBSP* 1809–10 #683; *Times,* 24 September 1810, p. 3; Crook, *Complete Newgate Calendar* (London, 1926), vol. 5, p. 65.

[30] *Times,* 20 September 1819, p. 3; "A full, true and particular account of Mr. Henry Stent, butcher, who made an atrocious attempt to assassinate his wife, in the parlour of the Saracen's Head Inn, on Tuesday, August 5, 1819" [BL]. Lord Ellenborough's legislation of 1803 had expanded the definition of attempted murder to make a much wider range of acts capital.

imprisonment – a stiff sentence for the time for a mere attempt, particularly when the victim, who had run off with another man and then returned asking forgiveness, at the trial blamed herself and urged leniency for him.[31]

That same year John Holmesby's "most pathetic appeal" to the feelings of the Judge and the whole court "on the situation in which he was placed at discovering his wife's infidelity," already weakened by the highly premeditated and repulsive manner of his act – nearly chopping off her head while she slept – failed completely when it came out that he had previously been bound over to keep the peace for ill-treating her. He was convicted of murder without any mercy recommendation and hanged in front of Newgate.[32]

Judges began to specify more precisely for juries just what was required for provocation that would reduce to manslaughter. Justice Littledale noted in a Nottingham trial in 1826 that "there was no evidence . . . excepting the prisoner's own word" that he had personally seen his wife committing adultery. Therefore, "he conceived that [the jury] could scarcely bring in any other verdict than that of guilty [of murder]" (which they did).[33] Even witnessing adultery, judges informed juries, did not excuse but only mitigated even an immediate enraged killing. In the case of Nicholas Baker in 1828, in which Justice Park had explicitly denied the existence of a right of chastisement, he had also gone beyond the specifics of the case before him to remind the jury that "even if he had found his wife in the very commission of the act, which he only suspected to have been done a year before, and had so killed her in the fact, yet in this case the killing would be manslaughter at the least."[34] Even for this reduction, the killer had to witness the adultery. Baron Parke, in a phrase that entered the lawbooks, noted in an 1835 trial at Carlisle that it would be manslaughter only if the defendant had "ocular inspection" of

[31]The death sentence was very rarely carried out for attempted murder, though such an outcome was not unknown. Stent's being charged with the felony, rather than a lesser wounding charge, already suggests some stiffening of official response. Stent had aggravated his offense by stabbing his wife six times.

[32]*Times*, 30 October 1819, p. 3; *Morning Post*, 30 October 1819, p. 2; *OBSP* 1818–19 #1413; "A true and particular account of the last awful moments of John Holmesby, who was executed at the Old Bailey, London, on Monday last, November 1, 1819, for the wilful murder of his wife " [BL]. Holmesby appeared motivated more by the insult to his masculine honor than to any injured love, for it emerged in his statement that he had offered to forgive her if she would swear out a charge of rape against her lover (an offer she refused). This "traditional" concern with honor and repute seems to have forestalled the sympathy from either jury or judge that could have saved his life. [It also suggests one reason for the skepticism with which married women's claims of rape were often received in court (see Chapter 3).]

[33]*R.v. Wood:* 17 March 1826, p. 4; *Nottingham Gazette*, 18 March 1826, p. 3; "Some particulars of the life, trial, behaviour and execution of Samuel Wood (aged 30), who was executed on Nottingham Gallows, Thursday, March 16, 1826, for the wilful murder of his wife" [BL].

[34]*Times*, 25 July 1828, p. 3.

the adulterous act, but not otherwise; this man also hanged.[35] The "ocular inspection," or discovery *in flagrante*, standard was again called upon two years later in a slightly different kind of case. A man stood trial for willfully killing the man who had seduced his minor son. Justice Park ruled against the defendant that, as with killing upon the provocation of adultery, "in all [such] cases the party [on trial] must see the act done"; the jury nonetheless (no doubt specially horrified by sodomy) returned a verdict of manslaughter, adding a recommendation to mercy.[36]

In cases of violence against unfaithful wives, defense counsel called upon public sentiments more lenient than those of the judges. As one argued in an 1839 attempted murder trial at the Old Bailey of a man who had found his wife in bed drunk with a strange man, and while the man escaped attacked his wife with a knife, "persons in the same situation of life as the prisoner entertained a belief that if a husband discovered a man in bed with his wife he would be justified in killing either or both. Now, that was a notion which the law would not, and did not, justify, but at the same time, if a man should be so unfortunate as to take the life of another under such circumstances, the law, in pity to human frailty, would consider that the offense was not murder, but manslaughter." In this case the Recorder of London, hearing the case, made clear his sympathy with the defendant. Noting appreciatively the defense counsel's arguments, he observed that "every allowance ought to be made for his excited feelings" and that, moreover, "in proportion as a man's mind was pure and honorable, so would his passion be greater under the influence of such a grievous wrong." The defendant, who also vigorously claimed he thought at the time he was attacking the man and not his wife, was found guilty merely of common assault and got off with three months in the House of Correction.[37]

However, sentiments about wife killing were in motion. As already noted of wife killers generally, and unfaithful-wife killers in particular, in the course of Victoria's reign such men came to meet a harsher reception from the justice system. Yet each case had its own combination of circumstances, whose consideration exposed differences among and between judges, juries and the public, stimulated contention, and led to varying outcomes. The often clashing views of juries and judges were on display in George Atkinson's 1864 trial for attempted wife murder. The jurors found him guilty only of wounding with intent to do grievous bodily harm and then recommended him to mercy on account of the great provocation he had suffered, although

---

[35] *R.v. Pearson: Times*, 14 March 1835, p. 6; "Trial and Execution of John Pearson," "Execution of John Pearson" (Bodleian Library, Harding Collection); 168 *ER* 1108, 1133.

[36] *R.v. Fisher:* 173 *ER* 452. Park heeded this recommendation and gave Fisher only a year's imprisonment.

[37] *R.v. Miller: Times*, 24 October 1839, p. 7.

Justice Keating had told them that "it is not for you to judge of that immoral act, for although the woman has misconducted herself most grievously, she is not amenable to the law of the land for that offense, but is answerable at a much higher tribunal. Whatever provocation she may have given him, he was not authorized to use any violence to her." Despite citing other factors in the prisoner's favor, and of course the jury's recommendation, Keating still gave Atkinson six years' penal servitude, a particularly heavy sentence for the offense.[38]

### Acquittals

Acquittals ceased after 1872. Always unusual for this crime, they had been generally a result of sympathetic jurymen seizing upon a suggested interpretation of the act that could release the defendant. When William Ansell shot his wife to death soon after his return from the Crimea in 1856, he was greatly aided by the patriotic feelings still running high from the war. Even though he had acted merely on unproven suspicions, his military service won over the jury. "It was proved," the *Times* reported, "that the prisoner had been personally thanked by the Duke of Cambridge for his attention to him while he laboured under illness at Balaclava." Of course this hardly constituted legal grounds, but the now-sympathetic jury accepted Ansell's unsubstantiated claim that the gun went off accidentally during a quarrel and dismissed all charges.[39] Henry King, a London carpenter, also won this escape. In 1862, after three years of marriage, his wife left him, returning to her mother's house. She refused his pleas to return, instead aggravating her offense by taking up with another man. Her departure does not seem to have ended the marriage in anyone else's eyes. King visited her yet again to plead for a reconciliation; this time he found the other man there, and in a heated quarrel stabbed her to death with a chisel. At trial his counsel suggested (again without any corroborating evidence) that her death was perhaps merely an accident: it was "likely [that] he rushed at the [other man] . . . and that the deceased interposed . . . and thus received the fatal injury. . . ." The jury was out a long time, and returned to take up the latter suggestion, finding "not guilty." This acquittal was greeted by some courtroom applause.[40]

The next acquittal in these trials was produced two years later by a judge pushing a jury too hard. The wife of a Hampshire laborer, Robert Hallett,

---

[38] *Times*, 19 December 1864, p. 11. On the other hand, the same year Chief Baron Pollock, in sentencing to only six months' imprisonment another husband convicted of the same offense of wounding with intent to do grievous bodily harm, observed that "the case disclosed a story of disgusting depravity, and, under all the circumstances, and considering the provocation the prisoner had received, he thought that a comparatively mild sentence was sufficient." [*Times*, 21 March 1864, p. 11.]

[39] *Times*, 8 March 1856, p. 11.

[40] *Times*, 27 November 1862, p. 11.

had been found dead, with her throat cut. Hallett told the court that "on the night this occurred she told me she had been along with different men. She excited me, so I don't know what I did." That night doesn't seem to have been the beginning of the problem: it emerged during the trial that the victim "appeared to be a very abandoned woman, and was in the habit of going about with other men." Although the prosecution provided evidence of his having in preceding weeks threatened to cut her throat, Hallett's defense counsel urged that "for all that appeared, the woman had inflicted the wounds, or one of her paramours might have come in and inflicted them." The jury retired for about an hour and then came into court and asked whether, if they thought the man did it in a moment of passion arising from jealousy, they could return a verdict of manslaughter. "Certainly not," Baron Bramwell (a judge known for his attachment to the idea of the law as a system of logic) told them. "If [he explained] a man takes the life of another it is murder, unless he can satisfy the jury of something which shall reduce it to manslaughter. The only scrap of evidence to that effect," he observed, "was that some days after [her death] he said she had cut his throat first; but he did not make that excuse until he had had time to think about his defense." The jury then retired, and returned in an hour and a half to acquit altogether. It seems clear that if Bramwell had let them, they would have convicted Hallett of manslaughter, but given only the option of murder, for a man with such a persistently bad wife, they balked and let him go.[41]

The last Victorian acquittal took place in 1872 in Worcester, of a man whose wife had eloped with a Methodist preacher. The man, hitherto peaceable and well liked, rested his case explicitly on an implausible claim that she, not he, had cut her throat with three separate slashes, after first attempting to strangle herself. Implicitly, however, his case rested on his good character, her bad character, and specifically the grave provocation. Although the judge in his summation emphasized the medical and other evidence against the man's story, the jury nonetheless grasped the thin reed thus held out, and found him not guilty, producing "a great burst of applause" in the courtroom.[42] This was an outcome not to be repeated during the rest of the century. Thereafter, no Victorian man charged with this kind of murder escaped a homicide conviction except through a committal to Broadmoor.

### Manslaughter Verdicts

More common than acquittals were manslaughter verdicts, by which a jury marked the commission of a serious crime but preserved the defendant from the threat of the gallows. Sentences for manslaughter were completely at the discretion of the judge, who could award anything from a day to life in

[41] *Times*, 4 March 1864, p. 11; *Lloyds' Weekly*, 6 March 1864.
[42] *R.v. Beasley: Times*, 24 July 1872, p. 11.

prison. How were such verdicts arrived at, what pressures were operating, and is any change detectable over the Victorian era? Two chief legal grounds existed for a lesser verdict: lack of intent (although this was rarely argued in itself in this kind of highly "provoked" killing) and the existence of sufficient provocation to overcome the killer's self-government. On this latter ground most argument was based.

The most obvious kind of provocation was the only mitigation clearly accepted by the common law as reducing the crime to manslaughter even when murderous intent was proved – this was what Baron Parke in 1835 called "ocular inspection" of one's wife in the act, followed by a homicidal act. Yet this appears to have been a rare circumstance. "Ocular inspection" there may have been, but hardly ever did it produce an immediate fatal assault, as the law demanded.[43] There was only one case of this, that of a miner from a village near Barnsley, Isaac Hazlehurst. In 1887 he had been drinking at home with a group of men, and found his wife in the bedroom with one of the men, with several others looking on. He cleared the house of the men and nothing more was heard until the next morning, when he went to his brother and told him she was dead. Her body was found, marked by many blows and kicks. It was established that "the deceased was a drunkard and had been unfaithful to her husband. On several occasions she had run away with other men, but had been forgiven and taken back by her husband." Hazlehurst, the only Victorian to clearly fulfill the formal legal requirement for reduction to manslaughter, received a sentence of only twelve months' imprisonment.[44]

The closest approach to Hazlehurst's was the case of William Smith. In 1869 his wife had "formed adulterous intercourse with some soldiers in her

[43] At least by the evidence of murder prosecutions (coroner's juries and magistrates were supposed to charge all persons suspected of killing where any evidence existed of possible intent as murder). The closest case among my sample of 374 manslaughter prosecutions 1820–1905 was that of William Robson in 1902, who admitted striking his wife upon discovering a love letter to her. She was a known drunkard, and the jury acquitted him of her death, finding that "the deceased died from a fracture of the skull, but there is no evidence to show how it was caused." *Times*, 9 May 1902, p. 3.

[44] *Times*, 9 May 1887, p. 7; *Barnsley Independent*, 7 May 1887. In delivering his summation Justice Grantham denounced the men, not just for their fornication with the deceased, but even more for standing by outside the house door listening to him beating her to death and doing nothing to stop it; in his denunciation the judge let his class prejudices loose and implied such behavior reflected the more primitive moral state of their village and of the mining districts generally, an implication heatedly rejected by the local newspaper. The *Barnsley Independent* concluded its strongly worded editorial by noting that the people of the village of Wombwell "claim the right to stand before the world as a mining community as civilised, brave, and intelligent as any in the country" [*Barnsley Independent*, 14 May 1887, p. 8].

husband's absence." When he returned, he found her in their company, and mayhem ensued. After striking and kicking her, the prosecution brought forth evidence that Smith gave her a blow with a heavy iron implement that sent her falling down the stairs to her death. But neither judge nor jury accepted this claim, treating the case simply as a kicking death; the jury found manslaughter, with a strong recommendation to mercy, and the judge gave him only nine months imprisonment.[45]

On occasion, judges acknowledged one further allowance: if a wife's adultery were "aggravated" – if, for example, she added to a revelation of adultery taunts that she intended to continue in it – and if the defendant had then killed immediately. In this case, the general rule that provocation by words would not reduce the crime of murder to that of manslaughter might, as Justice Blackburn observed in Christopher Rothwell's 1871 trial, be waived. The heinousness of a wife's infidelity allowed, as nowhere else, for an exception to the rejection of verbal provocation as grounds for failing to convict of murder. After Blackburn's concession Rothwell, who had upon hearing this taunt beaten his wife to death, was convicted of manslaughter only, although still given ten years' penal servitude.[46] This ruling was cited thereafter as a precedent, though only sometimes successfully. One such success marked Samuel Thompson's trial in 1900. Justice Darling, apparently believing his story of taunting and immediate response, told the jury that while "no mere words" could reduce a murder to manslaughter and thus "the only possible verdict on the evidence seemed to be one of guilty of murder or of not guilty," Blackburn's 1871 ruling "that words of the kind attributed to the deceased woman in regard to her preference for the other man might be held to constitute such provocation" had never been rejected. Although Darling worried out loud that this acknowledgment "might seem to be straining the law in favor of the prisoner," it was enough for the jury, who found manslaughter.[47]

More often, however, judges failed to be firmly convinced that circumstances fit the Rothwell case, and told their juries so. In Thomas Mumford's 1879 trial for murdering his pregnant wife, his counsel described his client

[45] *Times*, 29 October 1869, p. 9. Unusually, the coroner's jury had returned a similar mercy recommendation to its reluctant finding of manslaughter. However, such leniency did not go uncriticized. The Tory newspaper the *Standard* published an editorial the next day complaining that "nine months seems to be the regulation sentence this session at the Central Criminal Court for manslaughter. On Thursday a man was sentenced to that term of imprisonment for causing the death of one of his workmen, by throwing him into a cauldron of boiling water; and yesterday SMITH, convicted of the manslaughter of his wife in a beerhouse at Hounslow, was also sentenced to nine month's hard labour" [30 October 1869].
[46] 12 Cox C.C. 145; *Times*, 9 December 1871, p. 11.
[47] *Times*, 16 November 1900, p. 10.

as "stung to madness by the taunts of his wife as to her previous adultery." "It was the law of England," he went on, not quite accurately, "that if a man detected his wife in the very act of adultery he might kill both her and the adulterer, and thence [citing *Rothwell*] if the husband were taunted with it, and he thereupon killed his wife, it would reduce the crime to manslaughter." Mumford, however, failed to win a manslaughter verdict, after Justice Cotton, doubting the prisoner's tale, warned the jury that they "must be satisfied, as a fact, that the supposed communication as to the infidelity of the wife was first made to the prisoner on the night in question – the night on which he committed the act."[48] More drastically, George Watt's claim in 1898 of such taunting (again citing *Rothwell*) was belittled by Justice Hawkins, and he went to the scaffold.[49] In such summations well into the twentieth century, judges patrolled the boundaries of this exception, warding off the extension efforts of defense counsel. At least three times in the single year of 1913 – in *Palmer* (23 Cox C.C. 377), *Birchall* (23 Cox C.C. 529), and *Greening* (23 Cox C.C. 601), defense efforts to extend the Rothwell allowance (to, for instance, a wife's sudden announcement that she was leaving to live with another man) were firmly rejected. By 1920 [in *Ellor*], the Court of Criminal Appeal gave this judicial resistance to any further allowance for such wife killers a formal imprimatur. Lord Chancellor Reading, speaking for the court, observed that "all cases subsequent to [*Rothwell*] have regarded that particular case as an exception to the general rule, which is that except under very special circumstances words do not constitute sufficient provocation to reduce the offense of murder to one of manslaughter."[50]

If judges made only the one specific Rothwell exception, juries were, as might be expected, more forgiving. A wife's taunts, despite judicial doubts and rejection, could yet serve as sufficient provocation for them. In an 1866 case a wife had twice left her husband for another man, returned each time, and then in a quarrel taunted him about the former lover; the husband responded by cutting her throat. The defense counsel, Fitzjames Stephen, made an eloquent speech arguing that "no amount of provocation could well be imagined greater than that which the prisoner had endured at the hands of his wife." Justice Byles insisted that since the defendant had known of her infidelity, the immediate provocation was simply a taunt about what he already knew, and as "mere words are not sufficient provocation," could not be the grounds for a lesser verdict. Nonetheless, the jury went with Stephen's plea and found manslaughter. Byles signaled his displeasure after sentencing the man to ten years' penal servitude by announcing that "if a remission

---

[48] *Times*, 17 January 1879, p. 11; HO144/33/80550.
[49] *Times*, 27 June 1898, p. 3; HO144/274/A60146.
[50] *R.v. Ellor* 1920: 26 Cox C.C. 680.

of part of the sentence was wished, it would have be applied to in another quarter" than his.[51]

A decade later even Stephen himself, now a commissioner of assize, rebuffed a similar jury judgment. In the trial of a man who, after a quarrel with his wife about her behavior with another man, stabbed her in the throat, almost but not quite killing her, he had summed up strongly for an attempted murder verdict. However the jury found the man guilty only of wounding with intent to inflict serious bodily injury and further recommended him to mercy. When Stephen asked the grounds for their recommendation, the foreman replied "on account of the provocation we think he had received." This hardly satisfied Stephen, and in sentencing the man he declared that "whatever the provocation in mere words might have been, it could not possibly excuse the cruel and cowardly act of stabbing her in the throat.... Besides, whatever the provocation might have been, it had passed hours before, and the prisoner had had ample time to get over it." He gave him the very stiff sentence for the crime of twelve years' penal servitude.[52] By no means infrequently, therefore, judges and juries displayed different views of this subject. Yet they also often agreed, and not always in the direction of severity.

If such taunts were made in public, the provocation could be perceived as still worse, particularly if the husband were a man of some local standing, with a reputation to lose. As late as 1880, this could lead a jury to find only manslaughter. In that year George Litchfield, described as "a man of very good character and respectable surroundings [who] belonged to the volunteer corps of [Northampton], and had on some occasions acted as a special constable," found his wife, by no means for the first time, out drinking with another man, and before all the patrons of the pub she refused to come home. The next day he cut her throat and made a weak effort to cut his own. He was able to retain the leading counsel of the day, Montague Williams. Williams beseeched the jury that "the prisoner's life was blasted, his home desecrated, and his name degraded by the conduct of his wife" and that the "fatal deed" was done in "a mad fit of jealousy." This appeal moved many of those in court to tears. The judge, while deprecating the notion of a mad fit, since Litchfield had had many hours to cool, sympathetically offered the jury another possible scenario, that in quarreling the next day she had informed him of and taunted him about her infidelity, pushing him (who may have had a razor in hand to do away with himself) to kill her. The jury grasped at this possibility and returned manslaughter; Justice Baggalay then awarded a light sentence of five years' penal servitude.[53] Clearly, judges did not always present a solid front, just as varying circumstances and characters could lead

[51] *R.v. Smith: Times,* 15 December 1866, p. 11; 176 *ER* 910.
[52] *R.v. Janes: Times,* 23 July 1877, p. 8.
[53] *Times,* 28 October 1880, p. 11; *Northampton Mercury,* 30 October 1880, pp. 6–7.

to different outcomes. Murder trials (and perhaps this is one reason for their enduring fascination) did not (and do not) follow a set formula but took, and still take, many not always predictable paths.

A manslaughter verdict could also be obtained when a wife's unfaithfulness was not only clear, but aggravated in some way, particularly when no lethal weapon had been used. The lack of use of a lethal weapon was, as we've seen, a strong argument for lack of intent to kill or even "grievously" harm and often smoothed the way to a manslaughter verdict. Henry Calvert, left in 1868 with three children when his wife ran off with their lodger, set out to find the guilty pair; finding them, he kicked his wife to death. Disregarding the time elapsed between the provocation and the lethal response, the sympathetic jury found Calvert guilty only of manslaughter, though Justice Brett then gave him twenty years' penal servitude.[54]

Even the use of an instrument did not bar a manslaughter verdict, if the provocation were strong and immediate enough. Both William Smith's judge and jury in 1869, as we have seen, rejected the strongly supported prosecution argument that after striking and kicking his wife he gave her a blow with a heavy iron implement that sent her falling down the stairs to her death. He received only nine months imprisonment. The same year (1869) a Liverpool pipe fitter whose wife told him that she was pregnant by another man, and who then fatally stabbed her, was convicted of manslaughter, having acted as his counsel put it under "provocation so recent and strong that he might not be considered at the moment the master of his own understanding." Justice Lush however, sentenced him to the maximum penalty of penal servitude for life.[55]

Far more lenient was the treatment in 1881 of the Yorkshire colliery worker Thomas Beckett. He was in such despair when his wife left him for another that when, some days after being returned by the lover she declared her intention to return to him, Beckett cut her throat and then his own. She died, but he survived to be tried. He had come close to death, a fact which seems to have brought out everyone's sympathy, and as a man of unchallenged previous good character he was readily portrayed as a victim of love and betrayal.[56] Even the judge was moved. Justice Manisty, severe on violence against women except apparently when a wife had committed adultery, remarked on "all the circumstances of a painful case" in passing only a nominal

---

[54] *Times,* 22 December 1868, p. 9.

[55] *R.v. Garbett: Times,* 31 March 1869, p. 9; *Liverpool Mercury,* 30 March 1869, p. 8.

[56] Even at the end of a century of war on violence a man's high character could make all the difference: in *R.v. Dickson* (*Times,* 16 September 1902, p. 13) the prosecuting counsel, only asked for a manslaughter verdict, observing that "the prisoner was a man with whom the jury would be able to sympathize. He was a highly respectable, sober, well-behaved man, an admirable husband, and an admirable father," whose wife had an ongoing affair with the lodger, throwing it in his face and refusing to cease. The judge called the circumstances ones of "extreme provocation" and sentenced him to only six months imprisonment.

sentence (and indeed a unique one in such cases) of four days' imprisonment, effectively discharging Beckett.[57]

In the first half of the Victorian era, even when a weapon was used, not much beyond a husband's unsupported belief in his wife's infidelity was often needed for juries to avoid finding murder. While judges usually in such cases made clear their preference for a murder conviction, jurors often went their own way. For instance, in Liverpool in 1844 the tailor Owen Leonard, accusing his wife of infidelity with a lodger, slashed her repeatedly with a razor and while she lay on the floor kicked her out into the hallway of their building; she died after a police constable got her to the hospital. When asked by the police why he did it, he said "she was an old bitch." At trial, he repeated his belief that she had been unfaithful, but provided no corroborating evidence; even his counsel showed less than full confidence in his client by suggesting to the jury that they could find insanity, though he offered for this no medical support. Despite the weakness of the defense, Leonard's claim was enough for the jury to find manslaughter.[58]

It was not unusual for juries before the later Victorian years to give no heed to judicial instructions to ignore mere suspicions. In 1862 Joseph Isott, a former soldier living in Rochdale, became convinced that his wife was carrying on with a young lodger. First he beat and threatened her life; some days later he shot her. A female neighbor was produced to tell of seeing the wife bending over the sleeping lodger and giving him a kiss, but that was the extent of corroboration. Isott's counsel observed that the case was about "one of the most powerful passions which operated upon human nature." He "did not ask [the jury] to say whether or not he had any grounds for being eaten up with that passion, but whether, rightly or wrongly, he was actuated by it." Despite its lack of legal grounding, this appeal was sufficient for them to return a verdict of manslaughter. Justice Willes, however, made a point of stating his "clear ... opinion that this was a case as nearly as possible approaching the crime of murder" and sentenced Isott to penal servitude for life.[59]

Nonetheless, as judicial pressure was joined by pressure from the expanding world of journalism, it became increasingly important for defendants to

[57] *Times*, 7 February 1881, p. 10. In the seven wife murder trials Manisty presided over where there had been no wifely adultery, there were four murder verdicts, all leading to executions, two sentences of penal servitude for life and one acquittal. Three more trials involved unfaithful wives, but in one the adultery had taken place a year before, and was known and forgiven by the husband at that time; the murder had other precipitents, and the defendant was executed. The two truly "caused" by a wife's unfaithfulness produced Beckett's uniquely light sentence of four days, and a sentence of seven years.

[58] *Times*, 26 August 1844, p. 6; *Liverpool Chronicle*, 31 August 1844, p. 6. However, Baron Pollock, repelled by Leonard's callousness and brutality, gave him the maximum sentence of transportation for life.

[59] *Times*, 31 March 1862, p. 11; *Liverpool Mercury*, 31 March 1862.

clearly establish the fact of their wives' infidelity. Though by itself of no direct legal weight, the fact in practice increasingly made the difference between a murder and a manslaughter verdict, and eventually between a reprieve and a hanging. As the century went on, suspicions alone ceased to avail such defendants. Indeed, without evidence of actual infidelity, a man (no matter how good his previous character, or how bad his wife's) in the latter half of the era rarely (other than by committal to Broadmoor) escaped hanging.

### Murder Verdict with Reprieve

In the course of the Victorian era, in this kind of killing verdicts of murder came to replace many manslaughter verdicts. Judges became more united in calling for this and juries more willing to find murder, even when a wife's adultery was not in dispute. And once they did so, the prisoner's fate became no longer a choice between verdicts but a choice between execution or re-prieve to penal servitude for life, an immediate question of life or death. As the choice changed, so did the locus of decision, moving from the courtroom to the Home Office in London, whose head exercised the royal prerogative to "interfere" with a death sentence. Tensions between judges and jurors were in these cases after the verdict and sentence succeeded by tensions between a wider public and the central government. Possible mitigations now received a second consideration in the offices of Whitehall.[60]

Two kinds of mitigation (already encountered earlier in the courtroom) were crucial in avoiding the Victorian and Edwardian gallows: circum-stances – whether the infidelity was in any way "aggravated" – and charac-ter – the previous good character of the perpetrator and/or the bad character of his victim. Playing on these two kinds of mitigating factor was an increas-ingly significant degree of public intervention. Such intervention, ironically, was encouraged by the increased tendency of judges to press for murder con-victions, which had the effect of shifting discretionary power over the lives of such defendants from a popular institution, the jury, to a secretive state body, the Home Office. As the attitudes of bureaucrats toward homicidal husbands became decisive for deciding life or death in more cases, mass pe-titions, lobbying of elected officials, and newspaper editorials became more frequent as the only available counterweights (if often unsuccessful ones) to this increasingly professionalized system of justice. This trend is most evident in regard to murders stimulated by wifely infidelity.[61]

[60] On the expanding role of the Home Office as a "tribunal of mercy," see R. Chadwick, *Bureaucratic Mercy* (New York, 1992).

[61] Yet even organized mass petitioning could not stop the trend towards more severe treatment of wife murderers. From 1841 through 1870 six men found guilty of murder while claiming their wife's infidelity as provocation drew public petitions in their favor, and four of them won reprieves; from 1871 through 1900 twenty-one such men drew increasingly numerously signed petitions, but only ten won reprieves.

Serial infidelity on the part of the wife – the most straightforward "aggravation" of the provocation – now no longer necessarily reduced to manslaughter, but it did sufficiently blacken her character and intensify the provocation to the husband to virtually assure a reprieve from execution. In 1879 a Cheshire man married twenty years, William Sherratt, strangled his wife, considered by his neighbors to be "drunken and profligate," with a rope. It was found that "besides indulging in drink," his wife "had on more than one occasion left her husband and gone off with other men, but he had always taken her back again, and, unless he was in drink himself, invariably treated her most kindly." His jury indeed took a considerable time reaching a decision, apparently torn between finding manslaughter or murder, but finally returned a murder verdict. The key consideration that seems to have won him sympathy from his judge and from the men at the Home Office was the claim he had made that the final straw had been the wife's declaration that she was determined to leave him for her latest lover.[62]

If not multiple, infidelities could be aggravated in other ways. For example, the wife of John Thomas Smith, a 39-year-old Durham puddler, ran off in 1884 with his own half-brother, leaving her children behind. When she refused his pleas to return Smith, known as "a quiet inoffensive man," picked up a table-knife and stabbed her to the heart. Not only did the jury strongly recommend mercy, but Justice Hawkins, though known for his severity, unusually seconded this recommendation, arguing to the Home Office that "the conduct of the murdered woman, though it would not have justified a verdict of manslaughter, renders this a fit case for commutation" – which was granted.[63]

Two years later a factory worker near Manchester, John Waite, was convicted of murder despite his claim, accepted as true, of extreme provocation given by his wife openly engaging in sexual play with the lodger. Justice Cave directed the jury "that the provocation required for manslaughter must come upon the prisoner with such suddenness as would cause a man of ordinary self-command to lose his self-control." However, the jury appended its "very strongest" recommendation to mercy, and Cave himself, while opposing a manslaughter verdict, supported the mercy recommendation when communicating with the Home Office. Officials there agreed that, as Charles Murdoch, the head of the Criminal Department, remarked, "the provocation was extreme," and Waite was reprieved (and released after twelve, rather than the more usual sixteen or twenty, years).[64]

A family member was again, as in Smith's case, the other man when Frank Harris cut his wife's throat near Exeter in 1895, several days after she had announced to him her infidelity with his younger brother and at the same

---

[62] *Times*, 30 April 1879, p. 13; HO144/38/83349.
[63] *Times*, 29 April 1884, p. 10; HO144/135/35383.
[64] *Times*, 19 July 1886, p. 6; HO144/287/B425.

time declared her intention to leave him and set up house with his brother. After his murder conviction and recommendation to mercy, it was noted at the Home Office that in several previous cases "the provocation of infidelity on the part of the wife (*where it has been of a specially aggravated character*) has been allowed to tip the scale in favour of mercy." It did so here.[65]

However, there are signs that horror at a wife's infidelity alone was, at least in Whitehall, growing dimmer. When Arthur Riches, convicted and reprieved in 1886 after his judge and jury joined in recommending mercy, petitioned for release ten years later (as was becoming more common as public criticism of long prison sentences mounted), he was denied. One official noted against him that "there is no evidence that the wife was drunk or made the home unhappy otherwise than by unfaithfulness."[66]

Alongside provocation as a crucial determinant of killers' fates was character – theirs and their victim's. Again and again, Victorian British spouse murder trials mixed the social category of character with the legal category of provocation (as to some degree it always is in such trials). If wives' intolerable behavior failed to win their killers a manslaughter verdict (and increasingly it would not), it still could save their lives. This mitigation often took the form of a general pattern of behavior over a period of time, rather than a single specific provocative action – "cumulative provocation" in the modern legal term. When in 1863 an Army pensioner in York, John Gair, suspecting his common-law wife of unfaithfulness, cut her throat, he could not establish that his suspicions had been justified, and he was found guilty of murder. However, her "drunken habits" and general bad behavior over a period of years were brought out at the trial, winning him a strong recommendation to mercy, concurred in by Justice Mellor, and not surprisingly a reprieve.[67]

Yet over time a wife's bad character alone gradually became less effective as a mitigation, and a reprieve came to depend more on the previous behavior and repute of the prisoner himself. One quality shared by Smith, Waite, and Harris was a "good character" in the eyes of their neighbors and acquaintances. Even when a wife's adultery was aggravated, and her character therefore blasted, and even when her other behavior was censurable, homicidal husbands still often needed good reputations to obtain a reprieve. The year following Gair's trial saw a similar case in which, though the dead wife's character was certainly attacked, center stage was held by the killer's excellent character. George Hall, a young Birmingham jeweler's stamper, had shot his new wife to death after she refused to return home. How much

[65] *Times*, 15 November 1895, p. 10; HO144/549/A57211 [italics added].
[66] HO144/288/B647.
[67] *Times*, 15 July 1863, p. 11. It probably did not hurt Gair's case that he fainted in court and had to be carried out, particularly as he was described as "a respectable looking, middle-aged man, with a pleasing and kindly expression of face."

blame could be placed on the victim in this case was limited by the fact that she had first left him the very day after their wedding and, though pressured by her parents to return to him, had left again within weeks; her "adultery" with her former sweetheart took place only after she had repudiated and left the extremely brief marriage. The main burden of the defense had to rest on evoking admiration for his character and sympathy for his situation and state of mind. His fellow workmen and employer provided multiple testimonials to his sober, religious, and hard-working nature, and he and his counsel worked the theme of a good man ruined by a bad woman and a despicable (Irish, in this case) rival.

The jury, pressed hard by Justice Byles, could not avoid a murder verdict, but Hall's response set up the case to be re-argued to the Home Office. Awakening from a seeming "state of stupor," Hall delivered an unusual, and remarkably eloquent, appeal for mercy. His "voice rose and fell with his varying passions, and now assumed a tone of piteous entreaty, which soon swelled into a loud cry of agony and scorn for the man to whom he imputed his ruin. Judge, Jury, Court, bar and spectators looked on and listened awe struck," declared a newspaper reporter.[68] "I have kept company with her," he avowed, "for more than three years; and during that time there is no man on the earth that loved a girl better; and all that time she loved another . . . she said she had no home to dwell in. I said, 'Sarah, I have a good home, will you share it?' She said, 'George, if you will give me one chair and a stool I will dwell with you till the day I die." The night after the wedding, he continued, "she said she was poorly and went home to her mother, and on Saturday night she slept with Martin. She came to me again after being in bed with that man. Is there a heart of a man in a Christian land who will condemn or sanction the condemnation of a poor man under such circumstances? . . . When I am dead and gone, there is no one here who will say that I harmed a hair of her head [until the fatal night]. . . . Let my parents visit me, and let my friends visit me and pray with me in the condemned cell, and let me then rise to the throne of God and be judged by our Lord Jesus Christ. I shall then see her where no man can tear her from me."[69] He then fainted into the arms of his guards, setting off a furor in the courtroom. "Every one present," a reporter noted, "was visibly affected, and the women who thronged the gallery sobbed aloud."[70] A mass petition

[68]This was the *Times'* account, but similar observations were made in the reports published in Birmingham newspapers as well.

[69]*Times*, 7 March 1864, p. 9.

[70]Hall's Christian rhetoric and the public response to it illustrate the movement in religious discourse in the middle decades of the century from judgment to forgiveness, from belief in eternal damnation to a much broader promise of salvation [see Geoffrey Rowell, *Hell and the Victorians* (Oxford, 1974); Boyd Hilton, *The Age of Atonement: the Influence of Evangelicalism on Social and Economic Thought, 1795–1865* (Oxford, 1988)].

in Birmingham for Hall eventually garnered the remarkable total of 69,000 signatures, local and even national newspapers wrote leaders urging mercy, and the two Members of Parliament for the town interceded with the Home Office. Against his personal judgment, Home Secretary Grey acceded to such pressure and granted Hall a reprieve.[71]

Hall's life was saved by a successful evocation of Victorian sentimentalism. The insistence of Hall and his defenders that his act sprang not merely out of humiliation but more deeply out of a shattered love resonated across lines of both class and gender, appealing to many women, high and low, as well as to men. As a vindicator of male honor Hall would have won far less pity; but as a good man who loved not wisely but too well, only to be betrayed by the object of his love, his case echoed one of the most powerful themes of nineteenth-century popular fiction and song. It was a theme which even the highly respectable *Times* could appreciate: it labeled the murder a "domestic tragedy" and called Hall "the victim of a cruel and overmastering sense of wrong, not imaginary but real, not transitory but permanent, blasting his happiness, withering his hopes, making tyrants of his tenderest and finest feelings. . . ."[72]

A similar close call with the gallows was had in a less romantic case in 1874 by a Surrey farm laborer, George Poplett, whose wife had left him with three children to live with another man. He went to them and fatally stabbed her. Like Hall, he acted with clear deliberation, and his judge, Baron Bramwell, reminded the jury of that by citing Poplett's previous expressions of his intention to kill her. Thus, although many neighbors testified to his good and peaceable conduct towards her and everyone, and her very bad conduct, and the police supported their testimony on the lack of any previous ill-treatment on his part, he was found guilty of murder. Verdict in hand, Bramwell then supported the jury's mercy recommendation in a letter to the Home Secretary, as "the prisoner was a man of very good character and conduct, the woman quite the reverse. Her leaving him was quite without any justification." The chair of the local Board of Guardians, the Surrey High Sheriff and his employers also wrote in support, citing Poplett's military service during the Indian Mutiny, as against his wife's notorious "drunken and profligate" character, while several hundred of his neighbors signed a petition describing his long provocation.[73]

---

[71] HO45/9400/52638.

[72] *Times*, 10 March 1864, p. 11. For more on this case, see M. Wiener, "The Sad Story of George Hall: Adultery, Murder and the Politics of Mercy in Mid-Victorian England," *Social History* 24. 2 (May 1999), 173–195.

[73] "Shortly after their marriage the deceased took to drinking and from that time she has wasted the money he earned, frequently compelling him though a good and reliable workman sober and hardworking, and earning capital wages at piece work, to break up his home and go into the Workhouse or lie out with his family in the

Questions of character (in this case the husband's good one, the wife's bad one), once central in practice (if not in law) to deciding whether a killing was murder or manslaughter, now would no longer necessarily determine a verdict; instead, they were being relegated to the two stages of the post-jury phase, the judge's determination of sentence in the case of manslaughter, and the Home Secretary's decision in a murder verdict whether to "interfere with the course of justice." At that stage their traditional importance continued, and in the latter phase contention over a prisoner's life if anything intensified. On the one hand, petitions from neighbors and fellow workers became the norm, and newspapers, now expanding their social reach beyond the middle class, by the last decade of the century and beyond more often supported reprieve efforts. On the other hand, the attitudes of judges and bureaucrats were if anything moving in the opposite direction from that of the outside "public." In Poplett's case, reprieve efforts included a widely signed petition, a local newspaper editorial urging mercy in strong terms, and even a letter from the victim's mother praising him and denouncing her dead daughter. This effort sounded many of the themes struck in the effort for Hall a decade earlier: the prisoner's good character, the awful nature of the provocation he had received, and, also like Hall's case, the comparative poverty that made it difficult if not impossible for him to properly defend himself (in this last regard, as Hall's supporters had cited the example of the well-off John Townley's escape from the gallows some months before on a trumped-up insanity claim, Poplett's cited the recent case of the Rev. John Selby Watson, another gentleman who was reprieved for murdering his wife where a poor man would probably have swung). The greater ability of men above the working class to ward off the gallows became a card successfully played in reprieve efforts for respectable workingmen like Hall and Poplett before an increasingly wide public to save them as well.

All these efforts for Poplett did not impress Home Secretary Cross, who noted that "the real question" was "whether it is right and just that a wilful and deliberate murder which this undoubtedly was should escape the punishment of death," as his predecessor, Sir George Grey, had similarly insisted, before yielding, in regard to Hall. Cross also had to yield, as public pressure mounted (and a second letter from Baron Bramwell, one even more sympathetic to the prisoner, arrived). Again as in Hall's case, a reprieve was reluctantly issued only hours before Poplett was to hang.[74]

---

field. Ultimately she became a confirmed drunkard and a loose dissolute character – she more than once left him to cohabit with other men.... He is not a quarrelsome man, some of his fellow labourers describe him as too easy...." HO45/9374/39497; see *Times*, 23, 26, 28 November and 15 December 1874 (pp. 11, 4, 12, 10).

[74] *Times*, 23, 26, 28 November 1874; HO45/9374/39497. An additional factor affecting chances of reprieve was the particular attitude of one's judge. Poplett's judge, Baron Bramwell, showed greater sympathy for put-upon husbands than most of his

In the course of the period a homicide defendant's character came more and more to be assessed not only by his previous behavior and reputation but also, as has already been seen in other kinds of wife killing, by the nature of his act. In particular, how "brutally" he had killed bore more and more on a man's chances of reprieve. A prolonged and bloody slaying was more disturbing to judges and Home Office clerks than a gun shot or even a stab in the heart. On one hand, such sensitivity favored those above the working classes, whose crimes were likely to be carried out more "cleanly," while on the other, it bore witness to a "democratization" of the civilizing offensive, as working-class and even lower working-class men were becoming expected to meet the same standard as men of the middle class; after all, their female victims were all working-class themselves, and outrages upon their bodies were for the first time coming to evoke almost as much horror as those upon women socially above them. In this way, the lives of working-class women were beginning to be valued by the law more similarly to the lives of women in the middle and upper classes.

When in 1868 a Liverpool man, Thomas Quigley, discovered his wife drunk in another man's home, he beat and kicked her to death. Despite his employing no weapons, the victim's not dying for four days, and the accepted view in the neighborhood that she had been a drunkard as well as an adulterer, Quigley had a harder time winning a reprieve than might have been expected. While his character, in the traditional sense of being liked and valued by his neighbors, was vouched for as good, his actions had been particularly offensive to a "respectable" sensibility increasingly revolted by violence. Justice Mellor noted not only the deliberate but the prolonged nature of the killing, and the jury returned a murder verdict, though with a strong recommendation to mercy which Mellor approvingly passed on. Yet it was almost denied. The trial testimony horrified the Permanent Secretary at the Home Office, A.F. Liddell. He observed to his subordinates that the man "dragged her into the house [and closed the shutters and shut the door] before he began to hammer her"; after stopping at one point and going down to the bottom of the yard, he then "went back and hammered her again." Her body was "smashed." In the end, it was thought too much to disregard the combined views of jury and judge, and a reprieve was granted. Still, Quigley had a closer brush with death than most like him before.[75]

colleagues. In this case he observed to Cross that while Poplett's act was certainly deliberate, he "was a man of very good character and conduct, the woman quite the reverse, and . . . her leaving him was without any justification." The man was clearly guilty of murder, "but it does seem strange that a slight blow should reduce such an act to manslaughter, and this conduct of the woman should not though it had goaded the man to desperation." HO45/9374/39497. For examples of Bramwell's sympathy for husbands, see *Times*, 5, 6 March 1863 (pp. 12, 11); 10 June 1864, p. 11; 24 July 1872, p. 11; 19 December 1872, p. 9; 28 November 1874, p. 12.
[75] *Times*, 27 March 1868, p. 12; HO144/30/75392.

The brutality of a murder, rarely cited earlier, became more of a factor in the later years of the century (in some part probably because of the greater role now played by the university men staffing the Home Office) and could bar early release for otherwise "deserving" prisoners. In 1896 the Home Office considered two wife-murderers, both convicted ten years before, for release. John Waite, as we have seen, had received "extreme provocation" from his wife and was a hard-working, esteemed workman. Despite feeling sympathy for him, the Home Office decided to delay his release another two years, after the head of the Criminal Department pointed out that "great brutality was used."[76] Similarly, Arthur Riches' release petition was denied altogether, in part because "great force and violence must have been used." Riches died in prison.[77]

## Executions

By the second half of the period, hanging had come to equal a reprieve as the most likely outcome in trials for the murder of a supposedly unfaithful wife. As has been noted, while in the first half of the period twelve such trials ended in manslaughter verdicts, five in reprieves, and five in executions, in the second half executions totaled fourteen, reprieves also fourteen, and manslaughter verdicts only eight. However, these figures by themselves are somewhat misleading, since the primary factor in denying a reprieve was the lack of certainty about the murdered wife's infidelity. A majority of these hangings took place in cases where the man's belief in his wife's infidelity had not been supported by fully convincing evidence.[78] In the twenty-four murder convictions during 1871–1900 in which it was reasonably certain that a legal wife had been unfaithful, only six men went to the gallows, well below the proportions for all convictions for spouse murder, or for murder of all kinds. In these numbers is apparent the "infidelity allowance" granted wife killers. A wife's sexual infidelity was indeed the greatest provocation a husband could receive, in the eyes of both the general public and the administrators of the criminal law. Just as its aggravation encouraged a conviction for manslaughter only or, if not that then a reprieve, so if it were reasonably certain, a reprieve was also favored. Yet even here, as we have seen,

---

[76] HO144/287/B425.

[77] HO144/288/B647.

[78] Claims of a murdered wife's infidelity raised *after* trial were hardly ever taken seriously: In 1853 Nathaniel Mobbs was hanged for cutting his wife's throat; a letter from some friends and neighbors attacking his wife's character ("a drunken worthless woman [who] spent her husband's wages instead of providing food and clothing for his children by his former wife"; they also claimed "she was unfaithful to her husband and was at one time infected with a loathsome disease in consequence of her connexion with other men") was disregarded. Whatever the truth of these claims, and they appeared far from convincing, "the lives of many women are at stake," observed Home Secretary Sir George Grey. [HO18/376/21.]

execution was becoming more likely, since during 1841–70 of the seventeen similarly convicted only one man had hanged. Moreover, this allowance did not extend to cases in which claims of a wife's infidelity were not satisfactorily established; these were treated much more severely, and increasingly so. Mere jealousy was not to be allowed as mitigation for taking life, and indeed was harshly condemned, especially so in the later years of the century, when such cases almost always produced murder verdicts, and nearly all of these convicts were left to hang.[79] Whereas in 1844 Owen Leonard won a manslaughter verdict without providing evidence of his wife's adultery, in 1885 a London housepainter, Henry Norman, who had immediately given himself up after stabbing his wife with a dagger while she lay in bed but was unable to substantiate his suspicions, hanged. At Norman's trial Justice Hawkins announced that the dead woman's character remained unsullied. "The crime of murder," he went on, "was not palliated by a [mere] suspicion of undue familiarity."[80] Others in Norman's situation now met the same fate.

After Richard Insole, who had shot his wife five times, was convicted of murder in 1887, Justice Field announced his satisfaction at the lack of a jury recommendation to mercy. Field "hoped that it would be long before English juries adopted a system which he believed was largely prevalent in some other countries of appending to their verdict a recommendation to mercy on the mere suggestion of infidelity unsupported by evidence." Even a large petition from his home town of Grimsby, an appeal by the Bishop of Lincoln, and some late evidence of his wife's infidelity failed to prevent Insole's execution.[81] Charles Wooldridge, a soldier, who was tried on the Oxford Circuit in 1896, cut his wife's throat after she told him she wanted a divorce. Described as a "nervous, excitable and passionate" man, he acted believing she had a lover, but though her friendship with another man was shown, no solid evidence of any illicit behavior could be produced. Even after Justice Hawkins rejected defense arguments for a manslaughter verdict, some members of the jury inclined that way. But when Hawkins gave the impression in his charge that he would support a jury recommendation to mercy, a murder conviction was returned, with such a recommendation. After extended deliberations, however – and in spite of being immortalized in Oscar Wilde's "Ballad of Reading Gaol," which appeared while reprieve deliberations were going on ("each man kills the thing he loves") – Wooldridge hanged.[82]

[79] See Table 4.
[80] *Times*, 18 September 1885, p. 12; HO144/157/A40949.
[81] *Times*, 10, 12, 22 February 1887 (pp. 5, 10, 10); *Grimsby Express*, 16, 21 February 1887; HO144/289/B836. If introduced at trial such evidence would have had more effect; the Home Office was not moved. As the Permanent Under Secretary noted, "these petitions do not alter the case. She may have been an unfaithful and bad wife, but she had separated from him and he deliberately murdered her."
[82] *Times*, 19 June 1896, p. 11; *Berkshire Chronicle*, 20 June 1896, p. 6; HO144/268/A58000. A mercy petition signed by all members of the jury claimed that they had been misled

When a wife's infidelity was more or less proved, to bring her killer to the gallows required some serious black mark against him, chiefly his own lack, in one way or another, of good character. The wife's bad character was already established by her adultery. The husband's came to attention in this type of trial less immediately, sometimes not until after conviction; but then it was often critical. If he could not show clean hands up to the killing, show, in other words, that he bore no obvious responsibility for provoking his wife's provocative behavior, a reprieve often moved out of reach. As early as 1841, when a Salisbury pig-dealer shot his wife to death after she had eloped with a lodger, it became clear that the prisoner had grossly ill-treated his wife before her desertion, and Justice Erskine pointedly refused to endorse the jury's recommendation to mercy. The man hanged.[83]

One man whose wife had left him, and whom he suspected with some reason of "intriguing" with another man roused no noticeable sympathy after cutting her throat in 1862. The tailor Walter Moore admitted to the police that the act was quite deliberate ("I asked her to go back with me this morning, but she wouldn't, so I killed her"), which virtually assured a murder verdict; more important for his post-conviction fate, it was shown at the trial that her departure was preceded by repeated beatings.[84] Moore was convicted without a jury recommendation to mercy and was duly hanged.[85]

William Frederick Horry, a publican and proprietor of a hotel in Burslem, Lincolnshire, who shot his wife to death hanged in 1872 despite his wife's established adultery and despite his class position because he had not only shot with forethought, he had on previous occasions beaten his wife and also been himself a gambler, a heavy drinker and incessantly unfaithful. In rejecting several petitions for him, Home Secretary Bruce observed to his clerks that "the argument from jealousy is much weakened, if not altogether destroyed" by the fact established of his "constant intercourse . . . during the whole of his married career . . . with loose women," and his having as a consequence "communicated disease to her."[86]

---

by Hawkins: "many of the jury," it said, "were deterred from giving a verdict of manslaughter only by the opinion that their strong recommendation to mercy would save the prisoner from the gallows." However, the Home Office saw the case as one of simple possessive jealousy: as one official put it, "it is the old phrase so often presented to the Home Office of if she would not be his wife she should be no one else's."

[83] *R.v. Taylor: Hampshire Advertiser,* 6 March 1841, p. 4; *Times* 4, 13, 18 March 1841 (pp. 6, 6, 3); HO18/45/31.

[84] Thus the importance of George Hall's claims in his 1864 trial that he had never struck his wife before killing her.

[85] *Times,* 10 April 1862, p. 9, and 15 August 1862, p. 10; *Annual Register for 1862,* Chronicle, pp. 163–164.

[86] *Lincolnshire Herald,* 23 January, 6 February, 19 March, 26 March, 2 April, 9 April 1872; HO45/9303/11410.

As in the preceding cases, John Wingfield's previous ill-treatment of his wife (as well as the exceptional brutality of her 1880 killing) cancelled the weight her highly provoking behavior would otherwise have exerted on jury, judge, and Home Office. She had left this laborer with four or five young children on his hands. His Paddington parish refused to take charge of them, even as he and the children were evicted for nonpayment of rent. All this time he knew that his wife was publicly keeping company with another man. When she refused his fresh appeal to return, adding, he claimed, "taunting and insulting language," he drew out a knife and in broad daylight on a public street stabbed her fourteen times. Despite his provocation, as the Permanent Undersecretary noted, it was proven that Wingfield "had exercised a long course of hostility towards his wife and if that ended with her leaving him and children, it is no excuse for him and the murder was a brutal one." Neither jury nor judge recommended mercy, and he too hanged.[87]

As Wingfield's case suggests, and as noted earlier in regard to releases, particular brutality in a killing was becoming an important consideration against granting a reprieve, by increasingly outraged officials. Unlike a "clean" killing like a single knife-thrust to the heart, a prolonged or savage attack, intensifying the victim's suffering, was becoming harder to mitigate (unless insanity could be found).[88] Such brutality was overwhelmingly a phenomenon of "rough" men in the working classes. Already in 1865, a miner, Matthew Atkinson, received no sympathy from jury, judge, or Home Office for his wife's blatant unfaithfulness after killing her in a particularly revolting manner. As the *Times* described it, the immediate cause of his attack was her refusal to prepare supper. She ran out to escape his beating, but he followed and dragged her back. "Then he began to kick her, a work on which he spent about an hour and a half. He beat her with the poker, the tongs, the fire-shovel, and a sweeping-brush. The shovel he broke over her head, and the tongs and poker he bent with the violence of his blows. Once, in the middle of the business, he stopped, went out of the house for about twenty minutes, returned, and fell to work again." Although Atkinson claimed that he had been gravely provoked, that "he had brought her home that night from another man's house, and that had occurred seven times," he was hanged.[89]

---

[87] *CCCSP* #273; *Times*, 28, 31 January; 4, 9 February; 5 March 1880; CRIM 1/7/8 and HO144/55/90932.

[88] On the increasing use of insanity defenses in cases such as Wingfield's, though not Atkinson's, see Chapter 7.

[89] *Times*, 20 December 1864, p. 9 and 6 March 1865, p. 11. Both the judge and the *Times*, in an editorial, denounced the many neighbors who listened outside without interfering while he slowly murdered his wife (after threatening to kill anyone who tried to stop him). Justice Mellor upbraided the "craven spirit" and the "want of manliness" which "so many persons" had exhibited. "We do not know," the *Times* wrote, "what foreigners may think of this story; but we must say, for the credit of

Although an Old Bailey jury in 1876 strongly recommended the laborer John Eblethrift to mercy, apparently because of both his provocation and his drunkenness at the time, Home Secretary Cross called it "a terrible case . . . the place where the stabs were given on the woman's body shows great savagery and brutality," and refused to interfere with his execution.[90] Thomas Berry, whose common-law wife had left and refused to return, prompting him in 1880 to stab her thirteen times with a chisel, "over and over again," as a Home Office clerk noted, "with ferocity and determination . . . piercing stomach, liver, lungs, throat and heart," also was denied a reprieve.[91]

When in 1887 a miner, Benjamin Terry, first gave his supposedly unfaithful wife a prolonged beating with a poker and then strangled her, infidelity, though not established beyond question, was not implausible. Yet the Home Office focused its attention in a different direction, that his crime was, in the words of Permanent Undersecretary Lushington, "a particularly brutal murder" and his character a bad one – one clerk emphasized that he had broken his wife's nose previously. Not surprisingly Terry hanged.[92]

James Taylor, a retired soldier, found in 1892 that his wife's repeated taunts about her intimacy with other men were insufficient to save him from the gallows. Taylor's sterling military record over twenty-two years – three medals and five good conduct badges – won a joint recommendation for mercy from jury and judge. However, a military record was less impressive to the civilians in the Home Office, especially as the killing was so deliberate and so brutal and his behavior towards her so bad. Home Secretary Matthews decided that "the prisoner's married life seems to have been wretched enough, but the most apparent cause was his own brutality. He gives his wife a black eye the second day she was married to him, and nine black eyes in three months. He commits upon her two assaults so serious that he is sentenced to two and four months' imprisonment." He went on to make an important distinction between a man's military and domestic character: "The jury [he observed] recommended him to mercy on two grounds, character and provocation. The military character is excellent. The prisoner's conduct since his marriage is less exemplary." His provocation was admittedly great, but not enough to tip the scales for such a bad man. Matthews declined to prevent Taylor's execution.[93]

Englishmen, that we believe the like of it was never reported before. Here are a number of big, sturdy men – seven actually gave evidence on the trial – who allow a woman to be killed by inches before their eyes without daring to stay the arm of the murderer." *Times*, 7 March 1865, p. 9.

[90] HO45/9417/57634; *Times*, 11 August 1876, p. 12.

[91] HO144/63/ 94963; HO347/15, p. 94 [Memorandum on Capital Cases]; see also the *Times*, 17, 23 June and 7 July 1880 (pp. 10, 12, 4).

[92] *Times*, 7 February 1887, p. 12; HO144/189/A46354.

[93] HO144/245/A54158; see also the *Times*, 14, 30 June and 29 July 1892 (pp. 13, 3, 11).

In 1894, the Liverpool baker John Langford hanged despite a jury recommendation to mercy, his victim's adultery and bad character cancelled out by his own brutality and bad character. "Another miserable episode of drunken low life at Liverpool ending in a murder," the head of the Home Office's Criminal Department characterized it. "She was drunken and unfaithful, he drunken and brutal."[94] In such a pairing of faults, the usual outcome now was a hanging.

As judges and civil servants hardened their faces towards the mitigating power of wifely adultery, more defense pleas even where great provocation could be shown focused instead on the defendant's state of mind and incapacity to form an intention to kill. John Wingfield's 1880 defense for stabbing his wife to death on a public street after she left him for another man rested primarily on the ground of having fallen into a "fit of temporary insanity," rather than on that of provocation. One medical man deposed, "I am distinctly of opinion that a man in the same condition as [he] was, in a short time when brain disease is better understood will be pronounced insane, indeed to be quite as much needing medical care as any patient now in any of the asylums." Very likely because his character was already bad (the victim had taken out a summons against him for his threats on her life, and at the inquest a Poor Law official described him as "a man who would not provide for his family"), the jury convicted. The judge sent on a stern warning against mercy ("a clear case of murder"), and when the Government's doctors found him sane Home Secretary Cross let him hang.[95]

When in the following year Thomas Brown cut his unfaithful common-law wife's throat in a drunken frenzy, his counsel followed a similar course and focused not on the provocation she gave him but on the effect of drunkenness in throwing him into a state of temporary insanity. However, Justice Stephen refused to allow what he saw as interpretative sleight-of-hand, and Brown was found guilty. Petitioners (including eight of the jurymen) then brought forward evidence both of insanity in his family and of his own "weakness of brain." But his own statement to the police that "I did it, I killed her, it's a wilful murder and I shall have to be hung for it" was too much to overcome, and Cross's successor, W. V. Harcourt, whose civil servants cited to him Cross's practice not to reprieve such cases, let him hang.[96]

Such pleas were, then as even now, often made in desperation, when it was clear that other defenses would not persuade and most of the time failed.

---

[94] HO144/259/A55879; see also the *Times*, 7 May 1894, p. 3. The trial judge in Terry's case felt the same, telling the jury that with such a man, "her unfaithfulness was a matter which it would be their duty to discard in this case." *Liverpool Daily Post*, 7 February 1887.

[95] *Times*, 28 January, 4, 9 February, 5 March 1880 (pp. 10, 11, 10, 12); *CCCSP* 1879–80 #273; HO144/45/90932.

[96] *Times*, 29 July 1881, p. 10; HO144/85/A7411.

Their increased frequency in the last years of the century was as much a testament to the diminished efficacy of provocation defenses as to the growing plausibility of insanity claims, when supported by medical men like the one testifying for Wingfield. Cross, standing behind the judges' resistance to such claims, held back the rising pressure for more "medicalized" evaluation of criminals. However, after he left office in 1880 such pressure began to break through with increasing frequency. Even for many men possessing such reasons to form an intent to kill as these did, insanity became a more important mitigation. Yet without strong backing from medical men such claims remained a last desperate throw of the dice, availing little. James Whitehead's counsel, fearing that to establish the victim's unfaithfulness, true as it seemed to be, would only strengthen the case for premeditation, instead stressed in his 1894 trial Whitehead's impaired mind: "There was," he urged, "no deeper feeling of irritation and provocation than even the supposed infidelity of a man's wife. It was shown that the prisoner had been suffering under that feeling for two or three years, and that it had been operating upon a mind which, according to the evidence for the prosecution, was to some extent tainted with insanity." Yet the medical evidence was ambiguous, and a murder verdict was returned. After this, reprieve efforts focused on the traditional mitigations of his previous good character and her bad one, but, as Permanent Undersecretary Lushington observed, "the real question is whether the premeditation was not too great to admit of commutation of the sentence." It was: Home Secretary Asquith conceded that "it is impossible not to be moved by deep compassion for this much-wronged and unhappy man," but he concluded that on principle he could not commute the death sentence.[97]

Condemnation of the murder of unfaithful wives was not confined to the institutions of criminal justice. Indeed, intolerance of such "crimes of passion" were increasingly noted as markers of British identity and superiority. Later Victorian newspapers frequently complained of the less civilized judicial practices in this regard of continental Europeans and Americans. For instance, the *Times* again and again deplored the habit of French juries of acquitting both husbands and wives of the murder of adulterous spouses, and boasted that that would not happen on the law-abiding side of the English Channel.[98] A wife murder trial in Paris in 1884 was typically and smugly characterized as "one of those cases in which French juries reduce the institution of trial by jury to the ridiculous." The situation was summed

---

[97] HO144/260/A56472; see also the *Times*, 12 November 1894, p. 11.
[98] On the treatment of such crimes of honor in France, see Joelle Guillais, *Crimes of passion: dramas of private life in nineteenth-century France* (Oxford, 1990) [original French edition 1986]; Ruth Harris, *Murders and Madness Medicine, Law, and Society in the Fin de Siecle* (Oxford, 1989) and, more fully, Louis Gruel, *Pardons et châtiments: Les jurés français face aux violences criminelles* (Paris, 1991).

up thusly: "A man returning after a fortnight's illness to his mistress finds she has consorted with another man. He stabs her with a file, strangles her with his pocket handkerchief, and, leaving her dead, endeavours to drown himself in the Seine. He does not succeed, and a few days afterwards gives himself up to the police. The jury have acquitted this heroic person on all counts."[99]

The same scorn was expressed when the tables were turned, as rarely happened in Britain. When the same year the wife of a French Radical deputy fired six shots, in a courtroom, into the man who had publicly slandered her sexual character and went on to announce that she had been planning to do so for some time, English papers had a field day. "The murder," the *Times* observed in a leading article, "would be thought startling indeed were all the parties to the affair English and had the offense been perpetrated at our Law Courts in the Strand." But of course "if Madame Clovis Hugues were an Englishwoman she would not have taken the law into her hands in this way." "In France," however, "people live in a heated atmosphere," and their legal administration does little to cool it.[100] "The whole affair," the *Illustrated London News* noted, "was looked upon by the tumultuous audience much like the first representation of some thrilling melodrama at a popular theatre. Madame Hugues was equal to the situation; she played her rôle of a superb and remorseless Roman to perfection, glorying in her crime, and declaiming in a theatrical manner about her honour and her virtues. The witnesses, taking their cue from the principal culprit, all sought to produce effects by their replies, and posed for the public. The end of it was the acquittal of Madame Hugues, who was loudly applauded, and who received her friends the next day in her drawing-room, decorated with flowers."[101] Even before her trial, *Lloyds' Weekly* predicted an acquittal, since as it put it, "French juries are accustomed to shut their eyes to the law when sentiment is involved." It went on to note that she and her husband, Deputy for Marseilles, a man who had previously fought several duels, and who had rushed to congratulate his wife upon the deed, "belong to that Southern France whose people are nearer akin in the warmth of their temperament to the Italians than to the people of Normandy or Eastern France. The avenging of private quarrels in this red-handed fashion is one of the things on which we have no reason to congratulate our neighbours."[102]

---

[99] *Times*, 27 September 1884, p. 5.

[100] *Times*, 28 November 1884, p. 9.

[101] *Illustrated London News*, 17 January 1885, p. 58.

[102] *Lloyds' Weekly*, November 30, 1884, pp. 6–7 [editorial]. She had even claimed the mantle of a duellist, telling the press that she believed her victim was armed at the time, as he had been at their last confrontation: "I was persuaded that this time also he was armed. It seemed to me something akin to a duel." *Lloyds' Weekly*, December 14, 1884, p. 2.

Such travesties of justice, it was agreed, could only encourage further de-civilization. As it was reporting Madame Clovis Hugues' acquittal, the *Illustrated London News* noted another honor shooting elsewhere in France and issued a smug lament: "Paris," it declared, "the luminous centre of civiliza- tion – according to Victor Hugo – has forgotten its duties of late, and been lapsing into violence and barbarism. Madame Clovis Hugues has already found imitators. A lady at Tonnerre has calmly shot an old Celadon, who worried her with his attentions; and one night last week two police officers, armed with swords and pistols, broke into the office of a Socialist newspaper and engaged in combat with the editorial staff, the result being wounds on both sides and a terrible scandal. If even policemen take justice into their own hands, what are we coming to? What is the cause of this stirring up of the blood and nerves of the excitable Gaul? Is it absinthe, or adulterated wine, or bad food, or a thirst for publicity at any price? Is it the fault of the journalists who turn people's heads by their analyses of neorose [sic], or of the novelists with their horrible dissections of eccentricities; or of the doctors, with their theories of the irresponsibility of criminals and their classification of crime as a simple disease, like measles or epilepsy?"[103]

These dangerous foreign miscarriages of justice, it was widely agreed within the legal world, had to be halted at the cliffs of Dover. Even Fitzjames Stephen had observed in 1865, though just shortly after he had assisted in the defense of a man who had committed a "murder of love" against an unfaith- ful wife, that "it would be deplorable if we came to look upon passion and sentiment as any excuse whatever for crime, after the fashion of Frenchmen and Mexicans."[104]

In 1860 a Frenchman living in London, Antonio Dherang, had provided a vivid public example of his countrymen's madness in regard to husbandly honor. Obsessively jealous of his English wife, he cut off her head, and then shot himself to death in Hyde Park. An examination of his body uncovered "on his breast . . . pricked in ink, 'Death to an unfaithful woman;' also on his arm a portrait of the Emperor Napoleon" – suggesting perhaps an affinity between intimate and political forms of "un-English" behavior.[105] The prece- dent of settling an affair of passion with a pistol in a fashionable park had been set a decade earlier, as we have seen, by another native of France, but a woman, Annette Myers. Although unlike Dherang in not turning her gun on herself as well, Myers similarly disregarded her own safety by letting herself

[103] *Illustrated London News*, 17 January 1885, p. 58.
[104] "Capital Punishments," *Fraser's Magazine* (June 1864), 763.
[105] *Times*, 29 June 1860, p. 12. After another Frenchman, Louis Bordier, killed his English wife in London in 1867, the judge, Mr. Justice Montague Smith, told the Home Office that though in France a jury would have found extenuating circum- stances, Bordier's English jury had quite properly convicted him of willful murder [HO12/174/78990].

calmly be apprehended. She was transported to Australia and released on license after a few years, after having served as another public example of French "hot-bloodedness" about sexual honor. As Wilkie Collins observed to Charles Dickens, "the morality of England is firmly based on the immorality of France."[106]

A number of conclusions can be drawn about "unfaithful-wife" murder in the Victorian criminal justice system. First of all, while such murderers were given more sympathy and were less likely to hang than other equally deliberate killers, they came to be treated with increasing severity and certainly by the latter half of the era were dealt with by the criminal justice system more harshly than has been assumed. Particularly if the infidelity was not clearly established, or if the couple were simply not legally married, the gallows was the most likely end. Even when a legally married man could satisfy the courts of his wife's infidelity, he was treated by the second half of the era with less leniency than earlier.

Murder prosecutions where the chief defense was the infidelity of the victim maintained their per capita frequency while other homicide prosecutions were diminishing – suggesting both that more such killings were being charged as murder and that they were continuing to occur as others were yielding to the "civilizing process," and thus could well have come to seem more threatening than they had been when a smaller proportion of all homicides. Whether actual incidence of this act was maintaining its frequency, or whether authorities were increasingly determined to see that all killings of this sort were charged as murder (to "send a message" about their seriousness) is not a question that can be resolved here; perhaps it will never be resolved.

Judges were increasingly determined to obtain murder convictions in these cases, not only where the two "conditions" did not both apply but even where they did. In these latter cases, the "true" unfaithful-wife murders, once a conviction had been returned, judges – and the men at the Home Office, to whom the matter then went – were frequently not averse to reprieving the man, if his behavior had not been darkened by some further aggravation.[107] Such inclinations were supported by the strength of public sympathies in most of these cases. If horror at such acts prevailed among judges,

---

[106] Quoted in R. Gibson, *Best of Enemies: Anglo-French Relations since the Norman Conquest* (London, 1995), p. 225.

[107] Judges who had worked to ensure that juries returned murder rather than manslaughter verdicts had a practical interest in seeing defendants whom juries had only reluctantly found guilty of murder reprieved. As Justice Field reminded the Home Office in the case of Arthur Riches, "it is good that juries should find verdicts in accordance with law rather than give way to sympathy and return a verdict not warranted by the evidence, and when such a verdict is accompanied by so strong a recommendation to mercy as in the present case it is worthy of every consideration" [HO144/288/B647].

Whitehall officials, Secretaries of State, and *Times* editorial writers, sympathies for gravely provoked husbands had wide currency in the public at large, and led to much contestation. Juries often resisted clearly stated judicial preferences, and public activities in favor of reprieves became numerous and quite large. Many of these convictions stimulated a vigorous mobilization of public and press. Popular petitions for mercy became common, and large, in this era.

From the dramatic rise in murder convictions in this type of trial it appears that the general shifts in English criminal justice in this era towards a higher ratio of murder to manslaughter charges and a diminishing proportion of acquittals went much further in this type of trial than in homicide or murder trials in general. The offense was unlike any other: on the one hand, the provocation in murders of unfaithful wives was the greatest imaginable and evoked sympathy through all levels of society, and among both genders, for many of their perpetrators; on the other, such murders were increasingly offensive to a legal establishment (and to some degree a public) more horrified than previously at serious violence inflicted upon women and more ready to break through the walls of "a man's castle," the home.

By the close of the century, as violence was less tolerated, with national identity becoming increasingly identified with "reasonableness" and "cool-headedness," the killing of unfaithful wives had become more stigmatized as both dangerous and evil in itself and as "un-English." While Frenchmen, Italians, Spaniards, Greeks, and other such peoples might be quick to anger and to act violently, good Englishmen were expected to resist such impulses. Similarly, those people were seen as misogynistic in a way that Englishmen were not, or at least no longer. "Englishness" involved both self-control and care for the weaker sex, restraints upon violence, and protection of women. Violence against wives certainly bulked larger in popular consciousness and sentiments than in the century's earlier years. In particular, wife killings had arguably become more symbolically significant to English life, law, and even national identity than ever before.

# 7

# Establishing Intention: Probing the Mind of a Wife Killer

When no major provocation was claimed, when in other words the murdered wife had not been egregiously "bad," the focus in a murder case was squarely on the accused killer himself, his mental processes and capacity of mind. Here the question of intent was explored. The intent to kill was the fundamental distinction between calling a killing manslaughter or murder; when no intent seemed present, a homicide was usually indicted only as manslaughter; when it was a definite possibility, a murder charge would typically be brought. Intent was the *mens rea* (the "guilty mind") required to establish the crime of murder. As much as or more than provocation, it was a locus of much revealing contention. Not only contention but change: as the bar for provocation sufficient to reduce a killing to manslaughter was gradually raised, so too was the bar for the lack of intent sufficient to accomplish the same task. However, where the story of provocation and its Victorian restriction is fairly straightforward, the story of intent and its fate is more complex. Even as the legal notion of intent was expanding, the complete denial of intent embodied in insanity pleas, determinations of unfitness to plead, and post-conviction mental evaluations was gaining acceptance. In fact, the very squeezing of traditional defenses like provocation and lack of intent through drunkenness or as shown by the lack of use of a lethal weapon was increasing the pressure for an alternative "escape" from the hangman. The alternative of insanity was thus the child not only of the advance of "medicalization" but also, paradoxical as it may seem, of the increased Victorian repulsion against violence and increased insistence on the standard of personal responsibility.

Potentially even more exculpatory than strong provocation, a lack of "malicious intent," that is, of a conscious intention to kill or at the least to cause "grievous bodily harm," as it was put in the law books, posed more difficult problems for both defense and prosecution.[1] Legal definitions of murder had

---

[1] Victorian judges pointed out at various times to juries that it was not necessary to intend to kill to be liable to the capital conviction for murder. A sharp example was provided in the trial of George Stonor, a middle-class commission agent, at York in 1898. The post-mortem examination of his prostitute common-law wife revealed that, as the *Times* put it, "brutality of a kind unfit for publication had been committed."

required such intent for many centuries (as they still do). This defense was usually employed in any of three situations, two of them potentially mitigating the offense and the last potentially excusing from criminal liability altogether: when no "lethal weapon" was used, or when the defendant had been drinking[2] (and frequently the two situations were found together) – or, most drastically, because of the claimed insanity of the defendant. The first two situations were common, at least one of them occurring in most wife-killing cases.[3] The third claim was less common and less successful in the justice system, but one that became more prominent and more important with time.

Just as defenses of provocation came to face rising courtroom hurdles, so too did defenses based on lack of intention to kill, as the determination to more effectually punish reckless or malevolent violence gained strength among judges and other legal actors. As provocation was being legally narrowed, intention was being broadened, in both cases making behavior more culpable. As we have seen, arguing eloquently in 1866 in defense of an accused wife murderer that "malice aforethought" had to be quite clearly proved, Fitzjames Stephen conceded that "the ordinary meaning of those words had been greatly extended by successive decisions of courts of law."[4] At the same time, as with provocation, the judicial broadening of intention called forth resistance, from juries and from members of the public, and

Indeed, "the medical witnesses said that a great deal of violence must have been used, that the woman must have suffered excruciating pain." When the jury returned with a verdict of "guilty of inflicting grievous bodily harm, but without premeditation of death" Justice Darling refused to accept it and sent them back to deliberate further, and kept them at it even after they announced that they could not agree. Finally, they came back with a verdict of "guilty of murder" and a strong recommendation to mercy. When defense counsel objected, the judge countered that "in strict logic I think that what [the jury] had said implied a verdict of guilty of murder. The words 'without premeditation of death' had no effect in law, whereas the finding 'guilty of doing grievous bodily harm' implies the intent to do it, because a man is prima facie understood to mean what he actively does. There was, therefore, a felonious act, and, if death ensued, a murder." He would, however, he implied, see that the recommendation to mercy would be heeded (even though he found "the circumstances of the case almost too revolting for words"). [*Times*, 2 December 1898, p. 6.]

[2] One way or another, drink played a prominent role in wife killing, either in the drunkenness of the perpetrating husband, or the provocation of the wife's drunkenness.

[3] The great majority of manslaughter prosecutions for the death of a wife involved beating or kicking, usually without significant use of any further weapon, as did also 183 of the 701 wife murder prosecutions 1841–1900 that I have located. In at least 262 of these 701 cases the husband was drunk at the time; the two categories of course overlap, but even after allowing for overlap they make up close to half of all wife murder prosecutions, as well as most wife manslaughter prosecutions.

[4] *R.v. Smith: Times*, 15 December 1866, p. 11.

stimulated ambivalence even within individuals, as the desire to support the ideal of personal responsibility struggled with sympathy for men facing the grim prospects of penal servitude or even the gallows.


### Lack of a Lethal Weapon

In the early Victorian years, as we have seen, even the use of lethal weapons did not necessarily bring a murder charge, if provocation existed. In 1836, both John Pritchard – whose wife was found dead, her skull fractured, after neighbors reported a fierce quarrel, and his bloodied hammer found – and James Pollitt – whose wife, also after a quarrel, was stabbed to death – were indicted only for manslaughter. Similarly, two years later Isaac Strudwell fatally stabbed his wife and also was charged with manslaughter.[5] And later, even when a murder charge had become the norm for killings with a weapon, manslaughter verdicts, with or without judicial sanction, abounded.

Yet judicial attitudes were hardening here also. A large number of manslaughter verdicts in trials for wife murder carried out with weapons were followed by maximum life sentences. When James Jones in 1851 cut the throat of a prostitute with whom he had been living for some time as man and wife, his sad story of loving a bad woman was most affecting: "during the trial," a reporter noted, "there was scarcely a dry eye in court." Yet after he was convicted of manslaughter he was transported for life.[6] The following year Thomas Bare's judge, after warning the jury not to let merciful sentiments determine their verdict in his stabbing case and then expressing his disappointment with their manslaughter decision, had him also transported for life.[7] In the same year Andrew Heath, killing his wife by repeated blows with a poker, was found guilty of manslaughter but sentenced to transportation for life. One reporter observed of this trial that since "cases of wife murder had lately become shockingly numerous [and] that in some cases of brutal assaults the Judges had passed sentences apparently inadequate to the offense; and that there had been some remarkable inequalities in the severity of the punishments awarded to different classes of crime, this case excited much comment. It was a general opinion that crimes of a homicidal nature were not at this time sufficiently dealt with."[8]

Although use of a lethal weapon had never been a legal requirement for a murder conviction, it had long been an accepted marker for intent to kill, or

[5] *Times,* 7 April 1836, p. 6; 18 August 1836, p. 6; 29 March 1838, p. 7.
[6] *Times,* 2 August 1851, p. 7.
[7] "Examination and committal of Thomas Bare for the wilful murder of his wife" (1851) [BL 1883.c.3]; *Times,* 18 December, p. 7.
[8] *Times,* 30 July 1852, p. 7. As this was being written, Parliament was taking up the Act for the Better Protection of Women and Children, to increase the penalties for non-lethal violence against wives.

at least to do grievous bodily harm (which sufficed to find murder).[9] It was not the only such marker, but it was the clearest. In establishing malicious intention or the lack of it, the nature of the violence was important.[10] A wife killing that did not involve use of a deadly weapon had been presumed legally to fail to suggest intent to kill or to cause grievous bodily harm, and socially to carry echoes of the now-discredited but "common-sensically" familiar notion of chastisement for wifely misbehavior. In the absence of previous declarations of murderous intent, such killing was normally liable only to a manslaughter verdict. Blows and kicks, produced by the "natural" weapons of the body, were the usual means of death in these instances. When Michael Carney was convicted of murder and hanged at the Old Bailey in 1803, it was not simply because he had repeatedly kicked and stamped on his wife's head when she failed to have his dinner ready at 12 o'clock. As Baron Hotham made clear to the jury, "yet if [Carney] had been ten times more furious and brutal in his behaviour to his wife than he was, and death had taken place in consequence, if it were proved that no previous intention of killing her had existed, it did not constitute the crime of murder." Rather, it was his previous threats to kill her, coupled with previous excessive beatings, that made intention plausible and a murder verdict possible.[11]

Thus, unless witnesses could testify to previous death threats to the victim, a murder verdict had usually required use of a weapon. As Justice Vaughan informed a jury in 1837 in a wife murder prosecution where the cause of the woman's death after a heated quarrel was in dispute, even if the jury decided that the deceased's death was occasioned by the prisoner's act, he would be guilty only of manslaughter, "as it did not appear that he used any instrument calculated to produce death."[12] Early Victorian popular expectations reflected this tradition. When a Liverpool ship-scraper, Owen Kehoe, beat his wife to death in 1840, he declared, while in the act of beating her, "that he would only get twelve months for murdering her."[13]

This legal distinction was also understood among the Scottish populace. Anna Clark has described several trials in that nation in 1830 in which

[9] As Justice Byles told a jury in 1866, "it is sufficient [to find murder] if, a deadly instrument being used, mischief was intended at the time." [*Times*, 15 December 1866, p. 11; 176 *ER* 910.]

[10] For determining the existence of malicious intention, in particular, the degree and duration of *violence* employed came increasingly to serve as indicators.

[11] As Hotham continued, if trial testimony satisfied the jury that Carney had previously intended the lethal violence, "then they must of course pronounce him guilty" (which they did). ["Trial & Execution of Michael Carney. . . ." (Bodleian Library: Harding Collection); *Times*, 17 September 1803, p. 3.]

[12] *R. v. Covus: Times*, 18 March 1837, p. 6.

[13] *Times*, 13 October 1840, p. 5. In the end he was never sentenced. The coroner's jury brought in a bill for willful murder, but by the time he came up for trial some months later he was found to have become insane. *Liverpool Mercury*, 9 April 1841, p. 123.

defendants readily admitted to beating their wives to death but vigorously denied using anything that could be construed as a weapon.[14] In England, even by 1857, when Michael Crawley was tried for killing his wife with a bill-hook, his son, visiting his father at the police station the day after, exclaimed despairingly, "Father, how came you to do it? You should have struck her with your fist, and not used an instrument!" But he had, and as Justice Williams told the jury, "It was quite enough to estimate the malice aforethought to consider the nature of the weapon and the nature of the blows." Despite his age of 62, Crawley hanged.[15]

Crawley's case was not exceptional. By the beginning of the 1860s killings of women with a lethal weapon were being normally indicted as murder. After cutting his wife's throat in 1861 William Cogan, as with Crawley, was charged with and convicted of murder, and a recommendation to mercy on the ground that his deed had not been premeditated failed to save him from execution.[16] Samuel Wright met a similar fate in 1863. After his murder conviction, petitions came in to the Home Office signed by thousands of working men and supported, very unusually, by the prosecuting counsel, claiming lack of premeditation and citing the victim's "violent and quarrelsome character." But Justice Blackburn observed that "the use of such a weapon as a razor shows an intention to take life," and his death sentence stood.[17]

Even while murder charges remained rare where a weapon was not used, killing wives by hand and foot had come to be liable to more severe punishment. Serious punishment for manslaughter had become possible only after the 1803 legislation that removed for this crime the existing punishment ceiling of one year's imprisonment. Even while, a generation later, punishments for property offenses were lessening, transportation for life (a sentence hitherto given to few besides offenders against property) began to be awarded for aggravated cases of manslaughter of one's wife. In 1837, while Justice Vaughan was reiterating the strict requirements for a murder finding, Baron Alderson, as we have seen earlier, tried four wife killers at one Liverpool assize, and

[14] Anna Clark, *The Struggle for the Breeches* (Berkeley and Los Angeles, 1995), p. 73.
[15] *Times*, 10 July 1857, p. 11; Annual Judicial Statistics for 1857.
[16] *CCCSP* 1860–61 #783; *Times*, 27 September 1861, p. 8.
[17] HO12/146/59140; *Times*, 15, 17 December 1863 & 12, 13, 14 January 1864. The next case Blackburn heard that day was a killing of one man by another. This case, he told the jury "was not a bad case of manslaughter. The prisoner had lost his temper and assaulted the man under circumstances of some provocation [having been publicly insulted], but not such as to justify an assault. At the same time the prisoner did not intend to cause death." He gave the defendant merely two weeks in jail. [*Times*, 17 December 1863, p. 11] This reflected a difference in the seriousness felt, not only between killings with and without intent, but between killings of women and killings of men. Indeed, the last hanging in Britain for a crime other than murder or high treason in time of war took place in that same year, for an attempted wife murder. [*Times*, 9 August 1861, p. 9; Patrick Wilson, *Murderess* (London, 1971), p. 129.]

although none had used a weapon he "threw the book" at all but one. All four juries found manslaughter, apparently because they had used only fists and (shod) feet, but Alderson awarded three of them the heaviest sentence he could give, transportation for life, despite evidence that three of the victims were heavy drinkers, as we've seen a well-accepted "provocation" to violence by a husband.[18] Even Justice Vaughan's narrower opinion did not mean that he was lenient with wife killings. A month after that opinion, John Hennessey came before him at the Old Bailey for beating and kicking his wife to death. The question of murder did not arise, as the man was charged only with manslaughter, but upon conviction Vaughan also pronounced transportation for life.[19] Two years later Justice Coleridge sentenced another homicidal wife-beater, the Cornish miner John Rusden, to transportation for life, even though in this instance the woman had struck him first, and moreover did not die for five weeks, medical witnesses wavering as to the cause of death.[20]

"Black letter law" was altered in 1838, when a prosecution presided over by Baron Alderson became a leading case. Though not domestic, it was in the category of "aggravated" homicide which wife killing was moving into – in this case the killing of a representative of authority. In a situation of a police constable beaten to death by several men Alderson ruled that although no deadly weapon had been used, "brutality and therefore malice might be inferred from acts of continued violence well after injury had been inflicted." The jury, probably showing their dislike of the aggressiveness of the new police, nonetheless convicted for manslaughter only. Still, this ruling came to be cited as a precedent in other cases.[21] In the course of his ruling, Alderson noted that such inference could often be made in cases where "a strong man attacks a weak one" – or, it seems fair to add, when a man attacks a woman.

In 1843, a beggar who had kicked his beggar wife so that she died several days later and who had been convicted of manslaughter, was sentenced to transportation by Baron Rolfe. The judge explained his refusal to simply award him imprisonment, which was still the option more commonly taken, by observing that "although no dangerous weapon had been used, still there was a degree of ferocity exhibited in the manner in which he treated his victim, which rendered a very severe punishment necessary."[22] Transportation for life for fatally kicking their wives was awarded in 1844 by Justice Wightman to William Janaway and by Justice Coleridge to Edward Butler (both cases with histories of past mistreatment), and similar sentences followed in succeeding

---

[18] See above, Chapter 6; *Liverpool Mercury*, 7 April 1837, p. 110; *Liverpool Mail*, 1 April 1837, p. 2.
[19] *R.v. Hennessey: CCCSP* 1836–37, #2163.
[20] HO18/6/1; *Times*, 8 August 1839, p. 7. Coleridge referred in correspondence with the Home Secretary to the need to civilize the mining districts of Cornwall.
[21] *R.v. Macklin:* 168 *ER* 1136.
[22] *R.v. Facey: Times*, 24 August 1843, p. 6.

years.[23] Richard Wignall's 1846 sentence of transportation for life, indeed, was questioned by the *Daily News*, which, its opposition to the death penalty notwithstanding, asked why he was not convicted of murder and hanged.[24]

Of course social class made some difference: brutality was not surprising in the working classes, but if found in those of higher station, it was particularly hard for magistrates, judges, and probably juries to condemn its perpetrator to the gallows, or even transportation together with "common" criminals. In 1862 a wealthy Kent farmer, Major Murton, was accused of beating his wife to death in their kitchen (and throwing in a few blows with tongs at hand) after one of the two prostitutes he had brought home for the evening complained about her presence. This was obviously an even more offensive situation than those surrounding most lower-class killings, yet Murton was charged only with manslaughter. Admittedly, there were several factors stressed by his counsel – his wife already being in bad health and her having taken ten days to die – that diminished his culpability for her death. After his conviction, Justice Byles declared that even considering such mitigations, the manslaughter was an "aggravated" one and sentenced Murton to three years' imprisonment. In the context of the time and the prevailing social hierarchy, it was not a light sentence. "I know," Byles told the prisoner, "that it will be severe punishment, for you have hitherto occupied a respectable position in life – you have filled the office of overseer, church-warden and surveyor." Murton himself was taken aback by the sentence: "But," he burst out, "I provided handsomely for her!"[25]

Even by Murton's time, his sentence was more typical than Janaway's, Butler's, or Wignall's. Scholars like A.J. Hammerton, Carolyn Conley and Shani D'Cruze have shown that manslaughter verdicts and even merely manslaughter charges remained common in such deaths and that sentences ranged down to the proverbial slap on the wrist.[26] But it is also true that in the more serious cases manslaughter charges were giving way to charges of murder.[27] Similarly, even as the ending of transportation led to the virtual disuse of life sentences except as the merciful alternative to execution for convicted murderers, sentences for wife manslaughter within the lighter range

[23] *Times*, 13 March 1844, p. 7; *Times*, 15 March 1844, p. 7. There were at least four such sentences in 1847: John Clark (*Times*, 24 March, p. 8), Gilbert M'Donald (*Times*, 18 June, p. 7), Henry Lamson (*Times*, 18 June, p. 7), Patrick McIntyre (*Times*, 20 December, p. 3); all four were charged with murder.
[24] *Daily News*, 28 August 1846; *Times*, 27 August 1846, p. 6. As the *Daily News* put it, "we are advocates for the abolition of death punishments, but while death continues the legal lot of murder, why is Richard Wignall to escape from it?"
[25] *Times*, 5 December 1862, p. 11.
[26] A.J. Hammerton, *Cruelty and Companionship* (London, 1992); Carolyn Conley, *The Unwritten Law* (Oxford, 1991); Shani D'Cruze, *Crimes of Outrage* (London, 1998).
[27] Neither Hammerton nor D'Cruze deals in any systematic way with spousal homicides; both their works focus on lesser, "everyday" domestic violence.

thereafter employed were becoming relatively somewhat tougher. For instance, in 1873 Baron Pigott gave a pensioner from the Royal Marines, James Gorman, twenty years penal servitude while, as Conley has noted, ten years before he had given another man in similar circumstances only three months.[28] After drawing a pattern of light sentencing in mid-Victorian Kent, Conley also acknowledged a trend thereafter to severity. "At the assizes between 1859 and 1866 five men were convicted of [manslaughter for] beating their wives to death. The maximum sentence given was Murton's three years. Between 1866 and 1880 nine similar cases were heard in Kent and seven of the men were sentenced to more than five years' penal servitude."[29]

A double portent of change had occurred north of the border in 1840, when only a few weeks apart two Scotsmen, one in Edinburgh and the other in Glasgow, went to the scaffold for beating their wives to death. Hangings in wife killings in Britain were certainly not unknown before them, but since until 1836 those convicted of murder were required to be executed within 48 hours, the great majority of men convicted of any type of murder up to that date were hanged without any further consideration. Only after the removal of this requirement was considered thought given, and input from officers of the court and others received, in most murder convictions, and thus only from then on is it possible to take hangings or reprieves as revealing something of the social values, both shared and contested, within which criminal justice operated.

As we have seen earlier, these Scotsmen had each killed a wife who had provided provocation by her drunken habits, yet in both cases widely supported reprieve appeals were rejected by Home Secretary Lord Normanby. Even a letter from the Lord Provost of Edinburgh concerning one of the men that argued that "there is scarcely a single instance upon record of the last sentence of the law being carried into effect in such circumstances" did not save the man.[30] The judicial and bureaucratic administrators of the law were now setting themselves to repress such domestic violence. However, such portents remained for the moment only that; these controversies also showed a public increasingly unhappy with capital punishment: in the other of these two cases, for instance, a petition signed by nearly 12,000 inhabitants of Glasgow observed that "the punishment of death is, every day, becoming more unpopular in this country, on account of its brutal tendency."[31] In these early Victorian years, greater sensitivity to brutal behavior worked in two opposing directions: to harden attitudes against wife-killers and at the same time to reinforce jury reluctance to return murder verdicts. As articulate

[28] *Times*, 4 December 1873, p. 10.
[29] Conley, *Unwritten Law*, p. 80.
[30] *R.v. Weymss:* HO18/16/29; see also *Times*, 21 April 1840, p. 6; *R.v. Templeton:* HO18/22/25; *Times*, 14 May 1840, p. 5.
[31] *R.v. Templeton:* ibid.

public feeling turned ever more against the death penalty, and transportation of felons rose to a peak in the 1830s and '40s, executions for such killings, in both England and Scotland, remained unusual, while few objections were made to the non-capital sentence of transportation, tougher as it was than what had been the more common previous penal practice.

In 1850 John Stuart Mill and Harriet Taylor attacked this reluctance to return a murder conviction. If wife-beaters who kill their victims were tried at all, they complained in the *Morning Chronicle*,

> (which in general they are not), the jury are not convinced that they intended death, and they consequently escape with a verdict of manslaughter. This interpretation of the law had the sanction of Mr. Baron Alderson, in the recent case of Alexander Moir. If it be a correct interpretation, the law is, in this matter, grossly inconsistent; for many acts, venial in comparison with Moir's, are led by law to be murder when death ensues as an unintended consequence.... But surely a man who, though he does not intend to kill, perpetrates such ruffian-like maltreatment that death is a natural consequence, commits an offense that is at least equal in depravity to cases of murder.[32]

Moir's case was somewhat more complicated than Mill and Taylor suggested. The inquest jury had called it manslaughter only, a ruling that was then rejected by the presiding magistrate who had issued an indictment for murder. It was a legally hard case, dwelling in the shadowy borderlands between simple definitions of murder and manslaughter. The *Times'* reporter observed that "death did not appear to be attributable to any one act of violence on the part of the prisoner, as was usual in charges of this description, but to a long continued course of brutality committed towards the unfortunate deceased, terminating in her death." Thus the jury found manslaughter, but, they added, "one of a very aggravated character." The judge strongly seconded their description, calling it "very little short of murder" and giving Moir the maximum sentence of transportation for life.[33] It was not as lenient a trial as Mill and Taylor suggested, but certainly their indignation was a telling sign of rising unwillingness on the part of opinion-formers to accept anything short of a war on violence against wives. Indeed, their feelings about the seriousness of persistent spousal violence and their argument about the law of murder were more and more shared by judges, who took to saying similar things in instructing juries (not that juries always accepted their interpretations, to be sure).

The tension between the newly evident sentiments of abhorrence of violence against wives and dislike of capital punishment was reflected in different understandings of intent by judges and juries. For most jurors, as Mill and

---

[32] *Morning Chronicle*, 31 May 1850, pp. 4–5.
[33] *Times*, 10 May 1850, p. 7.

Taylor lamented, a finding of intention required premeditation, which did not always exist even when a lethal weapon was used. Judges were taking to reminding juries that the law did not require premeditation; all that was necessary was an intent at the moment of the act.[34] When Mark Sherwood, a Sunderland army pensioner, cut his wife's throat in a drunken passion in 1844, despite his weapon the jury, as petitioners including the mayor and magistrates of that town insisted, "had great difficulty in being brought to deliver a verdict of murder." As another petition noted, a verdict of manslaughter "was fully expected by persons in court who heard the trial." The chief sticking point was intent: it was argued in court that there was no premeditation; after conviction, petitioners including many jurymen argued that even if a murder verdict were returned, an execution should be carried out only in cases of clear premeditation ("malicious design to murder," as one writer put it), which this was not. The judge however supported the verdict, and Sherwood hanged.[35] As Justice Willes observed in the trial of Matthew Francis in 1859, "It did not matter whether the impulse to kill her came into his mind on a sudden, or whether the intention was deliberately formed; for if the man gave way to the impulse he was guilty of murder."[36] A reprieve for a Liverpudlian shoemaker, Thomas Gallagher, in 1860 was urged not only by petitions but also by the *Liverpool Mercury*. "Several persons," it noted, "convicted of murder at the present summer assizes have been reprieved. One in particular, a young woman, tried at Leicester for deliberately poisoning her master with arsenic, she fully confessing her crime. In this case there was premeditation, and some time elapsed during the periods at which she administered the poison. In the case of Gallagher there was not premeditation, and the act was so instantaneous that the jury would have been fully warranted in bringing in a verdict of manslaughter." However, unlike the female poisoner and like Sherwood, Gallagher hanged.[37]

Even though use of a weapon was a simple way of signifying intent to judges and, increasingly, juries, killing without a weapon could also demonstrate intent by its often more prolonged nature. We have already encountered the case of Joseph Howes, a Sussex laborer who drunkenly beat his wife to death in 1863. Despite his lack of use of a weapon as well as his drunken state, Baron Channell found murderous intent to be clear. "If a man used such brutal violence towards a woman," he told the jury, "and continued to do so, after having been warned and cautioned not to kill her, it was difficult to see

---

[34]And, technically, not even that, if the result of the violence could be reasonably anticipated to be the victim's death.

[35]HO18/146/2; *Times*, 5 August 1844, p. 6; 174 *ER* 936; see "Execution of Mark Sherwood. . . ." and "Lamentation of Mark Sherwood. . . ." (Bodleian Library: Harding Collection).

[36]*Times*, 8 August 1859, p. 11.

[37]HO12/127/42050; *Times*, 17 August 1860, p. 10.

that he could have meant anything else than to cause her death." The judge went on to stress the legal principle often called the "felony murder rule" that had up to then been largely confined to killings in the course of robberies, and very rarely applied in domestic killings: "he was bound to tell them that, in point of law, it was not essential that the prisoner should have intended to deprive her of life. If death was caused by acts of violence, which amounted to a felony, it was murder; to wound with intent to do grievous bodily harm was a felony: so that if the prisoner had inflicted blows with intent only to do his wife serious injury, or knowing that they would have that effect, and they in the result caused her death, he would be guilty of murder." The jury nonetheless rejected this instruction and the murder charge and convicted only of manslaughter; the judge gave Howes ten years' penal servitude.[38]

However, jury members (who had to meet property qualifications to serve) were themselves "respectable" persons, and their greater reluctance than judges to find murderous intent (stemming from their reluctance to bear responsibility for a subsequent hanging) should not be taken to suppose that they were averse to severe punishment for extreme violence against women. In an 1851 Gloucester wife killing trial, after returning the manslaughter verdict indicated by Baron Martin, the jurymen, fearful that the judge would let the man off too lightly, insisted their foreman remind the judge of "the prisoner's very rough usage to his wife in her delicate condition." Martin took the point, if he did not already feel the same, and sentenced the defendant to transportation for life.[39] Magistrates, too, like juries often more lenient than judges, could yet be hard-nosed in such matters. In the 1847 case of John Clark, whose wife died after repeated beatings, the coroner's jury had found manslaughter, but the magistrate nonetheless upgraded the charge to murder (the man was convicted of manslaughter but transported for life).[40]

When Daniel Donovan's wife jumped out of a window to escape his beating in 1850, his Old Bailey jury quickly found him guilty of attempted murder (still then a capital offense), even though this required a finding that he had specifically intended to make her jump. Although by that date no one had hanged for this offense for a decade, and thus his judge, Baron Alderson, immediately recorded rather than pronounced the death sentence, Donovan did receive the maximum sentence of transportation for life. The jury no doubt understood that this verdict would not lead to an execution, and under this circumstance was less resistant to finding intent to kill.[41]

The first Victorian murder conviction in England and Wales for wife killing without use of a weapon took place in 1857. John Lewis, a house-servant of Merthyr, drunkenly beat his wife to death. His first murder trial

---

[38] *Times*, 6 August 1863, p. 8.
[39] *R.v. Halliday: Times*, 16 August 1851, p. 8.
[40] *Times*, 24 March 1847, p. 8.
[41] *Times*, 11 July 1850; CCCSP 1849–50, #1325; 4 Cox C.C. 399.

produced the rarity of a hung jury, but the second, unlike previous similar cases, convicted him of the full charge. Jury and judge both sympathized with him (the local newspaper described the audience and the judge himself in tears during the judge's pronouncing of sentence) but that did not prevent his execution.[42] Thereafter, as both the number and conviction rate of wife murder indictments rose, among these indictments and convictions a greater proportion than earlier involved only fists and boots. There were three more wife murder charges for cases without weapons brought in the last two years of the 1850s, eighteen in the 'sixties, twenty-six in the 'seventies, and thirty-one in the 'eighties. The next conviction and execution took place in 1862, and twenty-two more murder convictions (with thirteen leading to executions) during the rest of the century.

Especially from the later 1860s executions for wife killing without weapons increased. Magistrates appeared now readier to find intent without weapon use and readier to view this kind of killing with greater condemnation. Part of this rise seems due to an intensified hostility to physical abuse, a heightened repulsion against brutality: "mere" kicking or beating, if issuing in death, was now a good deal more likely to yield a murder charge and even to lead to the gallows. Also a factor, it seems, was the heightened determination to "civilize" the men of the lower classes, too many of whom, as we have seen judges complain, seemed to continue to believe in a right to beat their wives.[43] Humanitarianism and class feeling (clearly joined even in Mill and Taylor) thus strengthened one another.

In 1870, one man hanged and another came close to the scaffold for fatally kicking their wives. When a Lancashire miner, John Gregson, drunkenly kicked his wife to death with his iron-tipped clogs, his judge rejected defense claims that mere kicking did not evidence intent to kill, the jury followed his instruction, and Gregson hanged.[44] The same year another miner, Patrick Jennings, angered at his wife's drunkenness, beat and kicked her to death while they were walking home from a pub. Similar claims of lack of intent failed to convince either his judge or the Home Office; its Legal Adviser, after counting up the number of the deceased's broken bones, argued that "the prisoner may not have intended to kill her. But where death naturally ensues from such brutal ill-treatment can such a plea be admitted in his favour? There is a clear difference between death caused by a single kick or blow and death caused by repeated acts of violence." He warned that accepting that death caused by repeated acts of violence was not intended (which

[42] *Times*, 9 July 1857, p. 11; HO12/113/28478.
[43] The turn of the 1870s saw a further increase in concern about wife abuse; the 1853 Act now seemed to have been a failure. An editorial in the *Manchester City News* asked whether wife-beating was an "epidemic" like suicide or smallpox, as this offense was "far in excess" of what it had been a few years before [11 July 1874].
[44] *Times*, 21 December 1869, p. 11; HO12/189/89603.

FIGURE 10. "Wife Murder at Wolverhampton" (*Illustrated Police News*, March 12, 1870). Patrick Jennings' fatal wife-beating. The spectre of working-class brutality at its sharpest.

had commonly been done earlier) "would be a most dangerous doctrine." However, a group of local medical men intervened at the last moment with additional evidence of the victim's very poor state of health, and this tipped the scales, even though the evidence did not directly bear on the question of intention: Jennings was reprieved by a reluctant Home Secretary.[45]

In the similar case of the laborer William Lace in the West Country two years later, the man's brutality prevented his previous excellent character from saving his life. Justice Mellor emphasized to the Home Office the "extreme violence and savage character of his conduct" as justifying the murder conviction. "In point of law," he went on, the jury "had no alternative upon which they could have reduced their verdict to manslaughter." Though even the father and sister of the deceased woman pled for mercy for Lace, claiming that the murder had been committed in a paroxysm of jealousy and consequently was unpremeditated, he hanged.[46]

[45] HO144/14/35535 (comments of Godfrey Lushington); *Times*, 17 March 1870, p. 12. See Figure 10.
[46] *Times*, 6 August 1872, p. 11; HO45/9315/14993. Increasingly men who actively tried to stop such brutality were applauded, even though they had no duty in law to do so: in *R.v. Willsea* in 1861, a man who interfered with a husband's beating of his wife

Another jealous husband, an impoverished Londoner, James Godwin, in 1874 supplemented his fists with a bedpost to fracture his wife's skull. Several on the coroner's jury felt it to be manslaughter only, because of lack of evidence of premeditation, but "the Coroner pointed out to them the law." Despite the apparent lack of prior intent, his judge, Baron Cleasby, saw no reason to find the lesser charge: he acknowledged that "it does not appear there was any reason to suppose the act was done with premeditation, but under the influence of anger" but continued that "when anger leads a man to such an act it deserves the same punishment." A petition from both clergymen and doctors offering evidence of Godwin's weakmindedness had no effect, and he too hanged.[47]

Comparable outcomes in beating or kicking cases followed. Another Londoner, Charles O'Donnell, an army pensioner who had spent time in an asylum, hanged in 1876 in Newgate, after a jury was pressed by their judge to bring in a murder verdict. The following year John McKenna was more easily convicted for a similar act and also hanged, this time in Manchester's Strangeways prison.[48] Not infrequently, however, juries were resistant in such cases, as when Henry Dorricott kicked his common-law wife, a prostitute, to death in 1875, while claiming she fell downstairs. His more rustic Shrewsbury jury was out, most unusually, for two and a half hours, returning a verdict that "the death of the woman was caused by the violence of the prisoner, but without any premeditated intent on his part to cause her death." Justice Quain refused to accept such a verdict and directed them that "if by premeditation they meant planning or preparing to kill he must tell them that that was not essential to the crime of murder, and that if they were of opinion that great or dangerous bodily harm had been inflicted by the prisoner, such as would probably lead to death, and did, in fact, prove fatal, that would be wilful murder." The jury again retired, and came back with a manslaughter verdict, which, as the defense counsel later recalled, exasperated the judge,

and ended by stabbing him fatally with his own knife was sentenced merely to two months' imprisonment; his counsel argued persuasively that he "had only done in the first instance what would be expected from every Englishman – namely, interfered to protect a woman from violence on the part of a man who had evidently very much ill-treated her, and who was armed with a knife and in a position to be enabled to cause her still more serious mischief if some one had not interfered on her behalf" [*Times*, 26 September 1861, p. 9].
[47] *Times*, 7 May 1874, p. 10; HO45/9362/33644.
[48] On O'Donnell: *Times*, 3, 10 and 24 November 1876 (pp. 9, 10, 11); HO45/9422/59678. O'Donnell's Old Bailey jury wanted to find him insane, but Justice Hawkins ruled that they could not. On McKenna: *Times*, 6 March 1877, p. 11; HO45/9431/62405. Lack of jury sympathy for McKenna may be explained by the description of his neighborhood by the Protestant-inclined *Glasgow Evening News* as inhabited by "the lowest class of Rochdalian Irish, where squalor, misery and brutality are seen in the most hideous forms." [clipping in HO45/9431/62405]

who then observed that they "had taken an extremely humane view of the case; it appeared that he had been carrying on a course of crime for sixteen years, and had been eleven times convicted of deeds of violence and had now kicked this woman to death." Quain (despite his exasperation somewhat constrained by the jury's attitude) gave Dorricott fifteen years' penal servitude.[49]

More such prosecutions were also being brought about through more energetic police activity. When the wife of James Diplock, a farm laborer, was found dead in 1881 at the foot of their stairs, an inquest returned a verdict of accidental death. However, someone told the police that they had quarreled and that her injuries were caused not by a fall but by kicks. An examination confirmed this, strongly suggesting that the local surgeon who had first examined her had been in league with Diplock to hush it up. Diplock was put on trial for murder (while the surgeon was threatened with prosecution). He was convicted only of manslaughter, but the aroused Justice Coleridge declared that "the case was only one degree less than murder. It was one of cruel brutality" and pronounced the sentence of penal servitude for life.[50]

In the last three decades of the century, men who beat their wives to death (like those who killed unfaithful wives) could expect more severe treatment in the courts than their fathers would have received. Among manslaughter verdicts in killings without weapons, those with wife victims merited decidedly more severe punishments,[51] and most solo killings without weapons that were found to be murder and especially that led to the killer's execution had female, usually spousal, victims. The general end-of-the-century shift in the scale of criminal punishment away from severity did not much extend to cases of wife killing. Such offenders tended to receive longer manslaughter sentences than most other kinds of homicide. Moreover, while murder convictions for killings without weapons became again highly exceptional, in cases of wife killing they still occurred, as with Harry Mack in 1902 and Robert Gill in 1903.[52] In the case of Mack, a pimp, the head of the Home Office Criminal Department

[49] Ernest Plowden, *Grain or Chaff?* (London, 1903), pp. 118–120; *Times*, 23 March 1875, p. 11.

[50] *Times*, 4 Nov. 1881, p. 11.

[51] As Justice Stephen declared in an 1882 trial where the victim before dying insisted that her injuries came from a fall down stairs, despite her husband's well-established history of severely beating her: "it was of the greatest importance to all whom it might concern that it should be clearly understood that if any man beat a woman, more especially when she was his wife, and, above all, when she was pregnant, it was a most brutal act and that he took his chance if she died of a most exemplary punishment." [*R.v. M'Carthy, Times*, 13 January 1882, p. 10; CRIM 1/13/4 (inquest); *CCCSP* 1881–82 #215.]

[52] *Times*, 17 November 1902, p. 7; *Manchester Evening Chronicle*, 14 November 1902; *Times*, 17 March 1903, p. 11.

was moved to explicit description of the "absolutely sickening" details: "He kicked her all over her body and more especially in those parts where fatal injury was likely to ensue, and ended by punching on her stomach as she lay prostrate and helpless on the bed." No mercy was granted.[53] In general, as we have seen, wife killings formed a growing proportion of homicides prosecuted as murder, of murder convictions, and of executions.[54] If Victorian outrage at wife-beatings that went too far played its part, what made these trends legally possible was the judicial (and Home Office) broadening of the concept of evil intention to embrace a greater amount of "brutal" behavior.

### Drunkenness

A well-used defense to homicide had long been that of an inability to form a malicious intention because of one's drunkenness. Formal English law nominally allowed only a narrow scope for drunkenness as a defense in criminal prosecutions.[55] However, the actual treatment of the drunkenness defense through the eighteenth century never matched the prescribed legal response. "The scholarly debate," Dana Rabin has pointed out, "about whether intoxication was irrelevant to an assessment of guilt or whether it increased the defendant's culpability was overshadowed by the popular opinion expressed by defendants and their supporters that drunkenness decreased responsibility." Such opinions came readily from a social environment in which alehouses were central to village life, and alcohol was a part, and a growing part, of daily life for judicial authorities as well as defendants. The disorder of drunkenness, even the violence it often led to, was accepted as virtually inevitable, particularly for the poor. As a result of this acceptance, Rabin observed, "justice discourse allowed for the consequences of such disorders without criminalizing them because they were an integral part of the collective identity."[56]

In the nineteenth century, broad efforts arose to expunge such disorders from the collective identity, and as a consequence this tolerance began to wane. Probably the single most powerful and widespread social "cause" of the century was that of temperance, and if the prohibitionist aims of the more zealous of its activists were never attained, the movement did succeed in deeply coloring accepted notions of social respectability. Along with public

[53] HO144/681/102278.
[54] Moreover, the proportion of all prosecuted homicide formed by domestic killings (mostly of that of wives) continued to rise, peaking (at least for Kent) in the decade 1900–10. [J. Cockburn, "Patterns of Violence," *Past and Present*, no. 130 (February 1991), 70–106.]
[55] See Nigel Walker, *Crime and Insanity in England*, vol. 1 (Edinburgh, 1968), pp. 39, 177.
[56] Dana Rabin, " 'Of Persons Capable of Committing Crimes': Law and Responsibility in England, 1660–1800" (Ph.D. dissertation, University of Michigan, 1996), p. 167.

opinion, also deeply affected were justice discourse and practice. In the second half of the century the prosecution and punishment of public drunkenness rose markedly. With new professional police forces now in place, convictions rose from 57,251 in 1860, to 69,881 in 1864, 109,356 in 1870 and 185,837 in 1876. Although most convictions resulted in fines, the number of jail committals increased sixfold during these years, from 3,993 to 23,665.[57] Similarly increasing was the charging and punishment of drunken killers. The number of trials for murder in which a man had killed his wife while he was drunk rose from sixty-three in 1841–70 to 152 in 1871–1900, despite the increasing restrictions on liquor consumption; murder convictions rose even more, from twenty-seven to ninety, and executions still more, from twenty-one to seventy-four.[58]

Drunkenness was closely associated with violence. Indeed, such a large proportion of interpersonal violence was alcohol related that no major legal crackdown on it was possible without a changed attitude towards defenses of drunkenness.[59] Drunkenness, one way or another, played a dominating role not only in manslaughter but even murder cases. Just as a drunkard wife was a commonly cited provocation, even more frequent was a claim of lack of intent to kill because of drunkenness. That this link between drink and

[57]Brian Harrison, *Drink and the Victorians* (rev. ed., Keele, 1994), p. 376 (from the annual judicial statistics).
[58]At the same time the number of light manslaughter sentences (up to one year) in these trials rose only from 11 to 13.
[59]Of course, defenses were frequently *combined* in practice. In particular, drink was involved in many of the spousal killing cases already discussed, even when they were defended chiefly in terms of provocation. As with provocation, common legal views of the history of drunkenness as mitigation are misleading. Looking backward from the present and relying solely on leading cases, legal scholars have ignored everyday practice in favor of simple teleological models leading more or less directly to the present. John Hostettler QC has recently summed up the history of the intoxication defense as a long movement towards modern "enlightenment": "In Coke's time drunkenness could never be a defence unless induced by unskilled medical treatment or the action of a man's enemies." Hostettler saw flexibility slowly entering the law and "by the nineteenth century the rigidity of the old rule had been gradually relaxed. . . . Generally speaking, today drunkenness remains no excuse for crime, except where it is involuntary or where it results in permanent or temporary insanity. But it is of importance if it can be proved to negate a mental element essential to the charge. This particularly applies to crimes such as murder and theft where it may negate specific intent, recklessness or specific knowledge. The evidentiary burden is now on the prosecution to establish that, despite the evidence of intoxication, the accused had the necessary specific intent" [*The Politics of Punishment* (Chichester, 1994), pp. 159–60]. However, the development Hostettler describes is essentially a twentieth-century one, which has reversed the dominant trend of the nineteenth. During the nineteenth century, in regard to homicide drunkenness, like provocation, was *not* increasingly admitted as an excuse or mitigation; in fact quite the contrary.

crime, particularly violent crime, was a causal one was strongly asserted and widely accepted. The reforming chaplain of Preston jail, John Clay reported in 1854 that "if every prisoner's habit and history were fully inquired into, it would be placed beyond all doubt that nine-tenths of the English crime requiring to be dealt with by the law arises from the *English sin* which the same law scarcely discourages."[60] Although this was an Evangelical's view, even a medical man acknowledged that in regard to criminal justice "it was obvious that if drunkenness were to be readily admitted as a defence, three-fourths of the crimes committed in this country would go unpunished."[61]

Earlier this theme was already being much sounded. The *Liverpool Mercury* editorialized on the spring 1840 assizes in that city to highlight the social dangers of drink. "Almost the whole," it observed, "of the cases of violence might be traced to the use of intoxicating liquors." It went on to lament that "it is a sad and melancholy thing to reflect that so many human beings are sent momentarily and by violence into eternity from the use of stimulating drink." The paper pinpointed the problem as the fatal conjuncture of drink and ignorance: "When an ignorant man, unaccustomed to the exercise of any of the higher feelings on the mind, becomes excited with liquor (and being dead to the receipt of any other pleasures but what minister to his animal desires, it is little wonder that he indulges the only avenue to his tastes), his passions, hitherto uncontrolled by anything but instinct, burst forth with redoubled energy, and at last he is swallowed up the unhappy victim of his own fury." It closed by calling for "a most extended system of national education."[62]

Though Charles Dickens much supported it, popular education did not appear a sufficient remedy in his eyes for drunkenness. In 1851 his journal, *Household Words*, sharply protested against jury consideration of a wife-killer's drunkenness. "Esther Curtis, of Gloucester, goes to a public-house, where her husband is drinking, to beg of him to come home. She complains that, while she works hard, he spends harder at the alehouse. Whereupon he goes outside with her, and, taking her into the garden, flings her, doubled up, across an iron rail – throws his whole weight upon her – and beats her with his clenched fist until she dies on the spot. When this gentleman is informed that his wife is really dead, he makes an exulting remark, too coarse to be repeated. A jury, out of tender consideration for his irresponsible condition (the poor man being drunk, and all drunk men, howsoever amiable when

---

[60] Quoted in W.L. Clay, *The Prison Chaplain: A Memoir of the Reverend John Clay* (London, 1861), p. 554.

[61] A.S. Taylor, *The Principles and Practice of Medical Jurisprudence* (1865), quoted in Roger Smith, *Trial by Medicine: Insanity and Responsibility in Victorian Trials* (Edinburgh, 1981), p. 51.

[62] *Liverpool Mercury*, 4 April 1840.

sober, being necessarily impelled to murder their wives when in liquor) design this manslaughter."[63]

Mill and Taylor, though as Utilitarian radicals having mixed feelings about the sentimental Dickens and rather hostile feelings towards Evangelicals, held, as we have seen, even stronger views than Clay, Dickens, or the *Liverpool Mercury* about wife killing and about drunkenness as a defense. A sign of Mill's strength of feeling on this question is the way he worked even into his classic argument for libertarianism, *On Liberty* (1859), a call for heightened criminal sanctions against drunken offenders. Drunkenness in an offender previously convicted of any act of violence under the influence of drink, he there maintained, should be considered an aggravating rather than a mitigating factor (a position more punitive than even most Tories were willing to accept). "The making himself drunk," he claimed, "in a person whom drunkenness excites to do harm to others, is [itself] a crime against others."[64]

Change, under way before such public comments, took many years to have a decisive impact, while the social and cultural roots of indulgence for intoxication shriveled or were pulled up. In late nineteenth-century trials for assault, drunkenness became primarily an aggravating rather than a mitigating factor.[65] And when drunken violence resulted in death, the same condemnation of drink was increasingly evident. Even inquest verdicts were affected. Victor Bailey has observed that suicide inquests in Hull in the later nineteenth century show a marked rise in medium verdicts (that refused to declare the suicide either sane or insane) in cases of drunkenness and has suggested that "whereas drunkenness had once been proof of diminished responsibility, now it was seen as an impediment to judging the deceased's true state of mind." This change in attitude on the part of inquest juries seems to reflect what Bailey called either "a wider unwillingness to excuse drunkenness, or a shift in the law's approach to drink as a mitigating circumstance."[66] By that period, certainly, drunkenness was less effective, perhaps in public attitudes as well as in legal proceedings, in limiting the perceived responsibility for a killing. Philippe Chassaigne, examining all homicide trials at the Old Bailey in the last four decades of the century, found that by the 1890s, despite a growing humanitarian reaction against penal severity,

---

[63] *Household Words*, 10 May 1851, p. 148.
[64] J.S. Mill, *On Liberty*, ed. David Spitz (New York, 1975), p. 90.
[65] Barry S. Godfrey and Stephen Farrell, "Explaining differential patterns of punishment for men and women convicted of violent offences in the late Victorian period," unpublished paper, 2003. Such severe treatment of drunkenness appears to contrast with both pre-Victorian and modern judicial practice.
[66] Victor Bailey, '*This Rash Act*': *Suicide Across the Life-Cycle in the Victorian City* (Stanford, Calif., 1998), p. 75.

London murders "committed under the influence of drink were more frequently punished by death" than earlier.[67]

Similarly, the movement against drink gradually worked itself out in the treatment of wife murder. Changing discourses did not of course immediately and sweepingly translate into corresponding changes in the outcome of criminal justice processes. Diminishing tolerance for drunkenness affected these processes only gradually and never uniformly. Even as the balance was shifting, some judges as well as many ordinary people continued to show "understanding" of heavy drinkers who killed. Not infrequently in homicides, particularly in the early Victorian years, judges allowed drunkenness to permit a manslaughter verdict. If other mitigating grounds also existed, such as the non-use of a weapon, wife killers were often charged only with manslaughter in the first place. James Stuttard received only eighteen months from Baron Parke in 1839, and Thomas Casey just one month in 1842, both for drunkenly beating their wives to death. Both men had the same mitigating circumstance: each had struck his wife only one blow, and the subsequent deaths were something of a surprise. Intent, therefore, was difficult to establish.[68] At other times also, if their victims had themselves been drunk, or seriously provoking, for instance, drunken wife killers would tend to be treated lightly. Yet without additional grounds to argue for mitigation, simple drunkenness rarely did much even in these years to save them from long prison terms or execution.

With both alcohol consumption and temperance agitation mounting, most case rulings were in the direction of limiting the use of drunkenness as a mitigating factor in homicide. This second front in the judicial war against violence was initiated in the leading case of *Carroll* in 1835, a case of woman, though not wife, murder.[69] Patrick Carroll, an Irish Catholic marine corporal, had gotten thoroughly drunk in a Woolwich pub, and when his attentions were spurned by the landlady, he stabbed her seventeen times with his bayonet. Carroll's counsel sought a manslaughter verdict because of his client's lack of ability to form an intention and cited precedents for this. Mr. Justice Park (after consulting with Mr. Justice Littledale) made short work of this argument, rejecting the precedents cited by the defense as mistaken rulings.[70]

---

[67]Philippe Chassaigne, "La meurte à Londres" (Thèse de Doctorat, Univ. of Paris, 1991), p. 293.

[68]*Times*, 28 March 1839, p. 7; *CCCSP* 1841–42, #2354.

[69]"Trial of Patrick Carroll, with an account of his execution in front of the gaol at Maidstone, Kent, for the wilful murder of Mrs. Browning" (BL 1888.c.3); *Times*, 16 May 1835, p. 7; 173 *ER* 64.

[70]Speaking for Littledale also, he observed that "there is no doubt that [*R.v. Grindley* (1819), the most recent precedent cited by the defense] is not law. . . . I think that there would be no safety for human life if it were to be considered as law."

He went on to state firmly that drunkenness was not relevant to the question of intention. The jury followed the judge's direction, convicting Carroll of murder, and he was hanged.[71] In the wife murder case of John Pearson the same year, Baron Parke similarly declared that "voluntary drunkenness is no excuse for crime," and Pearson also hanged.[72]

Although drunkenness continued to be taken into account in determining the existence of intention in situations of sudden, unexpected provocation, and in lesser cases,[73] in most murder trials it began to receive shorter shrift. In the same year – 1839 – that James Stuttard was let off with a light sentence for drunkenly kicking his wife to death, the barber William Lees hanged before Newgate for cutting his wife's throat in a drunken jealous rage. Both Lees and his wife were drunkards, and his unsuccessful defense rested both on the provocation she offered and on his irresponsibility due to intoxication. Neither defense got far. In pronouncing sentence, Baron Parke observed that "the barbarity of the act admitted of no excuse, and only one circumstance could possibly be suggested as to the cause of the dreadful crime – namely, that he was intoxicated at the time. The law, however, could never admit intoxication as an excuse for such a heinous offense; for if it did, the most dreadful crimes, many of which were committed under the baneful excitement of drink would go unpunished." Earlier that year Parke had again declared in court that "when a man made himself drunk, he became responsible for all the crimes he committed in that state."[74] Such remarks had been made in court before, but they had often been disregarded in the practice of criminal justice. Now they were coming to be enforced in a novel way. There was public sympathy for Lees's argument of intoxication, and the sheriffs and under-sheriffs at the Old Bailey itself put their names to one of several petitions. A deputation that included at least one City alderman was got up to ask for a reprieve, but it was rebuffed at the Home Office, since, as Home

[71] Of course, Carroll's case was not helped by his Irishness or Catholicism, nor indeed by his military profession: the jury accompanied their verdict with a complaint about the practice of allowing soldiers to carry their arms around; as the prosecuting counsel had put it, they were "dangerous appendages in the hands of men who were in the habit of going about to public-houses and inflaming themselves with liquor."
[72] *Times*, 18 March 1835, p. 6; "Trial and Execution of John Pearson," and "Execution of John Pearson" (Bodleian Library: Harding Collection); Ian Ashbridge, *Cumbrian Crime from a Social Perspective 1834–1894* (Cramlington, 1999), pp. 5–11.
[73] Such as in *R.v. Cruse* (1838); 173 *ER* 610. It was crucial that this case, frequently cited in modern scholarship, was first of all one of attempted, not successful, murder. As Justice Patteson pointed out, the former required specific intent to kill, which the latter did not. Second, it was a case of a (drunk) father beating his child almost to death, a situation in which actual intent even to cause "grievous bodily harm," the usual minimum requirement for finding murder when death resulted, was much harder to believe in than in killings or near-killings of adults.
[74] *R.v. Ferray: Times*, 11 March 1839, p. 7 [a trial for attempted murder of a woman; the jury found only aggravated assault, however].

Secretary Lord Normanby put it, "murders committed under the excitement of drink had become of late so frequent, it was necessary an example should be made."[75]

Lees's fate, and that of others in his situation, became a peg for sermons on the evils of drink and of jealousy, and on the need both to punish drunken offenders and to take broader measures to elevate the masses. The *Liverpool Mercury's* comments already noted came within months of Lees's well publicized trial. In particular, after mid-century (and the remarks of Clay, Dickens, the Mills and others), judicial and official attitudes towards the drunkenness defense (as they were in regard to other defenses put forth by killers) clearly hardened.[76] A new "discursive system" was emerging and gaining strength, especially among the growing ranks of the "respectable," which insisted upon the duty and the ability of men to maintain self-management, an insistence that fit ill with drunkenness. In William Janaway's 1844 case, the fatal beating of his wife had come in response to her publicly and insultingly asking him to come home from the pub; he left with her only to beat her to death in the street. Justice Wightman observed of his claim of provocation that "the only provocation that this unfortunate woman could be said to have used towards him, was a most praiseworthy endeavour to take him home from a scene of dissipation and intemperance."[77] Even the easygoing Lord Palmerston refused the drunkenness pleas of petitions in two 1853 convictions of wife-murderers and let them both hang.[78]

Sympathy for intoxicated killers did not vanish, and juries often vexed toughening judges with their greater inclinations to leniency here as elsewhere. Sometimes inquest juries made the allowances for drunkenness, removing that task from trial juries. When John Biggs beat his aged common-law wife to death in 1865, her inquest jury found only manslaughter, apparently not bothered by the victim's general sobriety. That others higher in society were bothered is suggested by the *Times'* report of this inquest, which was headed "Only Manslaughter!"[79]

[75] One petition focused on his wife's supposed bad character, the other on his susceptibility to violent fits. Neither moved Lord Normanby. *Times*, 17 December 1839, p. 7; also *Times*, 30 November & 14 December 1839; "Life, Trial & EXECUTION! of William Lees" [BL 1888.c.3]; "Sorrowful Lamentation of William Lees, now under sentence of death at Newgate," and "Execution of William Lees..." [Bodleian Library: John Johnson Collection]; *CCCSP* 1839–40, #106; HO18/9/17. Lees is also discussed in Chapters 4 and 5; see Figure 8.
[76] Although drunkenness was to continue through the century, and increasingly down to the present, to often be in practice in homicide and lesser cases of violence an important mitigation.
[77] *Times*, 13 March 1844, p. 7.
[78] *R.v. Dobson:* HO18/355/49; *Times*, 19 March 1853, p. 8 ; *R.v. Pedder:* HO18/368/4; *Times*, 11 August 1853, p. 10.
[79] *Times*, 7 April 1865, p. 12.

Yet even in "mere" beating or kicking deaths, once a murder charge was brought, drunkenness defenses did not often prevent stiff sentences. Justice Pigott, more sympathetic than most of his fellow judges to those afflicted with what he called "the sad habit of drinking," declared in an 1871 wife murder trial that while drunkenness by itself "was no excuse for crime . . . when the jury had to inquire into the quality of an act drunkenness, with all the other circumstances, must be taken into consideration." Yet when the jury then not surprisingly returned a manslaughter verdict, Pigott gave the man twenty years' penal servitude in the increasingly harsh penal system.[80] The following year Baron Channell gave his jury in a similar trial instructions explicitly ruling out any excusatory character to drunkenness and concluded that "he could see nothing in this case to reduce the crime [from murder]."[81] When the jury nonetheless found manslaughter, he also sentenced the man to twenty years' penal servitude.[82] Pigott himself, perhaps hardening his own approach, in 1873 gave similarly strict instructions to a jury in a drunken fatal wife-beating and, when ignored by the jury, issued another sentence of twenty years' penal servitude.[83] When in 1886 prosecuting counsel asked only for a manslaughter verdict against a London cabman, Thomas Little, though he had been indicted for murder after one too many drunken wife-beatings, Chief Justice Coleridge was not happy, and made a point to remind the jury that drunkenness was no excuse for acts done and that "they must administer the law as they found it. . . . The prisoner [he continued] had been found guilty of manslaughter in circumstances which admitted of very little defense or extenuation. . . . In some classes of society a wife seemed to be regarded as a kind of inferior dog or horse. That, however, was not his opinion, and persons who were brought before him for having ill-used their wives would find that he was not a Judge from whom they were to expect any mercy." He gave Little twenty years' penal servitude which, since the man was already 56 years of age, was virtually the same as a life sentence.[84] Sentences for drunken killers could be tougher still, even when no weapons were employed. In the same month in 1868 two younger men who had drunkenly kicked their wives to death, James Harris of Leeds and Anthony Fillingham of the Liverpool area, were both given rare life sentences. That both their wives had also been drunk probably saved the men from murder convictions, but they received no indulgence from their judges.[85]

---

[80] *R.v. Bradshaw: Times,* 7 December 1871, p. 11. The defendant was reported to have expected to receive a "twelver" [twelve months].

[81] Though he did concede that "taken in conjunction with provocation from the deceased it might make a slight provocation an excuse, but drunkenness alone was not sufficient."

[82] *R.v. Brice: Times,* 10 July 1872, p. 11.

[83] *R.v. Gorman: Times,* 4 December 1873, p. 10.

[84] *Times,* 6 May 1886, p. 7.

[85] *Times,* 11, 13 and 24 August 1868 (pp. 9, 9, 11).

Drunkenness as a defense was not only drawing stiffer sentences with manslaughter verdicts, but such a defense was also becoming less likely to prevent a murder verdict. After the clerk Thomas Corrigan stabbed his wife to death during one of his habitual drinking bouts in 1856, he was convicted of murder though reprieved to transportation partly in sympathy with his fall in the world, to which the drunkenness of his wife also had contributed. His story had a suitable Victorian sequel, for in Australia after release he became a Christian missionary against drink.[86]

Two years later, a Manchester laborer, Henry Reid, who had drunkenly strangled his wife was also convicted of murder and in his case, despite a strong jury recommendation to mercy, executed. Justice Hill received the jury recommendation by doubting in court whether the recommendation would "carry any weight," for, he asserted forcefully, "drunkenness is not – it cannot ever in this country – be allowed to be a mitigation of the crime of murder."[87] In the 1865 murder trial of the collier Matthew Atkinson for beating and striking his unfaithful wife on the head with the fire-irons, killing her, the defense counsel argued for a manslaughter verdict on the ground of "the intense excitement the prisoner laboured under when influenced by drink or anger" and quoted in support some dicta of the law. But Justice Mellor rejoined, pointing out that they were not applicable to the circumstances of this case, and, more generally, "that to have one law for drunken or angry and another for sober or quiet people would be subversive of all justice and order in this country." Atkinson was also convicted and executed, in spite of the fact that his wife had also been drunk and had been frequently so (and probably unfaithful as well).[88]

Even use of a lethal weapon was not necessary for the gravest punishment. When Charles Davis, a Gloucestershire laborer, was convicted in 1866 of murder for beating his wife to death, the chief argument of his counsel and petitioners, apart from citing the provocation he had suffered from a drunkard and possibly unfaithful wife, was his lack of intent to kill through drunkenness. Justice Smith privately commented to Home Secretary Grey that "doubtless he was excited by drink and possessed by jealousy but he treated his wife most brutally and resumed his attacks on her several times in the course of the night." Davis was saved from hanging in part by his non-resort to major weapons but chiefly by the belief among officials that the law of murder was about to change, a Royal Commission having just recommended the introduction of degrees into the verdict.[89] Citing

---

[86] *Times*, 7 Feb. 1856, p. 9; *Lloyds' Weekly*, 10 February 1856; HO12/102/20497; "Life, Trial, Confession and EXECUTION of Thomas Corrigan" (BL 1888.c.3); Roger Smith, *Trial by Medicine* (Edinburgh, 1981), p. 184.

[87] *Times*, 16 December 1858, p. 10; HO12/119/34777.

[88] *Times*, 20 December 1864, 6 and 7 March 1865 (pp. 9, 11, 9).

[89] In the end this recommendation was never adopted, a bill embodying that recommendation being rejected in Parliament.

this, Smith did not oppose the petitions, and Davis was reprieved to penal servitude.[90]

In the following year [1869], John Gregson's drunken fatal kicking of his wife near Liverpool produced, as we have seen, not only a murder conviction, but his execution. Gregson could not successfully claim that his wife had herself been drunk or otherwise grievously provoking; furthermore, his case displayed a tightening in judicial interpretation of "malicious intent." When his counsel argued that from mere drunken kicking itself one could not find an intent to kill, or even to do serious bodily injury, Baron Martin immediately interjected to say that this statement of the law was "not so": "if a man does an unlawful act, and death ensues, he is guilty of murder." The hesitant jury's recommendation to mercy as well as a petition campaign for reprieve that followed (joined by the coroner who had conducted the original inquest) were of no avail, since in addition the Home Office believed that he did in fact intend to kill her.[91]

As all murder convictions came as a matter of course to be considered for reprieve, the Home Office's role in the punishment of spousal killing expanded, while at the same time its line on such cases was hardening. In 1867 a new Permanent Under-Secretary (department head) was appointed: unlike Horatio Waddington, his predecessor for many years, Adolphus Liddell was a barrister, a Queen's Counsel in fact, and had prosecuted as well as defended many criminal cases, and also judged them as Recorder of Newark. His extensive practical experience with criminal justice gave him more confidence in his ability to evaluate murder cases than his predecessor had shown; it also seems to have given him a very low opinion of most offenders. The following year Henry Austin Bruce, who before entering Parliament had been a magistrate for five years, became Home Secretary. Bruce, who was responsible for the 1872 Licensing Act, intended to sharply reduce drunkenness, nearly always agreed with Liddell on reprieve issues. For twenty-one men convicted of the murder of their wives during his term, Bruce issued only six reprieves and one free pardon (all recommended by judges).[92]

In a non-domestic murder case in 1869 where the judge had suggested a reprieve on the ground of drunkenness, Liddell firmly objected, declaring

---

[90] *Times,* 7 April 1866, p. 11; HO12/163/70868.

[91] Permanent Undersecretary Liddell and Home Secretary Bruce rejected the opinion of the inquest jury that there had been no intent to kill and agreed with Martin: "The man," Liddell noted, "must have known well enough that to strike at a woman on the ground and kick her on the head with a 'clog' was likely to be dangerous and he certainly had had no provocation." "I fear so," Bruce added. "The kick behind the ear, combined with the expression 'If I have not done [killed her] I ought to do,' would seem to prove that at that moment, at any rate, he intended more than mere bodily injury."

[92] Other facets of his severity on crime are noted in Wiener, *Reconstructing the Criminal* (Cambridge, 1990), pp. 145–51.

to the Home Secretary that "it is a new doctrine to me that drunkenness is an excuse for crime." Although he acknowledged the practice in the Home Office to follow a judge's recommendation, this one "I cannot understand and do not agree with. The evidence all points to a wilful act, deliberately done, without the slightest provocation." When, however, Bruce had Liddell ask the judge, Chief Justice Bovill, to further explain and justify his recommendation, Bovill (one imagines quite put out at this "request") instructed him that "it is quite true that the law does not allow voluntary drunkenness to be set up as an excuse for crime, and judges are bound to, and so do lay down the law, but in most cases where crimes are committed under the influence of intoxication, and without any real malice or motive, the judge does take this somewhat into consideration in awarding the punishment." Bruce commuted the sentence, but Liddell maintained his view and was backed up in another similar case in 1874 by the even tougher Conservative Home Secretary, Richard Cross, who assured Liddell he agreed with his minute in the earlier case. Cross concluded by observing that "society in our towns would be quite unsafe if [Bovill's rule] were applied to such a case as present."[93]

Bruce and Cross (and briefly between their periods of office, Robert Lowe) were also establishing related rules on murder. In a case early in 1881 of a man who in a drunken frenzy killed his common-law wife by thrusting a red-hot poker into her abdomen, the recently appointed Home Secretary, the Liberal William Harcourt, was reminded of office precedent. "There was," one of his officials minuted, "most brutal violence and recklessness here, which according to Home Office practice constitutes murder though there was no premeditation." The official cited decisions to this effect by both the Liberal Bruce and the Conservative Cross, and the official next above him agreed, observing that "a more brutal act or a more reckless one than to shove a sharp pointed red hot poker into a woman's belly can hardly be conceived." Harcourt accepted these precedents, and in spite of recommendations to mercy from the judge as well as the jury, rejected the plea.[94] As Mill had wanted, the Government was now seeing voluntary drunkenness as opening the gates to recklessness and to brutality, and in that sense not as only not mitigating but perhaps even aggravating homicide.

The use of weapons of course sharply tilted the balance against their users, in drunkenness defenses as elsewhere. When Robert Davis, a middle-aged London carpenter, cut his wife's throat in a drunken rage in 1857, he claimed that "his brain was so excited at the time by the liquor he had taken that he did not know what he was about." However, since in the midst of his rage

---

[93] HO347/15: Memorandum on Capital Cases, pp. 125–26 (cases of William Murray [CCC] 1869 and Hugh Daley [Durham Assizes] 1874).
[94] *R.v. Stanway:* HO144/75/A1915; *Times,* 29 December 1880, p. 7 and 4 February 1881, p. 4; D'Cruze, *Crimes of Outrage* (London, 1998), pp. 76 and 78 provides further information from local newspapers on this case.

he had gone to lock the house doors to prevent her escape, he was unable to convince anyone of this supposed inability to form an intention and ended on the gallows. Chief Baron Pollock declared that "drunkenness was an excuse that could not for a moment be admitted for such an act as that committed by the prisoner, and it was clear that if it were it would tend very much to diminish the security of human life."[95]

In the 1874 murder trial of John Walter Coppen, keeper of a coffee-house in Camberwell, a determined Baron Bramwell laid down the law strongly enough, as the defense solicitor complained afterwards, to ensure that a manslaughter verdict would not be returned. Coppen, a frequent drunkard, had drunkenly stabbed his shrewish wife in the coffee-house with a knife that was already in his hand. As the defense counsel was telling the jury that they could not find murder in the absence of premeditation, the judge jumped in to strenuously reject that reading of the law, directing the jury that murder could be found "although the thought to do it never entered his mind till the moment he gave the fatal blow." The murder verdict that followed (though accompanied by a recommendation to mercy) aroused much public feeling: grand jurymen wrote the Home Secretary that if they had "had the slightest idea that this unfortunate man would have been convicted of willful murder . . . they would have returned a Bill for manslaughter only," and thousands of signatures were collected on a reprieve petition. However, leading newspapers kept aloof from this effort, and the Tory Home Secretary Cross, determined to end what he called "the shocking prevalence of the offense of stabbing, wounding and beating women by their husbands," refused to block execution.[96]

Two Old Bailey cases a month apart in 1877 showed the difference that the use of a weapon by drunken men might make: George Chapman received fifteen years' penal servitude for fatally beating and kicking his wife (who also was somewhat drunk, though not as much as he was), while Thomas Pratt, having stabbed his wife to death, hanged. Weapon use, as we've seen, was normally a marker of intent to at least grievously harm, and thus sufficient for a murder conviction. However, Pratt's counsel argued vigorously that he had been incapable of forming any intention, whether to kill or to grievously harm. He even cited Justice Hawkins' very recent allowance for this possibility in Chapman's case – ignoring, however Chapman's non-use of a weapon. Justice Lush rejected his argument: "Of course," the judge acknowledged,

---

[95]"It was dreadful to think," Pollock continued, "that in a Christian country such a scene could occur as that of a man almost deliberately, in the presence of his child, cutting the throat of his wife, whom he had sworn at the altar to cherish and protect. . . ." [*Times*, 2 November 1857, p. 11; *CCCSP* 1856–57, #1077; "Life, Trial, Sentence and Execution of Robert Davis, for the murder of his wife . . . in Islington"(BL 1888.c.3.).]
[96] *Times*, 28, 31 August, 4, 24 September, 14 & 17 Oct. 1874; *Lloyds' Weekly Newspaper*, 30 August 1874; *CCCSP* 1874, #423; HO45/9369/37745.

"if a man were lying in the road dead drunk, waving a sword about, and he thereby caused death, he would not be guilty of murder, but nothing short of that would reduce the crime to manslaughter."[97]

Another sign of intent was the length of an attack. When Edwin Hewett at Gloucester in 1886 put forth the defense that he was too drunk to know what he was doing, Justice Stephen accepted that drunkenness was a factor to be taken into account in determining intent but sharply restricted its influence by instructing the jury that "if a drunken man, because he was drunk, formed *a drunken intent* to do grievous bodily harm to another person, and in so doing caused death, he was just as responsible for his actions as if he had not been drunk." Since Hewett had spent several hours kicking his wife, the jury convicted of murder, though adding a mercy recommendation on the ground that he hadn't premeditated the crime. However, in pronouncing sentence Stephen declared that "it seems to me that your murder was as brutal and cruel a crime as has often come before me." A Home Office official commented in opposing the jury recommendation that "it would be dangerous to allow that sort of drunkenness which can frame and carry out a wicked idea to be considered a mitigating circumstance." Hewett hanged.[98] The length of his attack also contributed to its brutality, both factors providing evidence of intent.[99]

In some ways the most important factor affecting how much consideration might be given to a man's drunkenness remained, as in the past, the matter of his "character."[100] A bad previous record or repute would usually foreclose any leniency after conviction.[101] In 1880 a jury convicted William Distin, a carpenter, of murdering his wife and appended a recommendation to mercy, as was done in a majority of wife murder verdicts. Yet he went to the gallows, for he had seventeen previous convictions for lesser offenses.

[97] on Chapman: *Times*, 28 September 1877, p. 10; on Pratt: *Times*, 26 October 1877, p. 11; HO45/9447/68321.

[98] *Times*, 25 May 1886, p. 5; HO144/286/B318.

[99] The length of an attack was similarly noted within the Home Office in the 1910 case of a Leeds laborer, Henry Ison. After interviewing the presiding judge, an official minuted that "the crime was not due to a momentary explosion of rage nor to an irrational or unconnected impulse. The maltreatment of the woman continued for more than an hour during which time the prisoner was feeding his brutal passions by repeated acts of savage violence until at the end he killed her with the poker." Ison hanged, despite a strong recommendation to mercy from the jury and a numerously signed petition. [HO144/1107/200683]

[100] On the centrality of "character" in earlier periods, see P. King, *Crime, Justice and Discretion* (Oxford, 2000) and Cynthia Herrup, *The Common Peace: Participation and the Criminal Law in Seventeenth-Century England* (Cambridge, 1987).

[101] As we have seen with William Horry, whose bad repute made his drunkenness at the time of no avail even in saving him, a man of property, from the gallows in 1872 for the shooting murder of his unfaithful wife [see above Chapter 6].

For such a defendant drunkenness made no difference at all. Justice Denman pronounced in his summing up that "in no event would the fact of the prisoner being under the influence of drink be any excuse." A subsequent petition presented by a Member of Parliament and supported by the committing magistrate was countered by the Home Office view that though Distin "was in fact in liquor at the time . . . it appears that he has habitually when drunk on Saturday night beaten and knocked about the woman, and on this occasion he plunged a knife five inches deep into her."[102]

Even William Turner of Liverpool, who had not used any weapon beyond his boots, hanged in 1882. His drunkenness at the time was of no avail, for he like Distin was known to be a bad man, in his case chiefly through his persistent mistreatment of his helpless wife. "On the date mentioned," the *Times* reported, "he deliberately put on his boots and kicked her in a horrible manner. The poor woman, who was already ill and crippled, shrieked out, 'Oh, Will, don't kill me as thou hast near done many a time.' " Even the jury refrained from recommending mercy, and he hanged in short time.[103] The meaning of "character," however, can be seen in such cases to be shifting, as previous instances of violence came to count more than a reputation as a good worker or a good workmate.

On the other hand, the reputation for non-violence of the Hull pattern-maker Charles Newham, who kicked his sick wife downstairs to her death in 1884, did not prevent his murder conviction, but it at least won him a reprieve. Even though his wife had given him no provocation, a troop of character witnesses swore to his normal sobriety and mildness: the fatal events, all agreed, were most out of character for him. The jury, after Justice Day warned them against "allowing drunkenness to allow escape from responsibility," found him guilty, After this conviction, however, his employers started a petition, which collected 5,000 signatures (including that of Hull's mayor), making the familiar case that "he had no intention to commit murder, and that the assault upon his wife was the result of a fit of passion, induced by drink, and done at a time when he was not wholly responsible for his actions." Despite his warning to the jury, Justice Day supported the petition; once the verdict vindicated the principle of responsibility, he was apparently quite willing to show mercy to the well-thought-of prisoner. Newham won his reprieve.[104]

In the second half of the century it became a judicial cliché to blame the easy availability of drink for violent (and often nonviolent) crime, but such blame did not for a long time weaken the justification for severe punishment. Indeed, that was usually seen as an essential weapon in the war against drink.

[102] *Times,* 22 October 1880, p. 11; HO144/68/98910.
[103] *Times,* 22 August 1882, p. 5.
[104] *Times,* 2 February 1884, p. 10; *Hull News,* 2 and 9 February 1880; HO144/131/A34402.

John McKenna of Rochdale, who had as we have seen drunkenly kicked his wife to death in 1877, was cited by Justice Manisty as "a sad instance of the consequences of indulging in drink," but the sadness of his case did not prevent Manisty from leading the jury to a verdict of murder and omitting a recommendation to the Home Secretary for reprieve. After the verdict, the judge declared that "it is only owing to God's mercy that [drink] has not brought many more into a similar case. I am afraid that if this vice continues to be indulged in as it now so generally is indulged in throughout this country, many more will stand in like position to you. Oh that we could by administering the law put an end to it!"[105]

If the sanctions of the law alone might not be able to solve the problem of drunken violence, they were certainly seen as indispensable, particularly when women were the victims. Into the new century, when fears of crime and violence had much faded, drunkenness by itself continued to be given little slack in the justice process. In 1901, for instance, even a drunken wife killer provoked by a drunkard and improvident wife, for which the judge supported the jury's mercy recommendation, and for whom a strong petition effort was mounted, ended on the gallows. Indeed, this case displays clearly the gap we have seen between the concepts of "good character" that continued to be held by many in the offender's local community and by the Home Office at least from the mid-Victorian years on. Of a petition signed by the Mayor of Bolton, where the murder had taken place, and ten of the jury among others denouncing the man's wife and extolling his hard-working, fraternal, and "manly" character, an official noted that "he had a very good character from his employers certainly, but his [two previous] convictions of assault [on his wife (unmentioned by the petitioners)] and breaches of the peace show that he was a violent man at times."[106]

Two facets of drunken violence made it increasingly intolerable to Victorian officials and much of the public: its fundamental affront to the ideal of personal reasonableness and self-command, and its tendency to unchecked brutality. As we have seen, brutality grew as a consideration and, although by itself having no legal import, came to be used both as evidence of intent at the least to inflict "grievous bodily harm" and thus support a murder conviction, and as a strong factor weighing against a reprieve from the gallows. This was particularly so when the victim of brutality was a woman; the sight, or mere thought, of a broken and terribly bruised female body demanded severe punishment. Justice Lawrance justified his failure to support his jury's mercy recommendation in an 1898 case by noting that "it was a very brutal murder after habitual ill-usage." The Home Office shared this view: of a petition praising the convict's character from the town council

---

[105] *Times*, 6 March 1877, p. 11; HO45/9431/62405.
[106] *R.v. McKenna*: HO144/572/A62987; *Times*, 14 November 1901, p. 6.

of his home town, Aberdeen, the head of the Criminal Department, reflected that "it is curious that they seem to pity the man more than the
woman."[107]

However, at the same time that strict principles were maintained and reaffirmed against the drunkenness defense in homicide, judges continued the
long tradition of often taking drunkenness in practice into some account
as a mitigation of punishment, and in their recommendations on reprieves,
and even the Home Office began to show irregular signs in the years after
Cross of taking this point in weighing reprieves, though less often in domestic
than in public, man-on-man murders. As in other areas of the application
of homicide law, ever-more-firmly reiterated principles of strict personal responsibility and the intolerability of violent behavior, as they gained power
in determining verdicts and ultimate dispositions, had in practice to compromise with the continuing inclination of most men – whether we call it
pragmatism, resentment of teetotal preachiness, humanitarianism, or (in the
case of domestic violence) male chauvinism – to see drunkenness as some
mitigation of a homicide.

No systematic and invariable policy regarding wife killers could ever
emerge from the criminal justice process. First, the inevitable variation in
the particular circumstances of each case and the sentiments and notions of
each juryman and each judge guaranteed that outcomes would not be uniform and consistent. Second, clashing notions of culpability and the proper
relation of justice and mercy, along with clashing sympathies, meant an ongoing contestation over outcomes and a combination of continuity and change.
Yet even with the ambiguity and variability thus produced, a clear trend to
increasingly severe legal treatment nonetheless emerged, a trend which lasted
through the Queen's reign.

### Drunkenness and Insanity

The third and most drastic way to argue lack of intent and thus escape a
murder verdict (or at least hanging) was to claim insanity. It was drastic because if it succeeded, the defendant would not receive a lighter sentence, as
with such mitigations as the non-use of a weapon or simple drunkenness,
but be institutionalized at Broadmoor Criminal Lunatic Asylum often for
life. It was employed therefore normally only as a last shield against a murder conviction. As the effectiveness of drunkenness as a mitigating factor
diminished, this defense became more common in drunken killings. The
most obvious claim was that of "temporary insanity," but while that defense
was increasingly successful for women who killed their newborn children,
for men it was almost always dismissed in court. Men lacked the believable

---

[107]HO144/272/A59671; *Newcastle Daily Chronicle*, 4 March 1898.

organic basis for the claim which the great bodily changes of pregnancy and the trauma of birth provided women. For men, "temporary insanity" almost never succeeded, unless a link with some form of recognized mental disease or disability could be established. Its chances in court can be estimated from a judge's summary for Home Secretary Cross of an 1875 trial of a barge-owner, William Hole, who had fallen into habitual drunkenness, and in such a state cut his wife's throat: The act, he noted, "was certainly unpremeditated and done while the man was stupified by drink." Nonetheless, the effort of his counsel to establish a defense on the ground of insanity "of course failed." Also unsuccessful was a mass petition following the conviction praying for a commutation of the death sentence on this ground, specifically that Hole "was unconscious at the time of the crime, being maddened by drink."[108] Four years earlier, Liberal Home Secretary Bruce had dismissed the arguments of a psychiatrist for the drink-induced temporary insanity of Richard Addington, another wife murderer, by observing that "a man who inflicts three mortal wounds in different parts of the body must be assumed to have intended to kill."[109]

These difficulties in defending drunken killers had come to a head at the same time that the prestige of medical experts and the plausibility of medical explanations of deviant behavior had been rapidly advancing. One effect of that advance was to encourage increasingly active defense counsel to regularly employ medical witnesses to ascertain the mental state of their clients at the time of their criminal acts (a strategy which prompted the greater use of expert counter-witnesses by the prosecution). Although this employment has been characterized as a Foucauldian "professional invasion" or "medicalization" of criminal justice, it is better understood as the outcome of an interaction of the internal dynamics of criminal justice processes with shifts in outlook in the wider culture – a combination of increasingly professionalized defense and prosecution and the enhanced receptivity to medical experts on the part of jurymen and sometimes judges (helped along of course by the professional self-promotion of such experts).[110] Not only was medical evidence on the state of the prisoner's mind becoming commonplace in

[108] HO45/9381/43242; *Times*, 7, 8, 27 April 1875 (pp. 13, 11, 5); the presiding judge was Justice Lush. That this petition received as many as 30,000 signatures underlines the contestation continuing over these questions of criminal responsibility. But also see *Illustrated Police News*, 8 May 1875, p. 2 for a sharp criticism of the petition and a denunciation of the defense of drunkenness.

[109] HO45/9289/5490.

[110] On the latter, see Wiener, *Reconstructing the Criminal*, pp. 269–76. On the former, see Joel Eigen, *Witnessing Insanity: Madness and Mad-Doctors in the English Court 1760–1843* (New Haven, 1995). Also see Tony Ward, "Law, Common Sense and the Authority of Science: Expert Witnesses and Criminal Insanity in England, c. 1840–1940," *Social & Legal Studies* 6 (1997), 343–362.

court by the 1870s, but proceedings there could hardly help being affected by outside developments like the new statutory characterization of "habitual drunkenness" as at least in some cases a medical condition, by an act passing Parliament in 1879 to provide institutions for the treatment of persons suffering from this condition who voluntarily committed themselves.[111]

The conjuncture of developments in court and out encouraged defense counsel to put forward insanity defenses in drunkenness cases that linked drunkenness with some form of recognized mental disease or disability that could be seen as preventing the accused from forming a criminal intent. One possible avenue away from the growing likelihood of conviction and even execution was to place the prisoner's drunkenness within the context of a physical impairment out of his control – in particular, delirium tremens, a disease of physical tremblings and delusions of the senses, known to be brought on by prolonged drunkenness.[112]

This new argument however had a checkered reception from justice officials and the press. Raised for the first time in a wife murder in Corrigan's trial in 1856, it was rebuffed swiftly and the defendant convicted, although then reprieved. Even the popular *Lloyds' Weekly*, though critical of capital punishment, objected to the medical argument, seeing nothing but a fancy term for drunkenness: "The man murdered his wife in a frenzy of drunkenness," it wrote; "one vice is, then, to palliate a greater crime; the gin measure is to excuse the act of the knife."[113] Raised again in 1865, this defense had even less success; the defendant hanged.[114] Even when the victim was not a wife but a disreputable prostitute the defense was resisted. When a Swiss, Jacob Spinasa, beat a prostitute to death with a candlestick in 1870, he created a public sensation. Justice Channell rejected his delirium tremens defense and reminded the jury that a prostitute had the same right as anyone else to the protection of the law. Convicted of murder, Spinasa was reprieved by a reluctant Home Secretary Bruce only after the Swiss consul-general submitted evidence of Spinasa's previous hospital incarceration and statements from medical staff who had treated him.[115]

---

[111] Even while persons charged with crimes were explicitly excluded from the scope of the act.

[112] The term was first used in 1813, in a medical writing. On rare occasions other physical conditions might win an insanity verdict for a drunken murderer. In 1865 James Kelly was found insane because of medical evidence that he had for years had a physical brain disease which had defeated his repeated efforts to give up drink. [R. Smith, op. cit., p. 112.]

[113] *Lloyds' Weekly*, 9 March 1856.

[114] *R.v. Burke: Times*, 13 March 1865, p. 11 (the presiding judge was Mellor).

[115] *Times*, 3 and 4 March 1870; HO144/26/63070; *Illustrated Police News*, 29 January 1870; see Figure 11.

FIGURE 11. "The Finsbury Murder" (*Illustrated Police News,* January 29, 1870). Jacob Spinasa's killing of a prostitute.

The following year the third defense of delirium tremens in a wife murder trial finally produced an insanity verdict, the first, at least for a wife murderer, on these grounds.[116] But it was not successful again at least in such cases for another decade. The next year, in William Horry's trial for shooting down his unfaithful wife, delirium tremens was argued alongside the jealousy induced by her infidelity, but it too failed to save his life. Justice Quain told the jury that "If he was suffering from jealousy and from the effects of the drink, and the attacks of delirium tremens, that might form a moral excuse, but it would be no legal answer to the charge. Although this might justify them in recommending the prisoner to mercy, it would not justify them in acquitting him." In the event, Horry did not even receive a mercy recommendation.[117] It was next argued and rejected for wife murder in 1877, Justice Lush afterwards dismissing what he called the mental "theories" put forward in a petition.[118] Again the following year it was raised in James McGowan's trial, but Justice Manisty saw to it that it did not prevent a conviction. The jury did, however, in this case recommend mercy because of "temporary insanity caused by excessive drinking." Home Secretary Cross responded by having medical experts employed by the penal system evaluate McGowan (a practice his successor was to require in all cases where claims of insanity or other mental disability had been raised).[119] Even when these Government experts concluded that when he took his wife's life he was "under the influence of delirium [though] has since recovered from this condition of temporary

---

[116] *R.v. Cook: Times,* 31 July 1871, p. 11 (Justice Mellor was again presiding judge).

[117] *Times,* 14 March 1872, p. 11; HO45/9303/11410.

[118] *R.v. Bannister* (1877): HO45/9433/63057.

[119] This administrative practice was at least in part a response to the growth in use of insanity defenses supported by medical witnesses.

insanity," Cross was not satisfied, and sent a copy of the report with a factual query to Justice Manisty. The doctors, he told the judge, were

> of course only dealing with medical opinions, not as to what are or are not the actual facts of the case. Delirium tremens is a well known form of actual disease of the brain: absolute madness, and lasts for long. When a man is absolutely and *bona fide* insane, I conclude that the law does not stay to enquire into the cause of insanity. On the other hand, as the Doctors say they do not recognize the emotions and passions as sources of irresponsibility even when intensified by drink. All drunkenness is surely accompanied more or less by hallucinations and unreal impressions. The question I would venture to ask really your opinion on a question of fact: Can it really be said in this case there is any real evidence of delirium tremens as I have above mentioned? The jury say 'No' – or they should have acquitted him on the ground of insanity.

Such evidence was lacking, Manisty agreed – indeed, he made his dislike for the whole argument apparent, writing back that he "could not conceive a more dangerous and mischievous doctrine than that advanced in the report, viz., that if a man only drinks enough to make himself insane for the time being, he is in the eye of the law an irresponsible being" – and the prisoner hanged.[120]

Three years later (after the passage of the 1879 Habitual Drunkards Act) Justice Manisty modified his opposition by ruling in a West Riding wife murder trial that the normal culpability of an offender with "a state of disease brought about by a person's own act – e.g., delirium tremens, caused by excessive drinking" could be modified or even eliminated by that condition's "permanence." The defendant had several times been under treatment for delirium tremens, and had had another attack two days after committing the killing. He was saved by the judge's ruling from a murder verdict, but Manisty then sentenced him to as stiff a penalty as he could – penal servitude for life.[121] Yet even now this issue was hardly settled; Manisty's ruling recognizing the relevance of possible disease was explicitly rejected five years later (in 1886) by Justice Day in another wife murder trial. "The question," Day sternly pronounced, "was whether there was insanity or not; it was immaterial whether it was caused by the person himself or by the vices of his ancestors" as it was immaterial "whether the insanity was permanent or temporary." He "could not follow the decision of Mr. Justice Manisty" [in the previous case] and instead restated the traditional "intellectual" rule that an act would be excusable only if "a man were in such a state of intoxication that he did not

---

[120] HO45/9469/78542.
[121] *R.v. M'Gowen: Times*, 9 February 1881, p. 11.

know the nature of his act or that his act was wrongful." A murder verdict was returned, but then Day announced his "surprise" at the verdict's not being accompanied by a recommendation to mercy "as he considered the man was acting under insane delusions." He then supported a second medical examination by the Home Office. The Government's medical men found no clear evidence of insane delusions, and the man was left to hang.[122]

As habitual drunkenness began to be called "inebriety" and perceived medically, a DT defense – despite such rebuffs as Day's – had greater chances of succeeding, as long as there were sufficient evidence of such a condition existing prior to the crime. Charles Latham in 1888 had been "in consequence of his drinking habits" several times an inmate of the insane wards of St. Pancras Infirmary suffering from DT, and this allowed an insanity verdict; Thomas Baxendale was similarly found insane in 1893.[123] Even if not obtaining a finding of insanity, the claim of insanity through DT was not necessarily fruitless: several times at least in the eighties and nineties the evidence presented in the course of this defense would afterwards help win a reprieve or Broadmoor committal. Somewhat surprisingly, Job Hartland's 1894 defense of DT for the brutal killing of his wife and child led to a jury recommendation to mercy not specifically on that claim but "on account of his low type of character and drunken habits" (an example it would seem of reverse class favoritism). Justice Mathew supported the jury, describing the case to the Home Office as "one of those where jurors are reluctant to apply the strict rules of the criminal law, and where unless for very strong reasons it would be inadvisable that their recommendation to mercy should be disregarded." Faced with this joint recommendation, the Home Office gave Hartland a reprieve. Not without great doubts, however: Permanent Undersecretary Godfrey Lushington advised Home Secretary Asquith that

> the main question is whether he was suffering from DT or something tantamount to it. . . . He had been drinking heavily for a fortnight. . . . [He] had no motive for the crime; he killed them when asleep by cutting their throats and then when they were dead he hammered their skulls to pieces. All this looks like the conduct of an insane man. On the other hand he was or appeared to be sober all Monday . . . after he washed up part of his clothes in order to conceal the bloodstains and then went out he was treated as sober by the various publicans who served him. . . . The prison doctor saw him both that day and the next day – recognized that he had had a drinking bout, but found no DT.

---

[122] *R.v. Baines: Times,* 25 January 1886, p. 10; HO144/284/B81 and B99. Very likely his bad character kept a reprieve from him: Baines had been repeatedly before the magistrates for being drunk and abusing his wife.

[123] *Times,* 5 July 1888, p. 7; 2 August 1893, p. 7.

The man has a bad character from the police for ill-using his wife when drunk [and] if he was responsible, he deserves no mercy. But I incline to think he was not wholly responsible.[124]

However, few wife killers actually suffered from DT, and it remained easier to claim alcoholic insanity than to establish it sufficiently to win a verdict, or even a reprieve or committal. The claim still usually failed, caught in the general official hostility to drunken offenders. Latham's and Hartland's cases were atypical. Latham's in fact was the only one of twelve drunken wife murder trials in the 1880s in which insanity pleas were entered that had the plea fully accepted: in the other eleven, nine defendants hanged and the other two were found guilty though then reprieved. In the previous decade fourteen such cases had resulted in two insanity acquittals and eleven executions. Even in the following decade of the 1890s, when the number of insanity verdicts in all trials doubled, thirteen drunken insanity pleas in wife murder cases did produce more insanity acquittals – four – but they were still well outnumbered by executions (seven).[125] Taking the three decades together in wife murder trials there were eighty-four insanity pleas not related to drink, yielding forty-one insanity verdicts, but where the defendant had been drunk and claimed some version of alcoholic insanity, only seven of thirty-nine pleas were accepted.[126] A husband's drunkenness thus made an insanity claim, despite the growing acceptance of such pleas, still very much an uphill task. Far from making it easier to doubt a defendant's sanity, drunkenness offered an alternative and more culpable form of irresponsibility. Insanity

---

[124] *Times*, 22 November 1894, p. 5; HO144/262/A56500.

[125] On the total of insanity verdicts, see R. Chadwick, *Bureaucratic Mercy* (New York, 1992), p. 402 (table 6).

[126] In the 1870s there were twenty-six insanity pleas in wife murder trials where the drunkenness of the defendant was not an issue, which yielded eleven verdicts of insanity, fourteen murder convictions (five of these nonetheless were committed to Broadmoor, four were reprieved and five executed) and one manslaughter conviction. There were also fourteen insanity pleas in which the defendant was drunk; these produced only two insanity verdicts and twelve murder convictions. Of those convicted of murder, one was committed to Broadmoor and the other eleven hanged.

In the 1880s, twenty-two insanity pleas in wife murder trials where the drunkenness of the defendant was not an issue resulted in eleven insanity verdicts and eleven murder convictions (seven of these were committed to Broadmoor, two were reprieved and two hanged). Twelve insanity pleas in which the defendant was drunk led to just one insanity verdict, two reprieves and nine executions.

In the 1890s, the number of insanity pleas in wife murder trials rose (as they did in murder trials generally). Thirty-six insanity pleas in wife murder trials where the drunkenness of the defendant was not an issue produced nineteen insanity verdicts, two manslaughter verdicts and fifteen murder verdicts, of which three were committed to Broadmoor, one reprieved and eleven hanged. Thirteen insanity pleas in which the defendant was drunk resulted in four insanity verdicts and nine murder verdicts; of these two were reprieved and seven hanged.

was at least to the end of Victoria's reign for drunkard husbands largely a "desperation" plea.[127]

Another illness besides DT that had a relation to drunkenness was epilepsy, often stimulated though not caused by drink. Epilepsy had existed as a defined illness longer than DT and also seemed to be appearing in court more frequently in the later decades of the century. It had the advantage of having an origin independent of drink and thus bore no moral stigma. Even epilepsy claims, however, had to conquer much official skepticism. Although the first Victorian plea in wife murder of insanity through epilepsy (made by a solidly middle-class man, employing a Queen's Counsel) was accepted in 1874, when made by less distinguished counsel the claim was subject to severe scrutiny.[128] Hanged in the same year, 1878, as James McGowan with his DT claim was Thomas Smithers, a London cook who had stabbed his common-law wife and whose counsel brought in a series of lay witnesses to argue that he was subject to attacks of epilepsy. However, after the surgeon of Newgate found no evidence for this, Smithers was convicted (he had often expressed jealous feelings, which could place him in a familiar criminal category). Justice Denman then virtually ensured his execution by warning the Home Office that it "would be very dangerous to life if an opinion were to prevail that epileptics are irresponsible for murder. Epilepsy and a homicidal tendency are frequently connected."[129]

Yet epilepsy made a more winning insanity defense than DT. If the second epilepsy defense in a wife murder trial completely failed, the third, a mere two months later, succeeded, when another poor man, Thomas William Humphreys, was found insane at Stafford on this ground. Unlike Smithers, Humphreys had some history of mental problems; moreover, he had a medical witness testifying strongly for him. This doctor argued that Humphreys "suffered from epileptic mania, of which an irresistible homicidal impulse was one of the features." He held to this view under hostile questioning from Baron Bramwell. Medical judgment was becoming decisive in this area, and even Bramwell, in summing up ardently against the insanity defense, nonetheless allowed space for an insanity finding for such a man under the

---

[127]In an 1892 case where an insanity plea was not entered at trial, but only argued afterwards, a clerk observed that since the man had an expressed motive of jealousy, his mere suffering from the effects of drinking, even with a family history of insanity, was not persuasive. "The only question," he concluded, was "whether his constant drinking had so unhinged his mind as to make him practically irresponsible," and on this "the Home Office precedents especially since Lord Cross came into office would be against accepting this plea." [HO144/245/A54302; *Times*, 22, 24 September 1892 (pp. 6, 3).]

[128]*R.v. Sweet: Times*, 14 March 1874, p. 12; *Illustrated Police News*, 7 February 1874.

[129]HO45/9466/76890. After the trial the chief surgeon of the Metropolitan Police, having doubts, urged a further medical examination, which took place, but this turned up negative for Smithers, and he then went to the gallows.

restrictive "knowing right from wrong" criteria of the M'Naughton Rules, an option his jury immediately took.[130]

Sometimes epilepsy could serve as an excuse for saving the life of a sympathetic defendant. With provocation from a bad wife less exculpatory than in the past, in such a situation an illness like epilepsy offered the only chance of preventing a conviction. In the case of William Brown, a black former seaman in Sheerness, described as "a very quiet man in the ordinary way, but [one who] had a terrible temper when aroused or when in drink," who killed his wife with a hatchet in 1883 and then seriously wounded himself with the same weapon, a looming murder verdict and likely execution was averted by the discovery of epileptic fits in the man's past. As his counsel Henry Dickens recalled, Brown "had spent his life in the Royal Navy and [retired] on a pension with as high a character as any man could possibly have." After his first wife's death, he remarried:

> This was the tragedy of his life. She was a bad woman – a thoroughly bad woman. She drank to excess; went about with other men and used to taunt him with his black blood. He was patient and long-suffering; but his efforts to bring her to reason were unavailing and the happiness of his home was shattered. . . . [After killing her with a hatchet, he set fire to the house, and in a frenzy tried to throw his son, bent over her body, into the fire, and finally slashed at his own throat.] . . . These were terrible facts, facts which could not be contradicted. It was quite obvious to me what had happened. The woman had come home with another man, and in a state of drunken fury had taunted him with his black blood and goaded him to madness. I could not hint at such a thing, of course, as it supplied the motive for the act.[131] Insanity was the only defense; but the mere ghastliness of the deed afforded of itself no sufficient evidence

[130]Bramwell summed up: "If an insane man knew he was committing murder that man was responsible. It was not enough to have a homicidal mania. The object of the law was to guard against mischievous propensities and homicidal impulses. . . . He said this to the jury to disabuse their minds of a mischievous impression which existed, and which he believed had reached mad people themselves. He did not believe in uncontrollable impulse at all, had never heard of such an impulse leading to action where the means of prevention were present" – but, they could find insanity if they found he didn't know what he was doing was injurious, or wrong, or didn't know what he was doing at all – "pointing out the want of motive, and the absence of any indication of ill-will on the part of the prisoner against his wife, and observed that undoubtedly there were many circumstances in the case which would warrant the conclusion that he was insane in the sense he had pointed out." Even Bramwell found the case persuasive, observing that "the man is deeply to be pitied." *Times*, 7 November 1878, p. 10.
[131]Earlier in the century in such a case such "hints" would very likely have been made, supplying motive or not; it is revealing of the tightening treatment of cuckolded husbands that Dickens felt unable to do this in 1883.

of insanity such as must be shown to justify such a defense in law. . . . I was at my wit's end.

The man's life was saved when a sympathetic Crown solicitor told Dickens that the prisoner suffered from epileptic fits. " 'Thank God', I said, 'Thank God'." At the trial "there was much public sympathy for the poor fellow and I knew I was sure of help from the sympathetic doctor who was to be called for the Crown. . . . When I addressed the jury and drew attention to the character of the man, his love for his children. . . . 'Can you doubt that man was mad?' There were heads in the jury box nodding assent." Brown was found insane and sent to Broadmoor.[132]

Another time when a bad wife was murdered, the perpetrator's epilepsy was found to fall short of legal insanity yet was sufficient to avoid a murder conviction. In William Barnaby's 1902 trial for stabbing his wife to death with a sharp Swedish knife, the traditional complaints about her character were made in court. "Mrs. Barnaby," a policeman stated, "was known as an intemperate, violent woman, while her husband bore the character of a sober, respectable man." However, knowing that such a line would not get as far as it once had, the defense made its chief argument the man's epileptic insanity, combined with general low intelligence. The prison medical officer acknowledged that the prisoner was an epileptic and of weak mind but insisted that he was not insane (after all, he was well known as a "sober, respectable man"). However, in a rigorous cross-examination, the doctor was drawn to agree that "in some cases epileptics were subject to violent impulses, under which they did violent things without malevolence, although a fit was not upon them." Barnaby was convicted of manslaughter only, receiving a sentence of merely five years.[133]

### Insanity

When drunkenness was not a significant factor, and where no clearly physical disease like epilepsy existed, insanity defenses still were increasingly resorted to in murder cases. By 1875, even Dr. Forbes Winslow, a psychiatrist frequently called to testify for the defense, observed that "a murder is rarely committed [nowadays] without the sanity of the prisoner being questioned."[134] The M'Naughton Rules laid down in 1843, which set a high standard for insanity – the inability to understand the wrongful nature of the act committed – had operated through the Victorian period to hold down the number of insanity verdicts.[135] Particularly in the early years after the Rules were set down

---

[132] *Recollections of Sir Henry Dickens* (London, 1934), pp. 178–182; *Times*, 21 April 1883, p. 12.
[133] *Times*, 23 October 1902, p. 10.
[134] Letter, *Times*, 3 September 1875.
[135] See R. Smith, op. cit.

judges set themselves against almost every insanity defense. A year after M'Naughton, as one instance, Baron Alderson kept a jury locked up without food, drink, or heat for twenty-two hours until it rejected one insanity defense and convicted a wife-killer of murder. He then urged the Home Secretary not to stay execution, arguing that "this plea of madness is palliative of unruly passions leading to murder, and is very dangerous."[136] Such judicial aggressiveness in defending against insanity claims generally succeeded in the decades following M'Naughton.[137] Yet pressure later began to mount from within and without the courtroom on the narrowness of the Rules.

Despite the plethora of scornful judicial *obiter dicta* on the insanity defense, by the 1870s the rising number of claims were poking cracks in the official wall of resistance. A celebrated case in late 1871 brought the insanity defense into perhaps its greatest prominence since M'Naughton. A few weeks after the Rev. John Selby Watson, former headmaster of Stockwell Grammar School in South London, completed his four-volume *History of the Papacy to the Reformation*, he beat his nagging wife to death. After concealing her body for two days, he wrote a suicide note, declaring that "I have killed my wife in a fit of rage to which she provoked me," and took prussic acid which, however, failed to kill him. Despite this note and a history of bad feeling between husband and wife, defense counsel did not try to do anything with provocation. All efforts were thrown into an insanity defense, relying on what even the prosecuting counsel admitted was "an antecedent improbability in the deed which would lead everyone in the first instance to seek an explanation in insanity." But when two asylum superintendents attested only to his depression (he had recently been retired against his will from his headmastership) but not to any insanity, and Justice Byles summed up strongly against this defense, the jury, after deliberating for one and a half hours, returned a guilty verdict, with a strong recommendation to mercy on account of age and previous character. A wave of petitions and affidavits from medical men followed, arguing for his insanity at the time of the crime. Unusually, the judge himself now changed his tune and advised the Home Secretary that the medical evidence presented at the trial suggested to him that "this is not a case in which the sentence should be carried out." Prolonged debate ensued within the Home Office, and further medical opinion was solicited. Some kind of imprecise mental unsoundness was accepted, and Watson was reprieved, though

---

[136] *R.v. Crouch: Times*, 9, 10 May 1844 (pp. 6–7, 8); HO18/129/16. It was not only judges who were intensely suspicious of insanity pleas. Charles Dickens urged in 1862 that "in questions that concern the mind, the less heed we pay to the theorist, and the more distinctly we require none but the sort of evidence patent to the natural sense of ordinary men . . . the better it will be for us. Let us account no man a lunatic whom it requires a mad-doctor to prove insane." ["M.D. and MAD," *All the Year Round*, 22 February 1862, 510.]

[137] See R. Smith, op. cit.

FIGURE 12. "The Stockwell Tragedy" (*Illustrated Police News*, October 28, 1871).
The Rev. Watson's "loss of control."

(since he now showed no signs of lunacy) he was not committed to Broadmoor and spent the last twelve years of his life in prison. In his case, the incongruity of the crime and the lack of any lesser defense pushed the system to a controversial finding of "temporary" insanity to prevent the unedifying spectacle of the hanging of a clergyman of the Church of England. In a sense, for Watson provocation (by his nagging wife, under the stress of his forced retirement) had been reconceived as temporary insanity.[138] While Watson's case was being argued out at the Old Bailey, at the Home Office and in newspapers, a humbler wife killer was being tried in the North and also putting forth the claim of insanity. The shoemaker Samuel Wallis fatally stabbed his wife in an apparently motiveless act, and medical evidence emphasized his history of "melancholy" and a specific delusion of a "fearful thundering noise" in a disused colliery, where he had been hiding from apprehension. As usual, Justice Lush in his summation warned the jury against "permitting this kind of defence to prevail" and after several hours of deliberation they reluctantly returned a "guilty" verdict, but (despite his flight) recommended mercy on account of "the weak state of his mind." As with Watson's, Wallis's death sentence was commuted. Neither man was sent to Broadmoor, but both had been reprieved essentially if not formally, on doubts about their sanity.[139]

Official fear of insanity verdicts seems to have begun to ease after Broadmoor Criminal Lunatic Asylum opened in 1863, affording for the first time a secure institution within the penal system for placing those found unfit to

[138] *Annual Register for 1871*, part 2, pp. 110–111; *Lloyds' Weekly*, 14 January 1872; HO144/2/7940. For a thorough account of Watson's case, see R. Chadwick, *Bureaucratic Mercy* (New York, 1992), pp. 239–56. See also Beryl Bainbridge's absorbing fictionalized version, *Watson's Apology* (New York, 1985). See Figure 12.
[139] *Times*, 18 December 1871, p. 11; HO45/9296/9205.

plead or "acquitted" by reason of insanity.[140] Thereafter the Home Office instituted its own medical inquiries on capital convicts about whose sanity serious questions had been raised and, when on occasion the inquiries found insanity removed such convicts to Broadmoor.[141] Yet this policy, though it went further than many judges liked, did not necessarily satisfy the increasing resistance to the Rules visible among jurors. When in 1876 a heavy-drinking army pensioner who had spent time in a lunatic asylum beat his wife to death, his Old Bailey defense counsel, the eloquent Montague Williams, drew together his institutionalization, his excessive drinking, and the provocation offered by the victim, a "nag," into an impressive case for insanity. Yet, strongly opposed by the severe Justice Hawkins, it failed to prevent a guilty verdict. Afterwards, however, the jury protested their bullying by Hawkins: "Had we been directed," they wrote Home Secretary Cross, "that we were at liberty to act upon a probable presumption of insanity to be founded upon the antecedent, contemporaneous and subsequent acts of the prisoner we should at once have acquitted him." Other petitioners (including City of London aldermen) joined them in urging a finding of insanity. Cross felt obliged to have two physicians examine the prisoner. However, they found him sane, and he hanged.[142]

The combination of the greater legitimacy being given medico–psychiatric evidence and the continuing "de-legitimization" of provocation and drunkenness defenses in court and at the Home Office led late-Victorian and Edwardian defense counsel, partly in response to changing discourse on human nature and partly as a pragmatic "fallback" position, to employ the plea of insanity more, and sometimes successfully. If ordinary men were being expected to more tightly master their passions, then the only likely successful path to avoid a guilty verdict became that of showing the prisoner to be *not* ordinary (a situation coming to seem more likely, as the amount of insanity and mental disability acknowledged to exist in British society rose). If he were a man constitutionally incapable of being reasonable and self-controlling

---

[140]In 1863, Chief Baron Pollock did not object to an insanity verdict at the Old Bailey even against the evidence of the jail surgeon for Thomas Lidbetter. [*Times*, 14 July 1863, p. 10]. In 1865 Justice Montague Smith seemed to agree with an insanity verdict for the drunken wife murderer James Kelly, after the medical officer to the Burnley Poor Law Union testified that he had treated Kelly several years earlier and was convinced that he suffered from a "physical disease of the brain." These men became early inmates of Broadmoor [*Times*, 4 August 1865, p. 11]. The number of men indicted for wife murder who were either found unfit to plead, insane, or (from 1863) were sent to Broadmoor after conviction rose from one in 1850–54 and two in 1855–59 to nine in 1860–64, seven in 1865–69, and nine in 1870–74.

[141]The year 1865 saw the first cases of wife murder convictions in which the Home Secretary then ordered another medical examination and subsequently "reprieved" two convicts to Broadmoor.

[142]R.v. O'Donnell: *Times*, 24 Nov. 1876, p. 11; HO45/9422/59678.

under stress, then the legal standards of responsibility could not apply to him. Rather than his *situation*, the defendant's *constitution* more often became the key to his defense. As provocation or drunkenness became less effective preventatives of execution, mental disability was able to step into the gap and ward off a major increase in hangings.[143]

By 1888 Baron Pollock [son of the earlier judge] was noting to the Home Office the "difficulty that there is [now] of getting verdicts for murder" in insanity plea cases, and thus the value, once a jury is brought to convict, of acceding to its mercy recommendation.[144] In an 1896 case, the inquest jury itself reported that "we have come to the conclusion that the man was mad" and had to be upbraided by the coroner that "the question of insanity has nothing to do with you"; reluctantly, they then returned a verdict of "willful murder." At the man's trial several Government doctors testified that they found no signs of insanity, and the jury convicted, but with "a strong and unanimous recommendation to his Lordship to use every influence possible for the prisoner in mercy." The Home Office had him sent to Broadmoor.[145] As Pollock's comment suggests, by the end of the century, judges who now encountered less jury "difficulty" over the issues of provocation and drunkenness, were often chagrined to find themselves unable to prevent juries from returning insanity verdicts.[146] The increasing frequency of insanity pleas in murders of wives and others in the 1890s was matched by a marked rise

---

[143] In the 1895 Norwich trial of a well-liked former soldier, a provocation defense based on his wife's combined habitual drunkenness and her infidelity failed; petitioners then turned to insanity arguments that had not been introduced at the trial, citing sunstroke while in the army and an incident in which he had been knocked down by trolley some years before as having led to peculiar behavior. They won a reprieve. [*R.v. Miles: Times*, 15 June 1895, p. 6; HO144/548/A57035.]

[144] *R.v. Bulmer:* HO144/223/A49657; *Times,* 14 December 1888, p. 10.

[145] *R.v. Allison: Times,* 27 June 1896, p. 19; CRIM 6/19.

[146] The tough Justice Hawkins had a number of public run-ins with juries: in an 1898 case in which the chief engineer of a ferryboat shot a woman without apparent motive, but thereafter acted quite rationally, he was astonished at the insanity verdict. "Do you mean to say," he asked the foreman, "that [the defendant] did not know what he was doing?" "We do," was the reply. "It is your verdict," shrugged Hawkins, accepting defeat [*R.v. Sando: Times,* 19 May 1898, p. 3]. He also contended against post-trial claims of insanity made to the Home Secretary. One public rejection of such claims he later recalled with satisfaction: in the 1894 case of Walter Smith, who had shot to death a woman who had rejected him, "a question was asked [in the House of Commons] of the Secretary of State for the Home Department," Hawkins noted in his memoirs, "as to the prisoner being insane, and whether there was not abundant evidence of insanity at the trial" – a question that was thoroughly rebuffed by a written acknowledgment by the man's defense counsel that his argument had been that the shooting was entirely accidental, an argument that had rested in part on the entire absence of evidence of insanity. "After that statement," concluded Hawkins, "the humane questioner left the prisoner to his well-deserved fate." [Sir Henry Hawkins, *Reminiscences,* ed. Richard Harris (London, 1904), 2: 73.]

in verdicts of insanity or unfitness to plead, especially by the turn of the century.[147]

The clinical appreciation of alcoholism was by this point weakening moral denunciation (the 1898 Inebriates Act for the first time explicitly gave the courts latitude in the sentencing of crimes directly or indirectly due to intoxication), so that even drunken husbands, whether of high, middling, or low standing, were beginning to gain verdicts of insanity. The greengrocer James Flower in 1899, the businessman James Botton in 1901, and the street hawker John Devlin in 1906 all received this verdict after killing their wives in drunken fits. In these trials, prison medical officers played crucial roles by labeling the defendants' behavior as "alcoholic insanity" or conceding under cross-examination that "delirium tremens is insanity."[148] The very brutality or excessiveness of the killing might now be cited as evidence of insanity.[149] A new era of medically inspired allowance for drink-induced mental illness seems to have been dawning.[150]

[147] For total insanity resolutions, see Chadwick, *Bureaucratic Mercy*, tables 3, 5 and 6. In spouse murder cases, the number of jury insanity verdicts almost doubled from twelve in the 1880s to twenty-three in the 1890s; however, actual committals did not rise so sharply, for there had already also been seven cases in the 1880s of the Home Office certifying offenders as "unfit to plead" and removing them to Broadmoor without their ever being brought before a jury, but judicial protests had reduced this number to three in the 1890s; if they had gone to a jury, these cases would very likely have resulted in "unfit to plead" verdicts, increasing the total cited above. In the 1870s there had been thirteen insanity verdicts, and five cases of independent Home Office certification. The two ways of sending a prisoner to Broadmoor taken together rose but only modestly in wife murder cases from eighteen to nineteen to twenty-six in these three decades. However, after 1900 such committals increased a good deal further (in 1901 alone, there were five insanity verdicts and one certification after conviction in wife murder trials). Whereas in the mid-Victorian years about one in seven of those brought to trial for murder were either declared unfit to plead, acquitted as insane, or certified by a Home Office inquiry after conviction, by the years immediately preceding World War I the proportion had risen to more than one in three (Chadwick, table 5). [See also Nigel Walker, *Crime and Insanity* (Edinburgh, 1968), pp. 86–7, 122–123, 226–231, 264–265.]

[148] *Times:* 7 December 1899, p. 7, 14 September 1901, p. 13, 27 June 1906, p. 12. Botton was defended by a KC, but Flower by an unnamed barrister and Devlin by court-appointed counsel.

[149] At Devlin's trial, after acknowledging that DT was insanity, the prison medical officer observed that "in the case of murder committed by lunatics, or men not in their senses at the time, it is frequently the case that a great deal more violence is used upon the body than is necessary to accomplish the actual death. Murder is not usually cold-blooded in these cases."

[150] In his *Recollections*, published in 1934, Henry Dickens noted that "this principle [of leaving the jury leeway to find insanity] has, of later years, been extended to crimes in which 'intent' is of the essence of the crime, and where the accused have been entirely under the influence of drink" [p. 184].

The Home Office had responded to (and participated in) this trend by making post-conviction medical inquiries standard procedure under the Liberal W.V. Harcourt in the early 1880s, a practice formalized by legislation in 1884.[151] Such accommodation to "medicalization" increased the number of post-conviction committals in place of execution. Indeed, the *Times*, concerned about such committals in several recent cases, published an editorial to warn against this after the insanity plea had failed in an 1883 trial of a man convicted of murdering his three-year-old child. For the *Times* this was

> only too fairly representative of a class of cases frequently in English Courts. The prisoner Cole, who was a brick maker and labourer, and his wife were in great poverty. The husband was out of work, and the latter gained a living by mending chairs. One day they had been quarrelling, and the wife left the house for a short time. When she returned she found her husband holding the younger of their two children by the feet. She took the child away from him and went out again. When she came back she found him dashing this child's head against the wall. It was terribly injured, and it died on the following morning. There was the usual defense of insanity. It was urged that the prisoner had been so violent when in prison that he had to be put in a padded cell; that he had used, as was very probable, threats to his wife; and that he had frequently been in prison for crimes of violence. These not uncommon symptoms of lawlessness and ruffianism satisfied one doctor that Cole was "a typical lunatic with dangerous delusions." But the jury were not convinced by the familiar argument that a man who does anything particularly wicked must be insane, and they found the prisoner guilty of murder.[152]

However, after a further examination ordered by the Home Office Cole was certified as insane and committed to Broadmoor – just what the *Times* had feared.[153] Indeed, Harcourt's further step of urging prosecutors in capital cases to make greater use themselves of medical evidence seems to have contributed to rather than limited the subsequent rise in insanity verdicts, as Justice Willes complained in 1890. Upset by the unexpected evidence of an asylum superintendent called by the *prosecution*, which led to an insanity

[151] After the Conservative Cross's replacement by the Liberal Harcourt in 1880, the Home Office seems to have become somewhat more receptive to pleas of mental unsoundness, even in cases of unpopular defendants. In an 1881 case where a wife murderer's neighbors had attempted to lynch him, several alienists testified to his delusionality [of his wife's infidelity]. He was nonetheless convicted, but over the judge's objection Harcourt insisted on a further medical examination, and the man was committed to Broadmoor [*R.v. Payne: Times*, 14, 23 February, 10 May 1881 (pp. 9, 10, 4); HO144/A4796]. See also Wiener, *Reconstructing the Criminal*, pp. 275–276.
[152] *Times*, 20 October 1883, p. 9; see also its trial report in the previous day's issue.
[153] HO144/924/A32547.

verdict for a man who had cut his prostitute lover's throat, Willes declared in a private letter to the Home Secretary that he did not know "a more difficult or more anxious task than the conduct of an inquiry as to a man's sanity in a capital case, and the extreme and growing frequency of the defense in cases of murder shows that there is a great need for vigilance on the part of the judge" – a vigilance in this case blindsided by the prosecution itself.[154]

On the other hand, official medicalization also served to protect the principles of personal responsibility. The guarantee of a post-conviction medical inquiry that existed from 1884 gave judges a new tool to overcome jury reluctance to convict. It also preserved some Government control over the process by enhancing the role of the more "responsible" medical men employed in the penal system as against that of independent experts, who were often active in efforts to expand the boundaries of recognized insanity. In the late years of the century judges were sometimes able to fend off looming insanity verdicts by promising that the prisoner's mental state would be carefully examined after conviction. In the 1889 case of Richard Townsend, Justice Charles found the evidence (as he later informed the Home Office) "far short of . . . any legal justification for [a] finding that he was insane according to the legal definition of the word insanity," but the man's longtime peculiar behavior made the judge's assurance of expert examination after conviction essential to bringing a hesitant jury to convict. In the end Townsend's sentence was commuted to penal servitude for life.[155] Similarly, Justice Wright obtained convictions in this way in two fiancee murders tried before him in the same month of 1903. In the trial of Charles Howell at Chelmsford he conceded that "there might be a kind of insanity which would not excuse him, but which could be inquired into hereafter by those medical gentlemen whose duty it is to advise the Home Secretary"; the jury returned a verdict of guilty, appending a recommendation not to mercy but to a medical inquiry. After that inquiry Howell hanged

---

[154]"When it is taken into consideration," Willes went on, "how irreconciliable are the theories of responsibility entertained by lawyers and by medical men, it will, I think, be seen that the judge's task is one which entitles him to every help that can be properly given to him. I hope, therefore, that for the future in Treasury prosecutions the particular kind of evidence to which I refer ["proofs" of insanity] may be supplied to the judge a reasonable time before the trial. . . ." *R.v. Terry* (1890): HO144/236/A51751; also *Times*, 28 July 1890, p. 4. A similar situation took place the following year when John Miller, who had fatally fractured his wife's skull, was examined before trial by Home Office doctors. Miller's counsel happily made use of their findings that his family "had the hereditary taint of insanity and he himself was of a low mental organisation, weak to resist impulses to violence, and easily thrown off balance by drink." Justice Lawrance told the jury flatly that this was not enough to meet the insanity test; the jury responded however by finding manslaughter. [*Times*, 11 December 1891, p. 6].

[155]HO Printed Memorandum; *Times*, 13 July 1889, p. 13.

anyway.[156] Alfred Nelson's counsel, at Norwich, argued that "all the circumstances of the case showed that the act was that of an epileptic automaton." Nonetheless, Justice Wright instructed the jury that they had to be convinced that Nelson failed to know right from wrong or the nature of his acts. "Small eccentricities," such as the bizarre past behavior that had been brought into evidence, "would not justify an acquittal on ground of insanity." Even in a new century and a new reign, judges could continue to insist upon the authority of the M'Naughton Rules in the courtroom, because of the safety valve of an assured Home Office medical examination. As in Howell's case, after laying down M'Naughton, Wright suggested that the Home Secretary would have the prisoner's mind more thoroughly examined than it had yet been possible to do. The jury duly returned a murder verdict, urging both mercy and further inquiry into his mental state. Wright observed that he "entirely concurred" in both the verdict and the recommendations. Unlike Howell, Nelson succeeded in escaping death; in this case the Home Office's medical men found Nelson's mind disabled. Consequently, at the Home Office, "the only question is whether to sentence to penal servitude or Broadmoor." Penal servitude it was. He was released after twelve years.[157] Such post-conviction determinations not only preserved the principle of personal responsibility for all who were not proved insane, it of course ensured that those as well as the non-insane convicts would not be released back into society.

To the stricter "objective" legal standard that had emerged during the Victorian era of the self-disciplined "ordinary reasonable man," the gradually broadening recognition of mental unsoundness constituted less of a challenge, both practically and theoretically, than did provocation or drunkenness. Not only did this recognition ensure that defendants in whom insanity was recognized did not as a rule return to society, it did not offer a competing vision of "normal" behavior to that of the Victorian judiciary and Home Office. Rather, the shift to mental unsoundness as a defense left that vision and that standard untouched for the great majority of persons and great bulk of behavior and simply established that a small number of persons were incapable of attaining it – lay, as it were, outside "normal" humanity. Particularly when such persons could be, as was increasingly the case, removed from the criminal justice system before trial by a finding of "unfitness to plead," insanity pleas could be readily reconciled with Victorian expectations of personal self-discipline represented by the "reasonable man" standard.

Moreover, even as insanity pleas further increased their success after 1900, neither the judiciary nor the Home Office, under either Conservatives or

---

[156] *Times*, 20 June 1903, p. 5. The Home Office doctors found him to be of sound mind, adding that "we were able to satisfy ourselves that the murder was the outcome of jealousy complicated with the effects of drink" [HO144/712/109157].

[157] *Times*, 15 June 1903, p. 12; HO144/982/109009.

Liberals, relaxed their skeptical scrutiny, as Thomas Rawcliffe's 1910 case illustrates. There, two medical men gave their opinions that Rawcliffe was insane at the time he had murdered his wife, though admitting that he appeared sane by the time of the trial. A divided jury was pushed toward a conviction by the judge. They then recommended mercy, specifically on the grounds of previous head injuries. The reformist Home Secretary Winston Churchill privately acknowledged that "the case differs widely from murders like Crippen's" but refused to prevent the hanging, observing in the tones of his Victorian predecessors that "the murders of defenseless women are too common for the repressive power of the death penalty to be relaxed, except where circumstances of irresponsibility or provocation are clearly proved."[158]

Thus, in the course of the Victorian era in most ways exceptions to the expectation of personal responsibility were restricted, especially in the killings of women. Just as the bar was raised for provocations sufficient to reduce murder to manslaughter, or even to reprieve a convicted murder, the bar for demonstrating lack of intention to kill was also moved up in regard to the lack of use of lethal weapons or drunkenness. In one area only – insanity and the related conditions of delirium tremens or epilepsy – did it become easier to negate the existence of evil intention. The consequent shift in legal arguments in murder cases by the end of the century on the one hand bore witness to an "English compromise," in which stricter standards for most "ordinary and reasonable" men went together with increased acceptance of the possibility of organic breakdown in some men. Indeed, each side of the compromise enabled the acceptance of the other, insanity determinations being made acceptable by the maintenance of stern expectations for the great majority, and these expectations being supported by the "safety valve" of insanity recognitions. Overall, men who killed (and even more, who sexually assaulted) women were treated more severely in comparison to other offenders at the end of Victoria's reign than had been true at its start, and the increased number of insanity determinations if anything allowed this severity to grow and then maintain itself.

[158] HO144/1103/199430; a full account of Rawcliffe's trial is given in the copy of the *Lancaster Observer* held in this Home Office file.

# Conclusion:
# The New "Reasonable Man"
# and Twentieth-Century Britain

In the early years of the twentieth century the Victorian civilizing offensive eased, as the overall amount of interpersonal violence in England was by all accounts markedly falling. Certainly fear of such violence was less apparent. Not only was the reported homicide rate steadily declining from about 1.5 per hundred thousand in the early 1870s to a mere fifth of that sixty years later, but the number of cases prosecuted and convicted was declining even more: whereas in 1871–75 81% of homicides known to the police had resulted in trials and 37% in convictions, already by 1911–14 these percentages had dropped to 64 and 29.[1] The number of known cases of "felonious and malicious wounding" followed a parallel trajectory, in both incidence and legal outcome.[2] The criminal law's civilizing offensive was being wound down. However credit for the change should be apportioned between that offensive and other influences such as rising incomes, education levels and welfare provision, English life by the outbreak of the First World War was nearing culmination of the long process of pacification. The "ordinary reasonable man" of Victorian legal thinking was more in evidence through all social levels, exercising greater self-restraint and settling more disputes nonviolently. A crucial contributor to this social pacification was the changed conception of manliness at the heart of Victorian ideology. And appropriately enough, the greatest beneficiaries of this pacification were women, chiefly of the working class, victims of far more violence than they perpetrated.[3]

[1] Annual Judicial Statistics; see also John Briggs, C. Harrison, A. McInnes and D. Vincent, *Crime and Punishment in England: An Introductory Survey* (London, 1996), p. 178.
[2] The number of such wounding cases known declined from 4.8 per hundred thousand in 1871–75 to 3.3 in 1911–14, while the number prosecuted fell still more: in 1871–75 79% of the known cases had resulted in trials and 60% in full convictions, but in 1911–14 those percentages were 59 and 40 [Annual Judicial Statistics].
[3] Indeed, the increased legal recourse abused wives obtained during the nineteenth century may have helped reduce the incidence of husband killing as well, as most of this, today as in the nineteenth century, appears to be reactive to abusive situations, perpetrated when other avenues of relief seem closed. For this argument in a present-day context, see Elicka S.L. Peterson, "Murder as Self-Help: Women and Intimate Partner Homicide," *Homicide Studies* 3. 1 (February 1999), 30–46.

In a wider perspective, the Victorians laid the groundwork for the twentieth-century paradox of an historically and geographically unusually "peaceable kingdom" ruling a vast Empire that rested ultimately on force. As with the domestic story, this global one had a gender component, in the uneasy coexistence of two distinctive models of masculinity – that of an "imperial man" ready to be violent when violence appeared to be necessary to preserve British authority and that of a much more pacific "home Englishman."[4] Such a coexistence contributed to many of the ongoing tensions and conflicts between Parliament, Colonial Office and high judiciary on the one hand, and local officials, military, traders and settlers out in the empire down to the end of British rule. By the time the empire began to unravel, the more pacific version of masculine self-mastery stood without challenge, and as late as 1955 could be located by the sociologist Geoffrey Gorer at the heart of "English character."[5] Certainly the legal system had fully accepted that view, and expected self-restraint of an Englishman in even the most provoking circumstances. In the same year in which Gorer published his study of the national character *Le Monde* observed skeptically that "the Englishman ... believes himself to be a creature of *sang-froid,* and the legal system in force supports this fiction in overruling once and for all any emotional troubles or irresistible impulses."[6]

Britain remained largely Victorian in this respect, as in some others more familiar, like sexual mores, until the 1960s. That decade of liberation seems to have set in motion an unleashing of, along with other emotions and impulses, men's inclinations towards violence – toward other men and toward women. Certainly, reported incidences of criminal violence, including sexual, began in those years a marked rise that, with fluctuations, has continued to the present. However, this is a new story that will have to be told in another place. Here it is sufficient to appreciate the importance of the Victorian

---

[4]However, even the imperial masculine model, while more accepting of violence, increasingly limited its scope while ever more sharing the domestic model's exaltation of self-discipline as a core value. [See James Eli Adams, *Dandies and Desert Saints: Styles of Victorian Masculinity* (Ithaca, N.Y., 1995); Kenneth E. Hendrickson, *Making Saints: Religion and the Public Image of the British Army, 1809–1885* (Fairleigh Dickinson, N.J., 1998).] As Philip Holden has observed, "For colonial writers of the early twentieth century [the mid-Victorian era] took on the status of a golden age of untrammelled masculine self-expression on the as yet untamed frontier. ... Towards the end of the nineteenth century, with the formalization of British rule ... this ideal was replaced with another that stressed emotional and somatic continence." [*Modern Subjects/Colonial Texts: Hugh Clifford and the Discipline of English Literature in the Straits Settlements and Malaya 1895–1907* (Greensboro, N.C., 2000), p. 106.]

[5]Geoffrey Gorer, *Exploring English Character* (London, 1955).

[6]Quoted in *Times,* 13 July 1955, p. 6 (in reference to the trial of Ruth Ellis for shooting her faithless lover).

chapter in the history of English violence, criminal justice and masculinity, and its legacy that has shaped much of twentieth-century Britain, down in some ways even to today, as contemporary feminism, for all its repudiation of Victorian values, continues – usually without acknowledgment – to draw upon that well for nourishment.

# Index